FROM MIDTERMS TO MINISTRY

Practical Theologians on Pastoral Beginnings

Edited by

Allan Hugh Cole Jr.

WILLIAM B. EERDMANS PUBLISHING COMPANY
GRAND RAPIDS, MICHIGAN / CAMBRIDGE, U.K.

Published 2008 by
Wm. B. Eerdmans Publishing Co.
2140 Oak Industrial Drive N.E., Grand Rapids, Michigan 49505 /
P.O. Box 163, Cambridge CB3 9PU U.K.

Printed in the United States of America

13 12 11 10 09 08   7 6 5 4 3 2 1

Library of Congress Cataloging-in-Publication Data

From midterms to ministry: practical theologians on pastoral beginnings /
    edited by Allan Hugh Cole, Jr.
        p.   cm.
    Includes bibliographical references.
    ISBN 978-0-8028-4002-8 (pbk.: alk. paper)
    1. Pastoral theology.   2. Theology, Practical.
    I. Cole, Allan Hugh.

    BV4011.F75   2008
    253.2 — dc22
                                                    2008010805

www.eerdmans.com

For Meredith and Holly

Contents

Contents

Foreword

The twenty-four essays in this superb collection are consistently personal and often self-revelatory in their candor. They draw us into a story that many of us know as our own: those first awkward steps from the academic world of seminary (Greek exegesis and neo-Barthian theology) to the real world of the parish church (recruiting volunteers to rake leaves and fussing with a budget that won't balance). Time and again as I read these essays, a wave of recognition washed over me, as in "I've been there!" But more than recognition, these wonderfully winsome memoirs offer light to guide the way for those on that same journey from midterms to ministry, as the title of this collection aptly names it.

I have no doubt that new physicians fresh out of medical school and residency experience discontinuity as they move from their classrooms and teaching hospitals to the routine challenges of actual medical practice. Surely newly-minted lawyers experience more than a few vocational jolts as they make the leap from law school to law office. But by all reports, and based on the two dozen experiences detailed in the following pages, the parallel transition from seminary to parish ministry is particularly jarring for many new pastors. But dislocating as many may find it, this is largely as it should be. This movement from midterms to ministry is especially and necessarily challenging for two good reasons.

First, seminary is neither vocational nor professional school. A good theological education is perhaps the last classically broad graduate course of study that encompasses literature (the Bible mostly, but not alone), languages (Greek and Hebrew for many), history (of the church at least), and perhaps philosophy (of religion). This is precisely the wide and deep education that the church needs for its leaders if Christian faith is to be saved (as it must be again and again) from sliding into theological simplicities, and if the Christian ministry is to be saved (as it must be again and again) from becoming a bag of spiritual techniques and leadership gimmicks. This is precisely the kind of wide and deep education that churches at their best demand for their ministers. This is precisely the kind of education that will ground ministers firmly for their difficult work, even if it may not have been the "how to" instruction manual they might long for in the first years of ministry. Finally, it is precisely the kind of education that demands that those who have received it make the connections for themselves — the often subtle and nuanced connections between the classroom and the parish church.

Second, the transition from seminary to ministry is more jolting than that from business school to corporate office, medical school to medical practice, or law school to law office because most ministers are generalists, not specialists. Medical schools, for instance, no longer train many general practitioners; they more often train pediatricians and cardiologists. In fact, most pediatricians have sub-specialties. The same has become true of the practice of law. A world-class corporate tax lawyer may know little more about criminal law than I do.

But this is not generally true for the practice of ministry. A pastor may not be as strong in one aspect of ministry as another, but parish ministers may indeed be the "last generalists." This is a reality that makes the work of parish pastors both especially challenging and especially rewarding.

Though it will be of great interest to anyone who cares about theological education and the church, the following collection naturally commends itself to those about to move, or who have recently moved, from the world of theological education to the world of the parish church. As a way to illumine the significance of this book and its subject, I would suggest to the reader three metaphors about this transition from midterms to ministry.

The first metaphor — a map. If you have not been somewhere before, it is enormously helpful to have a map of the place when you first go. The following collection of essays, many of them candidly autobiographical, are maps drawn by men and women who have been to the place, ministry in the parish church. These maps are drawn for the benefit of those about to travel there or those who have already arrived there and are not quite sure where they have landed or how to get from point A to point B in this strange new land. Many new ministers have visited the place as student ministers, but frankly, they were really "tourists," though in the best sense of the word. Full-time ordained parish ministry means that this is now *home:* you are not a visitor and you need to know your way around. The maps drawn by these essays vary dramatically with each minister-cartographer, just like actual maps vary. I live in New York City, where we have lots of different kinds of maps: subway maps, bus maps, street maps, museum maps, restaurant maps, and so forth. When you live here, you need all of them sooner or later. Just so in ministry; it is helpful to have maps drawn by a variety of mapmakers who view the land from different angles, each marking different kinds of landmarks. This is why the multiple maps in this collection are so much better than just one, however fine it might be.

The second metaphor — a bicycle. You learn to ride a bicycle by riding a bicycle. Pre-riding instructions on the theory and practice of bicycling can be enormously helpful: "you put your feet on these pedal things and your hands here, and when you want to stop you squeeze these things." But you can only learn to do it by actually throwing a leg over the saddle and doing it. Indeed the first few hundred yards are usually terrifying no matter how thoroughly you were prepped. In fact, most new riders, whether young or old, fall over at least once. Just so in ministry. Seminary preparation is essential, but so much of what a pastor is called to do can be learned only in the actual doing of it. And just as in bicycle riding, there will be crashes and scraped knees — all a necessary part of learning.

The third metaphor — eyeglasses. When you get new glasses, especially for the first time, and put them on, the world may look very strange for the first few days. Your new glasses are disorienting and uncomfortable, even if you can actually now see clearly what was fuzzy before. I have always thought that the lenses of a pair of glasses are a fit image with which to speak of faith. Having faith is a way of seeing the world, and it is often disorienting at first even if it is in fact truer. Just so in ministry: to put on a clerical collar, literally or figuratively, invites you to be seen and to see most everything in a fresh way. You look into the lives of the people you serve with a "pastor's lens." You listen to their voices with your ears tuned to hear in a new way. There is a fresh set of expectations and assumptions about precisely who you are and the texture of your relationship with those you serve. All of this becomes a new way of seeing yourself, seeing your church, and seeing your vocation. My experience, my deepest trust, is that even though it may be disorienting at first, it is finally a truer way of seeing and being seen.

MICHAEL L. LINDVALL
New York City

Acknowledgments

Envisioning and assembling any book requires a good deal of support on the part of many. This book is no exception. I want to thank Jon Pott, Vice-President and Editor-in-Chief at Wm. B. Eerdmans Publishing Company, for agreeing to publish this book after I hounded him for many months about its virtues. Jon has supported my work in many ways, not the least of which has been through his willingness to sign up a newer scholar for this and another project. His kindness and generosity warrant the deep sense of gratitude that I feel but can only approximate in expression. I'm also grateful to Linda Bieze, Managing Editor at Eerdmans, Jennifer Hoffman, Associate Managing Editor, and Andrew Hoogheem for their support of this project and their contributions to its improvement.

I feel a similar kind gratitude and joy toward each person who has written an essay for this book. Some of them I have had the pleasure of knowing personally while I was a seminary student, a pastor, or as I began teaching in a seminary myself. Others I have known simply through their work, by reputation, and by virtue of the influences that they have had on me and others. I respect each of them, and I have been humbled both by their interest in participating in this project and by their willingness to give so generously of themselves to support it.

Speaking of generosity, I am grateful to Michael Lindvall for writing a foreword to the book. I have been a distant devotee of Michael for many years, having first "met" him in his wonderful book *Good News from North Haven* when I was in seminary. That book contains delightful stories about the ins and outs, ups and downs, and give and take of church life, offering up clever insights and lucid perspectives on life in ministry. A number of years after reading that book, I had the pleasure of meeting Michael face to face and spending some quality time together in conversation. My admiration of him and his ministry have continued to grow. I am honored by his contribution to this project.

Since this is really a book about the pastoral vocation and mentoring those preparing for it, a few more persons deserve mention in my expressions of gratitude. These persons have supported and guided me in my own vocational journeys, including before seminary, through seminary, and beyond seminary. William H. Terry, former Dean of Students at Davidson College, helped me discern a call to attend seminary. In my years at Davidson, he offered me, as he had to countless others through the years, a kind of ongoing care and hospitality that one rarely finds. While a seminarian, as I served as student pastor at Community Presbyterian Church in Edison, New Jersey, the Revs. Joseph C. Fowler and Joyce Stedge-Fowler mentored me in countless ways, patiently but deliberately encouraging growth and maturity in a ministry vocation when my eagerness and passion surely exceeded my preparation, wisdom, and capacities for discernment. Subsequently, as I prepared to transition from seminary to my first ministry call, and as I lived into that call and others for a number of years, the Revs. Norman D. Stanton and Charles W. Holsinger, laudable mentors, fine churchmen, and dear friends, provided more in the way of time, attention, support, wisdom, and advice than I could ever convey or repay. In one sense, this book is my attempt to thank all of these persons — Will, Joe, Joyce, Norman, and Chuck — for who they are and for what they have given to me and to innumerable others who have traveled this vocational path.

Of course, as mentioned a number of times in the essays that follow, ministers of various stripes must rely on their families and closest associates for support and nurture if they presume to offer the same to others in their care. My wife, Tracey, has for over sixteen years given me what I can only describe as a grace-filled life. In innumerable ways she teaches, supports, inspires, and makes me laugh each day of life that we share, while helping me strive to become a better husband, father, son, minister, and person. All who live partnered lives should be so fortunate. Our daughters Meredith and Holly have shown me depths of love and joy that I never imagined possible, making an already abundant life overflow with blessings and delight. While too young to understand who ministers are and what they do, I trust that they will come to know about that in due time and, as is true for so many of the world's children, that several ministers will play meaningful roles in their lives, helping them to grow into the persons God has called them to become. This book is dedicated to them. My parents, Allan and Jeri Cole, have remained tireless in their love and support of me and my vocation, generously making lots of sacrifices to enable me to study and learn through the years. They introduced me to the love of God and the community of the church, two of myriad gifts they have so graciously bestowed on my life.

I wish to thank too Aaron Findley, a Master of Divinity student at Austin Presbyterian Theological Seminary, who has generously and painstakingly assisted me with various research and editorial needs for this project.

Also, I wish to thank two colleagues and dear friends, David Jensen and Arun Jones, who read my contributions to this book and offered their typical wise and thoughtful feedback. Dave and Arun model admirably what friendship, collegiality, and living as servants of the church ought to entail. As Ralph Waldo Emerson wisely noted, "It is one of the blessings of old friends that you can afford to be stupid with them."

Finally, I want to express admiration and gratitude to all of my colleagues and our students at Austin Presbyterian Theological Seminary, a school of the church and its ministry that I cherish. One of my life's foremost blessings continues to spring from living and working among such a talented and devoted group of teachers, scholars, administrators, staff, and students who, in varying ways, seek to nurture persons whose lives and life's work center on the church of Jesus Christ. I'm particularly grateful to Ted Wardlaw and Michael Jinkins, contributors to this volume who serve as Austin Seminary's president and academic dean, respectively, for providing faithful, competent, creative, and courageous leadership that invites teachers, scholars, and budding ministers to thrive.

ALLAN HUGH COLE JR.
Austin, Texas

Introduction

Allan Hugh Cole Jr.

Seminary life differs from life in the church. That fact catches many who make the transition from seminary student to minister by surprise. I have heard many a new minister say things like the following: "I had no idea how complicated ministry can be." "I wasn't ready for the politics of church life and all the energy it takes to be with such a diverse group of people." "The ministerial life, though truly rewarding, has great dangers and pitfalls. One must be on guard all the time." Truth be told, I have made similar remarks myself, particularly in the first few weeks, months, and years of life as a pastor. Serving now as a seminary professor, I often hear recent graduates say these kinds of things too, usually when they return to campus after having just begun service in their first pastoral position.

In this collection of essays a seasoned group of ministers, scholars and theological educators seek to respond to such remarks and, more importantly, to the situations and experiences that give rise to them. These authors share reflections, born out of personal experiences, on the transition from being a seminarian to becoming a minister. All of the authors have worked with two assumptions: first, that the theological school and the local ministry setting constitute related but different "worlds"; second, that while these worlds share things in common they also differ in significant ways. Specifically, these worlds may, and often do, operate with dissimilar sets of expectations and values, with different cultures and ways of life, and also with their own set of distinct challenges, objectives, rewards, and focal points.

To cite but a few examples, the theological school tends to expect and reward particular types of activity and engagement, centering largely on intellectual pursuits. Such activity and engagement includes critical investigation into one's faith and traditions, more technical or academic writing, a focus on enhancing one's capacity for tolerating ambiguity and abstractness, and wrestling with the larger life and faith questions for their own sake. While theological education at its best will certainly include attention to the "so what" of this type of activity and engagement, examining how it informs concrete thinking, acting, and doing in life, that "so what" tends to receive less immediate attention and perhaps less emphasis in school than in local ministry settings.

In contrast, the local ministry setting — and we have limited our attention in this book to local congregations — tends to expect and reward other types of activity and engagement. That includes building strong interpersonal relationships, communicating the Bible and tradition in terms that laypersons can readily understand and make use of in their daily living, and maintaining efficiency with regard to a variety of duties and tasks that span the administrative, leadership, and political realms. It is not the case that the local ministry setting ignores or otherwise lacks entirely what the theological school values and rewards; in fact, vibrant ministries will surely embrace and make use of the theological school's primary areas of focus to some extent. Yet those points of focus tend not to receive as much attention or be assigned as much value in the local ministry setting, as pastors and congregations, for a number of reasons, deem other matters to be more interesting, important, and in need of their energies and immediate attention.

Furthermore, to a large extent each of these worlds engages a different primary audience. The theological school's main audience typically consists of scholars and teachers; administrators, governing boards and judicatories; clergy, Christian educators, and clergy- and educators-in-training. The local ministry setting typically has as its chief audience laypersons, the local community, and perhaps mission partners with whom congregations may work, whether locally, statewide, nationally, or globally. Consequently, living and serving in one of these worlds often differs significantly from living and serving in the other. What a seminary student operates with in terms of norms, values, goals, foci, and rewards tends to vary from what a new minister must operate with in a new ministry setting — that is, as she graduates from seminary and begins service in a new and different world.

Many seminarians discover these two worlds' existence as they begin internships or field education in a ministerial setting. If they were already aware of these distinct worlds — and some will have been while others will have not — internships may lead them to uncover stark differences, in degree and kind, among the worlds. More often than not these discoveries come as quite a surprise; and it is not unusual for those making them to feel unsettled in their wake. Persons who spend time with seminarians, especially theological educators and judicatory personnel responsible for mentoring students as they discern and grow into their vocation, know that they commonly report feelings and concerns like the following: "Church people have different interests and questions than what we spend time on in seminary." "I wish parishioners were more committed. They always seem to find a reason not to show up on Sunday or not to support the church's finances or programs." Or, "I don't see how my seminary courses, which are so concerned with theoretical matters, have anything to do with what happens in church life." If these experiences were not enough to complicate the seminarian's life, she also tends to remark about her encounters with conflict in congregations, with clergy evidencing fatigue if not cynicism about ministry, and with the seemingly growing emphasis that both laypersons and ministers place on church growth, new and innovative programs, and being attractive to what they have come to know as the church consumer. Having entered the theological school with a certain set of expectations for what ministry will be like — expectations which, incidentally, tend less and less to be tied to long and deep formative experiences in congregations — students come to realize that what the theological school emphasizes, prizes, expects, rewards, practices, and predicts may differ substantially from what they find in the congregational setting. In many cases, such a realization brings about confusion and unease if not a deepseated vocational crisis.

I am not suggesting that this kind of confusion, unease, or crisis will be every seminarian's experience. Some will transition more or less seamlessly from seminary to congregational life and thus may encounter few if any of the scenarios or challenges I cite. Nevertheless, many will struggle, whether in the last months before graduation or, more often, in the first months and years of life in ministry. And I am convinced that for most of those persons their pain and confusion will stem from having to negotiate the differences they discover among the worlds of the theological school and the local congregation, along with the personal, vocational, and even spiritual disorientation that their discovery prompts.

The fact that seminarians nearing the end of their programs will have begun to anticipate this transition from the vocation of seminary student to that of installed minister becomes evident in several ways. They may begin increasingly to ask professors for "practical advice" on "what to do" as they begin their ministry, noting how "unprepared" they feel for the "nuts and bolts" of pastoral life. Sometimes their queries are couched in the assumption that they should take as many courses as possible in the so-called practical areas of theological education — preaching, worship, pastoral care and counseling, Christian education, leadership and congregational studies — in order to get what they need in the way of "tools" for the "toolbox" they anxiously seek to fill. Sometimes students ponder whether they should take part in a longer period of internship in a congregation, if perhaps a year-long Clinical Pastoral Education residency would be in order, or whether they should begin thinking more about serving first in a larger, multi-staff congregation — which presumably would provide them with mentors, colleagues, and a smaller range of responsibility in their first ministry years — as opposed to serving as solo pastor of a smaller, and what they assume will be a more complex and demanding, congregation. Sometimes students will even begin to question their vocation, speculating if coming to seminary was right for them after all, asking if they are "cut out" for parish ministry, wondering if they are "thick skinned" enough to lead others in the faith, and growing uneasy about whether they "know enough" to serve as a pastor amid all the demands they have found out the ministerial life tends to bring.

Even though seminarians, seminary faculties, staffs and administrators, as well as church officials may anticipate the pending transition from midterms to ministry, the *degree* to which that transition will prove *challenging* for new ministers often goes unrecognized: by those making it or preparing to make it, by seminary personnel who teach and help to form those preparing to make it, and also by congregations, judicatories, and communities that receive new ministers into their fold. As a result, new ministers frequently experience disappointment over expectations that go unmet, confusion about what responsibilities they have signed on to meet, and various kinds of internal struggles and relational problems that go part and parcel with experiencing vocational distress and which may hinder their health, happiness, excellence, and faithfulness in their new ministry context.

Practical theologians, the term I have chosen to describe those who serve as pastors, church educators, professors and administrators in seminaries and divinity schools, and also bishops and other church leaders, have significant insights to offer to those in the midst of their own transition to ministry. I am confident that the reflections these practical theologians offer in this book provide useful perspectives, wisdom, and advice, and that this will benefit seminaries, seminarians, new ministers, and faith communities welcoming them. By engendering greater awareness of several potential challenges that new ministers face and imparting wisdom concerning how new ministers may best negotiate their own challenges as they move from the world of midterms to that of ministry, the insights contained in this book will add to the confidence, courage, and hope, not only among new ministers but also among those seeking to understand their needs and to offer them support.

While some contributors may not typically identify themselves as "practical theologians" in the technical sense, meaning those who teach and craft scholarship in homiletics, liturgics, religious education, pastoral theology, pastoral care, church leadership and administration, and congregational studies — the theological areas that tend to make up the academic field called "practical theology" — all who offer their reflections herein care deeply about the church and its ministries. Likewise, all of these contributors seek in their vocation to help educate, form, equip, and support persons who will serve as pastors. Consequently, all *practice* theology regularly. Moreover, all contributors have spent considerable time and have rich experiences working in the theological school, a congregational setting, or both; and all have experienced the transition between the two worlds. As each author's essay was written independently of the others, readers should feel free to read the essays in any order.

There are several new and wise books that focus on the well-being and health of clergy (including both new and seasoned), on excellence in pastoral leadership, and on how theological education might serve these ends when preparing women and men for ministry. Those books include Jackson W. Carroll's *God's Potters: Pastoral Leadership and the Shaping of Congregations* (Eerdmans, 2006); *Resurrecting Excellence: Shaping Faithful Christian Ministry* (Eerdmans, 2006) by L. Gregory Jones and Kevin R. Armstrong; *Pastors in Transition: Why Clergy Leave Local Church Ministry* (Eerdmans, 2005) by Dean R. Hoge and Jacqueline E. Wenger; Michael Jinkins's *Letters to New Pastors* (Eerdmans, 2006); Anthony B. Robinson's *Transforming Congregational Culture* (Eerdmans, 2003); Loren B. Mead's *A*

Introduction

Change of Pastors . . . And How It Affects Change in the Congregation (Alban Institute, 2005); *Educating Clergy: Teaching Practices and Pastoral Imagination* (Jossey-Bass 2006) by Charles Foster et al.; and *The Scope of Our Art: The Vocation of the Theological Teacher* (Eerdmans, 2002), co-edited by L. Gregory Jones and Stephanie Paulsell. I commend each of these works to anyone interested in knowing more about enhancing life in ministry.

This book differs from those resources and others that may be concerned with a similar subject — ministerial leadership in congregations — in several ways. First, this book consists of essays by an outstanding *group* of thinkers who bring diverse life experiences, perspectives, interests, training, and vocational histories to bear on their work. Second, this book focuses on the transition from seminary or divinity school to first ministry setting, which means that it was written principally for new ministers or those who soon will become new ministers. Yet I also believe the book will benefit those who seek to support new ministers. That includes those of us who teach and administer in theological schools; pastors and educators who work in multiple staff contexts and who welcome new ministers from time to time; judicatory executives who seek to nurture and support new ministers in their charge; and various kinds of mentors who journey with seminarians *and* new ministers as they grow into their vocations. Third, each essay grows out of its author's own experiences and thus has a *personal* tone and recounts *personal* stories. When inviting contributors to take part, I asked them to reflect on their own transition from seminary to first ministry position, and to write personally about what they experienced, questioned, struggled with, and learned. I added, "Think about a few 'nuggets of wisdom' you wish you would have had imparted to you and that you would like now to impart to others who are making, or soon will make, their transition from 'midterms to ministry.'" In different ways, these contributors have been faithful to that request, seeking in their essays to impart some of the wisdom, knowledge, and advice they have gleaned, not only from observing and supporting others making a transition from seminary to ministry, but also from their own transition.

No contributor would presume to speak for everyone who may read this book. Each person's experience with moving from the world of the theological school to that of the congregation will differ from others' and will have distinct qualities. Even so, I am confident that the wealth of experiences and wisdom shared here will benefit many persons who travel a similar vocational path. Any transition from seminary to congregational ministry will inevitably involve personal, relational, institutional, cultural, and spiritual questions, concerns, struggles, and triumphs that serve to shape the experience; and that experience will almost always bring both challenges and rewards that have not been envisioned. The assumption, then, is that contributors' experiences will have many points of contact with the experiences of theological students or new ministers in transit from one world to another, and as readers become more aware of those points of contact they will find help for traveling their own vocational path.

1. The Essential Untidiness of Ministry

Thomas G. Long

The Yawning Divide

In his fascinating book *Religious Experience in Earliest Christianity,* Roman Catholic biblical scholar Luke Johnson imaginatively takes his readers on a tour inside a typical Catholic church. He observes that there is a different religious world at the front of the church than there is at the back. At the front of the church are the altar, the pulpit, the missal, the Bible, and the priest's chair — all symbols of order, authority, and sound theology. At the back of the church, however, things are a bit messier. In the narthex, tacked to a bulletin board, are news clippings of the latest appearance of the Virgin Mary, brochures advertising pilgrimages to a local shrine, copies of novena prayers said to St. Jude, and notices of various charismatic prayer meetings and healing services. Johnson says, "At the front of the church, religion is much concerned with correctness of doctrine, morality, authority, procedure. Back in the vestibule, religion is much more about the experience of transforming power in any available form."[1]

Johnson's contrast between the front and back of the church could serve as a symbol for what many believe is wrong today with the education of clergy. Seminaries, it is said, if they are concerned about the local church at all, often train students to work only at the front of the church. When these students graduate and become pastors, however, they discover that the people, the programs, and the energy are clustered in the back. As a re-

---

1. Luke Timothy Johnson, *Religious Experience in Earliest Christianity: A Missing Dimension in New Testament Studies* (Minneapolis: Fortress Press, 1998), pp. 1-2.

1

sult, new pastors are often dismayed by the messy, undisciplined, and sometimes crude forms of religious life actually being practiced in their churches, while congregations find what new pastors preach and teach to be mystifying, or perhaps just irrelevant and uninteresting. New pastors look at the back of the church and see only a collection of idolatrous golden calves, while congregations gaze in puzzlement toward the front of the church and see only a remote Moses-like figure enigmatically breaking sacred tablets.

For decades now, educators, church officials, and pastors have been grumbling about the split between the theological school and the parish. It is now a widely accepted piece of folk wisdom that a yawning gap exists between the theological education ministers and priests receive and the actual life of the churches to which they are called. The official story goes something like this: once upon a time, ministers were educated through the apprentice model. Guided by wise and experienced pastors, students "read theology" as they followed their mentors on their clerical rounds, and there was an immediate and tight interweaving of theological knowledge and ministerial practice. But prompted by the birth of the modern university in Europe, denominations gradually abandoned the apprentice model in favor of established theological schools with specialized faculty, curricula, and degree programs. The result was that these schools, as they grew stronger and more independent, increasingly hearkened to standards intrinsic to universities rather than those valued by the churches that had founded them. They began to look lustfully at tenure, scholarly guilds, and book contracts rather than mission, worship, and evangelism. A wedge was driven between the seminary and the church, between the education clergy receive and the actual practice of ministry, so much so that new ministers are at a loss about how to make the shift between seminary and church.

If some people blame seminaries for hearing the siren song of academic prestige and lurching away from the parish, others point fingers at the North American church for creating the chasm by drifting away from the faith. In this version of the story, while seminaries continued to prepare candidates for ministry in the classical disciplines, the church became culturally co-opted and began to care little for the hard work of shaping their mission biblically, theologically, and ethically, instead demanding a no-cross, low-cost, stress-free suburban gospel of positive thinking fueled by fizzy, upbeat self-help sermons. Gibson Winter's 1961 diatribe, *The Suburban Captivity of the Churches*, and Pierre Berton's *The Comfortable Pew*, published in1965, were early warning shots regarding the shallowing out of the gospel in North American congregations.

In his book *Why Preach? Why Listen?* William Muehl, who was at the time a professor of preaching at Yale Divinity School, illustrates this market-place approach to church life when he tells of a student who, while in seminary, loved and devoured the theology of Karl Barth. But when this same student returned to campus for a reunion several years after graduation, he was sporting a lapel pin advertising the television program of one of America's most popular preachers, a power-of-positive-thinking guru and a man whose outlook could hardly be farther from Barth's. When Muehl asked him about this apparent shift in theological worldview, the graduate said, "I lost three churches before I figured out what people want."[2]

Regardless of blame, at a more functional level recent seminary graduates report that they have just spent three or more years learning very specialized bits of information — obscure figures in church history, the contributions of the Cappadocian Fathers to the doctrine of the Trinity, the impact of feminism upon biblical hermeneutics, the difference between deontological and consequentialist ethics, and the like. Then they leave the seminary and encounter the buzz saw of a church that couldn't care less about any of this, consumed as it is with budgets, youth programs, duking it out over worship styles, maintaining local traditions, and hungering for sermons that make sense and matter in day-to-day life. The result is that seminary graduates find themselves poorly equipped to practice ministry and unable to find much use for their expensive and lengthy seminary educations. Even the practical ministry courses they took seem out of touch with the press of actual ministry demands. No one taught them how to run a stewardship drive, figure out what to do with the praise band that has formed in the congregation, fire a recalcitrant organist, or deal with the adult church school teacher who wants to replace the approved curriculum with Eastern-style meditation or with Rush Limbaugh tapes.

A True Picture?

Where there is smoke, there is usually fire, and there is at least some truth in this picture of the divide between seminary education and parish minis-

2. William Muehl, *Why Preach? Why Listen?* (Philadelphia: Fortress Press, 1986).

try. But in many ways, the chasm between seminary and the practice of congregational ministry has been misunderstood and exaggerated. Yes, there are professors and courses in most seminaries that are almost laughably irrelevant to the practice of ministry and to the life of the church (and, alas, a few theological schools have more than their share of these). The fact is, though, most theological school faculty are quite involved in and aware of the local church, and they incorporate this experience of the real church into their teaching. And yes, there are know-nothing elements in almost every congregation who couldn't care less about the finer points of their pastors' theological education so long as those pastors have warm hearts, bubbling personalities, and expertise in growing churches. Truth be told, though, over time most congregations grow weary of thin theology and tire of leadership that does not rest on some substantive base.

This is not to say there is no gap between a theological school and the practice of ministry, no boundary to be crossed between seminary and parish (to employ Roy M. Oswald's metaphor, which he described so well in *Crossing the Boundary between Seminary and Parish*).[3] It is rather to say that there *ought* to be a gap between seminary and the practice of ministry and that negotiating it well is one of the marks of faithful ministry. It is part of the mission of a theological school to step back from the day-to-day practice of ministry and the rough-and-tumble life of any particular local church and to think about the past, the present, and the future of the church in ways that churchly scholars are called to do. In terms of the past, the theological school helps to preserve those treasures of doctrine and history that belong to the church, but which are sometimes lost from view in the press of the church's current struggles. In terms of the future, the theological school is called to bring to the surface issues emerging in culture and society that the church has not yet anticipated, or has resisted facing out of fear or inertia. In terms of the present, the theological school is not called to teach techniques and gimmicks but to help shape in students that theological habit of mind that enables pastors to engage whatever situations develop in ministry.

As for the parish, it stands in relation to the seminary as the court stands to the law school, as the clinic stands to the medical school, as the marketplace stands to the business school. The parish is the place where

3. Roy M. Oswald, *Crossing the Boundary between Seminary and Parish* (Washington: Alban Institute, 1980).

the work of the theological school finally comes to expression, where that work is tested and reframed, where questions and cries for help are hurled back to the school house. Seminary and local church are two different institutions with two different ways of being and serving, and yet they belong to the same faith culture. If they move too far apart, they become strangers and adversaries, but if they move too close together, they can no longer provide for each other the refining and resourcing ministries that each needs and each can offer the other.

When Luke Johnson described the front and back of a typical Catholic parish church, he did not despair over the divide; he celebrated it. "The genius of Catholicism," he observed, "has been its ability to hold these two worlds of religion — the world of formal discourse and the world of informal power — together in some sort of creative tension."[4] Good ministry is found not when seminary graduates hang their M.Div. diplomas on the wall, mop their brows, and say, "Well, that's over. Now on to real ministry." Good ministry is found, rather, where pastors stand with one foot firmly planted in their theological education and the other foot just as firmly planted in the parish, and allow the resulting tension to shape their pastoral practice.

Living in the Tension: Some Suggestions

Every minister is unique and every ministry setting is different, so negotiating the gap between seminary and the church involves, borrowing a line from Paul, "working out your own salvation with fear and trembling." In my experience, however, there are certain predictable "crossings" that can be anticipated from seminary to pastoral practice, certain bridges that pastors can expect to have to build. I want to name a few of them:

Reframing One's Theological Education

In the process of making one's way through a seminary curriculum and checking off the requisite courses in each of the areas of the curriculum, one can easily lose sight of the character of theological knowledge. Augustine said this, Wesley thought that, Schüssler Fiorenza claims this, Boff

---

4. Johnson, *Religious Experience in Earliest Christianity*, p. 2.

stands for that — it can easily all swirl by as a series of abstract, ahistorical, and disconnected ideas. To immerse oneself in the practice of ministry allows for a different view of theology: it emerges out of an actual, on-the-ground conversation in the life of the church. Between the lines of almost every theological textbook read in seminary can be heard the voices of real Christians asking urgent questions.

A friend of mine, a pastor who developed an interest in ancient Christian spirituality, took a year between pastorates to do a Master of Theology degree in patristics. About halfway through his degree program, in which he spent a great deal of time, of course, reading patristic writings, he came to a startling realization. "I get it!" he exclaimed. "The church fathers weren't philosophers. They were pastors!" He had discovered that patristic theology was not done in the abstract but by ministers like himself, pastors who preached to congregations, counseled the distressed, comforted the sick, and buried the dead. Suddenly, patristic theology took on a new cast. Instead of seeing the patristic writings as a collection of arcane and abstract theological ideas, my friend now saw them as the struggles of pastors trying to address concrete situations in their congregations.

I had a similar experience with Calvin's major work, *The Institutes of the Christian Religion.* I had read the whole of the *Institutes* twice as a teenager (signs of a misspent youth!) and misunderstood what I was reading both times. I had thought I was reading Calvin's theological system, a logically structured set of essential ideas and doctrines of the Christian faith. When I was a pastor, however, I reread the *Institutes* and saw them with new eyes. They were now not nearly so logical or systematic. Instead I understood them as conversations with parishioners. Behind every paragraph was some person in Calvin's community asking a question, some conversation with a church member in Strasbourg or Geneva asking about salvation, baptism, prayer, or some other faith concern.

Seeking Integration in the Life of the Church

It is a common complaint of recent seminary graduates that the curriculum they have just completed was fragmented and *dis*-integrated. They were served up shards of knowledge about the Bible, pastoral care, and church history, but what did any one of these pieces of information have to do with the others? If the many parts of their theological course of study didn't fit together in seminary, how can seminary education possibly serve as a coherent tool for ministry? This lack of integration is also a concern inside the walls of seminaries. The four traditional divisions of the curriculum — Scripture, theology, history, and ministry — are often experienced as thoroughly discrete disciplinary areas with their own methods, objectives, and internal standards and with firewalls built between them. So the frustration of graduates is often matched by an equal frustration inside theological schools, with faculties constantly fretting about the lack of integration in the curriculum. This prompts various pedagogical schemes and reform proposals, such as integrative courses or team-taught seminars aimed at forging some sort of unity in seminary education, which mostly fail miserably to achieve their goals.

The main problem is that this long-sought integration in theological education is not to be found in the theological curriculum at all; it is a property of the life of the worshiping and serving community of faith, the church. Despite all the turf wars and disciplinary independence, the fact is that seminary curricula still bear the marks of their parentage in the life of the church. The reason, for example, that biblical studies are taught in theological schools is not because there is some mystical unity in the great body of theology as a whole, of which biblical knowledge is an intrinsic part. Bible is taught in seminaries because Scripture is an intrinsic part of the church's life, and the church needs and wants to know all it can about its own Scripture.

Every now and then I dream about a hypothetical theological curriculum in which students would come on the first day of seminary not to the classroom but to the chapel. There they would participate in a rich, full, and well-planned service of worship. The rest of the three-year curriculum would be an exegesis of that act of worship. Who is the God who was both cause and object of that worship? Why were ancient Scriptures read and how did they function? Why these Scriptures and not others? What kind of ethical life is implied in this act of worship and why? What kind of community is required to engage in this act of worship, and what resources of care and education do they need to sustain their life together? A thousand questions could be asked; and to answer them the full array of disciplines and courses present in the theological school would be required.

But of course my dream curriculum is not hypothetical at all. The act of worship which serves as its unity and focus occurs in congregations every week. It is in the church that everything comes together. Seminary graduates seeking integration should not look back in resentment at the seminary, but should rather look around at the life of the congregation.

Ministry as a Change of Velocity, not a Change of Subject

In a recent interview, an NFL coach was asked what he thought was the biggest change for football players moving from college to the professional ranks. "Speed," he replied. "Players are surprised and amazed at how much faster the game is played up here."

The same is true when one moves from seminary to the parish. In an Introduction to Christian Ethics course, for example, a student can move with all deliberate speed in thinking through end-of-life issues, a luxury of time not granted to a pastor in a hospital corridor caring for the weeping and anxious family of a dying woman trying to decide whether to remove the respirator.

Weekly preaching is a superb case in point. Most basic preaching courses crawl slowly through an exploded diagram of the preaching process — a week to exegete the biblical text, another week to work on structure, and so on. Students are fortunate if they have been given the opportunity to craft three or four sermons by the time they complete seminary. But then, if they become solo pastors, they are suddenly thrust into the routine of weekly preaching where, to use the famous image, "Sundays fly by like telephone poles on the highway." One has barely uttered the "amen" for one sermon when the next one screams for attention, and the pulpit is a hungry place.

To paraphrase the coach, "Pastors are surprised and amazed at how much faster the game is played up here." This is why a seminary education can best be seen as the development of a certain habit of mind, a way of thinking and acting that has been studied so deeply and thought about so fully that it becomes almost intuitive and reflexive. It may take a long time to learn how to do the classic waltz, and a lot of looking at one's feet is required. But the goal is to get to the place that, when the music starts, one can glide across the floor with fluidity and grace. In my preaching classes, I tell my students that my educational goal for them as parish preachers is to become like great chefs educated at the Culinary Institute of Paris, but currently working as cooks at Denny's. The orders will come at them at breathtaking speed, and they will have to sling the hash and flip the omelets with all dispatch, but they will know what constitutes *haute cuisine,* and a taste of it will be there in every sermon they prepare.

Seeing Resistance and Messiness as Potentially Positive

Perhaps the greatest challenge for new ministers negotiating the gap between seminary and the church is facing the disappointment they feel in the church as an institution. In the seminary, they became inspired by images of the church as the called-out people of God, an alternative and inclusive community devoted to countercultural service and witness. But then they find themselves in congregations of very conventional people who seem far less interested in being a countercultural force than they are in selfishly demanding ministerial services to meet their latest whims and needs. Ministers went to theological school because they had a vision of themselves as change agents, but they often find that real ministry involves being chaplains to narcissists, and they soon grow tired and become discouraged. It's hard to put a finger on the problem. Did seminary education involve a lie about the real church, or has the church rejected its birthright for a mess of culturally compromised pottage?

Creative ministry, however, involves seeing resistance not as defeat but rather as something more positive.[5] When a pastor is genuinely attempting to help a congregation move to a more faithful place, and there is resistance, this is often an indication that the pastor is getting close to pay dirt. Theologically, we can affirm that the Holy Spirit is at work in congregations, stimulating growth and shaping the community into conformity with the image of Christ. Resistance is often a key indication that the battle is fully engaged between where the Spirit is leading a congregation and their fears about going there. Resistance is less about where a congregation is permanently lodged and more about a people anguishing over the possibility of responding to the Spirit's call.

The first church I served after leaving seminary was a small congregation in a very conservative branch of the Presbyterian family. At that time, this particular denomination of Presbyterians, based upon what I consider to be a misreading of the Scripture, stubbornly refused to allow women to serve in any official leadership role. Women were forbidden to serve as church officers at any level: pastors, elders, or deacons. After more than a decade of reform efforts, though, one year at its annual meeting the

---

5. No scholar has addressed more helpfully the positive dimensions of resistance in ministry than James E. Dittes. Two of his books — *The Church in the Way* (New York: Scribners, 1967) and *When the People Say No: Conflict and the Call to Ministry* (San Francisco: Harper and Row, 1979) — are particularly insightful.

denomination changed its polity to allow any congregation that insisted to elect women to the office of deacon, considered the "lowest" rank of leadership. It was a small victory, but a victory nonetheless.

I thought that my own congregation, which had been largely free of theological nitpicking and infighting, was a good candidate to put this new policy into immediate effect. As it so happened, only a couple weeks after the polity change was made, our governing body, called the session, was meeting to nominate a deacon to take the place of a person who had moved away to a new community, and this seemed to me a providential moment. I practically bristled with pride over the prospect that we could become the first congregation in our denomination to elect a female officer.

As the members of the session gathered that Sunday afternoon, they passed by my office on the way to the meeting room. I was on the lookout for the clerk of session, an older member of the congregation who was the key leader of the church. Finally I saw him coming, and I motioned for him to come into my office. He did, and I closed the door. "Listen," I whispered conspiratorially, "this is an exciting opportunity. We have a chance to become the first congregation in our denomination to have a woman as an officer. People respect you and I think things will go more smoothly if you would be . . . you know . . . the one to nominate . . . you know . . . a woman."

Ah, naïve young pastor was I. To my astonishment, the clerk erupted in rage. "You're going against two thousand years of church history!" he screamed in my face. "Women try to run everything," he shouted, "and if we have a woman deacon the men will resent it and drop out like flies!" We stared at each other for a tense moment. Then the clerk said, "We've got a meeting to go to," and he turned away with disgust.

We opened the door to the meeting room only to be greeted by a table full of anxious faces. The other members of the session had overheard every word of our exchange. Right at that moment, I was considering what other vocation I might enter, since this one seemed to be turning to dust. Dutifully I called the meeting to order and opened with a prayer that the Spirit would be present and would guide us into the ways of Christ. I then said, "Well, we all know why we are here. There is a vacant slot on the Board of Deacons, and we need to nominate a person to fill that place. The floor is open for nominations."

Everybody stared at the linoleum, and the silence was awkward and profound. For a long, long time, no one said a word. Then the clerk shifted uneasily in his seat, cleared his throat, and began, haltingly, to speak. "There comes a time when . . . it seems to me that sometimes the needs of the church . . . I believe that every now and then you have to set aside your own opinions and . . . I guess that there are larger concerns than. . . ." Then he stopped abruptly, as if he couldn't find the words. He looked at every face around the table, and then he blurted out, "Aw, what I'm trying to say is, I nominate Ethel Sauls."

I could hardly believe my ears. The clerk who had shouted his resistance only minutes before had now inaugurated a new era, not only in the life of our congregation but also in the history of a denomination. I would love to claim this as a victory of my ministry, but I know better. This was more about resistance as a sign that the Spirit was at work in the trenches of life; this is less about skillful ministry and more about answered prayer.

This points, I think, to one of the sharpest distinctions between seminary and the church. The seminary is, in essence, a laboratory, and as every lab technician knows, lab tests are quite necessary but also quite different from real life experience. An electric motor that runs at 2500 rpm under a hypothetical load in the bench test will not necessarily run the same when hooked up to a real-world load.

For instance, it is considered common knowledge in the seminary that the biblical Book of Jonah is a piece of imaginative fiction — wise and valuable; and all that business about being swallowed by a big fish is theologically generative, but not historically factual. In the lab, congregations would welcome this insight into Jonah, but in the real world of my first church, the congregation was not thrilled to have their innocent view of the Bible disturbed. If I had launched into a sermon saying, "Now, as we all know, Jonah is a piece of imaginative fiction. No fish really ever swallowed this prophet," I would have paid the consequences.

What I discovered, though, is that many of my most traditional members were holding onto their view of the Bible only through a heroic and very costly act of compartmentalization. They desperately wanted to believe that the Bible was inspired, and they also wanted to use their full minds in serving God, but they couldn't figure out a way to do both. My seminary education was replete with ways to navigate this difficult passage, and I could see in their balking over the Bible an invitation to help them love God with their minds as well as their hearts.

Conclusion

Although we could wish that ministry were neat and clean, the fact is that it is messy and full of ambiguities and contradictions. An old teacher of preaching, Robert E. C. Brown, in his book *The Ministry of the Word*, speaks of "the essential untidiness" necessary in preaching, the ability to connect the gospel to the amazingly conflicted realities of life. This, it seems to me, is the necessary instinct for faithful and effective parish ministry. Ministers need to be able to learn much in the front of the church, but they then need to move to the messier place at the back of the church where people are thirsty for transforming power in any form. Such is the unending task of any minister serving the Word that became messy and ambiguous by becoming flesh and dwelling among us, full of grace and truth.

2. Leadership, Pastoral Identity, and Friendship: Navigating the Transition from Seminary to the Parish

L. Gregory Jones and Susan Pendleton Jones

Strangers in a Strange Land

Strangers in a strange land. That's what it often feels like in moving from life as a seminary student to the first setting of full-time pastoral ministry. It is a time of significant transitions and enormous changes. During this transition, new pastors often feel loss and loneliness, as so much that was known and familiar in the seminary setting has to be left behind and so many new things — people, places, responsibilities — have to be encountered. New pastors need to reorient themselves, to be sure, but they also need to grieve, for typically they will have left behind a strong network of friends with mutual interests and shared concerns. For pastors in appointive systems, the transition can be especially trying, for their relationship with their new church is somewhat like an arranged marriage. They neither chose the church, nor did the church choose them. Change like this, even change for the good, can be challenging and frightening.

Recently we saw a bumper sticker that said, "People don't fear change; what they fear is loss." It was a perceptive insight, for there is almost always an element of loss during times of change, and this is often what causes people the most anxiety. Even when there is more gain than loss, change can still be challenging. During times of pastoral transition, both congregations and pastors are experiencing loss and gain — and they need to help each other understand this dynamic of change. On the congregation's side, the former pastor's departure has almost certainly made some people mad, some people sad, and some people glad. When the new pastor arrives, he or she enters into the thick of these complex feelings. The

13

new pastor needs to be aware of this dynamic, just as parishioners need to be aware of the losses that their new pastor is experiencing. A pastoral transition means change on many different levels, and change always entails loss.

This change is also challenging for new pastors because it places them face to face with the unknown and the uncertain. For young, inexperienced pastors it can be hard to learn how to navigate unfamiliar territory. Indeed, the early years of ministry are a good time to learn from mistakes because they will inevitably happen. Early in her first appointment Susan spent so much time reading commentaries and various study guides in preparation for a weekly Bible study she was leading that she failed to attend to details of the pastoral care needs of those in the congregation. She had been accustomed to the seminarian's emphasis on study, but her mistake helped her see that a shift in focus to the rich, complex relationships of pastor and parishioners was needed. Study was still important, but not more so than getting to know the people of the congregation, particularly in those early months of a new pastorate.

Yet embracing change can also be very positive. With change comes new energy, new opportunities, and a chance to deepen one's "pastoral imagination," because no one can say, "We've already tried that under your leadership." With change comes a steep learning curve which gives the new pastor a unique opportunity to rise to the occasion. Never again will the pastor have this kind of opportunity with this particular community to put names and faces of church members together within the first week or two, to establish a strong pastoral presence among the people, to instill confidence, to convey to the congregation a sense that people will be able to see God through the pastor's life. One minister we knew took vacation time and study leave for six of the twelve weeks of his first summer at a new church. In doing so, he missed his opportunity to make early connections with the people. He was therefore never able to establish strong credibility with the congregation and was asked to leave that church just a few years later.

Recent studies have shown that most pastors who leave local church ministry do so in their first five years.[1] One obvious reason is the gap that too often exists between seminaries and local congregations, creating a dy-

---

1. See, for example, the study by Dean R. Hoge and Jacqueline E. Wenger, *Pastors in Transition* (Grand Rapids: Eerdmans, 2005).

namic wherein new pastors are either ill-equipped or unwilling to appreciate the distinctive contours of their new setting and to love the people in it. In addition, denominations often send new pastors into some of the most difficult settings for ministry, settings where congregations are often ill-equipped or unwilling to provide the kind of support that new pastors need. This is especially the case when either the pastor or the church has special needs — during times of conflict in the church, for example, or when pastors are struggling with issues of loneliness and isolation or when they have particular personal needs regarding marriage and family. "Conflict, burnout, feeling unfulfilled, and experiencing family and marriage problems are the main culprits in draining the supply of parish ministers."[2]

When we arrived at Susan's appointment as the pastor-in-charge of two congregations, we were greeted at the parsonage by numerous parishioners from one of the churches wanting to tell us "their" side of the story. From what we could piece together, it seems that there had been a very heated administrative board meeting a few months earlier. During the meeting, disagreements arose and several board members left to start their own meeting down the hall, declaring themselves the official board. They returned about forty-five minutes later, ready to pronounce their decisions to the rest of the group. Arguments ensued and toward the end of the meeting board members were throwing chairs across the room. When Susan attended the first board meeting of the summer a month later, the final question that one parishioner asked was, "Why is our church not growing?" They seemed to be totally oblivious to the unhealthy dynamics of their interactions and how that might affect whether others would want to join their community — or whether we as pastors could thrive or even survive there.

Yet there are also local churches that are very good at receiving and nurturing "first call" pastors. We celebrated when some of our classmates discovered that the congregations to which they were assigned out of seminary were welcoming places with people gifted at nurturing new pastors; we only wish we had been similarly placed! Such churches play a beautiful and powerful role in the lives of new pastors as "transitional congregations." They intentionally and purposefully claim as part of their mission to receive and support pastors with little or no pastoral experience. They commit to providing the kind of material support — includ-

2. Hoge and Wenger, *Pastors in Transition*, p. 198.

15

ing a livable salary and opportunities for continuing education — that new pastors need.

We hope that denominations will increasingly recognize, value, and nurture such transitional congregations, identifying those that already embody a gift for welcoming new pastors as well as equipping others to do the same. Together these churches would form a network to enhance seminarians' transitions into full-time ministry. They would familiarize themselves with the research that has been done on pastoral transitions; they would discuss the various issues with which "first call" pastors typically deal. In effect, they would live out their calling from God to nurture and care for inexperienced pastors and create supportive environments to encourage them in their first years of pastoral ministry.

How, then, might we cultivate stronger relationships among institutions in order to nurture stronger and better transitions from seminary to the parish? Are there ways to nurture those relationships during seminary itself as well as in the first years of parish ministry? Can we avoid thinking of the transition simply as a baton being passed in a relay race, the person being "passed off" from one institution to another?[3] Can we envision partnerships between the seminary, the parish, and the judicatory that can nurture good transitions into the first setting of full-time ministry?

Building Bridges

Last week we received an e-mail message from a rising third-year Duke Divinity School student. It began with a question: "Forgive me for my ignorance, but I was wondering if there are seminars for seniors in their last year at Div School which help one to prepare for life in the parish?" This young student is from Louisiana, and in the wake of Hurricane Katrina's destruction across the southern end of his home state last year his question is particularly poignant. Next year upon graduation, he will almost certainly be sent to serve as pastor of a church that is still grappling with issues of destruction, grief, and loss related to the extensive damage caused

---

3. For a longer critique of this "relay race" model approach to theological education, see L. Gregory Jones, "Beliefs, Desires, Practices, and the Ends of Theological Education," in *Practicing Theology: Beliefs and Practices in Christian Life,* ed. Miroslav Volf and Dorothy Bass (Grand Rapids: Eerdmans, 2002), pp. 185-205.

by the hurricane. Most students nearing graduation from seminary are not facing the kinds of challenges in parish life that Jon will be facing, yet they are asking the very same question. They wonder if their coursework and studies, field education and spiritual formation, and community life and worship experiences in seminary have given them the basic preparation they need for the transitions that will take place in moving from being a seminary student to being a full-time pastor.

In their book *Pastors in Transition,* Dean Hoge and Jacqueline Wenger report the findings of their extensive research on clergy who have left local church ministry. The single most important recommendation Hoge and Wenger make based on this research is that "seminaries should do more to prepare their students for the practical aspects of ministry."[4] We agree: better bridges need to be built between the experience of seminary and the realities of full-time ministry. We were happy to be able to respond to our student Jon's e-mail by letting him know that there are several seminars on this topic offered by the divinity school each year and that he was welcome and indeed encouraged to attend any and all of them. We also told him about a recent curriculum revision in which we approved a requirement that every senior divinity student take a "bridge" course focusing on the connections between their seminary education and formation and life in parish ministry. These bridge courses are taught in fields across the curriculum, and have a distinctive focus on Christian ministry. We also invited him to help us start a monthly mentoring group — a gathering in which students like him meet with other graduating seniors along with pastoral mentors to explore their concerns, fears, and hopes as they move into full-time local church ministry.

Even so, much of what needs to be learned about pastoral ministry can only be learned in the practice of pastoral ministry. This is why seminaries require contextual (or field) education, and why they typically expect students to meet regularly with their peers and clergy mentors to reflect theologically upon those real-life church experiences. Seminaries need to offer a wide array of opportunities for learning and reflecting on the practical aspects of parish ministry, but they should not become "skills-based" or "how-to" programs. Ideally, such opportunities will be found throughout the curriculum. Theological education needs to provide a strong foundation for understanding and interpreting Scripture, reason,

4. Hoge and Wenger, *Pastors in Transition,* p. 202.

history, tradition, and experience so that pastors are able to make discerning judgments based on well formulated understandings and broad reasoning abilities rather than on "quick-fix" solutions.

Recently we overhead a young pastor telling a friend how much she had appreciated the kind of education she received in seminary. She said, "I've come to see that it's similar to the old proverb: 'Give a man a fish and he'll eat for a day; teach a man to fish and he'll eat for a lifetime.' I feel more prepared now to serve the church faithfully, not because I was told in seminary what the right answer is, but because I was taught to read, study, converse, and think carefully and wisely about the things that really matter — and apply those judgments to a variety of situations that arise in my day-to-day ministry." Excellent seminaries build on the formation that students ideally have already received in congregational contexts by forming people for the practical wisdom that pastors need, while also recognizing that there are aspects of a gifted pastoral imagination that can only be cultivated in the midst of parish ministry.

To be sure, seminaries must continually be evaluating how well they are doing in fulfilling their vocation, even as the crucial transitional years need more attention and evaluation by congregations and judicatories. Even so, no matter how well prepared seminary students are for life in the parish, they still have concerns about making the transition. As we prepared for life in full-time ministry, we discovered that our concerns fell into three broad categories: leadership, pastoral identity, and friendships. We believe they remain high on the list of current seminarians as they prepare for their first assignments:

- Will they be able to handle the challenges of leadership in the parish, which include issues as wide-ranging as navigating cultural, regional, and potentially ethnic and racial differences; developing effective communication styles; managing committee responsibilities and budgets; and dealing with difficult parishioners and the conflicts that inevitably arise, and often fester, in parish settings?
- Will they have a strong sense of their own pastoral identity? Will they be able to maintain spiritual disciplines and theological inquiry while pastoring full-time and keeping the Sabbath? Will they be able to understand the opportunities and burdens that accompany being seen as a representative of Christ in the community? Will they be able to stay healthy in body, mind, and soul?

• Will they find adequate mentors and friends who will support them and hold them accountable through times of decision, loneliness, and blessing that they will experience in parish ministry?

To be sure, these three categories are not exhaustive. But taken together, they give us insight into some of the key issues that pastors, seminaries, and congregations need to be in conversation about in order to nurture well-lived pastoral lives during the first years of ministry.

Rising to the Challenges

"So you're moving here from North Carolina? Then let me be the first to tell you, now that you're in Baltimore, you don't have to hide your beer in the crisper." The chairwoman of the pastor-parish relations committee greeted us at our new parsonage with these words. We knew we weren't in the South anymore. To serve effectively as a local church minister in the U.S., you must take into account regional and cultural differences that exist in different parts of the country — not to mention the challenges that multiply in those contexts of ethnic and racial diversity.

Greg grew up in Colorado in the shadow of the Coors brewery. When he moved to Durham, North Carolina, for seminary, he discovered he had entered the strange world of tobacco warehouses and the home of the Liggett and Myers Tobacco Company. It was then that he discovered the regionality of sin. In Colorado, most church members thought drinking alcohol was just fine, but smoking was a sin against God; in Durham, smoking was sanctioned, while drinking a beer in public would cause heads to turn in polite company. Getting to know the people of your church, their histories, the church and community's traditions, listening to their stories, and understanding what makes them and their community unique, are all challenges, but they are key to a healthy pastoral transition.

Just as important is the challenge for the new pastor to hone his or her communication skills. We learned that the transition from seminary meant less time listening to professors and insights from books and more time listening to people and gleaning insights from the local cultures. We arrived full of ideas and insights, but we discovered that one of the key skills of leadership is the capacity to read well one's congregation and surrounding community. As you listen for the "heartbeat" of your church community, you are also expected to communicate with its members effectively. The primary tasks of pastoral ministry involve communication: preaching, teaching, praying, leading, listening. If you are an effective communicator, with God and with God's people, and if you regularly and faithfully practice the art of good communication, you will experience fewer misunderstandings and will gain the respect, trust, and support of the congregation. Good communication skills are essential in every aspect of effective pastoral ministry — from proclaiming the Word and listening to others, to leading meetings and negotiating conflict situations.

We knew of a church committee that was having difficulty with effective communication every time they met. Finally they called in a consultant who offered them what seemed to be a simple solution, but it proved very effective. At their subsequent meetings, the only time someone was allowed to speak was after he or she had adequately restated the previous speaker's argument to his or her satisfaction. Only then could the current speaker add new information to the conversation. This required all members to listen carefully to others' opinions and to understand those opinions well enough to state them in their own words.

Sometimes leadership requires very hard decisions. In the first month of serving a new appointment, a pastor we knew discovered that a key staff member was having an affair with a married church member. The pastor immediately called the head of the staff-parish relations committee and together they called for a meeting with the staff person and the married woman with whom he was having the affair. They began the meeting with prayer. After hearing from both parties, each of whom admitted to the affair but was not remorseful, the pastor told the staff person that he had one of two choices: either end the affair or turn in his keys. The staff person reached into his pocket and handed the pastor his keys. The following Sunday — only five Sundays into the new pastor's tenure at that church — she had to announce the resignation of that individual to the congregation. Difficult situations require strong action. We communicate what we believe by what we say and by what we do, not only with our words, but also with our actions. One of our favorite sayings is Maryland's state motto: "Strong in action; gentle in manner."

Seminaries can and increasingly do provide courses in leadership of congregations, and it is important for them to attend carefully to how their whole education and formation is directed toward cultivating pastoral leaders with gifts for shaping faithful communities. Yet many of the challenges of leadership can only be learned in practice. As we will suggest below, it is crucial to cultivate relationships and programs that enable wise elders to mentor young pastors learning excellent practices of leadership.

Developing an Identity

During their first years of ministry, pastors need to develop a sense of patience in learning that vocational satisfaction doesn't come immediately. It must be cultivated over many, many years, with the help of faithful parishioners who both support and challenge the pastor in good ways. During these early years, each pastor makes the transition from being primarily a learner to being the primary teacher of a congregation (while also continuing to learn); from being one who is mentored to becoming the one who often mentors others (while also continuing to learn from different mentors, including practicing pastors and other leaders). Throughout life we continue to teach and learn, to mentor and to be mentored, but the emphasis on which is primary changes over time.

During a telephone conversation Susan had with a recent divinity school graduate, the new pastor was reflecting on a retreat she had led the previous weekend for lay leaders in her congregation. During that retreat she realized for the first time that they were turning to her for leadership, for advice, that she was being looked up to by them — rather than the other way around. Many times during college and again in seminary she had been the one looking up to others while on retreat. Now, for the first time, she realized that the roles had reversed. It was unsettling; it called her up short. She realized that she was now called primarily to mentor others while also needing the continued mentoring of older, wiser pastors and friends.

Gregory the Great wrote in his *Pastoral Care* that those "who carry the vessels of the Lord are those who undertake, in reliance on their way of living, to draw the souls of their neighbors to the everlasting holy places."[5] Pastors are those who "carry the vessels of the Lord" and if we do that faithfully then we need to live before the people "a life worthy of the calling to which [we] have been called" (Eph. 4:1).

That is an unnerving notion for seminarians. When Greg was doing

---

5. Gregory the Great, *Pastoral Care,* trans. Henry Davis (New York: Newman Press, 1950), II/2, p. 46.

a field education assignment as he began seminary, he made a pastoral call on a family. When the young girl in the family opened the door, she saw Greg, and her jaw dropped as she stepped back and then said in a loud voice: "Momma, come quickly, God is at the door." Well, Greg knew that wasn't right, but it was unnerving even to think about the fact that this girl saw him as the representative of Christ in that community.

We use Gregory the Great's *Pastoral Care* in a course we team-teach for first-year seminarians at Duke on "The Pastor's Vocation." St. Gregory's emphasis on the formation of a pastoral identity, one grounded in a holy life, invariably triggers significant discussion, because it seems so far from many people's conception of the ministry as a "helping profession" or a vocation designed only to care for others. Yet when seminaries are fulfilling their vocation well, they understand that they are called to participate in the cultivation of a pastoral identity — even though the discernment of a person's gifts and character for ministry is the responsibility of churches and judicatories, and even though the embodiment of a pastoral identity is discovered most fully only in the practice of ministry.

How do we cultivate the disciplines and practices that support and sustain a pastoral identity? In part, the elements of pastoral identity are the same disciplines and practices that are central in the formation of Christian identity: prayer, fasting, searching the Scriptures, hospitality, singing our lives to God, practicing Sabbath, and the like. Yet there are also particular practices that are crucial to a pastoral identity: preaching and teaching the Scriptures, celebrating and living the sacraments, cultivating a pastoral imagination, and nurturing the agility to move from situation to situation, and relationship to relationship, with grace and skill. Further, there are the challenges of learning to sustain one's own disciplines and practices in the midst of being asked to cultivate and nurture others' practices. How and where, for example, do pastors worship without being responsible for leading it? How and when do we read Scripture for our own spiritual life, without focusing on how to preach or teach it? How do pastors learn to practice keeping the Sabbath that we call all Christians to keep?

After a few years of serving as pastor of a very demanding new church start, the pastor began showing early signs of burnout: he was easily agitated, somewhat depressed, functioning on a much lower level than usual, and beginning to express concerns about the future. His congregation loved him and his family deeply, but they realized he needed help. The pastoral support committee called him in for a meeting and told him that they were requiring that he take a three-month sabbatical. At first he was hurt and angry, but after a few weeks of much-needed rest, reading, and family time, he realized that they had been right. He returned to the church after those three months ready to be the pastor they had first come to love.

If God needed to rest on the seventh day, so does every local church pastor. Pastors need to be creative in carving out Sabbath time each week. It may not be a 24-hour period of time each week, but it does need to be intentional time that is shaped by renewing, worshipful, energizing activities. It needs to be life-giving. After years of studying nonstop, we discovered in our first years of ministry that we were not paying attention to the rhythms of life that God calls us to if we are to sustain our own pastoral identities as well as the Christian life of our congregation.

If pastors are to be faithful in the practices of ministry, then they must commit to being lifelong learners; and their congregations need to support them both financially and with appropriate amounts of time for study, reading, and reflection. A few weeks before graduation several years ago, one of our "second-career" students stopped by to talk about how she was feeling about the prospect of leaving a place she had come to love over the previous three years. "I can't believe how much I'm going to miss all these people," she said. "Oh yes, you do become attached to so many new friends during these years — faculty, staff, and students — don't you?" Susan offered in response. "No," she replied. "I'm not talking about them, though, yes, I will miss them, too. I'm talking about Yoder and Barth and Taylor and so many others. Never again will I have this kind of intensive time to read, to study, to hear lectures and to have such intentional conversations with others who are also preparing for ministry. I'm going to miss that terribly. I know I'll have the books on the shelves of my study, and I can refer to them when I want to, but will I ever again have such a period of time set aside just for study and learning?" One pastor we know has set a goal of reading fifty pages a day. That kind of goal may not be possible every day for every pastor, but the most effective pastors never stop being learners and people who engage intentionally in Christian practices, not just professionally but also personally.

Cultivating Friendships

Contemporary American images of pastoral ministry, especially in mainline Protestant denominations, often envision a "lone ranger" out in a parish doing ministry. This has been compounded by messages, sometimes explicitly articulated and often left implicit, that pastors should not develop friendships in their congregations. The reasons given for this range from the dangers of showing partiality to the potential for friendship to compromise the pastoral role. We find these reasons unpersuasive, and think it is important to begin to talk more candidly and positively about the importance of friendships for pastors.[6] To be sure, there are challenges that need to be addressed in nurturing friendships with parishioners. But challenges are meant to be navigated, not retreated from.

In any event, new pastors in contemporary American culture often discover a profound sense of loneliness in their first parishes. They have gone from an educational setting where they had close friends and fellow-travelers through school, to professional settings that are often in rural or isolated places where social networks are more difficult to sustain. Ironically, the transition into full-time ministry is precisely when friendships of accountability and support are especially important. New pastors are asking: "How can I make sense of this new identity I have?" "How can I navigate the challenges I face and the opportunities I have to be in ministry with people at particularly important and poignant times of their lives?" "How do I deal with these new tasks, and how do I deal with the complexities of these people I am called to serve?"

It is important for new pastors to have what we call "holy friends" to whom they can turn for both accountability and support. Holy friends are those people who will challenge the sins we have come to love, affirm the gifts we are afraid to claim, and help us dream dreams we otherwise would not have dreamed. New ministers may cultivate such friends through the networks of their seminary classmates, with whom they covenant to get together once or twice a year for several days. Some groups of recent seminary graduates have been doing so, and we only wish we had thought to do so when we graduated. We made phone calls to friends from time to time, but those amounted to little more than opportunities to swap "war stories" about the parish.

Ministers might also cultivate such friendships with ministers in other denominations, or with other people in the surrounding area

---

6. For a more extensive discussion of the significance of friendships for faithful Christian ministry, see L. Gregory Jones and Kevin R. Armstrong, *Resurrecting Excellence: Shaping Faithful Christian Ministry* (Grand Rapids: Eerdmans, 2006).

through other social arrangements found in civic groups, sports teams, or shared interests. There are varieties of ways to ensure that we have networks of accountability and support. It's crucial for new pastors to be intentional in seeking out such relationships and making them a priority.

Perhaps most important, however, is cultivating a relationship with a mentor — an older, wiser pastor who can help orient and initiate new pastors into the craft of ministry. As new physicians learn the craft of practicing medicine as apprentices to a senior attending physician, so should new ministers have the opportunity to learn the practice of ministry, as well as to reflect thoughtfully on that practice, with a mentor. Sometimes effective mentoring relationships can occur through the formal structures provided by a judicatory, and we have been heartened to see such structures being developed. Often, however, the best mentoring relationships develop out of voluntary, intentional relationships. Either a wise pastor seeks out some younger pastors to take under her wing, or the younger pastor seeks out a pastor whom he particularly admires, and asks if they can set aside regular time to focus on the joys and griefs, opportunities and challenges, and hopes and fears of pastoral ministry.

It took us too long in our first settings of pastoral ministry to discover the importance of mentors and to identify those from whom we could learn. Eventually we found a couple of people whose friendship and wisdom became critically important to our being sustained in ministry and in learning better practices. Yet we have also grieved as we have learned, after the fact, of gifted young pastors whose loneliness and isolation were key factors leading them to leave the pastorate and seek other vocations.

Holy friendships are important throughout the practice of Christian ministry, and they are especially critical during the transition into full-time pastoral ministry. They can be some of the most important relationships for our own soul as well as for increasing our capacities to be effective Christian ministers. Denominations can and should do more, and seasoned pastors can and should be more intentional in reaching out and taking responsibility for mentoring new generations of pastors into the crafts of ministry. At the same time, new pastors can and should be intentional in paying attention to the importance of holy friendships, and making their care and sustenance a priority in the rhythms of pastoral life.

In Conclusion

Too often, transitions into ministry become problematic because no one takes responsibility for cultivating strong relationships among the partners involved: the seminary from which the person is graduating, the parish and the judicatory to which the person is going, and the person (and, in many cases, the family) that is making the transition. If, rather than treating this time as a "spiritual Bermuda Triangle," we instead cultivate conversations and partnerships to enhance our capacity to navigate the challenges and build on the opportunities, we will be able to provide a much stronger start for new pastors than we ourselves experienced two decades ago. No one in particular is to blame, and a variety of institutions can and should work together to support and sustain such transitions.

Our hope is that upon graduating from divinity school, Jon — and all the other students in his senior class — will be well prepared not only to help their people deal with the unusual challenges of situations in ministry like Katrina but also to shepherd their people through times of pastoral transition, and indeed even through the normal, everyday seasons of their life together in the Body of Christ.

3. Making the Transition: From a Theology of Ministry to a Ministry of Theology

Ray S. Anderson

I was installed as the first pastor of a newly forming congregation just a week after graduating from seminary. In my mind, I was well prepared theologically to preach the knowledge I had acquired in seminary. In my congregation's experience, however, the theological mantle that I draped over my sermons in hopes of imparting truths about God was a poor disguise for an absence of practical wisdom that failed to connect the soul of God with the soul of humanity. The emperor had no clothes!

While in seminary, I had typed up all of my notes for systematic theology, believing that these would provide me a resource for sermon preparation. I found texts of Scripture that lent themselves to my homiletic design and proclaimed with passion the doctrine of God as I had been taught. Only a few months went by before one of my congregation's members ventured a word of affirmation along with a note of complaint. "We know that you really like theology, Pastor, and some of what you have been telling us about God we already knew and some we didn't know. But it is all quite irrelevant to our daily lives." I had already begun to suspect as much, for my passion for preaching did not seem to be met on their part with a penchant for learning. As it turned out, they were hungry for bread and I was passing out stones. The menu from which I was serving them was, at the same time, leaving me undernourished in my own soul.

Turning away from the instinct to defend myself — surely an early sign of God's grace! — I encouraged the man to explain further what he meant. "It's this doctrine of God stuff," he blurted out. "You say that we should come to understand that God is omnipotent — that he is all powerful and can do everything. What we want to know is can he do anything in particular, something that affects our lives, for instance." He went on to list all the attributes of God that I had carefully transferred from my systematic theology notes to my sermons. (He had been listening!) "If God is omniscient, we can easily assent to the fact that he knows everything. What we want to know is does he know who we are in our small lives."

Ouch!

Then I remembered the little book recommended to me by my professor of practical theology, a volume titled *A Little Exercise for Young Theologians*, written by Helmut Thielicke. Thielecke was a pastor before he was a theologian. Referring to a recent graduate of a theological seminary who became a preacher, Thielicke describes his initial failure as due to the arrogance of a theological novice: "Under a considerable display of the apparatus of exegetical science and surrounded by the air of the initiated, he produces paralyzing and unhappy trivialities, and the inner muscular strength of a lively young Christian is horribly squeezed to death in a formal armor of abstract ideas." It is not that theology itself is the problem, he goes on to say: theology is a sacred task but it can become diabolical when it becomes "a coat of mail which crushes us and in which we freeze to death." The apostle Paul put it plainly: "the letter kills but the Spirit gives life" (2 Cor. 3:6). Thielicke added his own commentary when he wrote, "Whoever ceases to be a man of the spirit automatically furthers a false theology, even if in thought it is pure . . . but in that case death lurks in the kettle."[1]

A few years later I discovered the book in which the German theologian and pastor Dietrich Bonhoeffer had warned his students who were to become pastors of the danger of theology used as a device to arm the preacher with authority:

> The greatest difficulty for the pastor stems from his theology. He knows all there is to be known about sin and forgiveness. . . . The peak of theological craftiness is to conceal necessary and wholesome unrest under such self-justification. . . . The conscience has been put to sleep. Theology becomes a science by which one learns to excuse everything and justify everything. . . . The theologian knows that he cannot be

---

1. Helmut Thielicke, *A Little Exercise for Young Theologians* (Grand Rapids: Eerdmans, 1962), pp. 8, 36.

shot out of the saddle by other theologians. Everything his theology admits is justified. This is the curse of theology.[2]

Had the theology that blessed me become a curse to others?

Needless to say, this was a shattering realization. I was not shot out of the saddle by theologians from behind — the seminary gave me a very good rear-view mirror! Instead, I was caught in the headlights, so to speak, by the luminous faces of those who turned toward me seeking the person of God, not merely mental constructs about him. Theology becomes a curse when our concepts of God conceal the being of God. And so what the seminary neglected to teach me I learned in the "merciful shattering" of the mental wall broken through by God himself once I became involved in ministry. C. S. Lewis, who had his own shattering experience of emerging from unbelief to belief, wrote: "Every idea of Him we form, He must in mercy shatter."[3]

The apostle Paul, whose own constructs of God were shattered in his encounter with Jesus on the road to Damascus, confessed that true knowledge of God comes only through the self-revelation of God through the Spirit: "What no eye has seen, nor ear heard, nor the heart of man conceived, what God has prepared for those who love him, God has revealed to us through the Spirit" (1 Cor. 2:9; Isa. 64:4; 65:17). The God who is inconceivable from a human standpoint is now revealed to humans through the *mysterion* of Christ, the God revealed in the flesh of Jesus (1 Tim. 3:16).

Looking back now, after forty-five years of pastoral ministry and seminary teaching, I can see several transitional points that impacted my life and that may well provide some wisdom for others. I view the transition from the seminary setting to ministry service as one that begins with professors who mentor the mercy of God as well as those who measure our doctrine of God.

Being Mentored in Mercy

My professor of pastoral theology at seminary was Dr. Clarence Roddy, a former Baptist minister who brought years of pastoral experience to the

---

2. Dietrich Bonhoeffer, *Spiritual Care* (Philadelphia: Fortress Press, 1985), pp. 67-68.

3. C. S. Lewis, *Letters to Malcolm: Chiefly on Prayer* (New York: Harcourt, Brace, & World, 1964), p. 187.

classroom and a wealth of anecdotal wisdom to bear on his counsel to those of us preparing to be pastors. Indeed, I think that I learned more from his personal stories than from his professorial lectures. "I was a young man, pastor of my first church," he began. At that point we put down our pens and opened our hearts. "A young woman in the congregation became pregnant before she was married. The head elder of the church demanded that she appear before the entire congregation on a Sunday morning to confess her sin. I stood helplessly by, watching the shame flood her face, and knew that we had lost a soul. She disappeared from our midst and we never saw her again."

Roddy was a deeply emotional man. Tears glistened in his eyes as he paused, as if to peer back through the decades in search of another ending. But there was none. There never is. Each of has a historian self that diligently records the facts, and though we revisit the scene a thousand times, we stand rooted in the same place. Finally, he looked up and said, "I knew in that moment that something was wrong with what we had done. Our crime against her was greater than her sin against God. With God there is mercy; with a scolding and scathing spirit of judgment there is none. But I was young and unsure of myself. I was afraid of the elder. The power with which he acted as her judge could, in my mind, as quickly be turned against me."

He paused again, and this time the tears were gone and fire burned in their place. "Within a year that same elder left his wife and ran off with another woman." Now he was the professor again. Turning directly to us he said, "Don't ever fear to show mercy to those who need it most, and don't ever think that mercy is a minor virtue in favor of God's justice. I know better now."

I heard little of the rest of the lecture. I pondered what he had said and made something of a vow to myself that I would begin my ministry, if possible, where he had ended, with the wisdom to show mercy. Rather than leaving behind a trail of casualties caused by being too quick to punish and too slow to show mercy, I would practice the wisdom of a pastoral heart from the beginning in the lives of those who were abusing themselves with guilt and self-punishment.

It was not easy. The new congregation to which I was called was rife with situations that seemed to call for moral judgment, if not also discipline. Yet I searched the gospel accounts of Jesus' ministry in vain for instances where his first response was one of moral judgment rather than mercy. There were numerous occasions when he encountered persons who were treated as outside God's moral law and many who had no moral standing due to their own sin. Not once did he scold or act in a judgmental way toward those 'real sinners!' When he did pronounce righteous judgment, sometimes with scathing words, it was always directed toward the self-righteous and those who claimed moral superiority by virtue of their own religious practices. Mercy tempers justice, wrote Shakespeare: "It is enthroned in the hearts of kings, It is an attribute to God himself; And earthly power doth then show likest God's, When mercy seasons justice."[4] (That old elder got his "pound of flesh," but not without drawing some blood!)

I then began to rethink the relation of mercy to God's moral law. Jesus practiced the moral freedom of God in standing with persons condemned by God's moral law. The woman caught in adultery, for instance, was thrown at the feet of Jesus with self-righteous moral judgment by her accusers. They even had the text of Scripture on their side which prescribed death as punishment for such behavior. Instead of invoking the moral law of God, Jesus extended the moral freedom of God by making an intervention between her and the law which condemned her, so that the effect of the law was deflected by his words, I do not condemn you, "go your way, and from now on do not sin again" (John 8:11). God can act quite arbitrarily with regard to extending mercy because he acts out of freedom rather than having to satisfy some abstract moral law. "I will be gracious to whom I will be gracious, and I will show mercy on whom I will show mercy" (Exod. 33:19). The moral freedom of God does not lead to moral confusion, for the result of mercy is not moral ambivalence but the creation of a new moral structure of love and community.

It was Jesus himself, who is "close to the Father's heart," who dared to extend mercy to one who had no moral standing before the law. In doing so, he invested his own moral authority in her rather than in the law. Mercy is itself moral empowerment while punishment, even justice, tends to disempower those who have already lost their moral right to righteousness. I began to see that God's moral freedom reaches deeper into the divine heart than God's moral law. It is not justice but mercy that drives the moral law of God and so establishes God's moral nature. There is a time and place for justice, but not at the expense of mercy. There is a sense in which justice often

4. The reference to William Shakespeare is from *The Merchant of Venice,* act IV, scene 1.

can only be realized through mercy. Those who are victims of injustice look for mercy on the part of those who have the power to restore justice.

As I suggested above, a second transitional point came as a result of the candid commentary on my preaching by one of my parishioners. As I have said, the theologian in me was like the proverbial "deer caught in the headlights." When the glare subsided, I decided to recalibrate my way of doing theology. I knew that I had to make the transition from academic theology to practical theology. I soon realized that the moment I graduated from seminary all the theology I had learned became historical theology! I was well-grounded in Christology (including the humanity of Christ) but woefully ignorant of "humanology" (the humanity of actual human beings). To make up for the deficit I embarked on a reading curriculum that involved an exegesis of human nature — a subject not included in my seminary education!

I discovered and read all the novels of Thomas Wolfe, among them *Look Homeward, Angel!* and *You Can't Go Home Again.* I read the novels of Dostoyevsky and discovered the agonizing but spiritual core of the human self. I read all of Søren Kierkegaard's works, and pondered the paradox of the existential moment in which the eternal is grasped in time. I read Gibran; the plays of Arthur Miller; Christopher Fry; D. H. Lawrence; the bittersweet and poignant novel *A Death in the Family* by James Agee; Nikos Kazantzakis' *Zorba the Greek* and, yes, *The Last Temptation of Christ*! I read the luminous works of Alan Paton, *Cry, the Beloved Country* and *Ah, But Your Land Is Beautiful,* and discovered that the soul of South Africa is close to the soul of God. And through all this, I found the contours of the incarnation of God, a landscape my theology professors never acknowledged if, indeed, they ever saw it.

I am reminded of Dietrich Bonhoeffer, who had failed to satisfy the church authorities with the sample sermons he submitted as part of his ordination process. The examiners' report was sent to him by his father while he was in Barcelona (Spain) fulfilling an internship assignment. Along with the report, his father added his own comment quite to the contrary. He cited his own mentor who had supervised him in his clinical work in preparing to be a psychiatrist, who said, "Just don't read any psychiatric literature! It only makes one dumb!" Apparently Bonhoeffer took the advice seriously but still managed to pass his ordination exam.[5]

---

5. The citation about Bonhoeffer is from Thomas Day, *Dietrich Bonhoeffer on Christian Community and Common Sense* (New York: The Edwin Mellen Press, 1983), p. 183.

Strangely enough, the transition was not a detour away from the Bible, but a return to reading the Bible through a new lens, something like the experience of Karl Barth, who, during his first year of pastoral ministry, began to read the book of Romans as though he had never read it before. This "strange new world of the Bible," as Barth put it, was the beginning of the recalibration of his own theological method.[6] My experience was not as dramatic, but fully as significant. Without knowing it at the time, I was making the transition from the *study* of theology to the *doing* of theology.

Doing Practical Theology Is More than Making Theology Practical

I discovered that the transition from academic theology to practical theology was a process of "thinking backwards" from the person and ministry of Jesus to the reality and being of God. I took as a starting point the life, death, and resurrection of Jesus as the very self-revelation of God's own being. To carry out this project I began a series of sermons from the four Gospels tracing out the life of Jesus from conception and birth through his ministry to the point of crucifixion and resurrection. I did not conceal my approach nor my intention from the congregation. I announced that we were about to embark on a bold venture, seeking to probe the depths of that *mysterion* which is not a secret, but rather a 'revealed mystery' made accessible to us through the person of Jesus Christ, in whom the "whole fullness of deity dwells bodily" (Col. 2:9). I asked them, as I asked myself, to be willing to have our concepts of God reconceived, as it were, through the conception of God's being in human form.

From the beginning, the series of sermons began to reveal a common thread. At each point in his life and ministry, the work of Jesus following his baptism by the Holy Spirit revealed the innermost being of God, his Father. The apostle John captured this truth in the simple but elegant words of Jesus to his disciples: "The Father loves the Son and shows him all that he himself is doing" (John 5:20). The reality of God's being is not a concept that stands alone and apart from us, but a divine communion in

---

6. Eberhard Busch, *Karl Barth: His Life from Letters and Autobiographical Texts* (Philadelphia: Fortress Press, 1976), pp. 98, 101.

which we participate through the humanity of Jesus. Through this communion we enter into God's self-knowledge — which is the soul of theology — and are empowered to participate in God's self-revelation — which is the soul of ministry. It is the ministry of God toward the world that reveals the being of God as the one who loves the world (John 3:16).

When I began to practice ministry as God's continuing ministry through Christ, I came to see that every act of ministry reveals something of God. By "act of ministry," I mean a sermon preached, a lesson taught, a marriage performed, counsel offered, or any other word or act which people might construe as carrying God's blessing, warning, or judgment. What we may intend as a very practical application of a biblical principle or church rule says something about who God is. Not everything we say or do is ministry in that sense, of course. But when we speak and act as a pastor we give others reason to conclude that we are speaking on behalf of Christ. When we speak and act out of the authority of the church, we give others reason to think that God's nature and character, as well as his will for persons, is embodied in our words and actions.

If I say, "I'm sorry, but our church does not permit children to partake of the communion service," I may think that I am merely explaining church polity, but in reality, I am saying something about God. The parent of the child may well conclude that God does not want children to taste and touch of his own grace, even though they can freely feed on the same food their parents eat at home. While the motive might be to protect the "holy sacrament," the effect might be to portray God as accessible only to those who are qualified by an enlightened mind. Jesus expounded a theology of supreme importance when he took the children in his arms and blessed them, despite the protestations of his disciples, and thereby proclaimed, "Whoever does not receive the kingdom of God as a little child will never enter it" (Mark 10:15-16).

Suppose that I should even say, "I cannot perform this marriage because you have been divorced and it would be contrary to the Bible's teaching." Surely one might think that having a biblical text as support for one's ministry would be sufficient! But even here we must ask the question: What does this act of ministry — refusal to marry a divorced person — teach about God? If it should be construed as teaching that God can forgive all sin but the sin of a divorce, and that God's grace is not available to one who has committed that particular sin, would this be in accord with God's Word itself?

Every act of ministry teaches something about God. When Jesus forgave the sin of the woman caught in adultery and refused to sentence her to death — which the Law of Moses demanded — his act of ministry taught something about God that even the law did not teach. In this case it was not enough for the religious authorities to say, "the Bible teaches," but rather, they were responsible to recognize that the Word of God was even then incarnate in their midst and acting so as to reveal God's ultimate purpose, which is to liberate persons from the law of sin and death and to free them to recover their humanity as God intended.

Jesus was often condemned by the religious authorities for his actions and for his ministry of healing on the Sabbath. He responded by saying, "The Sabbath was made for humankind, and not humankind for the Sabbath" (Mark 2:27). When Jesus experienced the work of God in healing, even on the Sabbath, he taught that God's act of healing led to a new theology of the Sabbath. The ministry of God through the ministry of Christ became a hermeneutical criterion by which the text of Scripture could rightly be interpreted as Word of God. The prophet speaks for God when he says that the word "that goes out of my mouth shall not return to me empty, but it shall accomplish that which I purpose, and succeed in the thing for which I sent it" (Isa. 55:11). The effect of the Word of God is as much Word of God as the utterance of it. When Paul experienced the coming of the Holy Spirit upon uncircumcised Gentiles, he expounded the ministry of the Spirit of God as theological truth and said that circumcision no longer was a binding requirement following the resurrection of Christ (Gal. 6:15). The transition from seminary to ministry is more than making theology practical: it is the actual doing of practical theology.

From Leading the Servants to Servant Leadership

But having made this transition, one entering into ministry is not yet assured of success. A student about to graduate and take up a position as pastor of a small congregation once asked me what factors contribute to success in ministry. "Seventy-five percent of ineffective ministry can be attributed to poor preaching," was my response, "while only twenty-five percent of success in ministry can be attributed to good preaching." The student then asked, "What about the other seventy-five percent that contributes to success in ministry?" "Effective leadership," was my reply.

35

Most congregations expect good preaching, but will not excuse ineffective leadership. Moses was a pretty good preacher (despite his apparent speech impediment) and an even better theologian. But it was his servant leadership that brought the people to the threshold of the Promised Land.

My seminary preparation for ministry included classes in homiletics accompanied by critical evaluation of several practice sermons. Our professor of pastoral theology not only taught us about officiating at funerals and weddings, but had us practice with each other doing baptisms with real water — including immersion for those so inclined! Yet we were never instructed in principles of church leadership, nor were there any "practice" sessions of conducting congregational and church board meetings. Apparently it was assumed that these skills were acquired through on-the-job training — for better or for worse, which, as it turned out, was most often for worse!

"I don't believe in the concept of servant leadership," a pastor once told me. "I am not the paid servant of my congregation, but their spiritual leader." Yet I could tell from his tone of voice that this pastor was protesting as much as he was proclaiming. When pressed, he admitted that he felt like he spent more time serving the needs of the congregation than leading it. There was an angry edge to his emotions and a bit of defiance in his eyes.

More than one pastor has ended up feeling this way. Seminary graduates often enter pastoral ministry with idealistic visions of a spiritual ministry devoted largely to preparing rich and edifying sermons, giving wise counsel to lay leaders, and offering pastoral care and comfort to needy souls. After all, the call is to "full-time ministry." Sooner or later, these same pastors begin to realize that the congregation is reading from a different version of the script, one in which "full-time" is the name of the horse hitched to the cart with a dozen wheels with one or more dropping off at the most inopportune times, and "minister" is the code word for the driver who also doubles as the mechanic.

The fundamental misconception with servant leadership, as reflected by the pastor cited above, is that one ends up being the servant of the people or the organization. This leads to the "doormat" concept of leadership, wherein one lays down whatever dreams and plans one has and invites people to walk over them. "I am only the coach," one pastor said, "my people are the players." Or, to put it in more ecclesiastical terms, "I am only the pastor, my people are the ministers." This conception of servant leadership is really the abandonment of leadership. It leads to failure on the part of the leader and frustration among the members of the church.

Robert Greenleaf, who wrote the seminal work on servant leadership, made it clear that the servant leader is not subservient to the desires and goals of the organization, but rather is a servant of the mission of the organization. It is the vision of the specific mission or goal of the organization, says Greenleaf, which marks the effective leader. "Foresight is the 'lead' that the leader has. When he loses this lead and events start to force his hand, he is leader in name only. He is not leading; he is reacting to immediate events and he probably will not long be a leader."[7]

The congregation that called me to be their pastor when I graduated from seminary had been meeting in a temporary building for six months and was looking to buy property. While preaching twice on Sunday (morning and evening) I assumed leadership of the church board and found myself negotiating for the purchase of the property, arranging for the financing, securing an architect and building contractor, and then working alongside the small crew of about a dozen men in our congregation every Saturday for almost a year putting up the first building. Hundreds of decisions had to be made and processed through the lay leadership while avoiding the landmines of petty prejudices, passionately held opinions, and the power dynamics typical of strong egos!

I quickly realized that the major transition in my role as pastor was one of relinquishing the built-in power of the office of pastor in order to gain the authority of a pastoral leader. The temptation was to use a power-play when my authority was questioned. Transitioning into effective leadership meant letting go of power in order to define the vision in such a way that others were empowered to lead the way forward. This meant personal vulnerability (having nothing to defend at the expense of another's feelings) coupled with a persistent challenge to make the vision so compelling that it belonged to everyone (having nothing to gain at the expense of another's loss). I learned that effective leadership involves discipline that corrects disorder and direction that overcomes disorganization and confusion. Effective servant leadership means directing and coordinating the

---

7. Robert Greenleaf, *Servant Leadership* (New York: Paulist Press, 1977), p. 18. See also his book *The Servant as Religious Leader* (Peterborough, N.H.: Windy Row Press, 1982). On the vision of leadership, see Ray Anderson, *Minding God's Business* (Grand Rapids: Eerdmans, 1986), pp. 66-68.

energies and resources of the people of God; this is being a "faithful stew-ard" of God's vision.

I discovered that the authority of a leader is not in possessing a claim to know the will of God more than anyone else, but in having the vision, based on promise, which leads to the will of God through doing God's work. When leaders claim to know the will of God as a private revelation, they are close to misusing power and abusing the people. Any use of power to abuse the people is contrary to the will of God because God's desire and purpose is directed toward the ultimate good of his people.

By the grace and mercy of God I made the transition from seminary to pastoral ministry; many do not. In reading what I have written above, I wish that someone would have placed something like this essay in my hands during my last year of seminary or, even better, during my first year of ministry! The idealism and romanticism that often inspires many sem-inary students regarding the nature of the church and pastoral ministry can be reinforced with knowledge but be impervious to wisdom. "Get wis-dom," urges the author of the book of Proverbs. "The beginning of wis-dom is this: Get wisdom, and whatever else you get, get insight" (Prov. 4:5, 7). The good professor who mentored me in mercy found the chink in my armor of knowledge through the tears in his eyes and the theology in his soul — I got wisdom that day, in at least one dimension of ministry. The "soul of ministry" is caught as much as it is taught.[8] For those who are al-ready struggling in the trenches, it is not too late to "catch up." For those who are breathless with anticipation of "receiving the call" and putting on the mantle of ministry, it may be a good time to pause and catch your breath. Gain insight into the kind of minister of Christ you want to be-come after a lifetime of ministry, and begin to practice it now. Mercy!

8. Ray S. Anderson, *The Soul of Ministry: Forming Leaders for God's People* (Louisville: Westminster John Knox, 1997).

4. Pulpit Supply

Stephanie Paulsell

It's hot, but not as hot as it's going to get. We're driving from Wilson to Oak City in the early morning, my dad and I, the windows of our green Impala wound down, fields of Bright Leaf tobacco shimmering in the heat on either side of the road. Most are nearly picked clean by migrant workers and local children working twelve-hour days, moving through the fields again and again, harvesting leaves from the bottom up. A few fields are neglected, the flowers growing out of the tops of the plants making breezy accusations of laziness, inattention. It's Sunday morning, and, except for the rattle and whine of insects, all the fields are quiet.

Oak City Christian Church is between pastors, and my dad is filling their pulpit. His plain, black, hardback Bible lies on the seat between us, his sermon neatly folded up between its pages.

Some Sundays we hurtle through the humming, green morning without saying much, just watching the fields go by and the fragile-looking barns where the tobacco will hang to cure. Other Sundays, we're more talkative. Once my dad told me about walking over the knob of a hill at the Abbey of Gethsemani in Kentucky, just as the setting sun washed the valley below in one last flood of brilliant light, and he felt God's presence just as surely as he had ever felt anything. Sometimes I ask questions. "Dad, do you think there's really a hell?" "No," he'd answer. "Why would God build a permanent place for evil?" This was the catechism of the car.

Back in the seventeenth century, the English poet and pastor George Herbert advised preachers to dip and season "all our words and sentences in our hearts" so that the congregation "may plainly perceive that every word is heart-deep." My dad types his sermons on a manual typewriter and then, with a pen in his hand, tests the depth his words have reached, scratching out, filling in. Even as a child I can see that this heart-deep work gets rewarded with attention. In Oak City, there's one young man in particular, in his late teens or maybe his early twenties, who leans forward in the pew, his chin in his hands, eyes bright, when my dad preaches. He looks like he would drink every word like water if he could.

My dad is serious about preaching, as those marked-up sermons testify, and he takes his listeners seriously, never hesitating, for example, to quote from Bernard of Clairvaux, a twelfth-century Cistercian writer he adores, when he feels Bernard can offer a clarifying word. Not that he's not funny. Like a lot of preachers, he often opens with a humorous story, the doorway across which he beckons his listeners, a place for the congregation to find their bearings and settle in to the work of listening. Sometimes these stories involve me, like the one about him overhearing my friend Jessica and me talking about the Blessed Virgin as we clamp skates onto our shoes, tighten them with a key, and skate back and forth across the smooth cement floor beneath our carport. At dinner he asks me, "Do you know who the Blessed Virgin is?" And I reply, "I thought you were a religion professor!" My dad thinks this is hilarious, and he laughs every time he tells it with the abandon and volume that have led his students to coin the phrase "the Wild Bill laugh." When he tells stories like that in front of whole congregations, I blush with real embarrassment, but I also kindle with real pride.

George Herbert also instructed preachers to choose "texts of Devotion, not Controversy." I can't say my dad always meets this standard. He tends to head straight for the most difficult knot in any passage of Scripture, and sometimes chooses something distasteful like Psalm 109, in which the psalmist prays that the wife of his enemy be made a widow and his children begging orphans. His friend, Matthew Kelty, a Trappist monk, says that "the one true purpose of monastic life is to discover reality." Substitute "religious" for "monastic" and you have my dad's own conviction, perfectly expressed. The really real is what he's after, and so he cannot do without even one of the Psalms, even though I've heard him say from the pulpit, "as I work my way through the Psalms day after day, I dread coming to number 109. I hate it. I wish it were not there." But it is there, every time through. And so he reminds himself of what his friend Matthew loves to say, that the Psalms take us "all the way in and all the way down." They shine a light into every corner of our selves. "If we can't face it," my dad asks as he looks out at congregations that are largely rural, largely white, wholly Southern, "how will we ever be able to change?"

This morning in Oak City my dad is preaching my favorite of his sermons: "Lost in the Mystery of God." I've heard him preach it in other churches, but I haven't gotten tired of it yet. This is what my dad wants for all of us, whether we're a farmer or a teacher or a teenager or a mother or a little girl: that we be lost in the mystery of God. Not that our dogma be airtight. Not that we be saved from the fires of hell. But that we become so lost in the mystery of God that we become permeable, available, vulnerable to what is really real.

I want to be lost like that. I've tried a few things: turning in circles in the front yard until I fall down, drunk and dizzy on the spinning earth. Swinging in the swing set my dad set up for my sister and me in the back yard, chanting *Narnia, Narnia,* in the hopes that I would suddenly break through. Pressing my hands against my closed eyes as I lay in bed, watching chips of pink and blue swirl against the dark. Kneeling in the woods behind our house, a cathedral of pine trees, building altars of moss and mud in its side chapels, well off the paths where the neighborhood boys raced around on banana seat bikes, playing cards clipped to their wheel spokes with clothing pins for maximum racket.

We pull into the dirt parking lot of Oak City Christian Church, and an elder smoking under the oak trees stubs out his cigarette and comes to greet us. "Morning, preacher," he says. "Going to be a hot one." "Sure is," my dad replies.

Once inside my dad disappears to do whatever it is ministers do behind the scenes before the service starts. I find a place in the pew that will be easy for him to see from the pulpit, on the aisle, about halfway up. When the organ music starts, and he walks out into the chancel with the elder who will lead the service, the first thing is does is look for me, and catch my eye, and smile.

The elder makes the announcements: a work day at the church next Saturday. Christian Women's Fellowship circles meeting in members' homes. The youth group will have a trip to the skating rink in Kinston. Who's in the hospital, who's just returned home, who's recently bereaved. He asks us to bow our heads, and he prays for all in need and that God will be with us this morning. We sing a hymn. The windows of the church are open to catch any stray breeze that might come along. I am wearing a short yellow dress that my mother made, and the bare skin of my thighs sticks to the pew. When my dad comes into the pulpit, though, I forget how hot it is. He reads the Scripture, offers a prayer, opens his whole attention to the congregation, and begins.

I wish I could remember the words of that sermon. When I asked recently if I could read a copy of "Lost in the Mystery of God," my dad told me that he had destroyed all his early sermons when he became pastor of a church in Indiana after decades of teaching so he wouldn't be tempted to pull an old one out of the bin on Saturday night instead of writing something new.

I find this wildly overscrupulous. "Lost in the Mystery of God" preached well in churches across eastern North Carolina when my dad was busy teaching full time and chairing a religion department and helping my mom raise my sister and me and writing books. Propelled out onto the back roads of eastern North Carolina by a vocation I could see clearly as a child and an economic need that is more visible to me now from the vantage point of adulthood, he had to have a bin to dip into. So many church parking lots we pulled into on so many Sunday mornings with "Lost in the Mystery of God" folded up between the pages of my father's Bible. Gold Point, Goldsboro, Wendell, Wilson, Greenville, Rocky Mount, Kinston, Morehead City, Ayden, Salem Fork. Nobody suffered from such bin-dipping it seems to me. And I sure wish I could read it again.

My dad says he can't remember what the Scripture text was for "Lost in the Mystery of God," and every time I bring it up, he says, "If we still had that sermon, it wouldn't look as wonderful to you as it does in your memory." My mother thinks the text was from the Psalms, and I think she's right. But not Psalm 109. Maybe Psalm 42: "As a deer longs for flowing streams, so my soul longs for you, O God." Or maybe Psalm 63: "O God, you are my God, I seek you; my soul thirsts for you; my flesh faints for you, as in a dry and weary land where there is no water."

Like many books I've read and loved, I don't remember the words of the sermon, but I do remember how it made me feel. It made me feel like the world was opening up all around me, on every side. It made me believe that it was the work of a lifetime to seek the presence of the living God and that there was nothing better to which one could devote one's life. It taught me that there were a thousand thousand places to seek that presence: in fields and barns, in marriages and families, in acts of mercy and justice, in books, in Scripture, in music, in silence, in prayer. Certainly in the Psalms. It convinced me that God's presence is available to all of us, not just the ministers and the monks and the saints. And it showed me that even for the ministers and monks and saints God's presence is a mystery so deep that we can swim and swim in it our whole lives long and never sound the bottom. We may feel God's claim on us, but we can never fully understand God, or know God's mind. The mystery of God, the really real, can't be put in a box. The world is full of faithful people, I've heard my dad preach from the pulpit, some Christian, some not. Anyone who has had an experience of God has something wonderful to teach us.

That sermon made me want to be better, more loving, more understanding, more good. It made me want to take risks for what is right. It made me want to pray. It made me want to stand with all the devoted, everywhere. It made me want to lose myself in the mystery of God.

After the sermon, the elders pray over the bread and grape juice, and we share communion, passing the plates, serving each other. A deacon bends down at the end of the pew where I am sitting and hands me a tray piled with tiny rectangles of pressed bread. I stand up and walk the length of the pew to bring the tray to an elderly couple sitting at the pew's opposite end. After everyone is served, one of the elders says a prayer, and we all eat together, placing those hard pellets of bread in our mouths, letting it soften on our tongues, or crunching down with our teeth. It's hard as a brick, but oddly delicious, and, like most kids, I always wish we got more than one tiny piece.

Next the deacons fan out through the church with trays filled with tiny glass cups of grape juice. They are heavier than the bread trays, and when I carry one to the elderly couple, I hold it while they fish out the little cups with their papery fingers. They beam smiles at me, the preacher's child.

After the last hymn and the invitation to join the church, my dad stands at the door to greet folks as they leave, and I walk out into sunshine so bright it blinds me. Now it is as hot as it is going to get. Everything that shimmered in the early morning sunshine — the fields, the barns, the church, the trees — is flattened and drained of color in the noonday heat. Even with the windows rolled all the way down, our car is a furnace, and my dad touches the baked steering wheel gingerly as we follow the car of a family in the church to their home for lunch.

The house is cooled by shade trees, and the food is delicious: fried chicken, green beans, boiled potatoes, and coleslaw. Fried corn bread and hush puppies drying on paper towels. Pie. Daddy thanks God for the food and the company and God's own sweet presence, and we start passing the food like we're still in church, serving one another. But this time, there is more than we can eat.

The table conversation always begins the same way, with the adults asking me and any other kids at the table how things are going in school. After we deliver our monosyllabic answers, avoiding one another's eyes, the conversation inevitably turns to tobacco. "Tobacco's over," I remember one farmer saying. "We'd do better to plant marijuana."

If there are children in the family close to my age, my time at the table is mercifully short. After we're excused, we disappear into pink bedrooms with the frilly canopy beds that I secretly covet and play board games or Barbies. Or we race up and down the rows of the tobacco fields behind the house. Or climb up two by fours nailed to the trunk of a pine tree to reach a treehouse built in its branches. If I'm lucky, the kids will show me their treasures: a pet snake, a litter of kittens, a secret stash of cigarettes. Once I remember squatting with another girl in a ditch that ran below a train track, pressing wet leaves between flat rocks and imagining the people thousands of years hence who would find our ready-made fossils, wondering if they would wonder about us.

By 2:30 or 3:00 my dad and I are usually on our way back home, quiet after a day full of words. Once home, Dad would disappear into the back bedroom to take a nap, and I'd curl up with a book or play records in my room. Once, I remember taking a sheet of loose-leaf notebook paper, writing "Lost in the Mystery of God" across the top line and filling half the page with my own sermon. I can see it in my memory, one long paragraph in looping cursive. Like the sermon itself, that sheet of paper is lost too.

Eighteen years later, I am a preacher. I don't drive through tobacco fields to get to my pulpit. I walk four and a half city blocks, from the basement apartment I share with my husband on the 5400 block of South Woodlawn Avenue in Chicago to the university chapel that rises up, a great pile of Indiana limestone, from the 5800 block of the same street. My congregation is not made up of farmers worrying over the viability of their crops, although some of them did grow up on farms in southern Illinois. My congregation is made up of city dwellers looking for a place to be quiet, or to find a way to be of use, or to move, tentatively, back to practicing a faith they thought they had abandoned long ago. They worry about paying the bills and random violence; they worry about doctoral exams, the job market, retirement; about whether they'll ever meet the right person; about cancer and AIDS. Like the members of the congregations my dad served on weekends, they are looking for a way to bring their inner and outer lives closer together. They are looking for a place to bring their anxieties, their fears, their gratitude for being alive. They are looking for a community, people with whom they might study and laugh and work and pray.

It was not my intention to become a minister. I did not go to seminary; I do not have an M.Div. degree. I have never done field education, taken a preaching class, or read a book on pastoral care and counseling. I am a doctoral student in religion and literature, interested in how women writers have understood the spiritual dimension of the practice of writing. I am studying literary criticism and medieval history, feminist theory and theology, twentieth-century novels and thirteenth-century manuals of spiritual instruction. But Clark Gilpin, the Dean of Disciples Divinity House, my denomination's house of studies at the University of Chicago, urges me to meet with the regional committee on ministry — the committee that recommends candidates for ordination in the Christian Church (Disciples of Christ) in Illinois and Wisconsin — that meets at the House twice a year. "They will help you think about your life and work differently than the faculty will," he says. "They will ask you different questions."

So I meet with them, twice a year for several years. And they do ask questions different from the ones my teachers ask me, questions about my calling, and how doing what I love might make a difference to others. My best friend asks me to ask the committee if they will license me as a minister in order to perform her wedding. Of course not, they say, that's not what ministerial licensing is for. But when I take an evening job leading a study group on classic texts of Christian spirituality at the university chapel, they agree to license me. And when I become licensed as a minister, not only do I perform my friend's wedding, but the dean of the chapel, an Episcopal priest named Bernard Brown, asks me to join his staff as the assistant minister. I have never preached a sermon or said a prayer at a hospital bed. So I apprentice myself to Bernie Brown, following him from hospital room to soup kitchen, from staff meeting to the dining room table where he and his wife, Carol Jean, welcome everyone: the joyful, the lonely, the broken-hearted, the confused. He listens to my sermons and comments on them; he invites me to sit in on his counseling sessions and to preach from his pulpit. Somewhere at the intersection of my studies and the practices of ministry, a vocation to ministry comes into view. I practice my way into ministry, upheld by Bernie who gives me both wise counsel and enough room to make my own mistakes. I walk from the chapel to the divinity school every morning after morning prayers with the readings and the collects still knocking around inside me; I walk back in the afternoon after my classes are over, my brain humming with Ricoeur and Derrida, George Eliot and Hildegard of Bingen. The connections between my life at church and my life at school are not always visible. But the space between the study of religion and the practices of faith seems less an unbridgeable gulf than a place of endless intersections. I spend two years as a licensed minister and then I am ordained and join the staff full-time.

The world of graduate study in religion and the world of the congregation are the not the only worlds between which I have to find points of intersection. There is also the world of a congregation gathered by a weekly Eucharist in the tradition of the Book of Common Prayer and the world of Lord's Supper in which I grew up. Every Sunday, Bernie celebrates the Eucharist at an enormous wooden altar that sits in the middle of a vast chancel. I assist him, receiving bread and wine from the people who bring it up out of the congregation, handing him neatly pressed linen napkins to wipe the lip of the cup. When there is too much consecrated bread and wine for us to consume at the end, Bernie and I carry it outdoors, pour the wine onto the earth, and spread out the bread for the birds. After a few weeks, when it seems I have gotten the hang of things, he asks me to serve as the celebrant.

Good graduate student that I am, I know how important it is to give an account of my intellectual positions. I think it over and then say, "In my tradition, we share a meal around a table, not a sacrifice at an altar. I don't know if I can lead this ritual, because I don't really know what it means.

And Bernie replies, "We don't do this because we know what it means. We do it in order to find out what it means."

I take Bernie's words to heart, and they help me live among the worlds of school and church, theory and practice, contemplation and action. What does it mean to celebrate the Eucharist? What does it mean to set a theory of religion down next to a prayer? What does it mean to study the knowledge produced in a classroom through the lens of the knowledge produced in a congregation, or a soup kitchen, or a hospital room? And what does it mean to study the knowledge produced in congregation, soup kitchen, hospital room through the lens of the knowledge produced in a classroom? As any student in field education knows, it's impossible to know the answers in advance.

Bernie's words not only shape my approach to ministry, they also influence my approach to my studies. As a graduate student, I am awash in books and arguments that I just barely understand. Occasionally I see glimmers of something I recognize studded along the bottom of those fathomless texts like starfish on the ocean floor. If I stare straight at them, they shimmer, then disappear. But if I look at them slantwise, or catch an accidental glimpse of them from the corner of my eye, they sometimes float upward into my waiting hands.

Preaching is a similar mystery; it requires a slantwise view, a willingness to be led by peripheral vision. It is also, by turns, the most exhilarating and the most utterly defeating work I've ever tried to do. When it is going well, making a sermon is the most satisfying work I can imagine. When it is not, my life (and the life of those around me) becomes what my medievalist husband christens *sermo inferno:* sermon hell.

It was a great conviction of George Herbert's that the minister should be "full of all knowledge" because "people by what they understand, are best led to what they understand not." Nothing human is alien to the minister, and so, for the minister, there is no such thing as useless knowledge. There's nothing a minister can know that can't be turned toward the work of ministry. "It is an ill mason," Herbert writes, "that refuseth any stone."

In his ministry, my dad needed to know the Psalms, Bernard of Clairvaux, the politics of tobacco subsidies. What is it I need to know? When my dad brought Bernard of Clairvaux into a sermon on a hot summer morning in eastern North Carolina, he always seemed to be bringing some important news, some information we all needed in order to get on with our lives. My first sermons, by contrast, sound like historical lectures with a little high-minded scolding at the end.

Over time, I discover that writing a sermon is not like writing an academic paper in which I lift myself carefully hand over hand up the rungs of my evidence into an argument meant to convince. It is more like lowering a ladder into the dark and feeling around until I touch something solid. Gradually I learn to trust that if I follow a word, a phrase, a connection that strikes me, something wholly unexpected, but possibly worthwhile, might happen. My best sermons stay close to the mysteries of the text, like my dad's, but turn those mysteries in the light of whatever I've been reading, or the concerns of whomever I've been counseling or teaching, or whatever I've caught from the corner of my eye as I've moved between school and church.

47

But I have to begin each sermon early enough for the stuff of my life, the lives of those around me, and the stories of Scripture to have time to coalesce into something with a shape, something I can preach. When I begin early enough, I can write the way I like best: going back over and over to the beginning, drawing a comb through the tangles of my sentences, pulling an idea through each paragraph until I see something I couldn't have seen when I began. I learn early on that I hate the feeling of racing through the parts of a sermon I don't like — the paragraphs where I lose hold on what I'm thinking, and instead of following the idea down to the ground, papering it over with something pretty instead. Coming to those paragraphs in the pulpit, I can feel myself speeding up, feel my neck stiffen as I hunch over my manuscript for cover from my own sloppy thinking. Years later, when I hear Lucinda Williams sing, "could tell a lie, but my heart would know," I hear those words as words about preaching. I make my preaching students listen to her, and I tell them: better to start early and mean every word.

But some weeks that's not possible. Some weeks a crisis comes late in the week and there's nothing to do but the best I can. Some weeks I don't manage my time well. Some weeks I do, and even then, a sermon never arrives any place significant, never opens any window on the really real. I see I am going to have to learn to live with not loving every word I speak from the pulpit. I begin to think that maybe this is just part of the job.

At my ordination, my dad prayed that I would live intimately with Scripture. And I find that good sermons do seem to come from the kind of intimacy I associate with the closest relationships, the ones not based on clarity and understanding but of living closely enough to see each other's strangeness. Sometimes I hit a groove, and week after week sermons I can preach with my head up come. In those weeks, I feel connected to my words and the people to whom I am speaking them; although I'm the one standing in the pulpit, I feel we are doing something together.

Inevitably, though, I fall into a trough and cannot climb out for weeks and weeks. What am I doing? Why is anyone listening? What in God's name can it possibly mean to *preach*?

It's not like my school studies, where I can feel myself gaining mastery — over languages, over theories, over ideas and methodologies. I can feel myself better able to back up my claims, to prove my points. Preaching is not like that at all. Every time out, everything is at stake. The literary theorists I read in school write about the endless chain of signifiers. As a preacher, I feel suspended from that chain, twirling at the end of it. Talk about an endless chain of signification, where one thing leads to another and another and another with no end in sight. The texts preachers must consider each week are potentially endless — Scripture from the Hebrew Bible, the New Testament, the Psalms; the language of the hymns and the prayers; the embodied realities of the lives of the people to whom we speak; the life of the world, every corner of it. Every week the texts change, and some of those changes are wrought in secret. Our mastery over "the material" is not the issue; our attention to the ways all these "texts" intersect, or might intersect, is.

I find this exhilarating. And I find it terrifying. Barbara Brown Taylor compares watching a preacher enter a pulpit to watching a tightrope walker get ready to mount the high wire. True enough. But if, as a preacher, you are alive to that fact, alive to the risk you are taking, it can become difficult to gather courage week after week to write a sermon. Some preachers protect themselves by developing a shtick and sticking to it. Some steal the sermons of others from the internet. George Herbert composed a panicky "Prayer before a Sermon" full of exclamations like "Oh Lord hear, Oh Lord forgive!" My strategy, when I hit a slump, is to console myself with thoughts like these: Who's perfect? Certainly not me! I'm doing the best I can.

On a visit home, I share this hard-won wisdom with my dad. We're two preachers, talking about our shared work. I chatter away, filling him in on all the pastoral insights I've acquired over the last eventful year. I am particularly proud of how I've learned to deal with the terror of preaching. "I've finally come to accept" (*finally* — as if I've been at this half my life, not just twelve short months) "that I won't preach a great sermon every time."

I see immediately that I have shocked him. My dad's quiet for a minute and then he says, gently, "Well, those people who come to church each week deserve your best."

Well. Even as I feel a red wave of shame wash through me, I know that my dad would forgive me a mediocre sermon. He would forgive me a hundred mediocre sermons, a thousand. What shocks him is the complicity with mediocrity I've expressed, the refusal of the risk that good preaching requires, my attempt to protect myself from spectacular failure by getting comfortable with little failures along the way. He can't abide my forgetting that what's at stake in preaching is not my sense of my own cleverness, nor the compliments I might receive, nor how I feel up there in the pulpit or at the back of the church shaking hands, nor even whether I do my father proud.

The preacher, George Herbert writes, should capture the attention of the congregation "by all possible art." But what makes a sermon a sermon, he insists, is Holiness. The preacher, he maintains, "is not witty, or learned, or eloquent, but Holy." Lest holiness seem so out of reach that there's no point in striving for it, Herbert is quick to give holiness definition: "there is no greater sign of holiness," he writes, "than the procuring, and rejoicing in another's good."

The people who come to church on Sunday morning deserve our very best: our willingness to take risks, to go deep, to employ "all possible art." And so do our students. And so do the dead whose work we study as scholars in pursuit of knowledge. To move between the worlds of school and church, we will have to build some bridges. But there is nothing we can bring across those bridges that won't be needed somewhere in all the worlds in which we serve.

5. Blackduck

James F. Kay

Late in the winter of 1974, an unexpected call reached me in St. Louis, Missouri. "How would you like a church?" said the voice on the telephone. The question took me by surprise. I had given up looking for a pastorate after spending some months in a fruitless search following graduation from Harvard Divinity School. The Vietnam War had swelled the ranks of America's draft-deferred seminary grads, and, after having come in second among sixty applicants for a small rural parish in Vermont, I had taken a job with Little, Brown and Company selling college textbooks among the Big Ten universities in the Midwest. Moving to St. Louis to begin my new career, I had largely disposed of my theological library.

The voice calling me that day was that of the Rev. Ronald Geisman, an intelligent, multi-talented classmate at Harvard. In retrospect, I believe that through Ron the Lord was interrupting and re-calling me into an unexpected new life. (As I would later hear Jim Forbes tell his preaching class at Union Seminary in New York, "First you got to get called. And, then, you got to get re-called!") Ron had lived across the corridor from me in Divinity Hall, where the memory of Emerson's Divinity School Address was still cherished. A liberal Presbyterian, Ron was now the pastor at Red Lake Falls, Minnesota, and moderator of not one, but two, vacant parishes yoked together in adjacent Beltrami County. "Adjacent," as I was to discover, meant in Ron's case over 100 miles — one way.

"How would you like a church?" Hearing Ron's question, I laughingly asked, "Where?" Ron replied, "Blackduck," to which I could only say, "Where the hell is Blackduck?" Little did I know that the civic leaders of Blackduck had actually printed a bumper sticker with that very question on it as a way of generating tourism! Blackduck lies between Tenstrike and Funkley, about two hours south of the Canadian border on U.S. Highway 71 (which runs from New Orleans, Louisiana, to International Falls, Minnesota). The church in Blackduck was yoked to another twenty-five miles farther north at Kelliher, near good walleye fishing at Waskish. Each Sunday, I would drive from Blackduck north to Kelliher, preach there at 9:30 a.m. and then return (at high speed!) to Blackduck for the 11:00 a.m. service. The church in Kelliher consisted of about twenty-five members on the roll; the one in Blackduck about a hundred. Salary: $7,000. Car allowance: $300. While this was extremely low compensation, even by 1974 standards, it was apparently still in sight of what starting schoolteachers were then making. (That did not prevent me from later feeling embarrassed when I filed my "low income" Minnesota tax form with one of my church elders who was an accountant.) There was a two-story renovated manse in Blackduck, right next to the 1911 green cement-block church on Summit Avenue, replete with an Allen electronic organ and Cokesbury-style liturgical furnishings, including an "altar" in place of a proper Lord's table.

Summit Avenue in Blackduck, Minnesota, is a long way, culturally, sociologically, and geographically, from Lindell Boulevard in St. Louis, Missouri, and even farther from Harvard Square. If the church of Jesus Christ were simply what Elton Trueblood once decried as the "company of the congenial," then placing guys like me in parishes like this would be by definition a recipe for disaster. What I learned from the Christians in Blackduck and Kelliher is that all that is necessary for a true church is the gospel of Jesus Christ; it is this story that creates the "ties that bind" the multiple stories of ordinary and strange people into the common story of the uncommon people of God.

Preparation for Ministry?

Looking back at my theological education, I have to say I was poorly prepared, at the level of course transcripts, to become a pastor. I'd never had a course in preaching, worship, Christian education, or Christian ethics. While I could still use my Greek, my Hebrew was fading fast. I had taken courses primarily in history and theology, and my wonderful days at Harvard (with an equally wonderful middler year at St. Andrews in Scotland) were more a high-class continuation of my liberal arts college education, which focused on philosophy, religion, and European history, than a specialization or training in ministerial practice or skills. The one exception was a life-changing year doing what today we would call Clinical Pastoral Education (CPE) at the Peter Bent Brigham Hospital under the supervision of an Episcopal priest, Bill Leach (reputedly a cousin of Archie Leach, better known as Cary Grant) and Dr. Samuel Bojar, a psychiatrist on the staff of the Harvard Medical School. My patients, many of them with life-threatening diseases, were my teachers as well. I learned here about fears, angers, and insecurities, my patients' and my own, and about the need to give patients the space to reject my ministrations in order to preserve some semblance of their own freedom and responsibility, often diminished by critical illness and hospitalization. As Muslims rightly say, "God is Great!" and this being the case, I learned not to "defend" the Deity in the face of pain or suffering, but to embody and signify, sometimes by simply listening, the all sufficient grace of God.

What I did gain from my college and theological education was historical perspective and a kind of Augustinian realism about the human condition. Both served me well, not only in the pastorate but later in the theological professorate where the usual religious sins are compounded by the academic ones. While in Minnesota, I was also able to undertake significant continuing education in preaching and liturgy. This included two summer stints at St. John's Abbey and University in Collegeville, Minnesota, in the wake of Vatican II. Here my first official preaching professor turned out to be a Roman Catholic Benedictine, Bill Skudlarek, a graduate of the Princeton Theological Seminary Ph.D. program in homiletics in which I now teach. It was also at St. John's that I took a hymnody course from Erik Routley (doing poorly, but loving the learning) and a church architecture course from Edward A. Sövik, whom I greatly admired, and with whom I later worked so collegially in renovating Miller Chapel at Princeton Theological Seminary between 1995 and 2000.

As a result of my summer experiences both at St. John's and at Pacific School of Religion in Berkeley, California, I became a strong proponent of post-seminary continuing education. Not everything gets covered in three years of seminary (actually about a year and a half if you count only classroom instructional time). As with marriage, so in the ministry we become more receptive to instruction and counsel *after* the wedding or the ordination than before. Life experiences, whether in marriage or in the ministry, generate the kinds of questions that open up new theological and personal insights enabling our closest relationships to become deeper, more textured, and more enriching.

Reflecting back on my time in the parish, I think the education that mattered most to me, in the abrupt and unexpected transition from sales rep to pastor, was the formation I received in childhood and adolescence from my family — my mother read me Bible stories each day before leaving for kindergarten — from the people and pastors of the First (now College Avenue) Church of the Nazarene in Whittier, California, and later from the professors at Pasadena College (now Point Loma Nazarene University), also in southern California. First Church in Whittier was my extended family. Even as a fairly young person, I was given responsibilities for teaching in the vacation Bible school as well as the Sunday school, and I was licensed there as a local preacher while still a teenager. (I am boggled now at the thought of a congregation enduring a sermon from a sixteen-year-old, or hearing temperance orations from youngsters schooled by the good ladies of the Women's Christian Temperance Union! The people of God are patient!) At times, I was also lovingly corrected by the church when I did something wrong.

My principal pastors growing up were B. Edgar Johnson and the late Ross W. Hayslip. "Brother" Johnson was a beloved pastor, once showing up on my dad's construction job in his overalls to do a day's work as part of his evangelism of presence. He taught me about integrity in ministry, about compassion for others, and the need for a "shepherd's heart." "Brother" Hayslip was a great preacher. The pulpit was not for him the trivial piece of furniture it has become today in so many evangelical churches. From it, Ross preached sermons carved in oak that held our attention Sunday by Sunday for a good half hour. There were no rhetorical tricks or clever methods. There was no "pretty preaching." For Ross, the gospel mattered. Something was at stake for the living of life. And he conveyed that. As I child, I am sure that I internalized from these two pastors a model of ministry that embraced an ethos of the minister as pastoral caregiver, as one present to need, and as a minister of the Word of God, which calls to us from on high. My formal theological education was a continuation, more critical to be sure, but still a continuation of the Christian nurture I received at home and at church.

At Pasadena College, where I majored in philosophy, the principal influences upon me were Reuben Welch and Frank G. Carver. Reuben, who became the college chaplain, conveyed from the pulpit what "Doc"

Carver, with his recently minted New Testament Ph.D. from Edinburgh, taught in the classroom, namely, that the gospel is about grace, about God "coming all the way down" to meet us where we are with transforming acceptance and accomplishing in us what the law (and legalistic versions of Christian perfectionism) could not do. Reuben preached a series of expository sermons on Romans that simply opened up this "strange new world" of a gracious and active God, and Frank walked with me one summer session through the Greek texts of "John and His Letters." I don't know how to say this any more plainly, but if you do not know what grace is, you can never be a true pastor or a preacher. If you do know what grace is, not simply as an idea, but as Jesus Christ, actively working in the world and in your life, then you can be a pastor and a preacher, however poorly you are "trained" and however great the distance seemingly lies between that training and your congregation.

When I drove my brand new 1974 Chevy four-door Impala north from Kansas City, Missouri, some 700 miles to Blackduck, Minnesota, I decided to avoid the interstates and drive up old U.S. 71 to get a feel for the topography and geography of Minnesota. My trip took me across the Missouri River, through the fertile farmland of Iowa, into southern Minnesota and Sauk Center of Sinclair Lewis's *Main Street,* and then, finally, into the region of lakes and forests known as "outstate" Minnesota.

This region of Minnesota was one of the last frontiers of the lower 48 American states. In fact, there had been an Indian uprising at Cass Lake as late as 1901, the year the Blackduck congregation was organized, as the timber rush gave way to homesteads and new towns in the closing decade of the nineteenth century. After the timber was cut, the land was sold by speculators to homesteaders, many of whom were Scandinavian immigrants. In time, it was realized that the land was far more suited to forestry than to farming, but, even in 1974, after years of steady depopulation, family farming, logging and its byproduct industries, together with tourism and resorts catering to fishermen and their families, were the economic mainstays in an otherwise economically depressed area. Indian reservations, one completely self-governing at Red Lake, the other an "open reservation" at Cass Lake, were home to a sizable tribe of Ojibway.

My congregations at Blackduck and Kelliher consisted almost entirely of Euro-Americans, mostly businessmen, tradespeople, and schoolteachers, and, because of intermarriage, some had Lutheran or Catholic backgrounds, just as some Lutherans and Catholics in each town, through intermarriage, were now former Presbyterians. The nearest hospital was in Bemidji, the county seat, about thirty miles southwest of Blackduck; more major hospitals were in Duluth or Fargo, some 140 to 170 miles one way, respectively. Winters were long. It could snow as early as September and as late as April. I was ordained amid a January blizzard that left the preacher, Peter Gomes, stranded at the Fargo airport. He never did make it to Blackduck, retreating on the next available plane to the relatively mild winters of his native New England! Temperatures could reach twenty, thirty, even forty degrees below zero, so every winter night I literally plugged in an electric heater under the hood of the car so that the engine was warm enough to start the next morning. ("If we can just get through February," I used to say.) In short, with its bakery café, post office, five churches (two of them Lutheran), village-operated liquor store, Laundromat, public school, two grocery stores, campground, and three gas stations, the village of Blackduck (900 souls) bore striking resemblance in its accustomed ways and mores to Garrison Keillor's Lake Wobegon.

Things Rarely Are What They Seem

There is a commonplace often instilled into today's theological students that one must be suspicious of master narratives, hegemonies, and traditional readings and expositions of authoritative texts. In the transition from seminary to congregation, one can be served well by summoning the moral courage to apply this "hermeneutics of suspicion" to oneself and one's own practices of ministry. By becoming self-critical, and not just critical, you can begin to move from despising folk religion and folk piety, a colonial attitude well-entrenched in America's liberal educational establishment, to a more empathic understanding of how people actually lead and live their lives with meaning and purpose. This is not to say that the minister should simply applaud and baptize folk religion, but one will have an easier time calling into question some of its more pernicious aspects if people sense that the Word of God also calls into question the religion and piety of their preacher.

My own awakening to the fact that the Presbyterian Church is not morally bankrupt simply because it happens to be for most of its members "the Republican Party at prayer," came home to me after an honor graduate of a local high school, and part Native American in his ethnic and cultural heritage, was arrested in Bemidji for allegedly assaulting a police officer at a school dance. When I visited him in jail, he said to me, "It's hopeless." With some fear and trembling, I brought this case to the attention of my board of elders, the session, in an attempt to secure some presbytery "justice funds" for bail money. Because my session of eight members had seven Republicans on it, one of whom had a son who was a deputy sheriff, I figured that my resignation might be demanded. (Earlier, I had received an unintended, if cautionary, warning when I called on a local merchant, who knew the arrested youth, and who slipped me some bills for bail money only on condition of anonymity.) What happened at the session meeting surprised me and forced me to reconsider my own prejudices. "Jim," said one elder, a woman who was a respected schoolteacher in the community, "we know what you've been doing, and we have already met and unanimously decided to support you." Whether the young man was guilty or not, I do not know, but the fact that charges were finally dropped and he headed off to law school in the West gave me hope that amid so much hopelessness things are not always what they seem. It began to occur to me, far too slowly to be sure, that many of my congregants were far more Christian than I, and that it was unworthy of me to dismiss them simply because their piety, whether political or religious, was not my own. Often God is at work outside what we deem to be the politically or theologically correct channels. It was, after all, Mikhail Gorbachev and Ronald Reagan, and not the nuclear freeze movement, who ended the Cold War. *Things are often not what they seem!*

Efficiency Is Not Efficacy

One of our uniquely Protestant sins, if Max Weber and company are right, is to equate capitalism and Christianity and thereby mistake business for holiness. For Presbyterians, this sin manifests itself as an inordinate desire for organizational efficiency, managerial competence, parliamentary procedure, and detailed record-keeping (whether of baptisms or of finances). In my lifetime there have been two major reorganizations of the national Presbyterian Church, one of which was arguably unnecessary and both of which were exceedingly costly, but which were discussed and implemented with the kind of gusto Southern Baptists reserve for "soul-winning." I think an argument can be made that these virtues of organizational purity quickly become ends in themselves and thereby turn into obsessive-compulsive vices bedeviling the spiritual health of a denomination or congregation. If you doubt this, just look at the Presbyterian Program Calendar. If you tried to implement all that it decrees, you would be hospitalized for exhaustion. Aldous Huxley once opined that "lives are saved by the holy, not by the busy." While my own holiness is empirically negligible, I confess that my witness to God's holy love was diminished at times by miring myself into the satisfying routines of administration and organization.

Let me give one example by way of confession. For years, First Presbyterian Church at Blackduck had two governing boards: The trustees, who held legal title to the property and managed finances, and the session or board of elders who were responsible for spiritual oversight, policy, and programming. One can see immediately the "two kingdoms" theology at work here, namely, of "the temporal" and "the spiritual," and how it is nigh to impossible to compartmentalize stringently these matters in any community holding to the Incarnation of the Word of God. Nevertheless, from the standpoint of folk piety, what the spiritual-temporal dichotomy enables is akin to what happens in a European state-church context where you have a geographical parish (temporal) within which is situated the gathered congregation (spiritual). This gives rise, to be sure, to a double-decker Christianity, or to a dual membership divided between a kind of halfway- and full-covenant status, or between "inactive" and "active" members, but what this distinction in its various expressions also does is to enable a continuing connection between the church and the culture or general population at large. In my view, this is not to be despised despite our current mainline love affair with Anabaptism and the Duke ecclesiology of "resident aliens." In Blackduck, that separate board of trustees kept several cigarette-smoking, "have a drink" veterans of the armed services active in the life of the church, at a level where they could make a genuine contribution without compromising their "worldly" consciences or their sense of their own manhood. When I finally, more in the name of efficiency than ecclesiology, got the congregation to consolidate the two boards, effectively eliminating the separate board of trustees, I unwittingly contributed to the excommunication of "regular Joes" from the life of the church, leaving institutional matters entirely to the women and the few "holy Joes" who felt "worthy" to serve as elders. The emasculation of the church is already far advanced in North America, and one ought to think twice before contributing to it further.

All this is to say that while it may be tempting for a seminary-educated pastor to impose a dogmatically correct ecclesiology on his or her congregation (for example, the dogma of "efficiency" hidden in the guise of opposing any distinction between sacred and profane, between secular and religious, or between temporal and spiritual), it is also necessary for a seminary-educated pastor to ask, in accord with practical theology, what is fitting and appropriate in signifying the gospel in a particular context. If, over time, a congregation has provided a way for the less pious males in the community to participate in its life, is it really faithful to the gospel to destroy that institutional wisdom in the name of some dogmatic norm, whether taken from the seminary or from the business school?

Nearness and Distance

From my speech colleagues at Princeton Theological Seminary I have learned about rhetorical "nearness" and "distance." Every sermon must negotiate these twin aspects of communication. On the one hand, as a preacher I must be "near" to my audience; that, is, I must convey by word, gesture, and delivery that I am present to them, that I am speaking directly to them, that their presence affects my presence. On the other hand, if I am too "near," too present, too overpowering, too intrusive, I may be experienced as tyrannical or suffocating, reminiscent of the ethos conveyed by many evangelists as they give their "altar calls." So, genuine communication requires that the preacher give his audience "distance," that is, space and room to breathe and to think. I find these rules of art helpful guides for preaching, and I likewise find rhetorical "nearness" and "distance" apt metaphors for the relation of a pastor to the members of his or her parish.

On the one hand, I need to be "near." I need to be out of my office and in public view with some regularity. For one thing, as a Catholic priest once said to me, "Death demands your immediate presence." So do serious hospitalization and medical emergencies. To leave parishioners abandoned at such times of crisis borders on ministerial malpractice. I also need to be present to the wider community. And, in retrospect, I now regret that I rarely attended high school sporting events and other community-wide gatherings. As an academic, I have a tendency toward "aloofness" and "reclusiveness." Temperamentally, I am more an introvert than an extrovert. So, my challenge in ministry was clearly on the "nearness" side.

On the other hand, I also need to be somewhat "distant," in the sense of maintaining appropriate boundaries. As a twenty-something, single pastor in an economically hard-pressed rural area, I worked 60-70 hours a week. By Sunday afternoon, I was exhausted. I found myself gravitating on those afternoons and evenings to two families in particular, who generously opened their homes and their families to me, including wonderful home-cooked meals, afternoon outings, and sometimes naps on the couch. This was for me a great blessing, but hidden in it was a danger. It is questionable whether we can really be "friends" or "family" to our parishioners, or to some parishioners and not others. As pastors, in our exhaustion and personal vulnerability we may gratefully accept this hospitality, but in the process subtly move out of the pastor-parishioner role into another defined by friendship. What may happen then is that when our parishioners-turned-friends need a pastor, we are no longer able to fulfill that role for them, the very role which brought us together in the first place. For this reason, I have come to believe that a pastor's legitimate needs for recreation, renewal, and friendship, and even for family — broadly conceived — as well as appropriate affectional relationships, should ordinarily be met from outside the congregation rather than from within it. Often clergy of other denominations or in nearby towns can become supportive friends and true colleagues for otherwise isolated pastors. (It is no accident that Jesus sent out disciples two by two.) With regard to these questions of appropriate boundaries and friendship there can be no rigid rules, such as the mainline church loves to adopt. There is a need for discernment and wisdom in navigating between nearness and distance, necessary ingredients not only to preaching but to all the other practices of pastoral ministry as well.

What's a Heaven For?

We may leave seminary with a necessary element of utopianism and enthusiasm. The work of ministry, when attempted with faithfulness to the gospel of Jesus Christ, is demanding work, calling forth from us our best efforts amid changing circumstances and complex contexts in gratitude for the grace we have known and continue to know. But in time, utopianism and enthusiasm are insufficient supports for the ministry of the gospel. This is because death circumscribes all our best efforts, including our managerial competence and pulpit eloquence.

In a village, death is very visible. People die daily, people one knows or at least knows by sight. Some of these deaths are tragic: a logging truck brakes too hard, sending its load through the cab with deadly force; a high school student is killed in a car accident on prom night; a stroke cuts short the life of a mother with small children; a hunter mistakes another hunter for a deer; and, while at Blackduck and Kelliher, two parishioners, one in each congregation, took their own lives. At times, I felt I was hemorrhaging emotionally by these continual losses.

Additionally, however sentimentally Garrison Keillor can paint the citizens of Lake Wobegon, the truth is that every one of the Ten Commandments has been and will be broken with regularity even in these rustic surroundings. This, too, is a sign of the death that infects our common life. Spousal abuse, sexual abuse, lying, cheating, stealing, adultery, and even murder, not to mention idolatries and covetousness of all kinds, do not end once we flee the teeming cities. And these sins are not confined to the non-churchgoers! As Martin Luther said, "God saves real, not imaginary, sinners." Every Sunday, the wicked and the violent walk into our churches, because the line between good and evil does not run *between* the religious and irreligious, or *between* the pastors and their people, but *through* them *all*.

In the face of this crisis besetting and besieging our true humanity mirrored in Jesus Christ, the gospel had better be more than good advice on parade or the charade of an ostensibly good preacher preaching to ostensibly good people. (I have seen a homiletics textbook that actually purports that this is what is happening in preaching! One can only ask if its authors have ever spent five minutes in a parish.) What keeps us going in a world like this is something called "heaven," which is not only our final destination, but which also breaks into our life and death in parables that point us to what is finally true and real about ourselves and about God.

Looking out on a congregation, there are many sins and circumstances of which I have knowledge, but over which I literally have no control. As a pastor, I can often see the train wrecks coming, years in advance, and despite my pleas, my warnings, or my prayers, they happen anyway. If this world is our only frame of reference, does anything ultimately make any sense or even matter? But if our world of sin and death is truly bracketed and ultimately subjected to the heavenly world of freedom and life, where the will and way of the crucified Jesus Christ is acknowledged by all creation, then I can stand in solidarity with real sinners in cemeteries, in

61

courthouses, in hospitals, in jail cells, in board meetings, or at the Lord's font and table where there may be on any given occasion no obvious evidence that God exists or that what I am doing actually matters.

So, what kept me going in the pastorate, and what keeps me going in the professorate, are the parables, that is, those contemporary patterns of events that we find already in the revelation of Jesus Christ, and which unexpectedly encounter us in this world and provide the basis and final hope for the ministry of the Word. I recall one winter morning, on my way to go cross-country skiing, I was driving far too fast on a county road that came to an end as it junctioned with U.S. Highway 2. Over this major east-west highway trucks from North Dakota passed at high speed to deliver their grain to waiting cargo ships docked at Duluth. The county road was icy, and by the time I stopped daydreaming at the wheel (a pastoral hazard), I realized that I could not make the stop. The choice was clear: either skid into U.S. Highway 2 into almost certain death, or simply drive the car off the road into the snow-filled ditch. When I finally forced open the car door and clambered out of the ditch, I walked over to Highway 2 and stuck out my thumb.

Car after car whizzed by. In jeans, woolen stockings serving as leggings, big sunglasses, and with a woolen cap pulled over my ears, I did not look very clergy-like. The speeding cars were filled with busy people on their way, no doubt, to important meetings. I wondered, too: would I stop if I were driving past this hitchhiker? After a while, fifteen degrees above zero begins to get rather cold, even for an adopted Minnesotan. Each time a big eighteen-wheeler whizzed by, the wind whipped my face like a saw. One of those big trucks flew by again, and then I heard the brakes and saw the emergency flashers. I ran what seemed like a very fast 440 to catch up to that stopped truck before the driver changed his mind. When I pulled myself up into the cab, there was a Native American at the wheel — a fact that struck me when I realized how many white people had passed me by. "I didn't stop sooner because I didn't see your car in the ditch until after I passed you. You look like a hippie! Get in!" In that moment, Luke's parable of the Good Samaritan was fulfilled in my hearing. This tough trucker had literally proven to be this white man's unexpected, and undeserved, salvation.

Because we have the witness of the Scriptures, we are able to thematize, identify, and recognize the gospel today as it takes place, as it "eventuates" all around us even in Blackduck and Kelliher, Minnesota.

Thanks to the Holy Spirit, Jesus Christ is not confined to the first century A.D., to the geography of some alleged "Holy Land," or to the pages of the Bible, but is becoming flesh in ever new circumstances "in accordance with the Scriptures." As the recognition scenes of the gospel recur in our lives, preaching becomes possible. Not only are our eyes opened, but so are our minds and our mouths as we share with others what the triune God is still up to in the world. This turns preaching into good news and frees the preacher from the impossible burdens of being the community moralist or public censor.

Letting Go

While the preaching office, under whatever name it operates in a particular denomination, belongs, in my judgment to the essence of the true church, it would be wrong to identify it exclusively with the ordained minister or with the Sunday morning sermon. The people of God have received the promise of the Holy Spirit at their baptism, and the whole company of the faithful bears responsibility for the ministry of reconciliation. For this reason, when the time comes, pastors can move on and the people can stay. (In some communities, the people move on and the pastors stay.) In American higher education, we are used to non-collaborative, competitive learning, developing skills that may be antithetical to the need for dialogue, consensus, compromise, and collaboration that are essential to a community ordered by love and the vision of a coming Kingdom of God rather than by the personality of any single member, including the preacher. We must not pit the office-holding of some against the priesthood of all in a kind of tyrannical prelacy; on the other hand, we must not pit the priesthood of all against the office-holding of some in a kind of free-for-all anarchy. Both pastoral tyranny and congregational anarchy are the enemies of love. I believe our goal as ministers is not to create congregations of those who adore us, or to abdicate our leadership and symbolic power in the name of the laity, but rather to shape communities where the difficult issues that tear our body politic to pieces can be discussed, debated, and, when appropriate, acted upon in faithfulness to Jesus Christ. But this means letting go of the need for always "winning," of always being "liked," of always needing the approval of others, or of always having in advance of a dialogue the right "answers."

When my Chevy finally brought me to Blackduck and Kelliher in 1974, I did not know these things in the way I know them now, but I remain grateful to those congregations for all they gave to me and for all they taught me. The people of God *are* patient, and the school of faith does not end in seminary. Thanks be to God!

6. Have You Asked a Good Question Today?

Elizabeth F. Caldwell

For eleven years I lived out my call working as an educational consultant with three Presbyterian Church (U.S.A.) congregations in Alabama. At various times during those years, I received inquiries about other jobs. Often these inquiries began with an observation regarding how long I had been working in my current position. "Haven't you been there long enough? Aren't you ready to move? We have a church for you." Each time my answer was "No," until a day in 1984 when I received a phone call that asked me a question which caused me to pause. "McCormick Theological Seminary has a faculty position open in religious education. Have you ever considered teaching in a seminary?" "No, I haven't; but let's talk," was my immediate response. From there the conversation continued, the chair of the search committee sharing information about the school, the position, and their hopes for the person who would be hired. I was both intrigued and challenged by the question.

Over the course of the years I worked as a church educator, it was not unusual to receive calls from pastors who wanted help with the Christian education programs of their church. Usually the calls focused on concerns about curriculum selection, resources for ministry with children, youth, or adults, or leading workshops for teachers in the church school. Occasionally pastors wanted consultation with their Christian education committees for help with planning and visioning for this area of ministry in their congregation.

I was always amazed that seminary graduates, who were quite capable in many areas of pastoral ministry, seemed so clueless about what I considered to be the basics of educational ministry in a congregation. Many questions came to mind:

- Why did their theological education not prepare them for leadership as an educational leader in a congregation? Was their theological education more focused on other areas of practical theology such as preaching, worship, or pastoral care?
- Had they ever taken a course in Christian education?
- Was Christian education really not important when compared with everything else a pastor has to do? And consequently, if it was not that important, did they believe it was just something they could pick up or hire someone to do?

After that conversation, I sat down and immediately made a list of everything I would want seminary graduates preparing for ministry to know and experience in the field of religious education. Included on that list were these competencies that focused on the work of the pastor as educator. I wanted seminary graduates to be able to do the following:

1. **Consider their role as teacher:**
   - Be attentive to their own development as a pastor who is also an educator/teacher;
   - Work on their skills as a teacher/educational leader and make commitments to gain experience teaching with every age level in the church (preschool, elementary, youth, and adults) within the first three to five years of their ministry;
   - Become familiar with (through class experience) and use a variety of methods of teaching and learning;
   - Know human development theory and appreciate its usefulness for teaching and learning with different age groups in ministry settings.

2. **Become familiar with theory and practice:**
   - Use course projects to address issues or concerns for educational ministry (theory and practice) in congregations in which they are active members/leaders;
   - Become familiar with and critically evaluate current literature in the field of religious education;
   - Integrate learning in other fields (Bible, history, theology, ethics, and the fields within practical theology — pastoral care, preaching, worship, urban ministry, spirituality) and make connections with their study and work in courses in religious education;

66

- Have the ability to assess and evaluate congregational models of religious education.

3. **Become comfortable creating and evaluating resources for ministry:**
   - Evaluate, design, and write curriculum for educational settings in ministry contexts;
   - Become familiar with and be able to evaluate resources for educational ministry from a variety of perspectives (e.g., theological, educational).

This list of knowledge, skills, and values in the field of religious education that I expected seminary graduates to possess evolved from my own questions and experiences in ministry. It became the basis for the development of a curriculum of courses offered over a three-year cycle which prepares theological students for ministry in a variety of settings: as pastors in congregations, staff in social agencies, teachers, chaplains, librarians, and church musicians.

Elie Wiesel tells the story of his mother, who asked him each day when he came home from school, "Have you had a good question today?" The call to the vocation of Christian ministry begins with questions that have no immediate answers. Questions that were once easily answered now require reflective pauses. For example, someone who knows you and your life of faith looks you in the eye and asks, "What are you going to do with your life? Have you thought about ministry?"

This chapter considers the transition from theological education to the practice of ministry through the lens of education. Daniel Aleshire has written that "Christian education involves those tasks and expressions of ministry that enable people: (1) to learn the Christian story, both ancient and present; (2) to develop the skills they need to act out their faith; (3) to reflect on that story in order to live self-aware to its truth; (4) to nurture the sensitivities they need to live together as a covenant community."[1] Women and men practice "a faithful ecology" when they focus on the ways that head, heart, and hands necessarily inform the vocation of Christian ministry.[2]

---

1. Daniel Aleshire, "Finding Eagles in the Turkeys' Nest: Pastoral Theology and Christian Education," *Review and Expositor* 85 (1988): 699.

2. This term has been used as a way to describe a network of both institutional and individual practices and commitments that together nurture the life of the Christian in the world. See "The Ecology for Nurturing Faith: Education, Disciplines and Programs for Faith Devel-

Elizabeth F. Caldwell

Head

In one of the three churches in which I worked, a small group of adults was interested in having a conversation about adult education. They wanted to form a new class for the Sunday morning church school hour. Three adult classes (two for older adults and one discussion class) were being offered but these people wanted something different. They wanted classes that employed teaching methods that were experiential and based around discussion rather than lecture. They also wanted more freedom with regard to topics than was offered in the denominational curriculum that was available for adults. Eventually, as they met for conversation, they identified one additional goal as well: they wanted the classes to have relevance for their daily lives.

They eventually named themselves the Peripatetic Class because they were committed to wandering around a variety of topics relating to faith and life: politics, including local and national elections and the role of the Christian as citizen; ethics and life concerns; justice issues and the world economy; and connecting faith and life at church and home through celebration of the church seasons.

Three things were important in the success of this model of adult religious education. First, the planning group was a visible example of the varieties of gifts that Paul writes about in 1 Corinthians 12. Some were knowledgeable about content — full of interesting ideas for topics of study. Others were very familiar with methods of teaching and learning with adults. One was very skilled in group process and knew the importance of enabling individual learners to become a community. And then there were the extroverts in the group who met visitors at the door and invited them to try this class. They all came together from the various places in their lives — their work, their homes, their roles as leaders in the congregation and the community — and modeled the kind of formation in Christian identity and practice that they sought to enable in the class that they were leading.

Second, this class modeled shared leadership in planning and teaching. Teachers emerged from within the group based on topic and time of year. Since many of these adults also taught children or youth in the church school, short-term topics in this class allowed them the flexibility

---

opment," in Milton J. Coalter, John M. Mulder, and Louis B. Weeks, *The Reforming Tradition: Presbyterians and Mainstream Protestantism* (Louisville: Westminster/John Knox Press, 1992).

to move in and out. Adults enjoyed volunteering to teach this group because there was a level of commitment on the part of the participants to be present and engaged with the topic.

The third key to this group's success was their commitment to gathering together once a quarter outside the class for a community event, such as a meal at someone's home, a Shrove Tuesday pancake dinner which they hosted for the congregation, or a mission project in the community.

My role with this group was that of resource person. I met twice a year with a planning team, once in the summer and again in late fall. We gathered in someone's home and I unloaded a bag of books which became the sources for thinking and planning for the class's discussion topics. Three hours later, a proposed curriculum was in place for the planning team to take to the class for consideration. My work with this group of intelligent and faithful Christians challenged me to think, to create, and to design curriculum that would, in turn, enable them to grapple thoughtfully with issues of life, belief, and faith.

Preparing students for their vocation as pastor requires helping them see the connections between their theological studies and their ministerial formation. One student recently said of her seminary experience that "the chance to study is the greatest gift of all." In commenting on her experience of both the challenges and rewards faced in the transition from her work in a corporate environment to academics in preparation for the call to ministry, another student expressed it this way:

> There is a wonderful tension between learning for the sake of learning and learning to be a professional minister. Sometimes I'm amazed by the way a professor is able to take an esoteric topic and help us think about how it would apply in the parish. For example, in a class I took on Genesis we applied each text to a contemporary issue, and at the end of the study, we had a question to answer: If you are a pastor asked to speak to a local school board about creationism or intelligent design, what do you say, based on your study of the creation story? Or, now that you have studied God's gift of the land to the Israelites, what do you believe is the biblical claim of the State of Israel?[3]

3. Thanks to the following McCormick Theological Seminary Master of Divinity students whose thoughtful reflections on transitions in ministry helped with this writing: Amy Pagliarella, Tahir Golden, Irene Pak, Paige Stephan, Andrew Baker, Malene Minor, and Mary Beth Shapley.

In the transition from theological education to ministry contexts, the work of the head, whose primary task is thinking theologically, continues. Having experienced teaching and learning contexts in theological education that require both knowledge and connection to ministry contexts, adults preparing for ministry are formed as teachers, ones capable of enabling that ability in others.

Heart

Graduation from seminary is a special day. Family and friends gather to celebrate the occasion; often church buses and vans unload teenagers and adults who have come to know this man or woman who will soon be called "Pastor" or "Reverend." I love meeting such companies of celebrants, for they are the ones who have supported an individual preparing for ministry among all God's people. They are the ones who have been praying for this woman; they are the ones who have gone on mission trips with this young man. They are the family members who have loved them, nurtured them, and supported them in their growth in the life of the Christian faith. This company of the faithful knows this person's *heart*.

One informal assessment tool I use at graduation is to look one more time at each graduate as she or he comes forward to receive a diploma. I say a prayer, and I ask a question: Can this person be my pastor? Could she be the pastor for my teenage nephews and niece? Does he have the pastoral heart necessary for visiting the elderly, sitting with parents who are awaiting their trip to China to meet and adopt their new daughter, or talking on the phone and e-mailing the young adult who struggles to understand and make meaning of her mother's untimely death? Does her pastoral heart reach out to the child whose beloved pet has died?

In writing about her transition to seminary, one student said that she "didn't want to lose touch with 'reality' or the experience of everyday folks like myself in the midst of academics and theological studies." This comment came from meeting pastors whom she believed had no connection with youth or young adults: "I knew I wanted to be a pastor, but I didn't want to be *that* pastor." Hopefully, over the course of a theological education, students make those connections, gaining clarity both about the role of pastor and their own abilities in ministry. For as a student's heart grows in its ability to nourish her own formation in the life of the Christian faith, so too is she enabled to be that presence for others, and this will help her in those pastoral care situations in which no fully sufficient preparation exists, nor any easy how-to steps.

One of my favorite gospel stories is John's account of Jesus meeting the Samaritan woman at the well. So many boundaries are crossed in this story. She simply wants water to drink, yet when he arrives, Jesus asks her to give him a drink as well. She can't believe that he, a Jew, speaks to her, a Samaritan woman! And then Jesus uses this moment to talk about "living water." "Where do you get that living water?" she asks. As Jesus explains about the "living water" which he offers, water which would satisfy all thirst, she asks for some. The conversation continues, and the woman comes to believe she is talking to a prophet. Eventually, Jesus reveals himself as the Messiah — to her, a woman whom many viewed as unrespectable due to her many marriages. Yet "many Samaritans from that city believed in him because of the woman's testimony." In her witness to others about her conversation with Jesus, she was a disciple. Writing about this passage, biblical scholar Gail O'Day says that "To witness to Jesus — to see Jesus and tell others about that experience — is one of the primary marks of discipleship in John."[4]

So many informal moments over the course of my ministry have become opportunities not unlike those when that woman who simply wanted water to drink met Jesus at the well. Conversations with teachers in the church school, or over a cup of coffee in the kitchen, have led to moments of listening and caring, that which in seminary we call pastoral care. My heart as an educator and pastor has been wisely and tenderly supported by friends in the church, by people who met me as Jesus met the woman at the well. Sometimes my bucket has been dry and these people have helped quench the thirst of my soul and my heart. Sometimes I have arrived at Sunday lunch and my bucket would be overflowing with stories and they have listened to me and I to them. Pastors develop hearts for ministry when they allow themselves to be open, and to be filled.

My sister is a church educator. Every now and then she calls and says, "I got to hold a baby today." After a child is born or adopted, she and one of her colleagues visit the family to meet the child. Together, the director of

---

4. Gail O'Day, "John," *Women's Bible Commentary,* ed. Carol A. Newsom and Sharon H. Ringe (Louisville: Westminster/John Knox Press, 1998), p. 384.

children's ministry and the pastor use this moment to talk with the parent or parents about this new life in their family and the ways that their congregation supports them educationally, pastorally, and liturgically. That, at any rate, is the "official" purpose of the visit. But I think that for my sister, the holding of the child fills her pastoral heart and reminds her of the living water of God's love that satisfies all thirsts and hungers.

Hands

I taught an introductory course entitled "The Educational Ministry of the Church" at another theological school during a summer term. Since it satisfied one of that school's five course requirements in the area of practical theology, it had a large registration. Before the first day of class I sent out a questionnaire requesting some basic information and was surprised by the answers to one of the questions: What is your faith tradition? Over half a dozen students responded with "unaffiliated," "unidentified," or "in transition."

In the weeks to come, I heard some of these students' stories. Some were actively searching for a new church home; others were unready to align themselves with any denomination. Yet there was a common thread uniting all these students who lacked connections to a particular tradition: a passion for doing ministry in the areas of social justice. Helping these students make the connections between religious education and the hands of ministry became my personal goal for the course. I wanted them to see that religious education, whether in the congregation or in another ministry setting, is essential to help individuals "develop the skills they need to act out their faith," as Aleshire says.

Opportunities for acting out our faith commitments have exploded in the years since I began my work as an educator. Mission trips to worksites both within this country and abroad; Habitat for Humanity housing projects; events such as CROP Walks and "Souper Sundays"; local church involvement in ministry with the homeless, the elderly, the very young, and those with mental and physical disabilities — all these are providing myriad opportunities for children, youth, and adults to learn experientially about the connection between the questions of the prophet Micah and those of Jesus: "What does the Lord require of you? Do justice, love kindness and walk humbly with God," Micah asks. And Jesus in the parable of the sheep and the goats asks, "When did you see me hungry, naked, thirsty, a stranger, sick, or in prison?"

If I had asked the young adults in that summer course, "Why are you here?" I think their responses would have focused on the acting out of their faith in specific contexts: immigration-related issues, care of the environment, housing issues, economic justice, the flourishing of all people, and the church as a welcoming place for everyone no matter their sexual orientation, economic status, race, or age. Having experienced churches that divide and separate people because of theological perspective or ideology, these young adults asked the simplest yet hardest question of all: How can people of faith, whether they are Protestant or Catholic or members of another religion, begin to listen to each other, to learn what we hold in common and how we differ? As Sharon Parks has written, they asked big questions and discovered worthy dreams.[5]

Children and youth in church school need to be encouraged to connect their hands, their head, and their heart as they become familiar with the stories of Jesus. They learn about Jesus breaking bread with strangers and with friends, when there was always enough for everyone. They learn that in breaking bread together at the Eucharist their hearts are full of love as they are surrounded by a community of the faithful: "This is the bread of life; it is for you." And as their hands prepare, serve, or share a meal with someone different from themselves, someone without a home, someone who needs help eating, or someone who is lonely and wants a friend, the integration of faith and life happens.

Asking Good Questions

Recently I asked some of my students to describe the challenges they faced in transitioning to seminary. Some students who had previously worked in a corporate environment commented on their need to rearrange their financial priorities and to adjust to a context not measured by material wealth or external accomplishments. Another student described feeling like she was "hiding from the real world . . . it has taken a lot to view this work of being a full-time student as valuable and necessary." Another student ob-

5. Sharon Parks, *Big Questions, Worthy Dreams: Mentoring Young Adults* (San Francisco: Jossey-Bass, 2000), p. 5.

served that "seminary requires an introspective and contemplative approach to development for ministry — the exact opposite of the business world . . . and also making the shift from being 'in front' to 'being among.'"

Some other young adults come to seminary fresh from work as mission volunteers, energized to gain theological perspective on their experience. One such student wrote about her experiences of seeing "many expressions of the face of God in the people with whom I lived in Kenya," and said that the difficult part of her transition to seminary has been in "finding that bridge between my head and my heart."

Hopefully a theological education provides space for asking good questions, for time to engage with others in a community of teaching and learning, and support for integrating heart, hands, and head. Sometimes this integration is easier said than done. Two more student comments illustrate the tension seminarians often experience:

> I worked for a church all last year during my first year of seminary. We had the usual assortment of crises, including a teenager in the youth group whose mother was seriously injured in an accident. As I was sitting there with this youth who was facing the death of his mother, I realized that he could care less how much I knew about Hebrew or history or theology.
>
> Seminary is a transformative space and has provided me the opportunity to think, pray, and reflect, all of which is priceless.

The second question I asked students to comment on had to do with the challenges they faced as they make the transition from seminary to ministry contexts — the focus of this entire book. One student wondered where her ministry would take her geographically; another questioned whether, as a black woman, her call would be validated by others. Another student wrote about her commitment to not lose touch with, as she says, "the experience of everyday Christians." As she thinks about the transition to her life and ministry as pastor, one of the challenges she will face is how "to be open to the real human ways people experience God." Yet another student identified his greatest fear as "the idea that I'm not fully equipped to journey with parishioners through the mysteries of life." He added, "The challenge of keeping a level and steady faithful presence as a minister regardless of my own circumstances is a fear that haunts me plaintively."

Having worked in the corporate world, one young adult realized that ministry is very different. It "is a lifestyle, not just a job. I think this is going to be the hardest part to balance. How will I be a mom, a wife, and also one of the girls with my friends? I also worry about the all-consuming nature of ministry. Because it's a call, not a job, how do you leave work at the office when you go home?"

Remarkable things happen over the course of three or four years of theological education. Students arrive with some questions and they leave with different ones. As I watch them walk forward to receive their diploma, I know some of the questions with which they have struggled. I also know they arrive having been formed in faithful Christian communities representing a variety of traditions: Presbyterian, Pentecostal, Baptist, AME, UCC, Mennonite, and Christian Reformed. In class discussions, in study breaks at night, in conversations over coffee and meals at the table, in worship, in articulations of challenges, and in learning through annual reviews with their faculty advisor, their formation for ministry is bounded by questions. If they don't leave different from the person they were when they entered, then we have failed them. Consider these thoughts from a student about to graduate:

> Sometimes my church and faith tradition seem foreign to me. My faith, theology, and politics have been transformed through the seminary experience and I question where and how I fit in back home. My friends tell me that they like how I think, but that my views on Christian ethics are too liberal and idealistic. I feel like I have to go back in a box in order to be heard or accepted in the church, but it's a compromise I am not willing to make. The challenge for me is finding a community where I can thrive as a faith leader and not feel encumbered by tradition or parochial views.

Students navigate their way through the transitions from their life before seminary to life in seminary. Through reading and study, papers and conversations, they are immersed in a culture that values both practice and reflection. As one student put it, "In a very consumption-driven world, where productivity and tangible items are most valued, I think it is sometimes difficult to view the work of ministry (prayer, study, thinking, reflection, and writing) as valuable and necessary. It requires constant reminding that this work is ultimately what brings meaning to everything else that people do."

What does the Lord require of you? Sometimes more than you expected!

Elizabeth F. Caldwell

Living into the Rhythms of Faith and Life

Twenty-two years later, the list of my hopes and dreams for persons preparing for ministry is still valid, and the goals for learning are explicit in the curriculum of courses in educational ministry offered at McCormick Theological Seminary. But the list is not exhaustive.

It's been said that good teachers are taught by their students. This is not just a nice thought but the truth. A number of factors have been influential in my formation and call to the vocation of teacher. In addition to reading, research, and writing, I am a different teacher and learner today because of my experiences in a theological school that is diverse in age, gender, race, culture, ethnicity, sexual orientation, nationality, class, and learning styles.

My perspective on the church's educational ministry has been challenged by engagement with my learning partners — the students, faculty and staff — with whom I teach and live in this community of theological education. And my teaching and learning with students and colleagues in the Association of Chicago Theological Schools has expanded my awareness of religious education and its practice across differing faith traditions.[6]

So now on my list of essential things I want students to know, learn, value, and experience as they prepare for their leadership roles in ministry are the following capacities, which focus on context, culture, spiritual formation, and developing abilities in areas of teaching and learning, educational design and resources:

- Experience settings of teaching and learning that provide hospitable space for thinking, reflecting, and creating, paying particular attention to space and learners;
- Intentionally reflect on what it means to teach and learn in a multicultural setting;
- Appreciate and learn from those who are different from oneself in language, learning style, culture, and faith tradition and generate applications for congregational models of educational ministry;

---

6. Faith traditions represented in these schools are Catholic, United Church of Christ, Unitarian Universalist, Evangelical Lutheran Church of America, United Methodist, Episcopalian, American Baptist, and Evangelical Covenant.

- Experience varieties of spiritual disciplines (e.g., prayer, *Lectio Divina, Examen,* music, meditation, space for quiet) in class and make connections for their practice with children, youth, and adults in the congregation;
- Gain experience teaching using methods which reflect attention to learning theory and multiple intelligences (linguistic, artistic, logical, musical, kinesthetic, naturalistic, intrapersonal, interpersonal);
- Become familiar with preferred learning styles and identify the implications for identity and formation as a teacher and a learner;
- Gain experience in teaching and leading groups in the church through experiential learning/field studies placements and reflect on these experiences in class;
- Nurture and support their creativity and skills in educational design;
- Develop criteria for and be able to evaluate Internet resources for use in settings of teaching and learning;
- Identify priorities for ministry in the role of pastor as educator.

In addition to learning the story (head), reflecting on the story (heart), and living the story (hands), religious education provides opportunities for people of all ages to understand and experience what it means to live together as a covenant community. The life of the Christian faith is formed in the rhythms of the seasons of the church year. As people walk together through Advent, Christmas and Epiphany, Lent, Holy Week, Easter and Pentecost, they tell and live the story of God's love and God's call to people of every age to live faithfully in the world.

Have you asked a good question today?

7. Ministry and Clouds of Witnesses

Michael Jinkins

The fields of central Texas range over softly rolling topography. Crops of wheat, sorghum, and cotton take their turns maturing in their own time under skies of blue that blaze white hot from May to late September. My daily walks as a young pastor took me past fields that stretched to a horizon bounded to the west, north, and south only by the curvature of the earth and to the east by "the Mountain," a hulking mesquite-covered plateau notorious for harboring diamondback rattlesnakes. If the scenery did not stop your heart, the occasional flock of blackbirds would as they exploded from a field on your approach. Lunchtime often found me standing flatfooted, watching birds break into the sky, turn, and turn again, like a living cloud of black wings, until they settled again in a distant field, or dipped to follow a tractor furrowing the black earth. There were moments when the only sound was a driving Texas wind, dry and hot, when the air was charged with the aromas of snuff and wildflowers, and the reign of God seemed to embrace creation right down to the roots of the blanched grass at my feet. In the midst of the land a collection of houses and buildings rose like stubble in a gleaned field, and in the midst of it all an old church tower, white as bleached bones, marked the gathering place of the congregation I served as pastor.

I was not a stranger to the country, having grown up on an East Texas farm. But I was a stranger to the world of vast family farms that made up my parish, a world largely vanished now. I had lived in larger towns and in cities for more than ten years as a student and in my first pastoral position. I had to become reacquainted with the agricultural calendar, the rhythms of the worked earth, of tilling, planting, cultivating, harvesting, laying fallow, and tilling again. I came to my first solo pastorate after serving for several years as an associate pastor in a busy congregation of suburban Dallas. My responsibilities as an associate pastor had been primarily administrative. I oversaw the educational, mission, and youth programs of the church, preached occasionally, visited in hospitals some, taught the odd class. I had become accustomed to the bustle of the city, and of a suburban congregation made up largely of busy professionals, attorneys, doctors, accountants, consultants, and executives.

The first time I visited the small town of Itasca, Texas, about an hour's drive south of Fort Worth, I was struck by how far it was from any metropolitan area. It could not even claim the distinction of being in the middle of nowhere. It was not that central to anything. It was just on the periphery of nowhere. Most travelers knew Itasca only because there was a Dairy Queen and a state-maintained rest stop (now gone) on the interstate where you would turn to go into town. Few turned. Most Presbyterians knew of Itasca simply because of the Presbyterian Children's Home nearby. Frankly, I worried about the remoteness of the parish. I wondered if my family and I would fit in, if we would get bored with the slower pace of life, if we would find the kinds of friends there we had known and loved in the city. My concerns on these scores were quickly put to rest. When we eventually left Itasca, after I had served almost five years as their pastor, I (and, indeed, my whole family) experienced a grief that took years to get over. We had become part of the community, the people, and the land.

"Someday you're going to look back on this time as the best of your life," a judicatory official said to me as we walked along the sidewalk in Itasca. He had made the trip from Dallas to visit with me about some presbytery committee work, and I had taken him to Rotary (it was Thursday and I never missed the Rotary Club if I was in town). It was also the week before Christmas, and we had sung Christmas carols accompanied by an ancient upright piano played by the wife of the Baptist preacher. The sustain pedal was broken so every carol sounded like a polka, even "Silent Night, Holy Night." My colleague winked at me as we walked along the sidewalk to my car. "Someday you're going to look back on this as the best time of your life." Oddly enough, there have been *few* times in my life that I don't look back on as the best time of my life, including last week, or yesterday. Usually I feel like "this moment, right now" is the best time ever in my life. But I have, in fact, looked back on this first solo pastorate as particularly wonderful, and I have often wondered why it was so good.

79

I think there are basically two reasons, and they are related to two things I learned then. First, I discovered in that first solo pastorate that the great voices of the church's past, including its distant past, are a living cloud of witnesses, that they are our exact contemporaries (to adapt a phrase from Søren Kierkegaard), that they have something to tell us and something to teach us that we would be infinitely poorer if we did not know. Second, I realized that the people with whom I served, the members of the congregation I knew and loved and cared for, were also among the great cloud of witnesses, that sainthood is a living category, that one does not have to die to be canonized.

These two discoveries transformed my ministry right at its beginning and made me understand that our salvation is a matter of our long-term transformation, and that this transformation occurs in real, concrete communities of faith. We are shaped as pastors by the congregations we shape. We change them (we hope, for the better); and often they transform us redemptively.

I think my learning these two things was somehow connected with the geography, the place, we inhabited together. Somehow I was able to focus on the sacrament of human community because distractions were subdued. I do not mean to idealize or sentimentalize or romanticize the country parson's life. To do so would diminish its sacred quality. The people I served were not paper cutouts. These were real people, often leading difficult lives. People suffered irreparable losses in that community. There were divorces, bankruptcies, illnesses, injuries, deaths. There were betrayals small and large. The "world," in a Johannine sense, was in that place too, as in any other. In certain ways, all of humanity, its good and bad, is only concentrated in a village. We knew each other well — sometimes one might feel we knew each other *too* well. There were not only comforting expressions of neighborly concern, there was also backbiting and harmful gossip. But there was integrity to the life, wholeness of earth, sky, and community that made our churchly life and my pastoral vocation come sharply into focus.

The ancient formula *extra ecclesiam nulla salus* (outside the church there is no salvation) took on new meaning for me as a statement of the most common and obvious sense: we are called into wholeness by God and we become all God created us to be only in communion with others. This may not be what the church fathers meant by this statement, but I came to believe it is the doctrine's truest meaning. God calls us from disintegration into a community that is grounded in the very being of God's own communal being. Father, Son, and Spirit, Creator, Redeemer, and Sustainer: these halting attempts to speak of God's own plurality in union, name the relationship that God is, in the image of which we were created. We were made to be together (this is the character of the God in whose likeness we were made), and without this togetherness we can't become who we were created to be.

I learned these lessons, the first about the contemporary nature of past saints and the second about the sanctity of my contemporaries, simply by paying attention in the particular setting in which we lived as a congregation, by allowing the classical witnesses to Christian faith to become my conversation partners and by privileging the wisdom of those with whom I broke bread. Of all the things I learned as a young pastor, these are the lessons that remain.

The Past Is Not Past

G. K. Chesterton once said that valuing tradition really amounts to extending the franchise to vote to our ancestors, "the most obscure of all classes." He called tradition "the democracy of the dead."[1] William Faulkner observed *somewhere* (and I can't recall where he said this) that the past is not dead, it's not even past. Today's church seems, by contrast, to celebrate the attitude of Henry Ford toward the past, that *history is bunk*. Such an attitude is not only arrogant, it is self-mutilating; it cuts us off from who we are.

I did not come to my first solo pastorate with a strong understanding of the meaning and significance of the past or of the wisdom of those who inhabited it. But I did come to the pastorate with a fairly strong theological bias that the Word of God was faithfully preached and the Holy Spirit had been at work in the church long before I was ordained as a minister. I had also been infected with an insatiable curiosity about what others think, and a visceral revulsion at the attitude that believes a new idea is better simply because everyone is talking about it right now.

Arriving in my first solo pastorate, I also had in my possession a practical gift given me by my wife, a complete set of *The Nicene, Ante-*

---

1. G. K. Chesterton, *Orthodoxy* (London: Bodley Head, 1908), pp. 82-83.

Nicene, and Post-Nicene Fathers of the Church, along with other classic
sources of Christian thought, for example, books by John Calvin and Martin Luther, Karl Barth, Reinhold Niebuhr, and Paul Tillich. And I arrived in
this pastorate with an assumption, the significance of which I had no real
idea at the time: that my seminary education was a launching pad for the
adventure of lifelong learning in ministry. Some of my colleagues assumed
that seminary was responsible for giving them everything they would ever
need to know for every time and place; and many of them became disillusioned, frustrated, and angry about their seminary education when they
discovered they did not know how to do some of the things they were
called upon to do. Such an attitude seemed to me bogus and irresponsible
from the beginning. They set themselves and their seminaries up for failure with their assumptions. I always assumed that seminary existed to provide an essential core of knowledge, especially regarding the Bible, Christian theology, and the history of the church; it provided a beginning
bibliography, a set of basic tools, and the opportunity to fall in love with
thinking about God and God's church. Consequently, far from being disillusioned, frustrated, and angry about seminary, I appreciated my seminary
experience for what it was: the burst of a starting pistol for a race to learn
as much as possible for as long as I can.

As a new pastor, I developed a habit of reading sermons and commentaries on every text I preached. In fact, I would generally read the texts
I planned to preach for six months in advance, preparing a separate folder
for each sermon over that period. Confronted with Ephesians 1, I might
read Calvin's commentary. "Christ alone, therefore, is the mirror in which
we can contemplate that which the weakness of the cross obscures in
us. . . . For these reasons, it is our good to transfer our thoughts to Christ,
that in Him, as in a mirror, we may see the glorious treasures of Divine
grace."[2] Then I might turn to St. John Chrysostom's sermons on Ephesians
to see an altogether different angle on the same passage: for instance, noting that Chrysostom emphasizes the idea that the power by which God
draws us into new life is identical with the power by which God raised Jesus from the dead.[3] I would read sermons by great pastors, ancient and

2. John Calvin, *Calvin's New Testament Commentaries: Galatians, Ephesians,
Philippians and Colossians: A New Translation,* trans. T. H. L. Parker, ed. David W. Torrance
and T. F. Torrance (Grand Rapids: Eerdmans, 1965), p. 136.

3. *Nicene and Post-Nicene Fathers of the Christian Church,* vol. XIII, St. John
Chrystostom, ed. Philip Schaff (Grand Rapids: Eerdmans, 1979), p. 60.

contemporary. I remember reading, virtually from cover to cover, the thirteen volumes of *Twenty Centuries of Great Preaching*.[4] At the suggestion of an experienced pastor, I started reading novels and serious poetry, at first thinking that I was reading for "illustrations," only gradually to realize I was reading in order to understand more deeply our common humanity and the intersection points of God and the lives we live.

It was, in fact, as a pastor and not as a college or seminary student that I became a voracious reader. Initially, as a new pastor, I was just worried that I might stand in the pulpit on a Sunday morning and have nothing to say. Within a couple of years, I discovered that my preparation to preach consisted largely of culling through the sheer impossible volume of possibilities to find just the right thing to say in response to a particular text on a particular day to my congregation. There were weeks when I literally had written two or three sermons when only one was needed, and in those cases I had to make tough choices about which sermon to preach.

During those years, John Calvin, Martin Luther, John Chrysostom, Karl Barth, Reinhold Niebuhr, Dietrich Bonhoeffer, Irenaeus, Paul Scherer, Will Campbell, Robert Farrar Capon, Annie Dillard, Frederick Buechner, and many, many others became conversation partners, beside whom, with whom, and through whom I learned to listen for the Word of God for my people. These saints and scholars, some living, many from the distant past, did not just have the right to vote. Often they had the responsibility to overrule me, especially when I got on some hobby horse or other. Sometimes they argued among themselves so vigorously that I could not get a word in edgewise, and sometimes they encouraged me to go ask members of my congregation to settle the argument. My love for these conversations was not merely academic, nor was it only scholarly (though there are worse things for a pastor to be than a scholar), it was churchly.

Maybe it was because I had served as an associate pastor for administration before becoming a solo pastor, but I never felt that the administrative side of ministry was particularly onerous. Good administration matters primarily because bad administration wastes so much time and energy, and because bad administration tends to exclude people and to underestimate their gifts and the contributions they can make to the life of the community. Good administration multiplies ministry, as an older pas-

---

4. Clyde E. Fant, Jr., and William M. Pinson, Jr., *Twenty Centuries of Great Preaching: An Encyclopedia of Preaching* (Waco: Word, 1971).

tor once told me. I had been reading for years on the subjects of leadership and management, and had found much (though certainly not all) of what I read valuable for organizing the church's ministry and building a larger body of leaders in the congregation. As a solo pastor, I found administration generally easy and straightforward, and I had a fairly clear understanding of my priorities, which meant I had lots of time to visit my congregation at home and in the hospital, to attend to their pastoral, spiritual, and emotional needs, and to prepare worship and sermons that were substantial and (I think) interesting. Perhaps this is an argument for new pastors to work hard at learning good administration. But it is also an argument for new pastors to attend to the core of our pastoral vocation rather than to forsake it to become mini-CEOs.

Joseph Sittler commented, "The principal work of the ordained ministry is reflection: cultivation of one's penetration into the depth of the Word so that the witness shall be poignant and strong."[5] These words have stuck with me since I first read them in 1986 while serving as a pastor in Itasca. Years later, while serving as the pastor of another congregation, I read Eugene Peterson's *Working the Angles,* which focuses eloquently on the essential matters at the heart of the pastoral calling. Peterson writes:

> There are a lot of other things to be done in this wrecked world and we are going to be doing at least some of them, but if we don't know the basic terms with which we are working, the foundational realities with which we are dealing — God, kingdom, gospel — we are going to end up living futile, fantasy lives. Your task is to keep telling the basic story, representing the presence of the Spirit, insisting on the priority of God, speaking the biblical words of command and promise and invitation.[6]

It seems to me that many of the concerns I hear articulated by pastors, especially by new pastors, about never having enough time and needing a better handle on "time management" are really misdirected. The problem is not so much time per se, but rather the need to gain pastoral focus on the use of our time, determining what to spend our best time on, where to

---

5. Joseph Sittler, *Gravity & Grace: Reflections and Provocations,* ed. Linda-Marie Delloff (Minneapolis: Augsburg, 1986), p. 49.

6. Eugene Peterson, *Working the Angles: The Shape of Pastoral Integrity* (Grand Rapids: Eerdmans, 1987), p. 18.

invest the lion's share of our days, sifting out the gold dust of the crucial from the sand of all the various demands that make their way to our doors. The only way to clarify focus as a pastor is to understand in one's heart the character of this calling. I wish every new pastor would reread two small classical treatises every year: Gregory of Nazianzus' "In Defense of His Flight to Pontus" and Chrysostom's "On the Priesthood."[7] In the former, Gregory explores the pastoral calling down to its deepest level, exploring what he calls "the art of arts and science of sciences," imploring us to a ministry of discernment so that we can wisely establish "what is gentle and dear to God . . . arbitrating between soul and body, not allowing the superior [concerns] to be overpowered by the inferior, which would be the greatest injustice," but living simply and consciously under the reign of God in the midst of God's people, remembering that "the scope of our art is to provide the soul with wings."[8]

Chrysostom, perhaps better than anyone else, reminds us that this ministry is not our own. "The initiative is with God, not man," as Graham Neville writes in his introduction to a popular edition of Chrysostom's classic. "No priest can force or restrain God's hand."[9] The pastoral office is not an executive office, in other words. We are sent on behalf of an Other; our authority is derived from Jesus Christ who called and sent us and from God in whose name we minister, and is mediated through the community with whom we serve. In a culture hell-bent on self-aggrandizement in the name of religion, Chrysostom encourages the sanity of humility and hospitality and a heart set on the good.

Reinhold Niebuhr's *Leaves from the Notebook of a Tamed Cynic* helped me differentiate the essential from the inessential. On the cover page of my worn copy of *Leaves,* I wrote long ago: "What is most wonderful about this book is not its originality, but its lack of originality. Honestly and humbly it speaks aloud what most all of us pastors have felt but were perhaps too timid to say."[10] Carlyle Marney's *Priests to Each Other* and *The*

---

7. *Nicene and Post-Nicene Fathers of the Christian Church,* vol. VII, Gregory of Nazianzus, ed. Philip Schaff and Henry Wace (Grand Rapids: Eerdmans, 1979); John Chrysostom, *On the Priesthood,* trans. Graham Neville (New York: St. Vladimir's Seminary Press, 1984).

8. Gregory, "In Defense of His Flight to Pontus," pp. 208-9.

9. See Neville's introduction to Chrysostom, *On the Priesthood,* p. 27.

10. Reinhold Niebuhr, *Leaves from the Notebook of a Tamed Cynic* (New York: Harper & Row, 1929).

Recovery of the Person rocked my world and made me rethink categories like "humanism" and "religion," and ideas like "the priesthood of all believers."[11] John Calvin's dictum, *"in tota vita negotium cum Deo"* (in all of life it is with God that we have our dealings), transformed the way I looked at the ordinary negotiations of each day, and taught me that "everything is illuminated" (to borrow a phrase from Jonathan Safran Foer's novel with this title).[12] And I will never forget first coming across Annie Dillard. Her poetic vision, for instance, in *Holy the Firm,* made me take seriously and pay more reverent attention to what is at hand; her understanding of vocation in "Living Like Weasels," and of worship in "An Expedition to the Pole,"[13] fired what Craig Dykstra has since referred to as the "pastoral imagination."[14] All of which brings me to the second thing I learned.

The Present Is Peopled by Saints

The manse was less than a mile from the church in Itasca, and often I walked to and from my study at the church. Not only was this good for my physical health; it was good for my spiritual health. I would stop along the way, especially in the afternoons, to visit with members of my congregation.

Late afternoons would often find me on Pauline Farrow's back porch, drinking iced tea and listening to the wisdom of the church. Pauline was one of the earliest ordained women elders in the Presbyterian Church in Texas. Pauline, then in her late eighties, taught me the hidden meanings of things. For instance, she explained why Mert got so upset when the little leg on the silver sugar dish got broken by a person who had used it for a church supper. It was not that Mert had made an idol of the silver service. For Mert the silver symbolized the devotion of the people in honor of whom it had been given to the church, people the memory of whom was

11. Carlyle Marney, *Priests to Each Other* (Valley Forge: Judson, 1974), and *The Recovery of the Person: A Christian Humanism* (Nashville: Abingdon, 1963).

12. John Calvin, *On God and Political Duty,* ed. John T. McNeill (Indianapolis: Bobbs-Merrill, 1956).

13. Annie Dillard, *Holy the Firm* (Boston: G. K. Hall & Co., 1977), and *Teaching a Stone to Talk: Expeditions and Encounters* (New York: Harper & Row, 1982).

14. Craig Dykstra, "Keys to Excellence: Pastoral Imagination and Holy Friendship," Remarks delivered at the Sustaining Pastoral Excellence forum, January 22, 2004.

already slipping from the congregation as years unfolded. Without ever telling me that I really ought to be more patient, Pauline showed me a more excellent way.

Pauline taught me to value the providence of God and to have an appropriate level of humility regarding my gifts for ministry in relation to my pastoral predecessors. "God called the right pastor here for whatever time we were going through," she told me. Mr. Cloud was here in the turbulent days of the early civil rights movement, and our congregation was the first in this area to integrate. She proudly told me that the Klan had burned a cross on the lawn of the manse, about where the monkey grass now grew. She went through the list of my recent predecessors, listing their gifts, each just right for the moment God called them. She reminded me that over the course of the last century there had been twelve pastors of this congregation. "And now you are here, with your gifts," she said with a smile. I may have been a fair organizer and a pretty good preacher, I saw immediately, but I would never have the prophetic gifts of Mr. Cloud or the pastoral gentleness of Reverend Stephens. I told Pauline this. She just smiled again as though to say, "Here endeth the lesson."

Vesta, Kenneth and Janie, Ollie and Paul, Debbie, Liz, Verl, Sally and Tom: I was surrounded by living saints that would redden with embarrassment to be labeled as such. In time I came to realize that sainthood is inextricably tied to locale (it always has been), and that the sainthood of the people with whom we serve is a living, almost tangible reality for every pastor willing to pay attention to his or her congregation. God has chosen to shape us into the likeness of Jesus Christ through the workings of the Spirit in ordinary communities of faith. This is where God does God's work of transformation, of conversion, if you will. Forgiveness, repentance and faith, grace and mercy and judgment, believing and being true, hoping and loving — these are all personal and relational categories. And for Christians, they have eternal significance. They transcend us. And we cannot get from here to transcendence in abstraction, only through community, through the concrete reality of life together in a practiced faith.

The church, spoken of eloquently by St. Paul as "the Body of Christ," is none other than the living, grumbling, combed-over, rouged-up gaggle of sinners that we live among. Saints have day jobs. And the church does not hover eight feet off the ground. The "People of God," whose names are carved upon the heart of the heavenly high priest, spit on the sidewalk and disappoint one another and forgive each other for real and imagined wrongs. And it is through all of this life together that we are becoming who we already are in Christ.

Pastoral ministry is most truly theological work when it is engaged in the ordinary pursuits of life. This is, I think, what Robert Frost meant when he wrote:

> But God's own descent
> Into flesh was meant
> As a demonstration
> That the supreme merit
> Lay in risking spirit
> In substantiation.[15]

When we argued with each other about the use of the church's silver in the church board meeting, we were also (to use John Calvin's language) negotiating with God. We were doing something profoundly spiritual and theological because we were coming to terms with who we were as a people of God, what we salvaged from our past, how alive (or dead) that past was to us, what claims it made on us, and where we could faithfully adapt as a congregation for the sake of the church's future (and the needs of the living) without betraying the memories of the dead.

When I arrived at the church building one Thursday afternoon and was greeted by the high school principal emerging from our sanctuary with a group of teachers, the band director, and some students with clarinets, trombones, and drums in hand, I was confronted with the human and communal dimensions of church-state relations. The principal told me that the band would be arriving at 10:00 a.m. this Sunday morning for the 11:00 baccalaureate service. They had already moved that "big table" from the middle of the "stage." I would need to have somebody put it back after the school finished its baccalaureate ceremony. I told him that this was all news to me, that this Sunday was *Pentecost Sunday,* a day *holy* to the *church,* and (as my sense of affront began to dawn on me and my emotions began to soar) *"What do you mean the school's got a ceremony here?! We're having church then!! Who gave you authority to commandeer our sanctuary for the use of the state!!!"*

Our church board assembled for a conversation, aware that half the

---

15. Robert Frost, "Kitty Hawk," in *The Poetry of Robert Frost,* ed. Edward Connery Lathem (New York: Holt, Rinehart and Winston, 1969), p. 435.

school board was made up of members of my church, and that several of our church members (including my wife) were employees of the school district, *and* that we had to work through a problem with community, congregational, and theological implications. As we negotiated a workable solution we were not just thinking about either the Constitution of the United States or that of the Presbyterian Church. We were thinking about who were we were as a people of God, how our values sometimes conflict even when the values are good, and what it means to be brothers and sisters in Christ at the end of a heated discussion. This is the work of saints.

I emerged from those years of pastoral ministry with a deep and abiding respect for the wisdom of deliberative groups of people and a distrust of my own bright ideas. I came to realize that I never had a good idea that was not made better by the community, and the best ideas I had ever witnessed were forged as we faced challenges together. James Surowiecki, in his *The Wisdom of Crowds,* has recently explored the thesis that "under the right circumstances, groups are remarkably intelligent, and are often smarter than the smartest people in them."[16] He is right. But the people in the congregations I served had already taught me this lesson, and it was not simply a lesson at the human level. It was also a theological lesson. God works through the people of God, not infallibly, not always efficiently, and sometimes not very quickly — but faithfully. When we speak of the Spirit of God at work in the world, we all too often these days think of the lonely prophetic individual or the prayer warrior alone in her closet. Mostly the Spirit works through a group of Christians arguing, thinking, praying together, just trying to muddle through, reaching the best decisions they can according to the best information they have at the time. God works this way among us.

These two things I learned listening to pages handed down for centuries and reading the congregations I served. Clouds of witnesses surround us like mists rising early before the heat of day settles in. Clouds of witnesses break from fields of stubble like black birds on the wing. And God is in the clouds.

---

16. James Surowiecki, *The Wisdom of Crowds* (New York: Doubleday, 2004), p. xiii.

8. Fragile Connections: Constructing an Identity in the First Year of Ministry

Carrie Doehring

I was twenty-one when I began theological studies in the Faculty of Religious Studies at McGill University in Montreal, Canada. I had just finished a bachelor degree in music that year (1975), also at McGill, and had become intrigued with theological studies while working as an organist at a small Presbyterian church. Raised a Roman Catholic, I stopped attending weekly Mass when I was an undergraduate, no longer able to tolerate the patriarchal authority structure of the Roman Catholic Church. I became an agnostic, and mentally argued with the minister at Park Street Presbyterian Church as I sat at the organ waiting for the sermon to finish. He was a second-career M.Div. student at McGill, and he enjoyed debating me when I started expressing my agnostic opinions aloud.

When he challenged me to read the Gospel According to John, I opened a Bible for the first time in my life and finished the Gospel in one sitting. Here I encountered John's complex portrayal of Jesus and experienced a transcendent reality whose existence I had easily dismissed when I left the Roman Catholic Church in anger. I was overwhelmed by the intensity of my emotional response to this reading, which, in retrospect, seemed characterized by all the feelings of grief and which I later identified as a conversion experience. For several days I experienced waves of sadness and found myself crying on the bus, during worship, and in bed at night. I cried because my life had been, up to this point, bereft of experiences of this awesome mystery, like a black-and-white picture that had only had shades of gray and not the full spectrum of colors. I cried because I had come very close to missing the opportunity of stepping into this new life. I cried because my old ways of defending myself against religious faith and its commitments were no longer available. I had stepped into a new world, and the old world of my naïve intellectual agnosticism was gone forever. In this new world, I was compelled to act upon my experience of God. I found myself voraciously hungry for more reading and study, and so I began graduate studies in theology.

At the same time, I joined the Presbyterian congregation where I worked. This small, working class congregation, founded by Scottish immigrants, was like the extended family I had never had. My family had always worshiped in large suburban Roman Catholic churches, where we attended weekly Mass and never spoke with anyone. Now I had a church home. I cherished its smells and its creaking wooden structure when I was alone practicing at the organ or when I participated in worship. I delighted in its Scottish heritage, enacted at the annual Robbie Burns Dinners, when haggis was paraded from the kitchen with bagpipes.

My participation in the life of this congregation, along with the deep sense of satisfaction I experienced in theological studies, led me to consider the ministry as a profession. I imagined how my intellectual ambitions would be fulfilled in weekly sermon preparation. My love of the arts, particularly music, could be expressed in preparing and leading worship. The enjoyment and delight I experienced in being part of a church family would likely become the basis for a pastoral care ministry.

After completing two years of academic courses at the Faculty of Religious Studies for a Bachelor of Theology degree, I did the In-Ministry year of practical and field education studies at Presbyterian College, Montreal. This degree program was typical of a "foundational" model of theological education: "The goal was to prepare students in the *academic foundations* for ministry, leaving the development of professional skills primarily to field work or summer institutes."[1] The "gap between academics and ministry practice and, more generally, between intellect and piety"[2] was deepened by the intellectualism that was so much part of my own approach to theological studies and the ministry.

I have only vague memories of going through the ordination process in the Presbytery of Montreal. At the time, there was no psychologi-

---

1. Charles R. Foster, Lisa E. Dahill, Lawrence A. Golemon, and Barbara Wang Tolentino, *Educating Clergy: Teaching Practices and Pastoral Imagination* (San Francisco: Jossey-Bass, 2006), p. 238.

2. Foster et al., *Educating Clergy,* p. 238.

cal testing of candidates, nor were there the written ordination exams that are now part of seeking ordination in the Presbyterian Church (U.S.A.). After an oral exam in which all eligible candidates met with a committee of the presbytery, the governing judicatory, I was approved for ordination. The only other requirement was that I accept a two-year mission appointment, which could be anywhere in Canada. My husband, whom I had married when I was twenty-two years old, agreed to any appointment that was close to a city where he could find work as a computer scientist. Though questions were raised about how a young woman like me, who had kept her family name when she married, would fit into a congregation with "traditional family values," I was appointed to two village churches in Rockwood and Eden Mills, Ontario, sixty miles west of Toronto.

And so, in 1978, at the age of twenty-four, I was ordained, and was among the first dozen female graduates of Presbyterian College to be ordained and was the second female minister in the Presbytery of Waterloo-Wellington, Ontario. I was well received in the two congregations. Although I didn't have much practical training or experience, I was able to do a good-enough job as a novice preacher and pastoral caregiver. Six months into my ministry, a young married man who was hospitalized for depression committed suicide. He had grown up in one of the congregations I was serving and his parents were church leaders there. I vividly recall the anxiety I felt as I met with the family, and planned and conducted the funeral service (compounding that anxiety was grief stemming from the fact that my own grandfather had committed suicide a few months earlier). The family expressed deep gratitude for my ministry, and this tragic event marked the real beginning of my ministry.

My first year, when I encountered many aspects of ministry for the first time, was like a supervisor-less internship year. These congregations had seen many student ministers come and go and were used to helping students and newly-ordained clergy take up the tasks of ministry. The challenges of constructing the public *persona* of being a minister was made more difficult by the fact that I had no office outside the study in my home, and no staff to whom I related on a daily basis.

I often sought advice from the only other ordained woman in my presbytery, a second-career clergywoman, who became a mentor. I received support from my local ministerial group, which elected me their president in my third year, when I was pregnant with my first child. I struggled with anxiety about sermon preparation, leading worship, preaching, and pastoral care responsibilities. My shyness and social anxiety made it initially painful for me to attend the family and social gatherings that were part of being a minister in two village churches. In spite of these challenges, I experienced being embraced and affirmed by members of the congregations, community, and the presbytery. In many ways, I began to realize the dreams of ministry I had envisioned when I first began my theological studies and became a member of the small congregation in Montreal.

I stayed for nine years. After three years I began part-time studies in a Master's in Pastoral Theology program at Wilfrid Laurier Lutheran Seminary, a program that included four units of clinical pastoral education (CPE). These studies were very helpful, allowing me the depth of integration that had not been possible in my studies at McGill, in part because of my age and lack of life experience, and in part because of the way that degree program separated academic studies from practical training.

Reflections

In reflecting on my transition from the world of theological studies to the world of congregational ministry, I will distinguish between aspects of my experiences that are likely *common to anyone* my age making this transition in a North American cultural context, aspects that were probably *similar to those of others like me,* meaning young, middle-class, Euroamerican women being ordained in theologically progressive Protestant denominations in the United States and Canada in the late seventies; and also aspects that were *peculiar to me.* In identifying the cultural, contextual, and idiosyncratic dimensions of my experiences, I am following Kluckholn and Murray's[3] maxim that "Every person is in certain respects (1) like all others, (2) like some others, and (3) like no other."[4]

---

3. C. Kluckholn and H. Murray, *Personality in Nature, Society and Culture* (Buckingham: Open University, 1984).

4. Emmanuel Y. Lartey, *In Living Color: An Intercultural Approach to Pastoral Care and Counseling,* 2d ed. (New York: Jessica Kingsley, 2003), p. 43.

Carrie Doehring

Cultural Aspects of My Experience

What aspects of my experience might be experienced by any young adult in a North American cultural context making this transition? Looking at my experience through the perspective of life cycle and faith development theories, I can see that my conversion experience was part of what Sharon Parks identifies as the critical years of young adulthood.[5] I had rejected the authority of the Roman Catholic Church, an authority that I had experienced throughout my childhood, particularly through my mother's conforming to the requirements of being a Catholic parent by taking her children to Mass every week and sending them to Roman Catholic schools. I had adopted the intellectual skepticism modeled by my father, and in turn had rejected that when I was faced with a complex, rather than simplistic, experience of Christianity. I began to construct a religious identity of my own, an identity which quickly gave rise to the dream of pursuing theological studies and subsequently the dream of being ordained.

Like many young adults my age, I was negotiating the developmental tasks of (1) psychologically and spiritually leaving home by differentiating myself from my parents; (2) establishing a unique identity of my own through finding meaningful work; and (3) negotiating a marital relationship based on feminist values of mutuality.[6] I didn't experience the phase of postadolescence[7] or prolonged "economic adolescence,"[8] perhaps because I had accumulated no tuition debts, enjoying both extremely low tuition fees in Canada and a low cost of living that allowed my husband and me to support ourselves through graduate school. However, the realities of supporting ourselves were somewhat deferred by living in a church manse and having the church treasurer pay the household bills in lieu of part of my salary. In many ways, my transition from graduate school to my first job was part

5. Sharon Parks, *The Critical Years* (San Francisco: Harper San Francisco, 1986).

6. Bonnie Cushing and Monica McGoldrick, "The Differentiation of Self and Faith in Young Adulthood," in *Human Development and Faith: Life-Cycle Stages of Body, Mind, and Soul*, ed. Felicity B. Kelcourse (St. Louis: Chalice, 2004), pp. 236-50.

7. "The term 'postadolescence' was introduced to denote what until then had been called late adolescence and/or early adulthood. It refers roughly to the third decade of life, but sometimes postadolescence is seen as starting at the age of eighteen or nineteen and as ending before or after one's thirtieth birthday." Friedrich L. Schweitzer, *The Postmodern Life Cycle: Challenges for Church and Theology* (St. Louis: Chalice, 2004).

8. A. Sum, N. Fogg, and T. Taggert, "The Economics of Despair," *American Prospect* 27 (July/August 1996): 83-84.

of "the phases of young adulthood — from launching to coupling to parenting — [a time during which] one begins to care for oneself, deal with one's own and others' sexuality, search for meaningful work, and negotiate and renegotiate relationships with parents, peers, and communities."[9]

For me, the transition from seminary to ministry came at a time in my life cycle when I had a lot of energy and motivation to establish myself professionally. The type of congregation in which I ministered — two small congregations in a small-town setting — made it easier for me to become a working mother. I worked out of my home, I could bring my child to work with me on many occasions, and there was a ready network of childcare providers at hand.

As graduates prepare to make this transition, they would do well to consider what life cycle issues face them, and whether the transition from seminary to ministry will be congruent with these life cycle issues, as it was for me, or whether the transition will be made more difficult. For example, a person entering ministry in his or her fifties may find that the time demands of beginning one's ministry in a low-paying profession may exacerbate the challenges of caring for aging parents and supporting children going to college. Being able to reflect upon such life cycle issues during one's academic studies, and in supervision and CPE, would greatly enhance one's ability to deal with such challenges.

Was I prepared for the stresses and challenges of this transition by those who educated me? My In-Ministry year did provide me with a field education experience, opportunities for preaching, and six weeks of CPE. Full integration of my academic coursework with field education was limited by several factors: the separation of academic studies from ministry studies in this M.Div. program, my own propensity to separate intellectual pursuits from experiential learning, and my age-related lack of life experience. My seminary educators fell short of fostering in me "a pastoral . . . imagination that integrate[d] knowledge and skill, moral integrity, and religious commitment in the roles, relationships, and responsibilities [I would] be assuming in clergy practice."[10] However, my education must have cultivated in me an aptitude for forming such an imagination, because within my first six months in the ministry I began to develop this imagination, which Dykstra describes as "a way of seeing into and inter-

9. Cushing and McGoldrick, "The Differentiation of Self and Faith," p. 249.
10. Foster et al., *Educating Clergy,* p. 13.

preting the world [that] shapes everything a pastor thinks and does."[11] I suspect that I would have been spared the anxieties of my first year in ministry if, during my graduate studies in theology, I had been able to form "dispositions and the intuitive knowledge, or *habitus,* of a given religious or intellectual tradition"[12] such that I could be not only literate but fluent in the academic and religious traditions in which I had been steeped during my studies.

Nowadays, most seminaries do a much better job of integrating the so-called foundational academic curriculum with the practical dimensions of ministry studies. Students should be encouraged to utilize fully all opportunities for integrative learning, so that they cultivate their capacity for pastoral imagination. As well, they ought seek out opportunities in their first several years of ministry to continue their integrative learning, particularly in the form of CPE programs. They may be more able to be open, and less defensive, about their vulnerabilities once they have been ordained and are no longer being evaluated by ordination committees.

Contextual Aspects of My Experience

Some of the anxiety I experienced in my early years of ministry arose from being different from my male peers. I was, first of all, a woman. Not only was I young, but I looked even younger than my biological age, being petite and often shy when first meeting people. I was married to someone who had very rarely attended church, and who did not identify himself as having a religious faith. While my Roman Catholic upbringing had given me lots of experience with women in religious orders, these women seemed very different from me. In other words, many aspects of my social identity — being a woman, being young, looking young for my age, being petite, being married to a nonbeliever — shaped the transition from the world of graduate studies to the world of congregational ministry.

I had an intense need for women role models and sought them out wherever I could. I hadn't encountered many during my theological education. The ones I did encounter often disappointed me, probably because

---

11. Craig R. Dykstra, "The Pastoral Imagination," *Initiatives in Religion* 9, no. 1 (Spring 2001): 2-3, 15.

12. Dykstra, "Pastoral Imagination," pp. 2, 15, as quoted in Foster et al., *Educating Clergy,* p. 23.

I had such high ideals and standards for both them and myself, up to which few could measure. I did find a mentor in the second-career female minister, who had moved to the Presbytery of Waterloo-Wellington about the same time I did. I called her as soon as I received the news of the suicide of a congregant, and we talked about how I could help the family make sense of this death. Her calm presence made me less anxious. Her appreciation of how hard it was for me to be a young woman learning how to function as a minister made me less critical of myself.

I also coped with stress the way I had all my life, by reading books. I remember poring over Penelope Washbourne's book, *Becoming Woman: The Quest for Wholeness in Female Experience,*[13] searching its pages for experiences similar to my own. I participated in a support group of female Presbyterian ministers that gathered every few months in Toronto, at the national offices of the Presbyterian Church in Canada. I was fortunate in being able to find various circles in which I could foster a sense of authentic spiritual identity.[14]

My academic coursework provided scant resources for helping me understand why I felt different and the intensity of my need to find women like me. The year of In-Ministry studies offered me some insights into myself. The half-unit of CPE had many puzzling moments, in which I couldn't identify or understand many of my own emotional needs, nor the enigmatic observations of my supervisor. Several years later, when I returned to CPE and had a more sympathetic supervisor, I began to understand myself better, and could look back and see how anxious I had been. Another illuminating experience was watching myself on a videotape in a preaching class and being struck by how young and shy I looked: like a deer caught in the headlights of a car. Now I could appreciate why a member of the presbytery had said I was "too little" to be ordained.

These moments of insight into the challenges I faced in constructing an identity as a minister were, sad to say, private epiphanies. There was no

13. Penelope Washbourne, *Becoming Woman: The Quest for Wholeness in Female Experience* (San Francisco: Harper & Row, 1977).

14. "A primary goal of spiritual formation is the capacity for personal *transparency* in relation to God or the ultimate truth of one's religious tradition. The capacity of the priest, rabbi, or pastor for authentic spiritual presence in the face of others' needs emerges from the depths of his or her encounters with the ultimate mystery of God and from the depths of religious tradition, as well as from experiences of loss, suffering, joy, transition, or death." Foster et al., *Educating Clergy,* p. 274.

forum for reflecting on such insights in my academic coursework or in the year of In-Ministry studies. I wonder now whether the Canadian, middle-class, male, Euroamerican cultural values of keeping emotional responses private led me to feel confused about and ashamed of my needs, leaving me with the responsibility of dealing with them. A few years later, in the culture of a supportive CPE program, I could begin to talk about what I was feeling.

Many students nowadays are in seminaries and CPE programs which foster much more self-reflection on aspects of social identity, and students are given many opportunities to think about how their gender, race, ethnicity, age, and sexual orientation inform the transition from seminary to ministry. Also, CPE programs are much less likely to use confrontation and are more likely to enhance students' reflections on their areas of vulnerability, like their propensity to anxiety or depression under stress. Psychological testing can be especially helpful in such reflection, as long as students do not become defensive about engaging in such reflection when being evaluated for ordination. Students can be encouraged to acknowledge such defensiveness, identify evaluative processes that inhibit self-reflection and sharing, and use every opportunity to reflect upon how their social identity and areas of psychological vulnerability shape the transition from seminary to ministry.

Idiosyncratic Aspects of My Experience

Looking back at the transition from the world of theological and ministry studies to the world of congregational ministry, I can see that some of my sources of stress and the ways I coped with them were unique to me. When I experienced a religious conversion through reading the Gospel of John and finding a church home, I transposed my love of the arts — both classical music and literature — onto my nascent spirituality. I quickly immersed myself in the beauty of choral music and in novels, like those of Iris Murdoch, which illuminated the existential dilemmas that now were of such interest to me. I delighted in portrayals of church life, like those found in the novels of Barbara Pym. Through the arts I appreciated a sense of the comic when events in the congregations where I pastored reminded me of some scene penned by one of my favorite novelists.

My introversion, along with an appreciation for the complex histories of the congregations, families, and persons I encountered, made me slow to assert my own agenda in my first year of ministry, saving me from making the mistake of initiating changes early on in my ministry. There were often moments when my quiet, unassuming manner made it easier for me to become part of a social circle, whether it was a gathering of the Women's Missionary Society, a poolside party at a congregation member's home, or even the ministerial association's curling league that gathered on Monday mornings during the winter.

As an introvert, having an office in my home was an advantage when I was worn out from being with people. Ministering in two small congregations meant that a lot of my work involved one-on-one pastoral care encounters, which were much more comfortable for me than having oversight of and participating in the many meetings and programs that would have been part of ministry in a single larger congregation. I remember in the first several years having many moments of "down" time, when I would immerse myself in a novel or play hymns at the piano in my dining room.

Another advantage of being in two small congregations was that I didn't need to have much administrative experience or background, something I surely lacked in both life experience and training. Like many small churches, the members of Rockwood and Eden Mills Presbyterian Church handled their finances in an informal way.[15] I did, however, have to master the weekly task of typing the orders of worship onto a flimsy transparency (I still remember the bright pink correcting fluid) and printing them out on an old Gestetner machine that I kept in my closet on a little dolly that I rolled out every week. The emphasis on pastoral care that is so much part of small-church ministry suited my calling very well.

Though I harbored a sense of skepticism about religious belief, which would later find expression in postmodern approaches to knowledge, specifically in notions about the social construction of reality, my sermons were formulated out of my pastoral experiences. For many years, this skepticism made me feel different from many of my ministerial colleagues. I had fears, which surfaced in dreams, that I would one day be called to account for my radical beliefs before a court of the church. I enjoyed expressing this radical side of my beliefs by participating in feminist social action organizations, like a local rape crisis group and a shelter for battered women, and also in further graduate studies and CPE programs.

15. Lyle E. Schaller, *The Small Church Is Different* (Nashville: Abingdon, 1982).

One aspect of my preparation for ministry that did ease the transition from school to parish was being part of a school — Presbyterian College, Montreal — and a denomination that were relatively small, where I could become known as an individual and my gifts could be appreciated. In my first years of ministry I was often affirmed and given responsibilities in my local ministerial organization, in the presbytery, and on committees that met at the denomination's national office in Toronto. While these responsibilities sometimes exacerbated my anxiety, I did learn that I could meet the challenges they offered, and I gained a sense of my unique identity and gifts for ministry.

When students form trusting relationships with field education supervisors, mentors, and CPE supervisors, they can more fully reflect upon the idiosyncratic aspects of themselves that both enhance and exacerbate the transition from seminary to ministry. Some students may, like me, find that the evaluative process inherent in CPE, field education, and the ordination process does not allow for the creation of deeply trusting relationships. If this is the case, they need to continue this important dimension of formation after they have graduated and been ordained. An internship year, and/or the opportunity to work closely with a mentor or be in a CPE program when they enter ministry, can be extremely beneficial.

In addition, students can and ought to alleviate stress in the first year of ministry by seeking out opportunities to reflect upon and cultivate spiritual ways of coping with stress. Nowadays, many seminaries incorporate a variety of ways for students to explore spiritual ways of coping with stress, and spiritual practices are often an important dimension of the formation process that is part of seminary education. Cultivating such spiritual practices can contribute to experiencing stress related growth in the first year of ministry.

Concluding Thoughts

The gap between the world of graduate studies in theology and the world of congregational ministry was wide for me, and as a result I experienced considerable anxiety in my first years of ministry. A major shortcoming of my preparation for ministry was lack of attention to what Foster and his colleagues call pedagogies of formation and contextualization (that is, teaching that attends to social identity and location).

Pedagogies of formation help students consolidate "the dispositions, habits, knowledge, and skills that cohere in professional identity and practice, commitments, and integrity"[16] and are usually found outside academic coursework and in the worship of the community, other community-life activities, field education, and CPE. The more students are able to draw connections between theological studies and the practice of ministry, the more they will be able to experience a pedagogy of formation within their theological education. The greater the gap between academic and practical studies, the more students will need to seek out integrative experiences, in the form of CPE, internship opportunities, and mentoring both at their seminaries and in their first year of ministry.

The second shortcoming of my theological education was its lack of attention to pedagogies of contextualization, which serve to "ground pedagogies of formation in the interplay of historical and contemporary contextual influences"[17] on the practice of ministry. Foster and his colleagues distinguish three such pedagogies. The first contextual pedagogy helps students develop "a consciousness of context" that helps them "learn to 'think contextually' about the 'theological task.'"[18] Such a pedagogy would have helped me understand the source of my anxiety in my role of pioneer, and would have made me better attuned to the differences between my social location and those of my congregants. Students and graduates need to seek out opportunities to reflect upon how aspects of their social identity inform their ministry in their coursework, field education, CPE, and, once in ministry, in mentoring and peer consultations.

The second participatory pedagogy "focuses attention on developing in students the ability to *participate constructively in the encounter of contexts . . .* [heightening] student attention to the dynamics of cultural or religious pluralism."[19] This pedagogy would have helped me understand the cross-cultural aspects of my ministry: the fact that I was an able-bodied middle-class woman from a highly intellectual home environment trying to understand and connect with congregants whose life experience was dramatically different from mine. The transition from seminary to ministry can be greatly enhanced when students and graduates have opportuni-

---

16. Foster et al., *Educating Clergy*, p. 100.
17. Foster et al., *Educating Clergy*, p. 128.
18. Foster et al., *Educating Clergy*, p. 132.
19. Foster et al., *Educating Clergy*, p. 132.

ties in coursework, field education, CPE, and peer consultation groups to reflect upon cross-cultural aspects of their ministry, specifically how differences and similarities in their social identities and those of their congregants shape their ministry.

The third transformative pedagogy "engages students in processes of social and systemic change in what might be called the *transformation of contexts*."[20] This pedagogy would have enabled me to co-construct visions of ministry with those in religious leadership, once we had gotten to know each other. Students and graduates can engage in transformative pedagogies when they learn how to do social and theological analyses of congregations in field education, and, once in ministry, through peer consultation and with mentors.

In some ways, the time was not right to incorporate these pedagogies of contextualization into the curriculum. Contextual theologies were new at the time of my studies. I remember that James Cone came to lecture, and was aware of the skeptical responses to his black theology. A few years later, there was a growing awareness of the need to understand what it meant to provide theological education in the bilingual context of Quebec, and there was growing attention to pedagogies of contextualization. At the same time, the traditional Western approach to the academic study of religion, and its separation from the pedagogies of formation, made it less likely that implicit pedagogies of contextualization would be utilized in academic coursework. Nowadays, in many seminaries and congregations, there is greater utilization of contextual theologies which enhance the transition from seminary to ministry by helping students reflect upon their social identity and the contextual theologies enacted in their own lives and with congregations.

I am fortunate to teach in an educational context and historical time in which there is more awareness of the gaps between academic studies and the practice of ministry, and more attention given to pedagogies of formation and contextualization. The fragile connections that I made between aspects of who I was, in constructing a sense of identity in my first year of ministry, are now given attention during the course of theological studies. However, it may be difficult for me, in my position of authority, to identify experiences of marginalization among the students in my classes or who appear before me during meetings of the Committee on Prepara-

20. Foster et al., *Educating Clergy*, p. 132.

tion for Ministry in the Presbytery of Denver. The challenge of educating clergy still has to do with developing ways to help students make strong the fragile connections between theory and practice, among the disparate aspects of themselves, and between themselves and their various circles of accountability and ministry.

Based upon my own experiences, I pay attention to students' needs for role models and mentors. We talk extensively about their social location, and what it is like to minister to those whose social location is similar to or different from their own. We also reflect upon personal assets and vulnerabilities, like tendencies toward depression or anxiety, which they bring to ministry, and we talk about how to draw upon their religious faith and spirituality in coping with stress. And, last but not least, I try to learn from them, as they describe what it is like for them to transition from midterms to ministry.

9. The Meandering Ministry

M. Craig Barnes

The Linear Journey

I write this essay on the twenty-fifth anniversary of my ordination to serve as a Presbyterian pastor. Frankly, this anniversary has taken me by surprise. This is not because I was so busy that I lost track of the time, but because effective pastoral work in a congregation is impossible to measure. And that was my biggest surprise after leaving seminary.

Maybe it's out of necessity, or perhaps just tradition, but we prepare people for ministry through highly structured, clearly graded, and easily evaluated programs of study. The goals are clear and so are the expectations that have to be met in order to make progress toward those goals. All this objective evaluation seemed stressful to me when I was a student, but I yearned for it after I became a young pastor who was no longer sure what progress even meant.

Since our training of pastors is essentially built on an academic model, I made my way through the ordination process in a linear approach toward a clear goal. Along the way there were lots of checkpoints at which my progress could be easily measured. Immediately after completing four years of college I was given a degree as a reward for my hard work, all-nighters, and cram sessions before exams. With this parchment proudly in hand, I then marched off to one of the theological institutions of my denomination, confident that I was prepared to do the reading, writing, and research that was going to be required of me.

Of course, like all seminarians I soon discovered I was not prepared as well as I assumed I was. How does one get ready for the inevitable and necessary stretching of faith that is a part of theological studies? Initially there was at least some encouragement in knowing that I had met all the academic requirements to be admitted to a master's degree program. And later, when it felt like I was struggling for the foundations of my beliefs (struggles which became the new reason for my all-nighters), the familiar reappearance of exams and due dates served as a tether that protected me from wandering into nihilism. I never had time for that; there was always another paper due. Nevertheless, I was far from completely prepared for the experience.

In the end, though, while seminary offered a more theologically focused experience in academic training, the model was essentially the same as the one I had survived in college. For three years I took classes that all required me to listen to lectures, read books, write papers, and study for exams. No class lasted longer than a few months, and each provided almost immediate evaluation in the form of a grade. Even the required two years of field education in a local congregation offered regular written assessments to help me develop skills required for ministry. When I completed the prescribed curriculum, I was again rewarded with a degree that certified me as theologically prepared to be a pastor.

In the Presbyterian Church, theological students must also make their way through a "candidating" process with their local governing body, the presbytery; this process, too, is essentially linear. It takes at least two years, which run concurrently with the three years of seminary studies. It's a rather detailed journey that includes psychological evaluations, a battery of standardized theological exams, periodic interviews with a Committee on the Preparation for Ministry, and final "trials of ordination" before an assembly of the pastors and elders of the presbytery.[1] As tedious as that process was, its conclusion, echoing those of college and seminary, provided a certification from which I also took encouragement. "Well, if the Presbyterian Church thinks I am now qualified to be a pastor," I remember thinking, "then I must be ready."

Even the friendships I made in seminary seemed purposeful and focused on common goals. At my seminary friends tended to find each other early, through the provocative introductory classes that quickly sifted us

---

1. The Committee on Preparation for Ministry in the Pittsburgh Presbytery, where I serve as a pastor, has published a handbook for their candidates that outlines 47 steps to the ordination process.

into theological camps. You could tell by the question another student asked, not to mention the pronoun that the questioner used for God, if this was going to be one of your friends or another challenge to your faith in the theological arena. It never really occurred to us to make friendships with the challengers, however obvious it seems now that friends should occasionally stretch us! I suppose that completing a rigorous theological program, rebuilding one's faith, and making one's way through all of the hurdles of a presbytery's candidating process seemed like enough of a challenge at the time; from my friends I was just looking for encouragement that I could be right about God, that I had not made a mistake in coming to seminary, and that the chances were good that I would be done one day.

The last semester of seminary included still another linear process that had the very spiritual name of "the call process," but which actually boiled down to finding a job. After completing a personal information form, I mailed it off to the denomination headquarters which matched my interests and skills, as limited as they were, with congregations who had submitted a church information form. Thus began the interviewing process, which consisted of letters, phone interviews, and on-site conversations with pastoral nominating committees. Eventually, a congregation offered me a call.

At the end of a very long, carefully measured process, I had been given a job, which was the clear goal of that process from the day I began it. But what it had not done was, well, prepare me to be a pastor. Certainly I was theologically equipped. I had rebuilt the naïve faith that had been all too easily dismantled my first semester of seminary, and I now was eager to offer my higher-critical insights to my new, unsuspecting parishioners. (I even went so far as to write a series of sermons on the significance of the Barth-Brunner debates.) But what seminary did not do, and I now believe did not know how to do, was show me how to love my parishioners who are all as lost as they can be in the wilderness. Ironically, as it turned out, the whole preparation process I had just completed presented ordination as the moment when the wannabe-pastor finally gets to leave the desert and cross the Jordan.

I vividly remember the day of my graduation from seminary. Having completed the graded programs of both my seminary and denomination, I was trained, certified, and about to be employed as *the Reverend* Craig Barnes. There I sat in the great cathedral chapel of Princeton University, beside my friends who had been with me every step of the journey. Our hearts were bursting with excitement and anticipation. We were even wearing our brand-new pulpit robes for the first time. It felt like our long sojourn through the wilderness was over and we were about to cross into the Promised Land of ministry. I already had business cards.

Then Henri Nouwen stood to give the commencement address. His text was from the twenty-first chapter of the Gospel of John, in which Jesus makes his prophecy about Peter's future ministry. But first, leaning over the great stone pulpit, Nouwen echoed the three questions of Jesus. "Do you love me? Do you love me? Do you love me?" He paused long enough for me to finish fidgeting in my seat as I joined Peter in assuring myself that of course I loved Jesus. But it suddenly occurred to me that I had not heard that question in a very long time. Not once had it appeared on the exams or evaluations along the way in my measured preparations to be a pastor. Did I love Jesus? I finally heard the question, and then remembered that I began the journey through seminary as a way of saying "Yes."

Nouwen continued in his sermon by simply reading the text: "Very truly I tell you, when you were younger, you used to fasten your own belt and go wherever you wished. But when you grow old, you will stretch out your hands, and someone else will fasten a belt around you and take you where you do not wish to go." He then assured us that if we said, "Yes, Jesus, I love you," if that was our motivation to spending our lives in ministry, then we were about to embark on a "downward journey in the midst of an upwardly mobile world." "I do not say this with sadness," Nouwen continued, "but joyfully, because the downward road of God is the road on which he reveals himself to us as God with us."

As I was still trying to absorb this startling news, he relentlessly continued by making the most confusing prophecy about my prospects as a pastor:

> If you say yes [to loving Jesus], it will mean meetings, meetings, and meetings because the world likes meetings. It means parishioners who only want one thing of you, not to rock the boat . . . it means being subjected to endless déjà vu experiences. It means all of that. But it also means anxious hearts waiting to hear a word of comfort, trembling hands waiting to be touched, and broken spirits with expectations to be healed. . . . Your life is not going to be easy, and it should not be easy.

> It ought to be hard. It ought to be radical; it ought to be restless; it ought to lead you to places where you would rather not go.[2]

I remember sitting in my pew thinking that I didn't have a clue what he meant. But it sure didn't sound like the Promised Land. What it sounded like was more time in the wilderness — but this time without a plan to get out. And that has been exactly my experience for the last twenty-five years.

The Meandering Ministry

My most vivid experience over the years of serving in congregations has been the déjà vu thing that Nouwen promised. It often seems to me that I have had the same conversations in three different churches about why the junior high youth group was eating pizza in the parlor that the Women's Association decorated, why we cannot find enough Sunday School teachers, why no one fills the church van with gas, why we better not have another special offering because it may hurt the church budget. The complaining rabble that I thought I had left in a previous church just kept appearing in the new church. Their names and faces were different, but in so many ways they were the same. Likewise, in pastoral counseling I seemed to just keep meandering my way through the same chronic issues of relationships and losses in life. Pastors never escape the rabble.

Pastors tend to think of themselves as Moses, whose job, we assume, is to get the people to the Promised Land. But in spite of all the carefully constructed sermons, strategic plans, and elder retreats, I cannot really say that I have left any of the congregations I served even on the banks of the Jordan. I may have helped provide them with more members, more worship services, more programs, and certainly more committees than when I arrived. But mostly all this was just a way of staying busy in the wilderness, born out of a longing to return to the measurable life I had experienced in seminary.

I now realize that my calling has been only to wander through the desert with the people I have vowed to love, pointing out the manna and the thin stream that flows along the way. That journey is never linear or

---

2. Henri Nouwen, Commencement Address, Princeton Theological Seminary, June 2, 1981. See Nouwen, "A Place You'd Rather Not Go," *Princeton Seminary Bulletin* 3 (1982): 237.

easily measured. It took me quite a while to figure this out, but it was never Moses' job to get anyone to the Promised Land. That was, and is, God's job. The pastor is simply called to journey with the people as God uses the adversities of the pilgrimage to turn their fear into faith. But watching faith develop is a long, slow, meandering way to spend one's life. It is also a far more wonderful life than I could have ever imagined.

These days my all-nighters begin when I receive a phone call asking me to come to the hospital because a dying parishioner has asked to see the pastor one last time. When I get there, I find that I'm so honored to be in such a holy place that I wonder if I shouldn't take off my shoes. After offering some holy words, I say goodbye and then finally sit quietly by the bed as the machines whirl away the last moments of life on earth. I know this man; I know this woman. I have also been called when a child was in trouble, when a job was lost, and when a spouse slowly slipped away through Alzheimer's disease. I know these people too. Driving home in the wee hours of the morning, I keep thinking about all the trials and losses that went into the creation of the saint who's finally crossed the Jordan. These thoughts linger in the back of my mind when, later in the week, I hold a baby for the sacrament of baptism. I smile gently as the parents vow too easily that they will raise their child to be a Christian.

I have learned to find this same saint-creating holiness at work in more subtle ways in ordinary congregational life. These days I more easily plop down into a metal folding chair at church dinners and enter into a lot of small talk that doesn't seem to have a thing to do with Apostle Paul's notions of sanctification. I don't really mind fretting over the budget with trustees. And I actually enjoy committee meetings in which we spend way too much time talking about the youth group's upcoming car wash. That's because I now see a holy mystery that is always at work just beneath the veneer of these ordinary routines. That's my job, my calling.

I'm the pastor who gets to witness God's ongoing creativity in human lives. All the chatting about the weather in the narthex; all the annual stewardship campaigns that struggle to find new ways of saying the same thing; all the trips across town just to pray for a parishioner in the hospital; and even all the repeated church arguments about things that don't really matter are moments of holiness. But holiness is not always apparent. That's why people need pastors. I'm there to point to the unapparent presence of God. The congregation needs to believe, at very least, that I believe we are not alone on our journey through all these circling years.

What is God doing to these people? How are they being formed along the way in their wilderness sojourn? When will the new creation of their life in Christ become more apparent? None of these good questions are for me to answer. God is the only creator, redeemer, and sanctifier of their lives. But I get to watch all this as it slowly develops.

I also get to spend every morning working on my sermon, which allows me to immerse myself in holy words before I spend the rest of the day hearing the ordinary words of the congregation. Thus my heart becomes something of a crucible in which the sacred and the common get ground together, and it is out of this holy mix that I find the words to speak from the pulpit every Sunday. And what do I say? In a hundred different ways, I just keep preaching the same sermon, really. I tell them to pay attention to the grace of God in their lives.

Making the Connections

Nouwen was certainly right: this has been a journey I would rather not have taken when I was completing seminary. Now I'm so thankful that I get to be on it. But like Moses, I've had moments along the way when I became exhausted.

About five years ago I left a parish I had served for nine years in order to become a full-time professor of ministry at one of our denominational seminaries. I am still not sure I know all my motivations for that move, but my hunch is that it had something to do with needing to take a break from the meandering ministry. I do love teaching and had long searched for an opportunity to work as a scholar on the art of pastoral ministry. But it eventually became clear that this was really just an effort to think about being a pastor without the bother of actually being one. It was a nice idea, but, as I soon discovered, it was essentially as silly as being a shepherd without having any sheep around to screw up his thinking about shepherding.

After my first year of teaching it was already abundantly clear that in spite of my love for it I would never last in the seminary. The hardest part was not making the transition back to the graded, linear life of academia, where the students are anxious about the faculty's evaluations and the faculty is anxious about the students' evaluations of their evaluations. The hardest part of teaching full-time was simply that I was no longer serving the parish, which I discovered I also still loved.

It came to a head for me one Sunday morning in a church I knew nothing about. I had been their guest preacher that day even though the pastor was there. I've never really understood the concept of the guest preacher; I have long thought of the sermon as a unique and sacred poetry that emerges out of the pastor's ongoing conversation with God and the people who have been carried all week in the pastor's heart. Guest preachers, on the other hand, I've tended to view as "rent-a-reverends." But just because I was always out of sorts, that didn't prevent me from being a guest preacher somewhere most Sundays for the better part of a year.

On this particular Sunday, however, I received a very clear epiphany at the door of the sanctuary following worship. The congregation formed themselves into two lines as they left church. Those standing in the line that made their way to me were very polite as they said things like, "Thank you for being with us today," before scurrying off to brunch. I noticed that the other line, which made its way to the pastor, was moving much more slowly than my line. As I caught pieces of the subdued conversations between the pastor and those who held onto his hand, it became clear that all many of those folks wanted from church that day was to tell their wilderness guide a thing or two about the journey. "Pastor, my husband Jim will be having surgery on Tuesday morning. Can you stop by?" "I won't make it to choir practice on Thursday because I have to help my mother move into a nursing home. Can you tell the choir director for me?" "Pastor, I missed hearing a sermon from you today."

Maybe all they really needed was just to hold onto his hand a bit. That may even have been the only grasp on the grace of God they were going to get for a while. As I saw the holiness of those moments, and remembered what it felt like to hold the "trembling hands" Nouwen had described, I knew I was in the wrong line. I had to find a way back into the parish.

For the last four years I've spent only half my time at the seminary, in order to spend the other half as an installed pastor in a local parish. The purpose of this arrangement is not only to find a way to do the two things I love, but also and more importantly to get at least a conversation started between the dramatically different cultures of the seminary and the congregation. Frankly, it's not been easy. The one is as linear, measurable, focused, and goal-oriented as it was when I was a student. The other one is meandering on a good day, and sometimes just as lost as it can be. But I am clear which one is the Bride of Christ. And I am blessed to be a part of a faculty whose members, in spite of their diversity, would agree that training pastors is central to our mission. Along the way, with the help of my colleagues and parishioners, I have discovered at least one significant insight about using the seminary to shape the soul of a pastor.

The most important thing I have learned is that it is more important to talk to seminarians about being a pastor than it is to explain how to do the work of ministry. As one of the handful of professors on our faculty charged with teaching practical theology, there is some expectation that I will show the students "how to do it." Actually, the students themselves often have this hope. And of course we do teach very practical classes that develop such essential skills as knowing which end of the baby to hold during a baptism. But those are not the most "practical" courses for our students. Nothing will have more nitty-gritty relevance to their future ministries than to get them thinking about pastoral identity.

No one fails at being a wilderness guide for lack of desert survival skills. The church will teach its pastor how to run a committee, read a financial sheet, and keep records of hospital calls. It won't necessarily be gentle in providing these lessons, but the church will offer on-the-job training. So the problem isn't really the absence of skills, and to reduce practical theology to the mastery of these skills is only to contribute further to the linear, goal-oriented culture of theological education that is already so out of touch with parish life.

When a pastor gets in trouble in a congregation, usually the problem begins as an identity issue. It is when pastors try to be something other than pastors — like saviors for instance — that they stray into a job description in which they cannot succeed. And pastors who are not clear about who they are soon discover that the members of their congregation will offer them a legion of conflicting identities that tear at their souls.

It's for this reason that I knock myself out to explain to my students how critical it is that they remain very, very clear about pastoral identity. The biblical paradigm for mission always begins with "being" and then proceeds to "doing." For example, it is only as we accept our identity in Christ that we can engage in the ethical and compassionate mission of *Christ*-ians. Similarly, it is only when pastors function out of their identity as Ministers of Word and Sacrament that they know how to survive the conflicts and confusions of parish life. They are not there to negotiate compromises, keep the peace, or service complaints. They are called only to look for the saving presence of the Word whose presence can still be found when the congregational waters get rough. But those who are tempted by role-anxiety to overfunction cannot accomplish such a critical ministry.

Only congregations create pastoral identity within seminary students. Seminaries can train and inform this identity, but they cannot transform their student interns into pastors. For that the student has to be subjected to all of the dynamics of a faith community, even the painful ones — indeed, *especially* the painful ones. This is why field education and internships are so critically important in pastoral formation. If it is possible to shape the curriculum to permit serious theological reflection to occur at the same time as students are organizing the youth group's bake sale, all the better. Every effective pastor I know struggles to hold together the contemplative and active dimensions of his or her work. It would be helpful, therefore, if the development of this balance could begin in seminary. But more importantly, it only makes sense to put the learning of theology into conversation with the actual doing of ministry even while the theology is being assimilated. It is one thing to be dismissive of Calvin's understanding of original sin while writing a paper in the back carrel of the library. That's quite another, and harder, thing to do after finishing a week of Vacation Bible School.

These days I am much less cynical about the limitations of theological education. I think that's because, like most things, once you come to accept what it cannot be it's easier to accept it for what it is. I have grave doubts that all that much will really change in spite of all the curriculum review committees of all the faculties that seem to be constantly in deliberation at nearly every theological school. No seminary will ever give up its need to be linear, measurable, goal-oriented, and focused on degree completion. Perhaps those traits are as central to seminaries' identity as not being all of those things is central to pastoral identity. But that does not mean that the seminarian cannot be shaped and even well prepared for ministry through his or her ordination process, including theological education. It just means that both students and professors need to remain clear that the seminary is attempting to equip future pastors to function in an environment in which the familiar measures of success, including those used by the seminary, will have to be left behind.

The seminary is the servant of the church and thus it must remain devoted to the fulfillment of the church's mission in the world. This means that seminaries cannot pretend that they are merely theological subcontractors to the denominations, free from the burden of worrying about pastoral formation. The burden that the churches need their seminaries to bear is indeed to prepare a theologically trained clergy, but with a clear focus. It's not enough to pour theological content into seminarians' brains so that they can repeat it back during examinations. What their future work as pastors will require is a theology that has informed and shaped their calling. In other words, before our students graduate they need, if nothing else, to be clear about who the pastor is. It's enough of a goal.

Even if the members of a faculty devoted all three years of a master's degree to this goal, they would only have provided their students enough insight to be dependent on the Savior who called them into pastoral service. But if that is clear, then it is also clear that they will be of service to the meandering church.

10. The Furnace of Humiliation

Pamela D. Couture

It was almost Christmas of 1979, my second year in seminary. The fall quarter had ended. For the winter quarter I had signed up for a biblical elective taught by Wolfgang M. W. Roth. Dr. Roth looked a lot like Albert Einstein, with wild, wavy hair of light brown and gray, and the sparkle of brilliance in his eye. One day I encountered Dr. Roth on the back stairwell of the seminary and told him that I was signed up for his class. And I told him that since I cared for two young children at home, I always tried to get some work for the semester done in advance. "What should I do?" I asked. The sparkle in his eye turned to a gleam of passion for his subject. He looked to the sky and gesticulated as if lots of little stars were falling. "Read the Book of Sirach twice. The first time it won't seem like much, but the second time you will find wonderful things." "I'll do that," I said. "Can I find it in the bookstore?" Dr. Roth's face turn somber, and he looked down over his glasses. "Mrs. Dunlap," — that was my name then — "it's in your Bible!"

As a young woman who had come forward to serve God, who was becoming educated in ministry for leadership in the church, I encountered three questions: *How to live? What to do? Where to stand?* When I have pondered these questions most self-consciously, my self-understanding of my gender, my ethnicity and race, and my class have shaped the answers. I would like to encourage all seminary students to drink deeply from the wells of these components of our identities, and toward that end, I offer this story.

Pamela D. Couture

How to Live?

The Christmas of 1979 was traumatic. At Thanksgiving my husband had announced that he wanted to leave the family after Christmas. We had two daughters, three and four years old. I will always remember the pain I felt as I watched him that year, struggling to stabilize the base of the tree in one of those rickety red cups with four green legs. It was excruciating when he looked up at me and said, "Well, at least next year I won't be here to do this." Later, I wondered if he would have stayed if I had agreed to quit seminary — but neither of us asked that question. A few nights after he left, I decided to try to be dignified. I put the girls in bed, put on my best nightgown, and sat down in front of the Christmas tree to read the Book of Sirach. On the first reading, I read, "My daughter, if you come forward to serve the Lord, prepare yourself for temptation. Accept whatever is brought upon you. And in changes that humble you be patient. For gold is tested in the fire, and acceptable people in the furnace of humiliation. Trust in God and God will help you, make your ways straight, and hope in God." I realized I was encountering the temptation of what contemporary praise music calls "the refiner's fire" over the question: How to live?

The foreshadowing of this encounter took place two decades earlier. When I was four, my Protestant family moved to a predominantly Roman Catholic neighborhood. When we drove downtown to the First Congregational Church, we passed St. Jude's Roman Catholic High School, where nuns in their habits walked the sidewalks. The shades on the windows were mysteriously drawn. My Catholic girlfriends in the neighborhood educated me: to be a nun you had to give up having a family. I couldn't imagine that. Still, I longed to know more. My friends gave me holy cards and a hand-me-down rosary that was broken and put back together with one bead of silly putty. They assured me that this rosary had been blessed by a priest. I learned to pray the rosary. I discovered that if I put a skirt at my waist, a skirt over my shoulders, a bobby sock across my forehead, and the right towel around my head, I could look a lot like a nun. This was before Vatican II, and my girlfriends knew they would go to hell if they went to Brownies with me in the Brethren Church down the street. And I knew that some Protestants, maybe even my own parents, didn't like Catholics. I could get in big trouble if someone found me dressed this way. Still, my walk-in closet, behind the clothes, was the perfect place to pray. It was the place to imitate the nuns and be holy. I loved the single-minded dedication of the nuns' life, and I also knew I would never give up having a family. But in early elementary school, I did not have to resolve this conflict.

On the way to church my family also passed the Jewish synagogue, Temple B'nai Abraham, which my confirmation class later visited. On the wall of the synagogue a stone carving read, "Love Your Neighbor as Yourself."[1] I pondered that saying as we drove. This synagogue, which was Orthodox at the time, reminded me each week to remember the teachings of Jesus! It helped to etch Jesus' Great Commandment in my mind.

First Congregational Church in the 1950s had the mark of a northern liberal church. Stations of the historic Underground Railroad were nearby, and the congregation taught of its importance. Yet at the time the church fostered no relationships between its members and living African Americans. The formation for my later interracial education came through my family, which proudly taught me my ethnic heritage. All my great-grandparents had arrived in the United States in the great waves of immigration between 1880 and 1920. My father proudly reminded us that the Swiss plate he displayed in our house came with his family when his mother's whole family — eight brothers and sisters, spouses, and my great-grandparents — arrived in Ohio together to farm. Only years later, after trying to grow a tomato plant in the Georgia clay, did I realize how they must have embraced the rich, flat, dark, rock-free soil of northern Ohio! My father's father, a French Canadian, worked the ships on the St. Lawrence Seaway, quickly becoming a first mate, then a Great Lakes ore freighter captain. My grandfather was known for his safety record, largely because he so deeply respected the transcendent forces of nature on the Great Lakes. The tragedy of the *Edmund Fitzgerald*, immortalized in the song by Gordon Lightfoot, later proclaimed the power of which my grandfather spoke to my brother and me.

On my mother's side, Hungary drew near as a country of origin every time we visited my grandmother and the family gathered for our first meal together — always stuffed cabbage, mashed potatoes, and green beans. This moment of identity-making happened within the family, not in society. As teenagers, grandmother and her sisters avoided any connec-

1. I wish to express my appreciation to Rabbi David Powers for confirming the wording of the carving.

tion with Hungary, finding themselves to be more acceptable in other people's eyes when they passed as Italians. My grandfather's mother, also a Hungarian, met my Liverpudlian great-grandfather when she worked as a soda jerk and he frequented her counter. They did not speak one another's language, but they communicated — and married. Such immigration stories germinated my ethnic identity.

Class consciousness, I believe, etches itself in the ethnic identify of immigrants. My great-grandparents sought economic security, and economic security compelled them and their descendents to work the family's way out of poverty, first performing menial tasks, then working at trades, next developing small family businesses, and finally achieving professions that required advanced education. As a child, though, I saw economic differences through the lens of houses. The size of the houses that my girlfriends lived in communicated their status in relation to mine. Through the car window on the way to church stately mansions and custom-built estates communicated elegant comfort and artistic creativity. My second-generation immigrant family emphasized small, practical homes. My mother stressed that we were a normal, middle-class family, giving me a class identity. All the people in the estate homes seemed to be old; only one acquaintance who lived in those houses attended my public school. I could no more imagine the lives of those families who drove into the garages of the big houses with doors closing behind them automatically than I could the lives of the nuns behind the drawn shades of their windows. As a child I wondered about those with larger, rather than smaller, houses.

Until the 1970s, my rising immigrant family avoided the shame and economic distress of divorce. Christmas of 1979 heralded a crisis in how to live. By shaking the foundations of my family life, the twin upheavals of my pursuing a seminary degree and my becoming the first single mother in the family quaked my gender, ethnic, and class identity. From this earthquake a theological fire heated beneath the meaning of the saying carved on the synagogue. Do we have three loves — love for God, the love for biological family, and the love for "neighbors" beyond the biological family — that inherently conflict with each other? Or do these loves complement and enhance one another? We *express* the right answer to the question in theology but we *resolve* it in practice. "How to live?" evolved into the slow, hot burn of my second encounter with the furnace of humiliation: "What to do?"

What to Do?

In 1978 I had experienced a call to ministry as I sat in worship at Overlook United Methodist Church in Woodstock, New York. The preacher was describing the long form of communion. I thought, "He's teaching. I can do that!" That week I visited with him about going to seminary. I had spent three weeks living on the pediatrics ward at the Albany Medical Center when my daughter had surgery; I had been a scribe for my friend's memoirs when she wanted to record the experience of living with and dying from a brain tumor. Rev. Osgood and I decided that I could go into chaplaincy. But there were childhood memories deep in my mind, full of confusing images.

During my preschool years at the First Congregational Church the choir had looked positively majestic as it processed in its robes. And I knew something mysterious happened when the black-robed minister, Dr. Linde, celebrated Communion. My Catholic girlfriends had already made their First Communion at seven years of age. I was curious about their white dresses and the idea that they had a party for an occasion other than a birthday, and I mourned the fact that I could not yet be part of the mystery. I knew what Communion looked like because I peeked at the wafers as I passed the plate to the adults next to me. But I could not take Communion until I was confirmed — and that would be years and years in the future.

In those days girls used rollers to set their hair. I got a piece of white bread, used the end of a roller to punch out round pieces, put the pieces in my dresser drawer to dry into wafers. A few days later I dressed up in my habit, took my rosary, prayer cards, and Communion wafers into my closet, and I celebrated communion for the first time.

I learned about ordination many years later. In 1963 or 1964, Virginia and Tom Eisentrout were seminary students from Oberlin College doing their field experience at the First Congregational Church. Virginia supervised the church school; Tom ran the youth groups. My mother told me they were going to be ordained on a Sunday afternoon, and she *required* that I attend. "It's historic for a clergy couple to be ordained in one ordination service," she said. "You will rarely see this." I can still see them kneeling together at the front of the church. I also hear the tone in my mother's voice saying, "Virginia will do Christian education. That's what they always make women do." Again, the messages were mixed: ministry is something women can do, but not quite.

As I prepared for college my father said I would make a good secretary or a good translator. No one — including myself — thought that I would ever have a job in which I would *need* a secretary or *need* a translator. In college I did as my mother advised me: I got a teaching certificate. For several years after college I harbored a secret desire to become a doctor. By choosing to go to seminary I thought I had finally narrowed my options. Yet I shortly realized that accepting a call to ministry was a lot like walking through the back of the wardrobe into Narnia: once I walked through the portal I could follow many possible paths.

Many women seemed to be quick studies for hospital chaplaincy, and I joined the crowd. My initial interest hit an abrupt reality check when, in my first year of seminary, I checked out the route to full credentialing. I discovered that I needed to study and practice for an unbearably long eight years before I would be a fully qualified chaplain. Still, in my first seminary year I volunteered as a hospital chaplain. For my first night I was assigned the day no employed chaplains wanted — July 4. My husband took the children to fireworks while I went to the hospital. While I was there, a teenager died from injuries sustained in an auto accident. I hovered over his mother. She taught me that sometimes a ministry of presence must be balanced by a ministry of appropriate distance. When I attended the funeral, her pastor was surprisingly affirming of my ministry — more so than I was of it myself, actually.

Chaplaincy training, though, was not parent-friendly. Early in my single parenthood, I concluded that the overnight rotations required by clinical pastoral education created an impossible barrier, and so I trained in pastoral counseling instead. I fell in love with parish work at the Arlington Heights United Methodist Church. The month after my marital separation one of the staff members took an appointment in another state, and I became a liturgical leader on Sunday morning in addition to being the youth leader. Charles Jarvis and Ted Rodd were wise mentors and guides, and for six months, as my public visibility in the congregation increased, they protected the knowledge of the crisis in my family life until I had gained more secure footing on the path before me. Most clergy must sometimes learn public leadership without taking private chaos into the pulpit. For me, the lesson came sooner rather than later. "This semester you became a professional," Charles commented.

When I was reviewed for eligibility for ordination, the registrar saw that my Wesleyan Theology course was categorized by the seminary as fulfilling a requirement for history, not theology. He sent me back to seminary to take Wesleyan theology — again. I took that second Wesleyan doctrine course; due to the weirdness of the course numbering system after Garrett and Evangelical Theological Seminaries merged, I never did take the basic Methodist history course. But it was meant to be. The first time I took Wesleyan theology, it circulated through my head; the second time Wesley's particular writings on the doctrine of perfection began to make sense in my heart. I read Wesley's treatises "On Marriage" and "On Celibacy" and found much the same conflict over ministry and family in his writings as I had absorbed in my childhood among my Roman Catholic girlfriends. This time I read Wesley not to pass the class but to think about my own life crisis. Now, I sought to find myself and my life in theology. Where students read theology not just to gain credentials for ordination but to find insight about their urgent life questions, vocation is being formed.

In my first appointment the senior pastor, Ron Graham, knew more about the challenges I would face as a woman entering ministry than I did. As chair of the Board of Ordained Ministry, Ron asked the bishop to assign every woman elder to the board in order to integrate it. He created parish policies that allowed me to function in nontraditional roles. I was responsible for visiting new members; he supervised the church school. We rotated the community calls for weddings, and those couples who came my way who insisted on a male pastor couldn't be married in our church. He also brought race and ethnicity a little closer to my pastoral consciousness. When Ron was in seminary at Boston University, a graduate student, Martin Luther King Jr., taught one of Ron's seminary classes. As one who usually pastored inner city congregations and transitional congregations, Ron aroused my curiosity about ministry beyond the suburbs. And Marilyn, his wife, did not hide her dismay at my inattention to social issues beyond family and congregation. Ron also modeled good clergy self-care, and he watched with some concern as I tried to adjust to pastoring, single-parenting, and dating. We enjoyed ministry together but he knew I wasn't quite settling in. He supported my desire for career counseling. The result, though, was unexpected. The career counselor looked at my psychological testing and concluded, "You get energy from reading and writing and educating. Go get a Ph.D. in pastoral theology."

I had struggled to find my vocation among the mixed messages that are a part of every person's life. As I wrestled with "What to do?" I was most able to verbalize the gender conflicts related to ministry. Still, expectations about education that were dictated by my ethnicity and class hung below the surface. My Midwestern and Eastern immigrant families shared the value that education should produce a practical skill, such as farming, business, or trades. We bore no professionals with advanced degrees, no clergy, doctors, or lawyers. When we considered higher education, we certainly did not imagine ourselves to be Ivy League stock. We never contemplated that I might seek a Doctor of Philosophy degree or that prestigious schools might be important to my opportunities. Instead of the family, the church now challenged me to seek to become a daughter of the University of Chicago. The rainbow of racial colors worshiping together in the Northern Illinois Annual Conference of the United Methodist Church challenged gender, ethnic, and class stereotypes that lay dormant within me. The church guided me through the crisis of "How to live?" and "What to do?" and tilled the soil so that during my graduate education the seeds of gender, race, and class could sprout and blossom into the third question of the furnace of humiliation: "Where to stand?" The question that heated the third refiner's fire was this: "Where do I stand as a white, now professional-class woman in American religion?"

Where to Stand?

I moved my daughters' and my belongings in the back of a parishioner's pickup truck to Hyde Park for our first inner city experience, where races and classes of people intermingled. This neighborhood surrounding the University of Chicago formed me even as the history of ideas I debated in the classroom educated me. Hyde Park was bordered by Lake Michigan on one side and low-income, African American neighborhoods on three other sides, forming a multicultural, educational ghetto island where the University of Chicago and other educational institutions reigned supreme. I depended on street smarts I'd learned from my seminary advisor, Stanley Hallett, when I took his class on "The City." The first day I thought I had to eat my dinner at Eduardo's Pizza and corral my children home before dark; a week later we knew we could roam around with our eyes open most evening hours. My children enjoyed their freedom to explore Chicago on public transportation and frequently did their homework in the university's Regenstein Library. In the end, Hyde Park helped to cultivate a social work career in my daughter, Meredith, and a career in public health in her best friend, Sibyl.

Two particularly formative neighborhood experiences relating family life, race, and class stand out. Three weeks after we moved to our Hyde Park apartment, well away from most friends and family, I fell ill. After making three trips to the University of Chicago health services office and draining a full bottle of Robitussin, I was unable to walk from one end of my apartment to another. With what energy I had I worried about my ten- and eleven-year-old daughters trying to adjust to their new environment by themselves. So a Hyde Park contact took me to the Cook County Hospital emergency room where one of his friends, a nurse, greeted me. Even in my debilitated state I was aware that the staff wheeled me, a sick white person, to the front of a very large room where rows and rows of African American patients waited, hoping for treatment. Yet I felt not hostility but sympathy from them as one patient murmured, "She looks really bad." The original *ER*, the one on which the television program was based, diagnosed double mycoplasma pneumonia. Thereafter, I watched *ER* with great appreciation for the time it saved *my* life, but on television I never saw the rooms with rows and rows of poor African American patients, waiting.

A few years later my daughters were well ensconced at Ray Elementary School, where twenty-eight nationalities and students from all over Chicago attended through the eighth grade. My daughters' friends ranged from children of professionals in Hyde Park to children from very poor neighborhoods further south in Chicago. The parents of the south side children had to make special efforts to get their children into Ray School, as they weren't immediate residents, and the children rode public buses every day. As with any group of elementary-aged children, the whole group were great friends, but didn't always get along. One day there had been some seemingly childish quarrel. One of my daughter's south side African American friends was offended at the way my daughter, Shannon, responded on the telephone, accusing Shannon of "playing black." The next day, Principal Sara Spurlark, the award-winning African American elementary school principal, called me to Ray School for a parent conference. When Shannon had arrived at school she had faced what Principal Spurlark called "a lynch mob." Yet rather than doling out detentions or blaming parents, Principal Spurlark gathered the children to talk to each other — that day, they discussed race relations. By the time she called me, everybody was back to being friends.

As I wrote my dissertation about the feminization of poverty, I could gaze over the athletic fields adjacent to John Dewey's Chicago Laboratory School to the Woodlawn neighborhood. There, single, African American mothers struggled to raise their children, as did I. A friend told me that the Dean of Students had commented about my attempt to do doctoral studies as a single parent, "She has so many strikes against her." I had reckoned, however, on the fact that graduate work would allow me scheduling flexibility in my children's upper elementary and junior high years, as they outgrew babysitters and became more independent. In Hyde Park I had elementary schools and doctors close at hand and graduate school friends and neighbors who understood and valued what I was trying to do. With the help of supportive friends I earned my doctorate in six years.

Even though I was now academically credentialed, my integration of gender, race and ethnicity, and class consciousness still needed to mature. In 1987, during the oral exam that followed my written qualifiers, Professor Martin Marty asked me a question about what happened at the women's tea party near Seneca Falls in 1848. It was the biggest event of the nineteenth century for women, and I think he thought this was a friendly, easy, conversation starter. But I hadn't studied women's religious history either at Garrett-Evangelical Theological Seminary, where women's history was in its heyday, or at the University of Chicago. I stumbled. I did not know what he was talking about. A knock on the door interrupted the conversation, and after the intruder was shooed away, we went on to territory that was happily much more familiar to me. But Marty didn't forget. When I did my first book review for *The Christian Century,* he sent me Susan B. Anthony's biography as payment.

Maybe I should have gotten it in that Methodist history course I never took, but I had clearly missed something big: the history of women in religion in the United States. I had significant make-up work to do. By the end of my second year of teaching I had read widely in women's history in order to include a historical chapter in my first book, *Blessed Are the Poor?* I studied the debate between middle-class women and lower-class women over "women's rights vs. women supports" and the contemporary androcentric and gynecentric voices in feminist scholarship. I learned that African American women in general and womanist theologians specifically understood the need for both rights *and* supports, as I did. I decided that a course that helped a woman seminarian to know her place in women's history, to know how the same struggles are recycled in new forms over and over again, would make a valuable contribution to the pastoral care of women, and so I created one, "Feminism, Psychoanalysis, and American Politics," to help women students find their historical companions for their journeys. Teaching this course several times over the course of a decade was, for me, a way to put words to gender, race, ethnicity, and class consciousness.

In my academic ministry I have frequently had to return to the question, "Where to stand?" in relation to gender, class, race, and ethnicity. In the 1980s, when I originally researched the feminization of poverty for my dissertation, the data that described the struggle of single-mother households spoke to the church and to society on their behalf — these data were used to demonstrate how single-parent mothers were among the contemporary "widows, orphans, and resident aliens" for whom the church should take especial care. In the 1990s the same data were interpreted much differently. In the hands of some it remained a gender argument — one that tried to argue that out-of-wedlock childbearing among poor women and the increasing divorce rate among middle-class women could be attributed to the irresponsibility of men who abandoned mothers and children. This strategy encouraged men not to take their marital responsibilities lightly. Yet I was concerned that this very well-intended argument directed at men failed to respond to the needs of single-parent women who desperately needed to hear from society how they, too, could parent well, even when support from fathers is not forthcoming. Furthermore, it failed to recognize men who did take their responsibilities for children seriously in the midst of divorce or out-of-wedlock parenting.

Too often, two valid concerns — one for holding parents accountable, the other for supporting their parenting efforts even in the midst of enormous obstacles — were pitted against one another. For example, the concern for holding men accountable led in some policy discussions to an attempt to reattach a stigma to all single parents, as had been widespread earlier in the twentieth century. Furthermore, the rhetoric through which these data were interpreted sorely offended my pastoral instincts. Although I was now an academic, I was also ordained. The bishop had laid hands on me and said, "Take thou authority . . . for the order of the church." I needed to dip into that well of pastoral authority to stand by the integrity of what I and many other single parents sought to do in raising their children, standing by modern day "widows, orphans, and resident aliens," even as an onslaught of blaming and shaming articles made their way into popular and academic press.

The argument about men was easily subverted for political purposes on behalf of different forms of "marriage movement" arguments. Marriage movement arguments became entangled in welfare reform legislation. Some legislators hoped to reduce the feminization of poverty by creating marriage incentives; yet studies by the University of Minnesota have shown that these efforts have been ineffective. Marriage movement arguments are now almost synonymous with defining marriage as "between a man and a woman" and legislating against committed gay and lesbian partnerships. In the end, paying attention to gender, race, ethnicity, and class helps me stand by a methodology that seeks to understand and articulate a vulnerable person's point of view, whether it is the point of view of a child or a parent with less than full support from others, over against pressures that promote social standards that some people can never achieve.

"Where to stand?" also became a critical question as I worked on the United Methodist Bishops Initiative on Children and Poverty from 1995 until 2004. Poor children have always been the most vulnerable people in the world. In 1995 the child poverty rate in the United States reached its height — 23% of children in the United States lived in poverty. The United Nations had drawn attention to children around the world, particularly girls, who suffered from destitution, violence, disease, and inadequate access to education. Yet as the project progressed, we discovered that the church in general had great difficulty conceiving of the direct relationship between children and poverty. Too often, the local implementation of the Initiative focused on "children," leaving out "poverty." Increasingly, therefore, my academic reputation became associated with children. And "children" invariably meant "middle-class children," without attention to the particular contexts or needs of children who live challenged by poverty. To stand by "children," I have had in recent years to reassert that I was primarily a theologian who researched poverty, and that I studied "children" as a subgroup of those who struggle with "poverty."

"Where to stand?" heated the refiner's fire as we recreated the contextual education program at Saint Paul School of Theology. The previous field education program had focused on dynamics internal to the congregation. With the introduction of contextual education we wanted to emphasize the relationship between congregations and their surrounding communities. To do this we needed also to focus on the relationship between the seminary and its local community — a low-income community of recent immigrants and African Americans left behind during the 1960s' "white flight" to the Kansas suburbs. Saint Paul School of Theology already had a long history of institutional involvement in the community; now, we wanted to translate that involvement into an educational experience. In my first year as dean I had preached about my formative experience traversing the boundaries between suburbs and the city. I had brought neighborhood residents to chapel to share their experiences. At students' request I had led a discussion about community involvement in an assembly. I had introduced the new curriculum, including the new goals for Contextual Education. The students seemed to be on board.

Yet when we actually implemented the program, one that was required for all Master of Divinity students, a large number of the students were outraged. Some were afraid of the neighborhood. Some didn't believe they could learn from the neighborhood. Some thought it took too much time to study the neighborhood. Some wanted the small groups in which they could talk over their own parish concerns. Other students were excited about the new program, but complained when we used class time to process the conflict. It turned out that we had clearly misread the preparedness of the community for this change; the students tested our convictions. Was it really worth it to insist that students actually do what both the church and academic practical theology societies had been promoting — learning from our contexts wherever we were?

The Director of Contextual Education, Dr. Jim Brandt, and I knew that this was a teachable moment — as much a moment for helping students learn about pastoral leadership in the midst of conflict as for opening up the relations between congregations and communities. We created time in class to hear the students in their anxieties and we modified the way some assignments could be fulfilled, even as we stood our ground about the importance of contextual experience in class and congregational learning. We believed we were being responsive to student concerns and that, in this semester of implementing the program, students could learn from our willingness to be open to their concerns, if not from their actual experiences in the neighborhood. In the end we learned that our attempts to hear students' concerns and to be flexible in the way they fulfilled their assignments, without giving up our core convictions, went almost entirely unnoticed as an experience from which students learned. Yet though they remained critical of many aspects of the class, over time they reported that many of their best educational experiences happened by way of their contacts and observations in the neighborhood. Although it followed almost two decades of very successful teaching, this class was my most difficult teaching experience.

Dr. Brandt and I remain convinced that the seminary *in its context* forms the learning crucible in which students learn about their congregations *in their own contexts*. Our pedagogies to communicate this conviction may differ year to year. But our belief about pastoral leadership of the church is clear: we believe that pastoral leaders need to learn how to cross the lines of gender, race, and class. In order to cross that most difficult line of class and privilege, pastoral leaders need to find out how the congregations they serve do and do not deal with the poverty of their local communities. Only then will they be able to equip their congregations for the postmodern task of re-knitting the social fabric of their communities.

The Furnace of Humiliation

The semester I studied the Book of Sirach Dr. Roth presented the book as a dialogue between a grandfather and his grandson, the latter of whom had edited the former's work. The grandfather was teaching the grandson about wisdom needed to take a leadership position in society. Wisdom, of course, is the attribute of God that is always portrayed in Scripture as female. This book is no exception. The grandfather had charted out seven stages of increasing complexity in the development of a leader: (1) Basic Duties; (2) Basic Relationships; (3) Mature Behavior, including a section on social authority; (4) Mature Reflection; (5) Responsible Citizenship; (6) Responsible Judgment and Adjudication; and (7) Comprehensive Theology. The grandfather placed the passage about the refiner's fire at the beginning of the first passage on basic duties — the refiner's fire is where it all begins. The fire prepares a person to stand by convictions based in wisdom.

Over several decades the refiner's fire has glowed hot in my life. At times, fortunately, it has cooled a bit. "... in changes that humble you, be patient." Twenty years ago such a difficult experience as introducing contextual education might have created significant self-doubt. Long years of being tempered in the fire of humiliation have made a difference. All my experiences of conflict over family, vocation, gender, race, ethnicity, and class provide a bit more solid ground for the next challenge to my convictions. I do not experience the intensity of such conflict over my convictions as shameful, as I once did. Rather, I experience my conflict as information that expands my worldview so that I can grow into being the kind of leader *this* particular institution needs me to be at *this* time. I would rather avoid such intensity — such a fire of humiliation — by accurately responding to institutional cues, anticipating institutional needs, and easing the institution through change. But I know that such foresight will not always be possible. Where it does not happen, the conflict that becomes the furnace of humiliation helps me to develop a more penetrating insight that allows me to see more clearly the needs and possibilities of this institution at this time and place. Long experience in the fire has taught me to use such experiences as a set of three-dimensional glasses. I cannot see through them immediately; but if I wait patiently and humbly my eyes will adjust, and I will see the contours of the landscape more fully. With the benefit of new insight, it is my hope that each year I will be a slightly better dean, scholar, and teacher than I was the previous year, and that over a lifetime, the increments will add up to faithfulness and accomplishment.

However your experience of gender, race, ethnicity, or class mediates your seminary experience, you will at times experience the furnace of humiliation as it grows hot. The furnace is a given. Hopefully, there are times when it will cool and let you have a rest. But the refiner's fire finds itself particularly at home in seminaries. It will meet you there. It will never give up its obligation to help you to resolve your personal conflicts. It will follow you wherever you go. It will always seek to purify your character and deepen your self-understanding; and, as certain elements in you are remolded, you will gain wisdom.

11. You Can Never Be Too Smart

Karen Marie Yust

Halfway through my seminary studies, the dean pulled me into his office for a chat. "Karen-Marie," he said, "I want to give you some advice." He then proceeded to tell me that congregations are afraid of really smart pastors, and especially of highly intelligent women, because they don't think intellectuals have much common sense or attunement to the basic needs of "regular" people. He suggested that I might "want to make a few B's" in my courses so that I wouldn't fall victim to this prejudice. I appreciated his concern and knew that his words realistically reflected the attitude of many congregations. But when I walked across the stage at commencement, I was an A student all the way, certain that the church needed stellar students of theology and ministerial practice far more than it needed academic subterfuge to maintain the comfortable lie that ministry is mostly about hands-on skill and not heads-up thinking.

The most important ministry practices I learned to cultivate in seminary were critical analysis and imaginative reflection. The first congregation I served after graduation was a street church ministering with recovering drug addicts and their families. Our worship and education space was a condemned three-story building in Roxbury, Massachusetts; the founders of the congregation had evicted drug-dealing squatters and claimed the site as a Christian mission. My primary responsibility there was to fashion a Christian education program for children, youth, and adults. The building only had three rooms — one on each floor — so the first floor functioned as a lobby/office, the third floor as the sanctuary, and the second floor was the church school classroom. All young people between two and sixteen years participated in a multi-age Sunday morning session. We would gather for an hour and a half or two hours each week before joining the adult congregation upstairs to share what we were learning and to celebrate the Eucharist. Adult study groups occurred on weeknights, usually just before or after one of the twenty-one Narcotics Anonymous meetings held in the building each week.

This is not the typical ministry setting envisioned by Christian publishers when they put together their curricular resources and teaching aids. Most of the materials marketed to pastors and teachers presuppose a more "traditional" congregation of at least moderately stable households for whom economic, health-related, and psychosocial crises are the exception rather than the norm. Mainstream Bible commentaries and Christian education texts say little (if anything) about integrating adequate attention to basic human needs for food, security, health care, and positive interpersonal interactions with preaching and teaching Christian faith. To fulfill my ministerial responsibilities, I needed to research the causes and challenges of drug addiction. I needed to investigate the availability of drug treatment programs in the area and understand standard treatment protocols. I needed a finger on the pulse of inner-city politics and an arm around a child who was being sent to live with Grandma while Mom was in rehab. I needed to dive more fully into personal Bible study so that I could hear the gospel anew in light of the Roxbury congregation's particular circumstances. And I needed to imagine how to incarnate Jesus' ministry of challenge and compassion to an ever-shifting population of young people who may not have had breakfast that morning before they hopped on the subway to come to church.

Seminary classrooms were the places where I gained many of the skills necessary to support this difficult work. My biblical exegesis courses taught me that the gospel is not easily interpreted, but that careful study and sustained reflection lead to fresh and transformative insights. Biblical Greek and Hebrew classes helped me to see that language matters when we tell faith narratives, and that the meaning of a story can change depending on the words we say and hear. Recalling my studies of church history provided me with examples of how Christians through the ages have responded in times of suffering, oppression, and trial. Pastoral care textbooks provided technical vocabulary and psychological frameworks within which to interpret addictive behavior, treatment protocols, and family dynamics. Theology class readings and discussions on sin, salvation, sanctification, justice, and other themes popped into my head as I wrestled with my own assumptions and prejudices and realized I needed to redefine what these doctrines meant for my practice of ministry. Even with high grades born of diligent study, I soon realized that I had so much more to learn. What seminary provided were a passion and strategies for study, along with a variety of practical theological foundations upon which to build a critically sound and creatively transformative ministry.

My first winter in Roxbury I led a women's Bible study session on the Annunciation. The group consisted of several women who had given birth to one or more children during adolescence, as well as three or four teenage girls. My preparation to teach the story of Mary's call to divine motherhood began with critical reflection on the life stages and experiences of the group members and how their social locations might affect their interpretations of the text. I read the passage in my Greek New Testament so that I might hear it afresh through the sound of its original language rather than through the very familiar cadences of my English translation.

As I worked with my reflections on the group and the text, I recalled an Amy Grant recording, "Breath of Heaven," that seemed to integrate the fears and misgivings of a pregnant adolescent with the story of Mary's decision to participate in the incarnation of God. I decided to begin the session by reading Luke 1:26-38 aloud and then playing the song. Silence filled the room when the recording ended and women of all ages wiped tears from their cheeks. "I never thought about Mary being a scared teenager," said one woman, "but it makes sense that she would feel alone and afraid and worried about whether she's doing the right thing. That's how I felt when I found out I was pregnant at fifteen." Other women remarked that Mary seemed more "real" to them when they imagined her struggling with the idea of having Jesus; they couldn't really picture her just saying "sure, God" and getting on with her life as if it was no big deal to be so spiritual. I knew what they meant, for my own understanding of the text had shifted and expanded as I applied the critical and imaginative tools I learned in seminary to the process of preparing a Bible study for "real life" ministry. I had come to realize that a call to teach in the church is much like Mary's call to bear a divine child: one must watch and listen to what God reveals about the world's needs and then, alongside one's anxious misgivings, permit a creative response to those needs to take shape within oneself for birthing when the time is right.

While seminary helped me learn how to listen and to imagine creative responses, managing the practical and eschatological anxieties inherent in this never-ending process of birthing effective ministry practices was something I had to learn after graduation. Completing a master's degree can give one the false impression that all knowledge necessary for being a good pastor and teacher has been, as the degree title suggests, "mastered." Even the non-straight-A student can feel as if she or he must be an expert because of the diploma now hanging on the office wall, and congregations often share this assumption. What I learned in Roxbury and have rediscovered in every congregation I have served is that I could never be smart enough to know everything necessary fully to incarnate God's love in my ministry. Every sermon, church school lesson, mission project, community event, Bible study, and other ministry I facilitated would teach me something I didn't already know, if only I would recognize my need to continue learning. An appropriate amount of doubt and uncertainty in the Roxbury ministry birthing process served to remind me that God was the true midwife of my work, and I was still (and always will be) a midwifery apprentice. I learned to welcome the butterflies in my stomach before each worship service and church school class, to see them as a sign that the Spirit was stirring up space within me for transformation. After eighteen years, I still experience a few unsettled moments before I preach and teach, a welcome reminder that Christ dwells within me, waiting to be reborn in my interaction with the congregation.

In addition to managing one's own sense of vulnerability and human frailty, pastors and educators must contend with the fact that many Christians are uncomfortable with natural spiritual birthing processes. Church members may prefer that their leaders stoically hide the struggle, suppress the pain, and mask the exhaustion that accompanies the development and implementation of critical and creative ministry practices. Thus the hours spent in private Bible study, contemplation, and prayer are deemed "unnecessary" or even "indulgent" rather than essential to good ministry. Parishioner demands that Christian leaders be visibly engaged in pastoral activities or program management can motivate even smart leaders to rest on already-acquired knowledge or to skip the full-course study menu and settle instead for the sermon nuggets and lesson-in-a-box take-out versions of ministry preparation. The pastoral brain does not stay sharp on a fast-food spiritual diet, yet many church leaders complain that they have little time to nurture their own spiritual lives while tending God's flock. Many of my Doctor of Ministry students confess that they have returned to seminary for another degree because they miss the intellectual challenge and creative jolt that regular theological study provides. My own experience echoes theirs, and I lament with them the lack of communal support for continued study and reflection after the seminary years are over.

What I do not share is the widespread belief among my clergy colleagues that congregations cannot learn to encourage and support their leaders as *theodidacti,* persons taught by God. While congregations may not list theological studiousness among the traits they are seeking in their leaders, those just out of seminary are uniquely situated to model engagement in regular study as one of the gifts they bring to ministry. For me, that modeling process was made easier by my decision to pursue a doctorate while pastoring congregations. Like the D.Min. students that I have taught over the years, I could point to the external requirements of my degree program to explain why I was *still* reading Augustine, Catherine of Siena, Rauschenbusch, and other theologians amid the work of planning Rally Sundays, Advent wreath rituals, Lenten forums, Pentecost celebrations, and Vacation Church Schools. What I discovered is that my determination to remain a student evoked the same kind of congregational support for my studies that my field education sites offered during seminary. My seriousness as a student and my gentle reminders that I was studying on behalf of all in the congregation who desired to know more about God and the Christian life generated acceptance of the time I spent in study and even anticipation about when and how ideas I was studying would crop up in sermons, Bible studies, and newsletter articles.

For a couple of years I taught the senior capstone course at a seminary in Indiana. One of the course requirements was that students construct an annotated bibliography of ten books they planned to read during their first year of post-graduation ministry. I told them that their list could include novels, theological texts, volumes of poetry, spiritual classics, commentaries on specific books of the Bible, and any other text they thought might contribute to their ability to remain students in God's school after graduation. Some students groaned at the assignment; they were looking forward to a practice of ministry uninterrupted by study and reflection. Others embraced the task, recognizing it as an opportunity to plan a personal course of study once the demands of an imposed curriculum end. It is often the latter students who, now colleagues in ministry, occasionally e-mail me with an insightful quotation gleaned from their current reading or a description of a congregational event planned in light of a discovery made because of a continuing education experience. These are pastors and educators who are beating the five-year-fifty-percent burnout rate and finding that repeated trips to the divine wellspring of study sustains and rejuvenates their ministry.

The power of continuing theological education to help church leaders avoid burnout lies in part in its ability to counterbalance the outward flow of spiritual energy inherent in the practice of ministry. We all orchestrate balancing acts in our lives to manage the choices that we have and the tensions between options or expectations that we feel. A mundane example of this balancing act is the debate we engage in with ourselves when we approach a yellow traffic signal while driving. As we head toward the intersection, we realize we have two choices. We can brake, or we can hit the gas. If we brake, we may feel virtuous and law-abiding in the moment, but as we stop for repeated yellow lights, we realize that we are running late for appointments or sitting through long yellows when we could have legally continued on our way. After a few such experiences, we decide to hit the gas at the next yellow light. Now we're making better time, but if we cut it too close, we risk getting a ticket for running a red light or involvement in an accident. Either outcome (or increased anxiety about the possibilities) encourages us to apply the brake more frequently when we approach yellow lights, at least until our next bout of anxiety about timeliness and efficient driving.

Maintaining balance in our ministerial journey is a similar process of applying spiritual brakes and hitting the spiritual gas pedal. Much of our work involves traveling briskly through a multitude of ministry tasks and situations, and we are constantly tempted to keep moving even when we see signs that slowing down or stopping for a time might be spiritually prudent. Competent ministry, however, requires that we sometimes come to a complete stop, giving ourselves sufficient time to study and pray before proceeding on our way so that we are not overwhelmed by unanticipated crises or troubling ethical dilemmas among the people we serve. Prayerful study and reflection sustains us as we use the gifts God has given us to serve the world, and regular spiritual breaks from godly service reminds us that we are gifted with strengths and abilities by God, but we cannot transform the world alone. Compassionate ministry is a movement inward and outward in a never-ending cycle, and smart pastors and teachers find a rhythm of study and service that's unlikely to leave them either perpetually on the sidelines of life's busy intersections or crushed by a church bus transporting too many human needs for any church leader to handle without God's help.

In the interest of full disclosure, I must confess that the idea of journeying inward and outward as a ministry rhythm originated in my seminary education, but the inward aspect was equated more frequently with prayer and quiet contemplation than with critical study of biblical texts and social contexts. It was during my first years of parish ministry that I came to appreciate the truth of Karl Barth's twin observations: prayer without study is dead, and study without prayer is blind. Without the critical tools of sociology, psychology, hermeneutics, ritual theory, and other disciplines shaping my reflections on the needs and mission of the congregation, my prayers lacked specificity and imagination. I could not join King David and other psalmists in a practice of lament containing informed complaints about the woeful state of human life and community and the need for explicit means of deliverance and care. I could not join my voice with the congregation's voice in the Lord's Prayer and picture actual ministry when we prayed, "thy kingdom come, thy will be done" or "give us this day our daily bread," for I had no clear understanding of what the tasks of helping to build God's realm or of receiving a daily measure of grace sufficient to the community's needs actually meant at any given time. I needed wisdom born of knowledge and inspiration, and prayerful study was the key.

When a parishioner with bipolar disorder called from a locked mental ward and uttered sexually explicit comments while asking me to come and visit him, I quickly realized that generic prayers for spiritual guidance would be insufficient to guide my response. I consulted with a mental health professional about the nature of bipolar disorder, studied biblical healing stories, and then prayerfully considered the therapeutic and theological implications of various responses. This process led me to ask a male colleague to visit this parishioner in my stead until the man's manic episode subsided and his illness-induced hyper-sexuality would no longer compromise his dignity, my safety, or our relationship as pastor and church member. My emerging theoretical awareness of the symptoms of bipolar disorder, my theological understanding of ministry as shared among many gifted by God with pastoral care abilities, and my spiritual commitment to imitate Christ in meeting the needs of those who are sick and oppressed shaped an appropriate response to a difficult situation. I was working "smart" by seeking out multiple forms of information needed to imagine other choices besides the obvious options and to decide what God was calling me to do.

Consulting experts and practitioners in other fields, as I did in the case described above, is only one of the ways I continued to develop my critical thinking skills after graduating from seminary. I also read journal articles recommended by parishioners who were psychologists, social workers, family practitioners, business consultants, and non-profit administrators. As the worldwide web emerged, I set up "favorites" on my Internet browser that included the American Cancer Society website (so I might better understand the treatments parishioners were undergoing, the latest research on cancer prevention, and general advice for assisting families struggling with diagnosis and treatment realities) and www.praythenews.com, a Carmelite site providing commentary on breaking news stories for thoughtful Christians. I added new sites for regular consultation, like the web page for the National Study of Youth and Religion, as new issues requiring research emerged in my congregation. I acquired Scripture search and Bible commentary software and subscribed to online discussion groups that would challenge my theological assumptions and encourage me to love God and the flock with whom God had entrusted me with my mind as well as my heart, soul, and strength.

Perhaps the most effective way I found to remain a student in God's school was by joining a clergy small group. Every Tuesday morning from 7:30-9:00 a.m., I and three or four of my ecumenical colleagues gathered for half an hour of silent meditation and an hour of breakfast and conversation. We took turns providing a short excerpt from a text we were reading as our meditation focus and rotated responsibility for the provision of physical sustenance (often muffins and orange juice) to accompany our spiritual feast. Over the six years I participated in the group, the "regulars" changed as clergy moved in and out of the community, but the ritual of sustained prayer and reflection in conversation with a text and one another's experiences remained the same. Not even the birth of children and the resulting exhaustion from infant care could keep me away from the early morning nurture of this dedicated group of *theodidacti*, for our work together in those weekly gatherings informed and transformed my ministry.

Scholars of spirituality suggest that Christians have historically recognized two distinctive aims of a spiritual journey. One aim is the illumination of the mind, which we call *speculative spirituality*, and a second is the illumination of the heart, which is labeled *affective spirituality*. These complementary aims have been pursued by two broad means: indirect (mediated) ways of knowing God, called *kataphatic* means, and direct (unmediated) ways of knowing God, identified as *apophatic* means. The recognition that we can never be too smart as a pastor and teacher motivates us to engage in speculative spiritual practices. Speculative reading and meditation challenge the intellect, the senses, and the imagination to work together such that God is made known to us in the encounter with text, feelings, and mental images. Perhaps we will not be blessed with divine theological dialogues like those to which God invited Catherine of Siena. We may not grasp as incisively as Howard Thurmann the theological and political implications of analyzing our social systems in light of Jesus' teachings. Our ability to visualize and analyze the gospel may not rival that of Julian of Norwich. Our commitment, however, to challenge our mind to work just as hard as our emotions and bodies as we seek to co-create with God a new heaven and a new earth increases the direct and indirect avenues by which God teaches us how to live and minister in God's name. Seminary studies habituate us to this mind-work; we abandon the habit to our and the church's peril.

When I was ordained, a friend sent me a card that I set on the shelf above my desk as a reminder of the mix of activities required in ministry. It read:

> Take time to work (it is the price of success),
> Play (it is the secret of perpetual youth),
> Think (it is the source of power),
> Read (it is the fountain of wisdom),
> Pray (it is conversation with God),
> Laugh (it is the music of the soul),
> Listen (it is the pathway to understanding),
> Dream (it is hitching your wagon to a star),
> Worship (it is the highway of reverence),
> Love and be loved (it is the gift of God).

Seminary did a good job of teaching me about some of these things, most notably the ones related to wisdom, power, effort, creativity, and understanding. Others, like play and laughter, were lessons better taught by friends and family than professors and field education sites. One of the hardest tasks since graduation has been learning to see all these elements as integrated aspects of a single spiritual life rather than compartmentalized components assigned to different parts of my life and work. In my current vocation as a seminary professor, I try to help my students attend to this integrative task more deliberately than I was encouraged to do while preparing for ministry leadership.

The card eventually grew yellowed and crumpled, and is now replaced by a framed print of the same words on my office windowsill. Joining it is a postcard image of a fifteenth-century painting called *The Magdalen Reading* by Rogier van der Weyden. In the figure of Mary Magdalene engrossed in the study of Scripture I see the studious young woman I remember being in seminary, caught up in the excitement and challenge of learning new information, making creative connections, wrestling with difficult issues and competing interpretative frameworks, wondering about the practical implications of theoretical claims, and trying to discern God's Word amidst the flood of words pouring into my life. I see, too, the congregational pastor and teacher I was for eleven years, putting the brakes on my "type A" ministry leadership in order to read, study, meditate, and pray so that I and the congregations I served might know and love God better. I note the reflection of the seminary professor I am today, marked up books piled all over my desk as I type this essay, prepare the class lectures and practica that are my ministry of teaching now, and hope to spark a mindful, studious love of God in those preparing for ministerial leadership. I even think I glimpse my future as a committed lifelong learner in the school of God's service advocated by Saint Benedict when he wrote his fourth-century monastic Rule.

In all these stages of my spiritual life of learning, I have been, am, and will be, like the Magdalen, a sinner in need of God's grace and guidance. The hard work I did in seminary in service of greater understanding and wisdom did not and cannot suffice to shape my ministry for a lifetime. With each day in parish work, new challenges and possibilities arose that required me to use my mind for the glory of God. My call to teach in a seminary multiplies the opportunities for intellectual growth in service to God's people. Every hour spent in lecture preparation and every session of class discussion reminds me that, for all my scholarship, I need the perspectives of other scholars and of the larger Christian community to keep my interpretation of the church's mission and purpose attentive to new and broader realities than I have previously assumed.

I wonder if this is how the poet of Psalm 119 felt as 176 verses on the desire to be taught by God welled up in his mind and heart. Like that ancient psalmist, my regular commitment to study is a plea to God: "Teach me your statutes" (verse 26b), "make me understand the way of your precepts" (verse 27a), "graciously teach me your law" (verse 29b). I, too, proclaim, "Your word is a lamp to my feet and a light to my path" (verse 105). My twenty-first-century words might be less elegant — a simple request for God's tutelage in whatever form God might elect — but this centuries-old longing for the blessing of God's wisdom shapes my life and ministry, and I commend that active desire to all who would serve God's people.

You can never be too smart in ministry, for even when it seems as if you have learned more than you ever imagined possible, even if you have been diligent in study and critically open to every new idea that came your way in seminary, there is a lifetime of learning still necessary for those in God's eternal school. You may be tempted to say, upon graduation, that you have all the ideas and strategies necessary for good ministry in hand and that you need only to refine that knowledge and those tools with experience. If so, I offer a story from the desert fathers as a different way to frame the movement from midterms to ministry.

> Abba Lot went to see Abba Joseph and said to him, "Abba, as far as I can I say my little office, I fast a little, I pray and meditate, I live in peace and as far as I can, I purify my thoughts. What else can I do?" Then the old man stood up and stretched his hands towards heaven. His fingers became like ten lamps of fire and he said to him, "If you will, you can become all flame."[1]

Whether we are like Abba Lot, knowing and doing all that seems right to us today, or like Abba Joseph, with the fire of Christ consuming a part of us, we have much more to learn before we are fully illuminated by divine wisdom and light. The pencil-and-paper exams come to an end, but God continues to examine our work in light of our vocation as *theodidacti* and persons called to church leadership. Our goal shouldn't be to make a few ministerial B's so we don't rock the ecclesial boat. Instead, we give our very best to the study of God, God's world, and God's will, so that we, as diligent and capable disciples, might reflect the glory of our teacher.

---

1. Benedicta Ward, trans., *The Sayings of the Desert Fathers*, rev. ed. (Kalamazoo, Mich.: Cistercian Publications, 1984), p. 103.

12. From Texas Pastor to Princeton Professor

Cleophus J. LaRue

An Early Spiritual Call and a Late Academic Start

In a manner of speaking, I put the cart before the horse as it relates to my seminary education and subsequent return to ministry. I moved in what many would consider to be the reverse order of the normal course of ministerial preparation since I was actively involved in pastoral ministry for fourteen years before I enrolled as an M.Div. student at Princeton Theological Seminary. In my pursuit of a theological education I moved from actual practice, to theory, and finally to reflection on practice and theory in my current capacity as a professor of homiletics.

I was called to the gospel ministry at the age of nineteen. Given the preeminence of preaching in Baptist circles, we usually referred to this as "the call to preach." In black Baptist circles formal education was not a requirement for Christian ministry. That longstanding de facto rule had its strengths and weaknesses. One of its strengths was that it allowed a young, untrained minister to plunge immediately into the thick of ministry. A weakness was that it left one without the benefit of a theological foundation in ministry and thus no means of engaging in informed reflection and formation on the how to, why, and what of Christian ministry.

A week after announcing my call, I was scheduled to preach my trial sermon. Shortly thereafter, I was licensed to preach by my home church — the Calvary First Baptist Church of Corpus Christi, Texas. In black Baptist polity there was no requirement for formal training before one could be licensed and ordained. If you sat under a highly respected pastor who had many years of experience and that pastor vouched for your faithfulness and diligence in learning the fundamentals of ministry, you were considered to have sufficient training to begin the work of ministry. I came to faith, and subsequently to ministry, under the watchful eye of a very seasoned pastor named Henry Clay Dilworth Jr. Rev. Dilworth was the founding pastor of our church and was held in high regard throughout the Corpus Christi community. He instilled in all of the young ministers who came under his protective care — as many as twenty-five in my formative years — a sense of ministry and commitment to the larger world. Our church supported the work of ministry in the local church, the district association, the state, and national Baptist conventions.

Growing up as a child in Corpus Christi, just about every day of my life was spent being around, thinking about, or participating in something pertaining to church life. I understand now that in some quarters my kind is a rare breed, as many times we get people in seminary who were not associated with the church as children and only came to Christ through a campus crusade ministry or later in life as an adult in search of meaning. That was not my experience. Rev. Dilworth drilled the faith into us at every opportunity. Sunday, Wednesday, and Friday evenings were spent expounding on the Scriptures. We were told to read the Bible before we read anything else in the morning. And that Bible we were instructed to read was none other than the King James Version. As a child, I just knew its stilted language was the way Jesus must have sounded. Along with the constant study of the Scriptures, a healthy dose of what Baptists believed and practiced was also thrown in for good measure.

Because the black church makes little distinction between the sacred and the secular, I learned to look for God's presence in every aspect of the human situation. Some mainliners are aghast when I tell them that politicians frequented our church and were allowed to speak from the lectern and make their cases on Sunday mornings. When they were done, however, Rev. Dilworth also thundered a prophetic note of justice right in the faces of the squirming politicians. The NAACP workers were allowed to solicit memberships in the narthex on Sunday mornings, but they were also called to account by the pastor if they didn't speak up for the poor and disenfranchised to his liking. From the participation of politicians, civic leaders, businesspeople, and others in our congregation, I learned that there were no "off-limits" for the church. I grew up believing that the church — the people of God — were to be involved in all of life, and that the Scriptures had something to say to the whole of the human situation.

In time, however, I came to realize that I lacked the ability to connect the secular with the sacred from an informed theological perspective.

We literally learned to do ministry by watching and being watched by Rev. Dilworth. Any number of us was in our teens when we announced our call and one minister was as young as six when he was allowed to go forward in the expression and use of his preaching gifts. Our parents totally entrusted us to Pastor Dilworth's care and guidance. He was the worship leader each Sunday morning. He appointed the devotion leaders (those responsible for the pre-service prayers and songs) and he decided who would participate and where in the worship service. He guided us not simply in the knowledge of the various functions of Christian ministry but in all of life. He instructed us on how to dress as well as how to conduct ourselves in the church and in the community. He insisted on a high standard of pulpit decorum and ministerial ethics. Rev. Dilworth was modest in his manner and frowned on any young minister who he thought had gotten "a little too big for his britches." If he detected any sense of entitlement in his young understudies he didn't hesitate to call us to account publicly and to insist that the offending minister mend his ways.

Rev. Dilworth was for many of us a walking seminary. He sat patiently with us and talked to us out of his vast wealth of experience about how to engage in effective pastoral care. He took us with him to visit the sick, the poor, and those who were struggling to overcome scandal or other unfortunate incidents in life. Moreover, he was our first homiletics teacher because he critiqued all of our sermons and would not hesitate to stop us midway through our sermon and ask us to sit down if he felt we had not made sufficient preparation. When it came time to license a minister a positive church vote was never a foregone conclusion. Some ministerial candidates were sent back to ponder a while longer what they believed God had called them to do. To this day all the young ministers who went through that grueling process under Rev. Dilworth's guidance are still actively involved in ministry.

I pastored my first church just like Rev. Dilworth pastored my home church. He was the model of a successful minister to me in the early years of my ministry. However, I came in time to recognize that I was doing ministry out of a preset mold. I was doing ministry strictly by Rev. Dilworth's book. Even though his pastoral experience shaped a faith community for over fifty years, I came to realize that a mere imitation of his ministry would never allow me the freedom to be my own person. I could never think through an issue on my own for I had no training or skill in how to engage in informed biblical and theological reflection. I could only think by way of a template that had been established for me by a much-beloved pastor. To think within the confines of a box because one has no other choice is a restrictive, confining process that causes ministers to become narrow in their clerical outlook and threatened by change and the different perspectives that inevitably come before them in the very public sphere of Christian ministry.

Any matter that did not conform to my traditional understanding of the faith was suspect to me. I felt threatened because I simply did not understand how so-called Christians could see the world so differently from Pastor Dilworth and the tradition in which I was shaped. Consequently, I felt I had no other recourse but to denigrate and speak disparagingly of anything different because I did not have the necessary tools to engage in theological vision and discernment. I didn't know how to think and reason theologically. I had no sense of the broader history of the church, no exposure to classical theology, no skill in different approaches to Scripture, interpretive strategies and other vitally important hermeneutical issues. And I was convinced that the Kingdom of God consisted only of the National Baptist Convention and its few faithful adherents. To imitate a tradition in the name of faithfulness eventually smothers the one who has embraced it as a source of life and sustenance.

An Unquenchable Desire to Attend Seminary

In the two churches I led prior to coming to seminary, I experienced many things in pastoral ministry which I literally had no clue how to deal with and absolutely no theological skills for thinking through. I could only go on the previous pastoral experience of others or the very painful trial and error which more often than not hurt the people who were the object of the trial and victims of the error. Let me cite a few examples.

In my early twenties I experienced one of the biggest church fights of my life. It could have been avoided with a better understanding of church polity, conflict management, and an understanding of systems and how they operate.

To cite another example, a little girl in our congregation was raped and brutally murdered by a neighbor who lived two doors down the street.

The police waited for me to arrive at the family's home before entering the house to tell the heartsick parents that their little girl had been found dead 150 yards from their home. I did not have the ability to deal with this horrendous tragedy, either in the lives of this distraught family or among the larger church family that agonized over this incident. I was literally flying by the seat of my pants. An informed understanding of issues surrounding grief and tragedy would have been most helpful to me in this situation.

For years young women in the congregation who became pregnant out of wedlock had to come before the church and beg the church's pardon. It was one of the most humiliating things I had ever witnessed in my life, even when growing up as a child in my home church. When I became a pastor I continued to inflict this inhumane sentence on young women. No such burden was ever placed on the male offender in this out-of-wedlock apology. In my heart I knew this was wrong and wanted to stop it, but just did not have sufficient grounding in theology or pastoral care to accomplish it. When we finally stopped it, it came at a heavy price to the congregation, especially for those who felt the church's moral standards were being weakened. Again, I acted from gut instinct as opposed to informed theological insight.

My die-hard stance against women preachers was another area of my ministry that I so desperately wanted to change as a young pastor and I simply did not know how to accomplish it without tearing my church apart. There were many in the congregation who were adamantly opposed to women taking any kind of leadership role that had traditionally been relegated to men. More often than not they based their discriminatory stance against women on the Scriptures. And to make bad matters worse, the Scriptures they cited were often interpreted by white fundamentalist preachers who were on the wrong side of all the social justice issues with respect to the advancement of black people in this country. Yet the black church used the biblical and theological arguments of conservative whites to bar black women from the ministry. I wanted to argue for women and against the tradition, but I felt I did not have sufficient biblical and theological grounding.

A quiet, unassuming member of our church was beaten to death by her husband one night. I had no sense of the telltale signs of her misery. I learned later that other church members knew of the abuse, but as I reflected on the tragedy I worried that there had been nothing in my preaching or teaching to lead that woman to believe she could confide in me. To

145

this day I regret that I was not of more help to her in her struggle to break free from her repressive and abusive husband. Again, I knew I needed to broaden my preaching and teaching, but I simply did not know how.

Moreover, as the years unfolded it began to dawn on me that I was not really developing as a preacher. Even though my church provided me with a generous book allowance, I really had no idea of what kind of books to buy and why. I was not being educated in a particular school of theological thought, rather I was being trained to imitate outstanding black pastors I knew and loved. Along with many of my peers, I had my own favorites among pastors and I tried to imitate them in every way.

I also came in time to distrust my preaching in broader circles. I felt that I could handle myself in the small, regional circles in which I had grown up, but when opportunities came to preach before statewide audiences I began to feel the weight of not having made sufficient preparation. Moreover, preaching outside my African American context was an even greater challenge. It was pure agony trying to prepare for such occasions, and each time I had to do so I was overcome by a deep sense of dread and despair. I decided from those gut-wrenching episodes that I would not become the most effective minister I could be if I did not take time out to prepare for Christian ministry instead of winging it by mimicking the preaching styles and experiences of others. I desperately wanted to attend seminary in order to determine if there was any method to this madness, in a manner of speaking. I purposed in my heart to seek formal training no matter the cost — even if it meant giving up my church and very fulfilling ministry.

A Second Chance to Prepare

When I finally began my studies in seminary in the 1980s, I had more hands-on pastoral experience than many of the professors who were teaching me. I had already served as pastor of two Baptist churches in Texas — one with a membership of one thousand plus — and had participated at every level of my denomination's work and witness throughout the world. Entering seminary on the heels of two pastorates, I had already filed away over 600 sermons, preached and/or participated in over 400 funerals, and presided at an untold number of weddings and special celebrations. And all of this by the time I reached thirty. I came to seminary not out of a desire to learn how to do ministry, but rather to be more effective in the ministry I was already doing. I in no way saw seminary as a repudiation of the ministry I had been involved in, but rather I saw it in terms of strengthening and grounding the work I was already doing.

My student days at Princeton turned out to be a second chance at formal study. When I graduated from Baylor University with my undergraduate degree in the late 1970s, I felt that my education would not be complete without a seminary degree. I wanted to commute 90 miles up the road to Fort Worth, Texas, to attend Southwestern Baptist Theological Seminary. When I mentioned my plans to my very supportive chairman of deacons he informed me that he felt the members of the Toliver Chapel Baptist Church would not support such a move. Never really a fan of formal training, he said I already had more education than I needed to pastor people in central Texas. Thus, I gave up any hope of attending seminary and decided to pursue a graduate degree at Baylor instead. The church promised that if I stayed at Baylor they would pick up all costs. I graduated a second time from Baylor in 1982 with a Master of Arts in religion. That degree was my consolation prize for not being able to attend Southwestern Baptist as I had originally hoped. The following year, still unable to move beyond the confines of Waco, Texas, because of my pastoral responsibilities, I was accepted into Baylor's Ph.D. program in church history. The workload of that program soon forced me to face up to the fact that I could not effectively juggle so many different responsibilities — family, church, school, community, and so forth. Even though I had to drop out of the Ph.D. program, I still could not bring myself to give up on the chance of a seminary education one day. However, I knew from past failures and hindrances that getting there would not be easy.

John B. Davidson was a crusty but prescient religion professor at Baylor. Watching me frantically jump from pillar to post, he cornered me long enough one day to tell me what I already knew in my heart: I would have to content myself with being a pastor of a fairly sizeable congregation in central Texas or make a complete break with my church and head to a different part of the country, where I could concentrate fully on my seminary education without the burden of pastoral responsibilities. By this time, in the mid-1980s, I had given up on attending a Baptist seminary because of the fundamentalist fight raging in Southern Baptist circles at the time. Professors for whom I had the highest regard — many of whom had given the best years of their lives preparing men and women for ministry —

147

were hurt in that internecine conflict and I wanted no part of it. Baylor professors Daniel B. McGee and Ray Summers were among those encouraging me to move beyond the narrow confines of Baptist life. They urged me on as I pondered making that leap of faith from Waco to a different part of the country. Robert Sloan, a Southern Baptist graduate of Princeton Theological Seminary, had just been appointed to the Baylor faculty. With his support I set my sights on Princeton, in large part because of its longstanding history of scholastic excellence, and also because I desired an academic environment where I could study and pursue learning without fear of reprisal.

Once ensconced in seminary there were a couple of foundational questions I always asked myself in each and every class I was privileged to take: Will it fly in the black church? And is this something that would uplift and transform the people I have known and served in the years before I came to seminary? Those questions kept me centered and focused in my educational pursuits. They helped me not to forget why I always believed seminary was so important to my spiritual journey. I was there to learn how better to serve the church I knew and loved. I never lost sight of that. In that regard I was different from many of my classmates. I was reflecting on fourteen years of pastoral ministry while many of them, because they had not the benefit of prior pastoral experience, were merely projecting on future possibilities for ministry.

No matter what you are exposed to in seminary, you must always keep before you the ultimate reason you are there. I wanted to learn how to be more effective in pastoral ministry. And I was never disappointed in that overall pursuit. For example, I could focus on people and actual situations as the professor talked about celebrating the Lord's Supper as a protest to the church's exclusivity and entrenched prejudices. While such lectures were provocative, because of my previous experience as a pastor I knew that the Lord's Supper was not the best place to protest wrongs in the black church. As professors talked about the different models of preaching, I knew there were people in my former congregations who were much more concerned about what I said as opposed to how I said it. I knew from experience that if people heard a ring of truth in your preaching you really didn't need an element of surprise to maintain their attention. They were simply glad to hear the good news. As professors introduced us to different ways of interpreting the biblical texts, and as they pointed out things to me that I had never seen in the Scriptures, I was always thinking in the back of my mind: how would I preach this to my former congregations?

Much of what I learned in my classes was quite helpful. Suffice it to say, however, that some of what I was exposed to was so far off the mark that I would have been voted out of any congregation the same day I tried to present it to them. I came in time to understand that one must make a distinction between what stretches you intellectually and what moves you beyond the bounds of the possible into the realm of the incredulous. I also came to understand that there were contextual decisions that come into play when one is considering how to think through and apply the benefits of one's theological education. More importantly, there was never any doubt in my mind that I was preparing myself to be of service to the church. I suggest to all seminarians that they begin with the faith that was once delivered to the saints and work their way from there into new and uncharted waters.

I was exposed to so much that broadened my understanding of the faith as well as the particulars of the practice of ministry. My exposure to Scripture and the biblical languages was both illuminating and empowering. To study the history of the church from its founding in the first century up to the present day gave me a sense of the breadth and depth of the church. Although I had been a pastor for fourteen years the practical theology courses were enlightening and inspiring. The practice preaching laboratory and the student-led critiques that came afterward strengthened me in my blind spots and challenged me to grow in areas where I had grown quite comfortable. The theory behind the practice made sense to me. The professors I found most helpful were those who had some sense of the church; those who were intent on making a connection between what they were teaching and what we would be exposed to in the ministries for which we were making preparation. I was most fortunate to have this in Old Testament Professor Dennis Olson. He never specifically said he was making a connection, but we all knew there was a point in his presentation when he stopped lecturing and starting connecting. The students longed for those connections, for in the early days of our seminary training we were not always able to make them with the same kind of precision and insight as the professor did. Preaching Professor Thomas Long made me want to preach each time I heard him lecture or critique student sermons. He had such a way about him that he could correct and uplift at the same time. He pointed us toward the church and he made us feel like our preaching could indeed make a difference in this world.

There were some things I desired in seminary that simply did not come to fruition. While biblical studies were quite helpful, I wished a few of the biblical studies professors could have taken my contextual point of departure more seriously. It seemed at times that some of them went out of their way to belittle my faith tradition's understanding of the Scriptures, as if no good had come out of my evangelical upbringing. I came to faith within the confines of a very conservative black Baptist church. In time, however, I wanted to break free and move beyond the narrow confines of that tradition, but I never wanted to completely abandon it. To have that tradition slighted made me suspicious of what these clearly gifted professors were trying to impart to me. Though few in number, there were those who seemed to take delight in stripping us of what they called our "Sunday School mentality." They apparently did not understand that it was that mentality that brought many of us to the doorsteps of the seminary in the first place, seeking a deeper understanding of the faith that had been imparted to us by "the school masters" — that is, the local church — "that led us to Christ."

Also, there was little in seminary to help me specifically with a better understanding of my Baptist heritage. I knew that I was going to a seminary where the Presbyterian expression of the Reformed tradition was taught. But there was little in the way of actual church practice with respect to the Baptist tradition that I found helpful in seminary. This was especially true with respect to the order of the worship service, ordinances of the church, Baptist polity, and other beliefs and practices. I found very little there that would make me a better Baptist pastor and get me ready to take on a Baptist church immediately upon leaving the seminary. As more and more students attend seminaries not of their own denomination, we run the risk of sending out ministers who have little or no knowledge of their own denomination and its requirements and thus little or no loyalty to its continuance. It may be that Baptists, Methodists, Pentecostals, and other faith traditions that have a large number of their students in seminaries of another denomination might need to require them to do a year of study at a seminary or divinity school of their own denomination.

The particulars of one's denomination will become even more important in the coming years as fewer and fewer students come to seminary out of religious backgrounds which provide a good foundation for the formation of their faith. The need to educate them in such matters becomes all the more important when they have not grown up in what we used to call "the total program of the church." How one overcomes this dilemma I am not sure. It should not be expected that Princeton Seminary, or any other denominationally related institution, should be charged with the responsibility of getting people from other traditions to pastor churches within the particular dictates of those traditions. Yet not to have exposure at that preparatory stage to the particulars of those traditions means that we are sending people out to pastor with a very low level of proficiency in their denominational requirements. And the people who call our students to pastor these churches are left to wonder what these trained people learned while they were in seminary.

Finally, there was and remains a vast gulf between the letter and the Spirit in my seminary education. Somehow or another I never felt the proper balance was struck. I, who had had some experience in the work and witness of the church, understood full well that the seminary was not going to be a Sunday school class. I knew it would be a place to learn how to think critically, gather information, sharpen skills, and ground one's self in the basics of the faith; but I had not expected such a chilly reception to matters pertaining to the Spirit. More often than not I had the sense that some of my classes amounted to little more than gathering information and that Spirit and Mystery had little or no place in our pursuit of the things of God.

Seminary and Beyond

I came to seminary with a different set of concerns than the average student. I did not come fretting over whether I had been called to ministry or trying to figure out what my gifts might be. Nor was I ever worried about whether I would be able to find a job once I had completed my studies. I received calls to seven different churches while I was studying at Princeton. In fact, I specifically remember that some of my grades suffered as a result of being on the road too often preaching for inquiring congregations and then trying to explain to them why I could not accept their offer to become their pastor. Upon the completion of my formal studies I decided to accept an invitation to join the faculty at Princeton Seminary, where I remain. I see my role as preparing women and men for leadership and service to the church.

Successful in my twenties by the standards of my denomination and considered an up-and-coming young minister clearly headed for bigger and better things (e.g., a larger church), I intentionally chose to give it all up and head to seminary in order to be sufficiently grounded in the faith and to come to a deeper understanding of biblical studies, church history, theology and, most assuredly, sound and informed reflection on the practice of ministry. To this day I do not regret stepping down from my pastoral charge in my early thirties and heading to seminary for what turned out to be an additional eight years of formal education. In some ways the experience was not all I thought it would be, while in others it was richer and more rewarding than I could have ever hoped. Though I entered Princeton as a second-career student, I came with a glad heart, an open mind, and an inquiring spirit, for I knew I had a lot to learn simply on the basis of what I had already been exposed to in the early years of my ministry.

Gardner C. Taylor, regarded by many as one of the greatest preachers of the twentieth century, invited me as a first-year seminary student to preach at the historic Concord Baptist Church of Christ in Brooklyn, New York. On the way to the sanctuary for the service, Taylor turned to me and asked how many years I had served my church in Texas as pastor before heading to Princeton Seminary. When I told him ten years he shook his head in disapproval and said to me, "I don't think I would have stepped down after so many years." Needless to say, his comments crushed me because of the deep respect I had for this great preacher and because he had been so influential in my desire to further my theological education. Taylor thought about what he said for a moment and then turned to me once again and said, "I take that back. You have done a noble thing and God will not allow himself to remain in your debt. God will honor your sacrifice." Looking back now over thirty odd years of ministry, I too believe, along with Taylor, that preparation for ministry is a noble thing. And I also believe that God will certainly honor the sacrifices we make in order to expose ourselves to that preparation.

13. Contemplation in Action

Anthony B. Robinson

It was a Monday evening in early July, about 8:00 p.m., when we heard a knock at the front door. My wife and I and our three-year-old son had arrived at the parsonage the day before after a cross-country train trip from New York to Seattle. I had finished seminary at New York's Union Theological Seminary in late May, and had been called to be the pastor of a small-town church in the foothills of the Cascades east of Seattle. My first day on the job, Thursday, was fast approaching. That Sunday I would preach my first sermon to my new congregation. Because our few belongings didn't begin to furnish the large old parsonage, the knock at the door echoed.

I opened the front door to a young woman, Betty, who I recognized as a member of the congregation. She looked anxious. "I think you had better come over to the trustees meeting," said Betty. "What's up?" I asked. "I just think you ought to come," she answered. I looked at my wife. She rolled her eyes as if to say, "I knew this would happen." "Okay, I'll be over in a minute." I went to change my clothes. Then, saying to my wife, "I don't know what it is, but I'm sure it won't take long," I went out the door and walked the block to the church.

The room where the meeting was in progress was packed, and though I didn't have a lot of experience when it came to board meetings, that seemed unusual. Moreover, the atmosphere was tense. It wasn't long before I figured out what was going on. The members of the group that filled the room and sat or stood around the edges were incensed by a recent action of our denomination's General Synod. The week before, that body had voted in support of a measure affirming civil rights for persons who were gay and lesbian. They had come to demand that the church cut off financial support for the denomination and withdraw the congregation.

When there was a break in the action, the chair of the trustees, a portly man who managed a large dairy farm and who had been on the pastoral search committee that called me, said, "Well, I see that our new pastor is here. Let's see what he thinks about all this." What I thought was, "O Lord, *what* am I doing here? Why did you think this was a good idea?" Only weeks before, as I finished my studies at New York's Union Theological Seminary, I had been working my way through Hans Küng's massive work of ecumenical ecclesiology, *The Church*. Looking around the room at the angry and anxious faces now looking at me I thought, "This is the church?"

It was not my first moment of abrupt transition between seminary and church. The previous autumn I had returned to Union Seminary after a year in upstate New York. I had spent that year serving as the student pastor of a small Scotch-Irish Presbyterian church that was part of a seminary program of "field-based studies" conducted in partnership with the Presbytery of the Susquehanna Valley. That program, which combined serving a congregation with classes and field-based mentors, proved an invaluable part of my preparation for pastoral ministry. It helped me to envision myself as a pastor as well as to get a better idea for what pastors really do and why it matters.

But after being immersed in the life of a parish, I found the transition back to seminary as challenging in its own way as the transition from seminary to church was proving to be on that Monday evening in the board of trustees meeting. When I came back to Union after serving a congregation for a year, few of my fellow students were interested in hearing about serving a little church in a small town. The buzz in classrooms was about God's "preferential option for the poor," and though most of the dairy farmers living on the west slope of the Catskills, where I had been for that year, were slipping off the edge of the economy, they were not "the poor" that excited my classmates or professors. That year some of the great Latin American liberation theologians were at Union. The little church I had served with its old people, farm wives, and awkward teenagers, seemed worlds away from the seminary. There seemed to be no point of connection between my year-long experience in the parish upstate and the world of the seminary. I found that difficult.

Earlier, when I had been making the transition from seminary to that small church and the field-based studies program, I worried about my ability to fit in and make a go of it. I sought the counsel of a trusted advisor, a pastor in the city who had been the supervisor for my fieldwork as a first-year seminary student. When I described the quite different world of smaller rural congregations where I might be spending the next year and my lack of certainty about the fit, he had suggested that I might try thinking of myself as an anthropologist. That is, instead of feeling that I needed to fully understand and embrace the ways of these taciturn rural Presbyterians, I could consider them an interesting sort of foreign culture, a tribe. I could be an anthropologist studying their ways and mores.

I laughed when he suggested it, but it turned out to be a brilliant suggestion. It may be good advice for anyone making the move from seminary to church, or the other way around. Take along your anthropologist's hat. Both worlds are, in their way, "cultures." That is, both are thick networks of symbols, language, story, status, and patterned activity. Moreover, they are quite different cultures which prize different things. Seminaries are, of course, degree-granting educational communities where the basic built-in social structure is that of faculty and students. Degrees, publications, grades, and being up on the latest thing are all important in seminaries. Almost none of that proved to be of any real significance in my student-pastorate or my first church. What mattered there was building relationships and being able to communicate, which includes listening. There was no interest in whether you could write a good paper. The question was, "Can you preach?" They were different worlds, as different as writing a paper that references scholarly sources for a professor and preaching a sermon that communicates to eighty- and eighteen-year-olds, and everyone in between. The overlap between the two was somehow the stuff and substance of Christian faith.

"Put on your anthropologist's hat," suggested my advisor. My hunch is that most successful pastors have a bit of the cultural anthropologist in them. They are able to look at a new situation with curiosity and interest, and begin to describe for themselves, and eventually for others, what this particular "culture" is about. They are able to see its patterns, symbols, and values. They are able to puzzle out who has power and how power works. They see how that tribe handles conflict. They notice what this particular culture and community sees and hears, as well as that to which it is deaf and blind.

Such a strategy, being a bit of an anthropologist, affords a new pastor

155

a way to ease into a new setting and ministry. It permits a certain amount of (probably healthy) distance from that new setting. Instead of feeling that you have to "get" everything right away and love it (and them) all, you can look at it, wonder about it, try to describe it and see what's going on. Moreover, this strategy fits with our emerging postmodern world where we recognize, increasingly, the particularity of contexts and communities. Each congregation and community has its own beauties and banes, triumphs and tragedies, potentials and challenges. However much one may have learned in seminary of theology, ecclesiology, and pastoral leadership, there is no "one size fits all" for churches. They are all unique — and yet, and at the same time, churches have much in common with one another. The task of a new pastor is to get a feel for that new and particular context, to hear its story, and to listen for the song that is being sung "beneath the words," to borrow a phrase from the teacher of leadership at the Kennedy School at Harvard, Ron Heifetz.[1]

Of course, someone reading this in seminary prior to graduation and a first pastoral call might nod and say, "That sounds okay, I think I can do that," and yet find that once they've arrived on the scene of a new congregation there seems very little time, if any, for reflection, and that whatever distance one had on the situation has been immediately swallowed up by the demands of that new congregation. Certainly as I sat at the trustees' table that Monday evening, and when the chairman turned to me saying, "Well, I see that our new pastor is here; let's see what he thinks about all this," it didn't feel as if I had much time or distance with which to make sense of it all.

My memory of the specifics of the conversation that evening has been blurred by time passing. I suspect that when the chairman put me on the spot, I began by asking questions, not by giving answers. In other words, I tried to find out what was going on, which is not a bad way for a pastor to proceed. Theologian H. Richard Niebuhr observed that for people shaped by the Scriptures the first question is never, "What shall we do?" Rather, it is, "What's going on?" We ask first, "What is God doing in this situation?" Only then do we formulate what we hope to be a faithful response.

That Monday evening my ignorance of both the issue and the people in the room was a gift. It allowed me to elicit information to fill in my own

---

1. See Ron Heifetz, *Leadership Without Easy Answers* (Cambridge, Mass.: Belknap Press, 1994).

knowledge gaps. Drawing out some of this information allowed the people in the room to step back from the heat of conflict to describe what was going on as they saw it.

I suggested to the assembled trustees and visitors that I, and probably they, needed more time and information to properly assess the situation. I indicated that I could see that people were concerned and upset. I said I cared about that and took it seriously. But I also made it clear that I felt a hurried decision or action was unwise. I managed to persuade them to table the motion to withdraw all support from the denomination. I staggered home that night at about 10:30. When I slipped into bed next to my wife she said, "Well?" "You won't believe it!" I answered, "I'll tell you in the morning."

Sometimes, in transitions from seminary to church, from classroom to pulpit, we don't get a lot of time to practice our anthropological skills. Nevertheless, the concept remains a useful one, a good tool for the pastoral toolbox and for transition between the different worlds of academy and congregation. It can help a person negotiate the transition between worlds. Moreover, and described in a slightly different way, it can become an ongoing tool and skill for ministry. The Jesuits speak of what I have been describing as "putting on your anthropologist's hat" in a somewhat different way, as "contemplation-in-action." The Jesuits are well known for their twofold commitment to spirituality and service. They encourage contemplation-in-action, which is something that most pastors need to aim for and practice as well.

What is contemplation-in-action? It is the capacity to participate simultaneously in the action of ministry, in the life and mission of a congregation, *and* to reflect on what is going on. It is the capacity to see the parts and the whole, the trees and the forest. It is a commitment to immersing oneself in a particular context and also to stepping back from it on a regular basis to ponder, "What's going on?"

Magic Johnson, the Los Angeles Lakers basketball star, was gifted at contemplation-in action on the basketball court, which is one reason that he was one of the few successful player-coaches in the NBA. He could play his game and see the game at the same time. He could play his position and yet also see the floor and unfolding patterns of the game. Pastors need to be able to do something like this. They need to be able to do their specific pastoral tasks, and yet, and at the same time, see the whole. They need to practice contemplation-in-action. In fact, if you don't kind of enjoy contemplation-in-action, pastoral ministry may not be a good fit for you. Pastoral ministry is a great vocation for the kind of person who is able to combine practice and reflection and who gets a kick out of doing so.

"Contemplation-in-action" is not, as the anthropologist move may be, a temporary coping skill useful for transitions between worlds and cultures. Contemplation-in-action, seeing the parts and the whole, a rhythm of practice and reflection, is at the heart of pastoral ministry and leadership. It is a skill and capacity that pastors need to recognize, affirm, and cultivate. It helps in the transitions, but it is also a necessary skill for pastoral leadership for the long haul.

Pastors who are early in their pastoral ministry might consider building in several tools and strategies that will aid them in developing the capacity for contemplation-in-action. Three such tools which I have found useful in this regard are "getting to the balcony," using a mentor or coach, and the periodic "state of the church" sermon.

"Getting to the balcony" is another term borrowed from Ron Heifetz's work *Leadership Without Easy Answers.* He suggests that organizations, including congregations, are like a dance. Every now and again, leaders need to get up above the dance floor, where they have been part of the dancing, and take a look from the balcony. On the balcony, you watch for patterns. Who is in the room, and who lingers outside the door? Which people and groups are up close to the music, and which ones are keeping their distance? Who is dancing with whom? I suspect that most clergy who are making the transition from seminary to congregation will be well-served by carving out a couple of times a year for getting to the balcony.

It is worth noting that "getting to the balcony" and reflecting on your experience is a different kind of thing than what many clergy do for professional development or continuing education. Often the latter means going off to a conference or going back to seminary to hear what's new, what's latest, and what's hot. There's a place for this, but reflecting on one's own experience, learning, and emerging insights may be more important. Seminaries could perform a useful role by creating contexts in which pastors can unpack their ongoing experience, rather than simply adding new material.

A coach or mentor can be a helpful partner in getting to the balcony and making sense of what you are seeing when you are up there. A new pastor can engage a coach or identify a seasoned pastor or another person with good judgment and experience to be a mentor. Ask that person to meet with you for an hour or so each month as you sort out what you are working on and what is working on you.

And there is value, I have found, in doing an annual or occasional "state of the church" sermon. Tell the congregation what you see. Remind them of things they have accomplished and are doing well. Name and frame a couple of the important challenges you see ahead. One organizing device for such a sermon is the SWOT analysis format ("strengths, weaknesses, opportunities, and threats"). Have the congregation or leadership do their own SWOT analysis and use that as grist for the mill when you are ready to offer your own SWOT or "state of the church." New pastors probably ought to be on the job a full year before attempting such a sermon.

A "state of the church" sermon is one form of leadership which brings up what may be the most important element of the transition from seminary to congregation. When, on that memorable Monday evening, the chair of the board of trustees turned to me, and said, "Well, I see our new pastor is here; I wonder what he thinks," he was giving me the opportunity and responsibility of leadership. Though I was all of twenty-eight years old, and probably the youngest person in the room, I was to play a leadership role in their midst. Often seminary has not prepared students for a leadership role or leadership functions. Normally, in seminary, a student spends a good deal of time on the receiving end and a good deal less time on point. Suddenly, I was on the spot, called to lead. "I see our new pastor is here; I wonder what he thinks." All eyes turned to me. All ears perked up. This was different from seminary! While I had occasionally taken leadership roles and responsibilities during my student years, this was a huge change of role!

How does a person make the shift from student, who may have part-time responsibilities in a church, to pastoral leader? What does that shift involve? The change and shift is a complex one. Probably the first step in making it is simply to be aware of the differences in role between student and pastoral leader. The two roles *are* different. The levels of status are different. The power and responsibility shifts are big. Some seminary students are eager for the transition while others find it daunting. In either case, there is a good bit of mystery to it all!

In many ways, seminaries as they have traditionally gone about their work do not help. By and large, seminaries prepare their students for the roles of chaplains and scholars. These are both worthy ventures, but being

159

a pastoral leader while including elements of both is different from either one. Moreover, the shift in roles is accentuated by shifts in the church and society in the last thirty years. The upshot of those changes is the need for many pastors, ministers, and priests to shift from being chaplains to being pastoral and congregational leaders.

There was a time when many pastors functioned largely as chaplains, that is, as providers of religious goods and services to their congregations and to the community. My first congregation expected me to be there for weddings, funerals, prayer, and pastoral care in times of death, crisis, and emergency. Not only did the congregation expect I would be there in those chaplaincy roles for the members of the church, they were accustomed to their minister playing a somewhat similar role for anyone in town who needed religious services and a religious presence. My first funeral in that town was for a thirteen-year-old girl, the victim of a violent death. Her family had no connection to the church, but when she died I was called, as I was the pastor of the town's most visible church.

There was a time when being a chaplain to the members of the congregation and community was the central role and work of pastoral ministry. That role and function fit well with the era of American Christendom in which the mainline Protestant churches were the established church of American society. But about the time I was learning the ropes in that first church, in the mid-1970s, Christendom, American-style, died. No longer was ours a nominally Christian culture where the church stood alongside bank, public school, and town hall as civic institutions. Increasingly, ours was a secular, religiously pluralistic, and ethnically diverse society. One consequence of this is that churches no longer need ministers who are mostly chaplains; they need spiritual leaders.

This is to say that overlaid on the transition from seminary to church, from student to pastor, there is another transition, a sea change really, in the culture itself. American Christendom has ended, and something new is emerging. With this shift, the role and responsibilities of ordained clergy have changed. Those making the move from seminary to church must not only negotiate those two different worlds, but they must do so in a time when the larger world and culture, as well as the church's role in it, are changing dramatically.

As I've suggested, one summary way to describe the meaning of this shift for ordained clergy is the move from being chaplains to spiritual leaders. Yes, we clergy will continue to conduct funerals and weddings, as well as preside at other ritual moments, and offer prayer and presence at times of need and crisis. But we must do and be more than that. We must be people who help congregations engage their most important challenges. We are called to help congregations deepen their capacity to grow, form, and sustain people who are disciples of Jesus Christ.

That is a change. In some ways, the bargain of the Christendom era was that clergy, in exchange for social status and a secure role, would be the religious people for the congregation and community. Increasingly, pastors are called to lead congregations that are vital communities of faith and to help people in those congregations discover their own gifts for ministry. This is different. If seminary has prepared a person to be only a chaplain or scholar, it may not help much. Increasingly, seminaries need to be preparing pastoral and spiritual leaders. That is what the church needs in this new time.

When I was interviewed by the pastoral search committee of the congregation where I was called for that Monday night meeting, I had gotten a glimpse of this shift in the role of pastors in our time. The interview seemed to be going well. I was enjoying the people, and I had a sense they were excited about my candidacy. In their excitement, they began to enumerate some of the many "wonderful things" they hoped their new minister would do in the community. These included, in no particular order of priority, attracting the town's wayward youth, playing a role at the new senior center, getting involved in town government, establishing relationships with other pastors in the area, and generally becoming known throughout the community as a good guy and as "their" pastor. And this was only the list of their hopes for their minister's role in the wider community! It didn't include the inner life of the church or the perceived needs of its members.

Feeling myself sink into my chair under the weight of their mounting expectations, I girded my loins and interrupted their excited enumeration of expectations. "Excuse me," I said, "there's something I need to make clear. I am very excited about being a Christian *with* you; I am not interested in being a Christian *for* you." Silence. I thought, "Now you've done it; kiss this job goodbye." I learned later than this had been a decisive point in the interview and a reason they called me. They appreciated my clarity and my courage.

This moment and conversation also gets to the shift in the pastoral role, consequent on the demise of Christendom, to which I have been alluding. They had been describing a role as community chaplain. I was interested in, and called to, a role that looked more like Christian and congregational formation. I was less interested in being the chaplain to the community (or congregation) than in being a spiritual leader and ministry mentor who helped the congregation's members grow in their own faith and discipleship. I believe that such a shift is a faithful response to what God is doing in our time.

Moreover, this distinction and shift is important to the transition from seminary to congregation. When making that shift, the new pastor may get drawn into the trap of trying to meet everyone else's definitions of "pastor," and their many and varied expectations for what you are to do. I can assure you that those expectations are many and diverse. Moreover, everyone knows what your job is, though no two of them fully agree! If you define success in ministry as fulfilling, meeting, or exceeding other people's expectations for you, you will be frustrated and soon depleted.

This is not to say that you are to be indifferent to people's expectations or to the needs of a congregation; these must be heard and taken seriously. But others' expectations and definitions regarding whom you are to be as a pastor and what you are to do as a pastor cannot be the source from which vital ministry flows. This, too, suggests a shift from seminary. In seminary, students are attentive to what their professors want and expect. They may be less aware of who they are and their own core passion.

That passionate core and deepest self is the source of vitality in ministry. It is who you are and whose you are in relation to God. When a new pastor tries to be all things to all people or falls into the trap of letting others' expectations and definitions define her, ministry sooner or later becomes untenable. To make the transition from seminary to church successfully and to be an effective pastoral leader, a person must know who they are and they must know whose they are. They must know themselves and how they are related to God. From this core, we minister and lead. Our job is, in the midst of the demands and delights of a congregation, to stay in touch with who we are and whose we are, and to lead from that place and center in us. Our leadership, in other words, is inextricably bound up with our spirituality.

To sum up, my own experience of the transition from seminary to church as well as my experience as a pastor, leads me to value several tools and insights, including the following:

- A capacity to "put on your anthropologist's hat" and to appreciatively explore another "culture" and its ways;
- The value and skill of "contemplation-in-action" as integral to pastoral ministry;
- An awareness of the large shifts in our culture and in the church's role, from American Christendom to a new time of religious pluralism;
- The related change in the role of clergy from cultural chaplains to spiritual leaders and ministry mentors;
- The grounding of spiritual leadership in one's deepest self and in one's relationship to God.

Like the perilous journey from adolescence to adulthood, the passage from seminary student to pastoral leader is a challenging one. It is also one that can be made and is well worth making!

14. Spinning Gold from Straw: A Matter of Multiple Vocations

Bonnie J. Miller-McLemore

Several months ago, when asked to speak on the topic of "Conducting Effective Research among Other Things" to a group of faculty, this is how I began: "I'm here" (so pleased I'd managed it). I'm here even though I'm female and the odds are against me (how many women faculty did you have when you were a graduate student?). I'm here because I'm white, middle-class, and organized, not to mention the beneficiary of two grandmothers who went to college. I'm here even though my husband's aunt has heart and kidney failure but hasn't died (yet). I'm here even though the plumbing company ripped us off on a water heater and I wasted hours trying to get money back. I'm here even though one son called and asked for a ride, another son called and asked me to go by Old Navy, buy him flip-flops, and deliver them to his dorm room, along with his official birth certificate and a book I'm right in the middle of reading because he wants to read it, and the third son didn't ask for anything (yet). I'm here because I refuse to let these things drive me crazy, because I'm good at ignoring the guy at the door with the mowing bill and the phone call from the dean, and because I think all this — children, family, household — deserves to be taken seriously. I'm here because I'd go crazy and be unfaithful if I didn't do what I'm doing (a ministry of teaching, writing, talking) and, one more essential quality, because I'm good at spinning gold from straw.

I have been thinking about the complexity of multiple vocations for a long time. Almost any kind of ministry — teaching, parish, chaplaincy, nonprofit work — as well as lots of other jobs come into daily conflict with our vocations as partners, spouses, and parents called to tend, care, nurture, and work for a living to sustain a home. Today the complexity of managing our lives just keeps getting more unmanageable.

Almost twenty years ago, I joined a circle of colleagues at a small academic meeting for a workshop on "problems in research." The facilitator began by asking each of us to identify a particular problem we had encountered. Unbidden one came immediately to mind. Looking around the all-male group, I didn't think it was what the facilitator had in mind. In the first trimester of pregnancy, I felt nauseated all the time. (Whoever came up with the term "morning sickness," anyway? "*Morning* sickness," with the promise of a little "*afternoon* health," would have been great.)

How does one focus or pay attention, among other things, when one's body will not cooperate? I've been pursuing some variation on this basic question for a long time. I've written about juggling motherhood and work.[1] I've wondered how the theological educator and the parish minister sustain a kind of contemplative vocation when faced with heavy professional demands.[2] I just finished a book on alternative ways to understand spirituality in the midst of family chaos,[3] and I am about to turn to a project reclaiming the devalued discipline of practical theology as a valuable way to understand embodied theological "know-how."

In each case, I have wondered about how to connect excellent ministry — whether seminary or congregational leadership — to the lived life. How does one focus or pay attention to ministry when one's body, broadly speaking, competes for attention, when one is otherwise preoccupied, whatever the preoccupation? For me it's not pregnancy anymore. Now it's teenagers and, of course, peri-menopause — that wonderful name for the ill-defined period before menopause when one starts to lose one's mind.

I loved the title given me when asked to speak — "Conducting Effective Research among Other Things." I didn't change it (well, to be exact, I didn't have time). How do we manage multiple vocations? This is what I want people to talk about as openly and candidly as possible. I consider this both a profound theological question, with political ramifications,

---

1. *Also a Mother: Work and Family as Theological Dilemma* (Nashville: Abingdon, 1994).

2. "Contemplation in the Midst of Chaos: Contesting the Maceration of the Theological Teacher," in *The Scope of Our Art: The Vocation of Theological Teachers*, ed. L. Gregory Jones and Stephanie Paulsell (Grand Rapids: Eerdmans, 2001), pp. 48-74.

3. *In the Midst of Chaos: Care of Children as Spiritual Practice* (San Francisco: Jossey-Bass, 2006).

and a spiritual and pragmatic matter, with concrete strategies. I want to look at both. First, however, let me comment briefly on how society has come to so utterly de-legitimize the "other things" that impact our work.

The De-Legitimization of "Other Things"

The easy person and period to blame is René Descartes and the modern Enlightenment detachment of mind from body. "I think, therefore I am" versus "I give birth, therefore I am" ("teenagers torment me, therefore I am"). We suffer what we might call "disembodiment syndrome." We act as if we have brains on wings that fly off somewhere to think, write, read Scripture, and pray. But the problem has deeper roots in Western history. Not just mind over body, but the severance of public from private and men from women has worked havoc. Philosophy has long protected elite men so that they might have time and space to generate ideas, theories, and sermons that then, in true Weberian fashion, make their way down to the masses. Theology in turn has privileged certain limited places where God is most likely to show up — early Christian monastic orders, medieval mystical visions, C. S. Lewis's study (where his housekeeper delivers tea), and the modern interior space of Catholic monk Thomas Merton and his imitators.

The problem also has profound political, social, and economic dimensions. The academy as a whole still largely presumes the "ideal worker" who "works forty years with no career interruptions, taking no time off for childbearing or child-rearing," as labor studies professor Robert Drago says.[4] The ideal worker in academe, according to work and family expert Joan Williams, "can move anywhere from Massachusetts to New Mexico, and can work like a fiend until tenure is granted or denied." She continues,

> In the old days, these job requirements did not bar the advancement of men and women who took academic jobs. Men were not affected because male academics had wives without careers who cared for the

4. Robert Drago, "A Half-Time Tenure Track Proposal," *Change: The Magazine of Higher Learning* 32, no. 6 (November/December 2000): 46-52, cited by Florence Caffrey Bourg, "Family Economics and the Lay Theologian," paper presented at the Catholic Theological Society of America, June 6, 2003, p. 5. Bourg has since published a book on family and work, *Where Two or Three Are Gathered: Christian Families as Domestic Church* (Notre Dame: University of Notre Dame Press, 2004).

children and moved from place to place as their husband's job required. Female academics back then were not hurt either, because, by and large, they were single and childless.[5]

The church is not much different. With few exceptions neither the market nor the institutions in which we work organize themselves around an employee's responsibility for intimate relationships, dependent family, personal health, or the welfare of the common good. And the market is where the rewards are.

In the 1980s poet and critic Nadya Aisenberg and lawyer and political scientist Mona Harrington decided to ask about sixty women what had impeded their entry into the "sacred grove" of the academy. They discovered that when a woman succeeds in combining a personal and professional life, "some extra measure has intervened" — extra finances or human resources, such as a partner, a mother or mother-in-law, or an understanding administrator. A "crucial condition" in all successes is that there are "no disaster or special trouble stories."[6] Interviewees who struggled had "unforeseen trouble in many forms" — divorce, a sick baby, a husband's illness, the care of an elderly parent, the birth of twins, and even seemingly less-significant factors, such as a husband's negative attitude or the desire to scale back.[7] In other words, the ideal worker is supported by hidden economic and social systems — other things — that are seldom valued or properly rewarded, assumptions that a Christian theology of work and family should find deeply troubling.

If there has been any change in work in the last twenty years, it is

---

5. Joan Williams, "How the Tenure Track Discriminates Against Women," *The Chronicle of Higher Education,* October 27, 2000, cited by Bourg, "Family Economics and the Lay Theologian," p. 6. See also Joan Williams, *Unbending Gender: Why Family and Work Conflict and What to Do about It* (Oxford: Oxford University Press, 2000). Even Williams, in her preface to *Unbending Gender,* admits, "Very few authors indeed have the luck to have the kind of family support system I have relied on" (p. xii).

6. Nadya Aisenberg and Mona Harrington, *Women of Academe: Outsiders in the Sacred Grove* (Amherst: University of Massachusetts Press, 1988), p. 129.

7. Aisenberg and Harrington, *Women of Academe,* p. 122. According to sociologists Phyllis Moen and Patricia Roehling, a woman who marries has a 17 percent increase in housework; a married man's housework decreases 33 percent. See their *The Career Mystique: Cracks in the American Dream* (Lanham, Md.: Rowman and Littlefield, 2004), cited by Linda Hirshman, "Homeward Bound," *The American Prospect,* available online at http://www.prospect.org/web/page.ww?section=root&name=ViewWeb&articleId=10659.

mostly its "intensification."[8] Aisenberg and Harrington focused on women. Now other things that worked against women plague men. The American Council on Education reports that young male faculty are "making sacrifices for parenting and caregiving at a much higher rate than their senior counterparts."[9] This is true in parish ministry also. Meanwhile, the bar for success, in the academy at least, just keeps rising (e.g., a terminal degree required to teach, timing and number of publications, the teaching "portfolio," use of technology). Consequently, as one young father told Catholic ethicist Florence Caffrey Bourg in her own exploration of how people manage multiple vocations, many people face an "unfortunate confluence of dramatically raised requirements for tenure [job success] and dramatically raised expectations for parental involvement."[10] The problems are simply heightened for populations still underrepresented in ministerial leadership and who otherwise might protest — women and men with primary family responsibilities, women in general, and minorities.

All this raises an old question, one previously foisted on women and now shared by many men as well: Can one write books or oversee a congregation and have a life? Or does "serious creative work," whether the work of seminary or church, require such concentration that the "nonwork life must be sacrificed"? Must one choose between "perfection of the life or of the work," in poet William Butler Yeats's words? Must the "claims of family, friendships, civic responsibilities, serious avocations, even recreation," as Aisenberg and Harrington ask, "give way before the claims of 'the work'?"[11]

---

8. Jennifer Gore, "Unsettling Academic/Feminist Identity," in *Everyday Knowledge and Uncommon Truths: Women of the Academy,* ed. Linda K. Christian-Smith and Kristine S. Kellor (Boulder: Westview Press, 1999), p. 17.

9. American Council on Education, Executive Summary of *An Agenda for Excellence: Creating Flexibility in Tenure-Track Faculty Careers* (Washington, D.C.: American Council on Education, 2005), p. 5. Available online at http://www.acenet.edu/bookstore/pdf/ 2005_tenure_flex_summary.pdf, accessed September 7, 2005. Cited by Linda Kerber, "A New Agenda for the Academic Workplace," *Chronicle of Higher Education,* March 18, 2005, B6-B8. An expanded version of the essay appeared as part of a forum in the *Journal of Women's History* 18, no. 1 (Spring 2006): 121-32 and a later version appears online at http://www.historians.org/perspectives/issues/2006/0602/0602pre1.cfm?pv=y. See also Mary Ann Mason and Marc Goulden, "Do Babies Matter (Part II)? Closing the Baby Gap," *Academe* (November/ December 2004): 10-15 and "Inequities Persist for Women and Non-Tenure Track Faculty," *Academe* (March/April 2005): 20-30.

10. Bourg, "Family Economics and the Lay Theologian," p. 7.

11. Aisenberg and Harrington, *Women of Academe,* p. 107.

How Do We Do It? A Theological Question of Vocation

Many of us have argued "no" for years. But whether theological education and society at large can achieve the new understandings of work and love required to make it genuinely possible is another question. The choice between perfection of the life or the work is, in fact, a false choice. There is no real choice when distorted ideals and social structures of work and other things go unquestioned. Such questioning is the responsibility of good theology.

Several years ago I wrote an essay, "Contemplation in the Midst of Chaos: Contesting the Maceration of the Theological Teacher," for a book on the vocation of the theological teacher, in which I asserted the importance of connecting a full life and work.[12] In particular, I challenged conventional understandings of spirituality as excluding the life of the busy teacher. I left the article partly unfinished. I concentrated on the need to redefine conventional models of spirituality that restrict it to solitude, silence, and prayer. I bracketed for another day the need to reorder the hectic patterns of our work lives, a "deserving topic to which I hope to return," I said.

On closer inspection, however, I question our common work ethic. I began with self-confession and a concern it raised for me about the state of our lived practice of study and teaching in the academy and its consequences as a model for those going into the ministry. We cannot restore the teaching of theology or the practice of parish ministry as a religious vocation without addressing one of the serious challenges of today's teaching context — the cacophony of demands. That so many of us have acquired an expertise in perpetual over-extension and distractibility gave me pause. Although a fast-paced, stress-filled life is not good for anyone, it raises particular problems for those called to ministry. In general, preaching and pastoral care, just like scholarship and good teaching, require periods of study and thought. Ministry for the sake of the church — whether teaching, preaching, or some other form — requires a mode of life that deepens understanding and wisdom. What, indeed, are scholars really teaching students and ministers teaching congregants through our hurried lives?

When Lutheran preacher and theologian Joseph Sittler wrote an essay, "The Maceration of the Minister," that is, the "chopping into small

---

12. "Contemplation in the Midst of Chaos."

pieces" of the work of ministry in the late 1950s, he called theological teachers to be "noisy advocates for our students, more concerned protectors of their reflective future."[13] He presumed wrongly, as it turns out, that theological schools have escaped the very iron cage of productivity and time management that he saw destroying ministerial life. Perhaps at the time he wrote, professors were still successfully resisting the "numbers game" of books assigned, pages read, papers written, students taught, evaluations tabulated, and articles published. When I first used his essay in a class in the late 1980s, I felt the duplicity of recommending a life of "unhurried reflection" that neither the school nor I modeled. Today we are still in poor position to act as advocates for reflective time. Indeed, we are just as often guilty of the reverse by both example and class requirements.

I had lunch with a student recently who told me that another professor assigned so much reading in a core course that it was impossible to do it. Others around the table nodded. Later another colleague told me that one of the biggest challenges in moving to our school was reestablishing his reputation as a real taskmaster. When I asked what he meant, he cited extensive reading and tough grading, among other things.

My knee-jerk response: Was I assigning enough tough reading? But I stymied insecurity long enough to remember that my most formative teacher, the one from whom I had learned the most and who influenced many of my peers to pursue graduate work in ministry and religion, focused on Augustine's *The City of God* or H. Richard Niebuhr's *The Responsible Self* for weeks. We soon learned not to buy all the books for his class. One semester we only had one text anyway: Alfred North Whitehead's *Religion in the Making*. It was plenty. I still draw on the scholars we studied.

Does ministry as a vocation require a certain quality of life that is sometimes difficult to realize mid-semester or mid-Advent amid competing fidelities to multiple vocational commitments? Does the way we live, the pace of our lives, convey inadvertently harmful messages about living in faith to those who must be able to approach the ultimate and lead others there?

I believe the answer is "yes" in both cases. In the way we live our lives, we have grossly underestimated the holy ground on which we tread. But the answer is even more complicated. Not only have we poorly understood

---

13. Joseph Sittler, "The Maceration of the Minister," *Christian Century*, June 10, 1959, pp. 698, 700.

the complex nature of spirituality, mistaking silence and serenity for genuine faith amid the noise and chaos, as I've argued elsewhere.[14] We have also truncated the nature of Christian vocation. A vocation is not a singular duty to which God calls each person. God's call is multi-vocal. Good Christians can receive more than one call. Women should no longer be forced to choose one vocation to the exclusion of others.[15] Nor, I would add, should men. Mothering is not women's supreme or only vocation, and bringing home the bacon is not the sole vocation to which men are called. Each person glorifies God in a variety of ways. This is, in fact, consistent with Martin Luther's own basic insight: each of us lives out a primary vocation to love God and neighbor within a variety of "offices."

So perhaps I wasn't so far off base when, in the first few years of teaching, I bucked the system and submitted an annual report to my seminary that stated "parenting my kids" right next to my list of publications. Even though no one else named "family" in their report, I've found seminaries quite receptive to recognizing the importance of multiple vocations. Perhaps seminaries can become "seedbeds," as their name suggests, for necessary changes in the church and wider world.

Professing multiple vocations goes against the social grain of seeing vocation as a singular pursuit: one person, one gender, one vocation. "A business card that lists more than one profession," author Barbara Kingsolver says with a smile, "does not go down well in the grown-up set. We're supposed to have one main thing we do well, and it's okay to have hobbies if they are victimless and don't get out of hand, but to confess to disparate passion is generally taken in our society as a sign of attention deficit disorder."[16] Multiple vocations do, indeed, contribute to disorder. Kingsolver again: "I'd like to think it's okay to do a lot of different kinds of things, even if we're not operating at genius level in every case."[17] Sometimes I'd be happy to reach average. Holding on to multiple vocations is

---

14. See *In the Midst of Chaos.* Some of my ideas in this chapter appear there in a chapter on "Giving Unto Others . . . But What about Myself?"

15. See my own work, *Also a Mother;* Nancy J. Duff, "Vocation, Motherhood, and Marriage," in *Women, Gender, and Christian Community* (Louisville: Westminister John Knox, 1997); and Cynthia L. Rigby, "Exploring Our Hesitation: Feminist Theologies and the Nurture of Children," *Theology Today* 56, no. 4 (January 2000): 540-54.

16. Barbara Kingsolver, *High Tide in Tucson: Essays from Now or Never* (New York: HarperCollins, 1995), pp. 130-31.

17. Kingsolver, *High Tide in Tucson,* p. 132.

difficult. Admitting this is itself an important step. Learning to live well within the demands of multiple vocations may even be the primary spiritual challenge of the pastoral life.

How Do We Do It? A Spiritual Question of Strategy

It is usually easier to call for normative change than to spell out practical ways to reach it. The routine work habits and expectations of our culture, including those related to hiring, tenure, and promotion or administrating and leading a congregation, are sometimes the last and hardest behaviors to change. The only real advice Sittler offers his readers, for example, is to "order" their study, preserving a substantial block of daily time for general reading and scriptural study. This is ultimately not enough.

The other day a doctoral student told me her third child is now eighteen months. "I don't know how you do it" slipped right out. I couldn't believe I said that. I'm uneasy when others say that to me. And there I was, blurting, "I don't know how you do it." It seemed to imply she shouldn't be doing this or she couldn't sanely be doing research and everything else or that research and other things are basically incompatible.

Next time I'll try to thwart the subtle disapproval behind the tiresome, even if sympathetic, "I don't know how you do it," and ask instead, "So how are you doing?" "What's working well and what isn't?"

So what are the other things for you? I'm imagining my readers, many of you newly appointed ministers, trying to envision your way forward in the midst of competing demands. How will you pursue your vocation to minister among all the other things? What are a few spiritual, pragmatic strategies that have worked for me?

Tricks of the Trade

One of my professors once told an audience of students how he conducted effective research. I've long lost my notes but I do recall one helpful piece of advice: "If you've done something once, do it again." Once you've finished studying Paul Tillich, do not think that you are done, even if you're eager to turn elsewhere. So have I found, even when this presentation turned into a chapter, I'm often not finished with something I've done before. It's good to figure out and build on one's strengths. In the academic world, that means: If you speak it, publish it — whether in the form of a conference paper or church workshop.

There are other such tricks for managing multiple vocations. If you attend a conference, come late, leave early (I know it'd be havoc if everyone followed this rule). See, treat, and schedule commitments for other things the same way that you treat work. Like the minister who named his boat *Business* so that he could tell people he was "away on *Business,*" find your "boat," whatever it may be, name it "Business," and sneak off. When the local school district schedules spring break, I take the week off with my kids and act as if I'm headed to a meeting. (Of course, it helps that I now have a dean who does this too.)

Last semester I asked students to do paper proposals. We talked about what a good question and thesis look like, and how critical an outline is (even for those who hate to do them or who can't follow them once they have). I asked students to share their own writing tips. I told them author Anne Lamott's "bird by bird" story and encouraged them to break down their paper, like Lamott's father encouraged his son to do with his overwhelming science project on birds, into its component parts, assigning each section its allotted pages and moving forward bird by bird.[18] Ministers should do the same kind of thing — get together and trade their secrets of living a whole life and working for the church too. We do not talk enough about any of this — this very personal revelation of how we work, whether it's our style of doing research or our knack for running a church — among ourselves or with our students and parishioners. We need to do so more.

Practices of Spiritual Attention

Besides proven tricks, however, there are also more complex practices akin to spiritual disciplines that can support doing ministry among other things. In an interview, Catholic systematic theologian David Tracy argues that moderns have lost a connection once present in our culture and still enduring in some other cultures between holy thinking and holy living or, in his words, between "theological and philosophical theories and spiritual exercises." "If you were an ancient Stoic," Tracy remarks, "every day you

---

18. Anne Lamott, *Bird by Bird: Some Instructions on Writing and Life* (New York: Anchor, 1995).

would practice certain exercises that would heighten awareness of 'my' logos and 'the' Logos." He admires Simone Weil and says she "loved the Stoics" because she "thought 'attention,' the ability to attend to the wider whole, was what we, her rushed contemporaries, most lacked."[19] With the multiple demands of ministry, we have to work even harder to learn and to practice disciplines of attention that bring together piety and daily life. How, then, can we live out well our spiritual conviction that we're called to multiple vocations? What are some of the practices?

Spinning Gold from Straw   My fifteen-year-old has a research paper due soon. He bemoaned the task, and when he moans the whole household labors under it. He couldn't, he declared, come up with a good "hook" for the first sentence or figure out how to state his argument. "I hate this." I suggested he say exactly what he thinks. "I can't use the word 'I,'" he declared. "Why not?" I asked, anticipating his answer. "Teachers say we can't."

Well, I say to him and to you: Use first person — and use everything that comes your way, including what often seem like inconsequential, frivolous, frustrating encounters like this one. Here he was, sitting in the chair next to my desk, whining, and I was trying to get my plenary address on conducting research among other things figured out. So I used the story.

I encourage you to spin your straw into gold, making concerns about which you are most passionate the heart and soul of your sermons, pastoral care, or congregational teaching. Use your own life as subject matter to propel you. A friend of mine teases me: "Of course you can balance work and family. Your research *is* your family." Although jobs often dictate the kind of work we can do and my area of teaching is quite amenable to work that emerges from existential and cultural conflict, everyone can find ways to use their own lives as inspiration for work that will connect to their life and hold wider meaning beyond themselves.

Use scraps and leftovers. I wrote a couple of articles from materials cut from my dissertation. When I revised it for publication, I'd cut ideas that didn't belong, that hinted at a different question and argument. I made something else out of them.

---

19. "Reasons to Hope for Reform: An Interview with David Tracy," by William R. Burrows, *America* 173, no. 11 (October 14, 1995): 16. See Simone Weil, "Reflections on the Right Use of School Studies with a View to the Love of God," in *Waiting on God*, trans. Emma Craufurd (New York: Harper & Row, 1951).

Let the pressures and reward of your other loves be an incentive. To finish this essay, I reminded myself that my twenty-year-old wanted a break from the dorm and was coming home Friday night. I didn't want an unfinished task hanging over me.

Honor the relevance of the other things. The commodification of work — the market-driven assumption that our worth or the value of a class is measured by how hard we work — leaves little space for anything that seems like "nonwork." However, if theological teaching and pastoral ministry depend partly on the personhood of the professor and minister as "instrument of God's love," then having a child, caring for a partner or her ailing mother, working at a soup kitchen, or playing the saxophone are not the negligible activities that they have often been made out to be.

Indeed, time away from work provides the "mental space for free play essential for the cultivation of critical creativity," according to two professors at Ohio University.[20] The institution in which I first taught pre-served each Friday as a day free from classes and meetings. Although the implications would be hard to quantify, time away and the preservation of space for other things sent a strong message about the proper pace of life in theological education. Sometimes churches mistake heavy programming for good ministry. They, too, could send a different message by cutting a few programs.

Several years ago I accompanied my seven-year-old on a field trip to the science museum. After our return to school at noon, he pleaded, "Please stay for lunch." When I said, "I have work to do — how will I get it done?" he replied succinctly, "work faster." I certainly knew how to do that. "Work faster," however, is not just the story of my life. It is a problem with far wider causes and consequences. I did stay for lunch. I was glad I did. But why do we so often feel we need to justify moments away from "work" rather than claiming their validity as essential to the gracious ministerial life?

Confessing Finitude and Rolling with It   In managing multiple vocations, one encounters limits constantly. We can never read everything on the subject or visit all the sick, dying, and needy. Valuing other things besides one's ministry just magnifies this. One encounters daily limits and must learn to live with finitude repeatedly. This involves living fully within

---

20. Mara Holt and Leon Anderson, "The Way We Work Now," *Profession* 1998: 137, 138. (*Profession* is an annual publication of the Modern Language Association.)

the boundaries of one's decisions. What is the good that I can accomplish here and now rather than if only I were elsewhere?

Embracing finitude does not stop here, however. Living within the boundaries of our decisions, in turn, means enduring the dread of knowing that in the midst of chaos we sometimes choose poorly or wrongly, and often meet expectations partially and inadequately. We face loss and failure continually. When pressed by many worthy demands, it is easy and common to fall short.

One way to live well with finitude is to recognize the different phases of our career. I'd studied life cycle theory to pass graduate exams. But I'd never thought about it in relationship to my own vocation until a senior colleague pointed it out. We cannot do everything (teaching, research, writing, administration, advising, speaking, editing) well all the time. In the first several years of teaching, I let teaching and committee work slide in order to write. In the past five years, I made up any previous institutional irresponsibility by over-functioning as a team player, chairing a curriculum review, co-chairing a planning grant, and serving on way too many search committees. I'm still trying to figure out how to teach better.

Recognition of the life cycle of our ministerial vocation in turn requires appreciation for colleagues. We do not have to do it all and can celebrate the success of others rather than experience it as competition and threat. We also depend heavily on the wider institutional community and the wisdom of its leadership to identify our talents and distribute well responsibilities for the wider church among all of us. Faculty and clergy "development" has, for this reason, become one of the more difficult and important arenas for deans and presidents as well as regional ministers and bishops.

My last sabbatical was partially funded by a grant, giving me an additional semester off. But for a long time I was miserable. I couldn't see any "progress" on a project not yet ripened. Repeatedly people asked me, "How's your work?" I wanted to scream, "I'm on sabbatical, darn it!" Moreover, one-half of my life — the other things of family — didn't go on sabbatical. Does the sabbatical suffer the same demise as the Sabbath itself? How might we do better at sustaining the fuller purpose for which sabbaticals were originally named — a Sabbath, a time of rest and renewal essential to creation, liberation, and redemption? Recognizing finitude suggests the need to salvage Sabbath. Like the days of the week, finitude revolves around rest.

Perhaps most difficult, finitude and effective ministry demand the discipline of saying "no." Making choices requires a careful, continuous re-assessment of one's vocational gifts as the best vantage point from which to decide. This becomes more difficult when one is called to multiple vocations. As much as we resist the idea, we need to recognize that saying "yes" means saying "no" to other possibilities and saying "no" actually opens up space for the responsibilities and challenges of a larger, life-affirming "yes" that, as ethicist Shawn Copeland says, "makes space for God."[21] For many, this discipline requires resisting offers that define success in terms that do not match our vocational call.

Turning Finitude to Gratitude   "Gratitude is very much a part of the writing process," comments author Kathleen Norris, "but unfortunately much of it is hidden from the reader, who encounters a finished poem or story but not all the pages full of false starts and scribbled revisions." So when she talks with high schoolers about effective writing, she takes a "pile of manuscript pages that came almost to my waist," pages "marked with sharp comments from my editor ('this sounds fatuous,' 'this doesn't go anywhere') and also the intense, line-by-line workings of a copy editor." This completely disabused them of any glorification of the writing process. When introduced with a list of her "successes," she makes it a practice to add the other side: "For 22 years . . . I was unable to get any kind of grant to support my writing."[22] Bestselling author Norris still gets rejection slips.

Just as Norris had to learn the "discipline" of coping with failure and congratulating other writers when they received grants and mean it, so also does she reach for gratitude. Without recognizing failure and reaching for gratitude, desire for success can quickly turn into envy, vanity, and complacency. We lose sight of gratitude because we forget the grace and good fortune that turns our shabby efforts to good. Some of her own success flows back to her in unexpected ways — a note scrawled on a cigarette carton from an appreciative truck driver or a letter from someone who had lost and sought renewed contact with Norris's mother. Such "success," she learns, isn't really a "goal that can be striven for. It is pure gift, and grati-

---

21. See M. Shawn Copeland, "Saying Yes and Saying No," in *Practicing Our Faith: A Way of Life for a Searching People*, ed. Dorothy C. Bass (San Francisco: Jossey-Bass, 1997), p. 60.

22. Kathleen Norris, "Gratitude at Last," *Christian Century*, June 3-10, 1998, p. 582.

tude is the only possible response." Gratitude refuses to "remain strictly private," but reverberates with unexpected returns. So she dubs gratitude "primary among the spiritual virtues, the wellspring, as it were."

On that note — what better note? — ends my rumination on the matter of multiple vocations. I'm grateful for colleagues like you with whom I have the good fortune to share the challenge and from whom to learn.

15. Sustaining the Pastoral Life

Earl F. Palmer

Getting Ready

When I graduated from Princeton Theological Seminary, the call that began my ordained ministry as a Presbyterian pastor was that of minister to students at University Presbyterian Church in Seattle, Washington. I served in that ministry with high school and university students for eight years. Afterwards, I served as solo pastor in an expatriate English-language church in the Philippines, the Union Church of Manila. After six years in Manila, I was called to serve as senior pastor at First Presbyterian Church of Berkeley, California, where I stayed for twenty-one years. In 1991, University Presbyterian Church in Seattle called me again, this time to my current position as senior pastor.

I begin this essay by reflecting on two things. The first centers on what Princeton Seminary gave me that helped me most to get ready, and actually to make it, in ministry. The second pertains to what it was that I discovered about ministry, which happened by being in the congregation of real people in a real place as their pastor.

My Princeton list begins with the friendships I made during three years as a student, friendships which continue to this day. I was in a support/prayer group during my Princeton years with fellow students. We were also involved in ministry opportunities together, primarily with Princeton University students. These friends were a source of encouragement for me and together we provided a healthy "check and balance" for each other, an arrangement that made us interpersonally responsible. As most of us left seminary to respond to our pastoral callings, and one went on for advanced schooling, we did not move on as loners. I think this atmosphere of inter-personal accountability was a stabilizing safety net for me. It also set up in me an expectation that I would always need to be in such a group.

I also owe to Princeton Seminary what happened intellectually and spiritually within me. Princeton provided me a mind-expanding theological framework from which ministry could happen. I was a young Christian when I arrived at seminary, and the whole world of theological study took me in and opened me up. I discovered intellectual mentors, both in person and in books, who would have a permanent impact on my outlook and my vision. I discovered Karl Barth, Dietrich Bonhoeffer, and C. S. Lewis. Each one became my guide toward biblical faith. Each pointed me to Jesus Christ as the faithful and grand center, as Lord and as friend. Added to this, I had the chance to watch the gospel make sense in practical experiences I had with students in the Princeton University small groups I was associated with. I left Princeton Seminary with confidence in the relevance of the gospel of Christ.

I learned strategy there, too. Those small groups of university students in weekly Bible study groups that I was a part of taught me how to be patient and to wait it out for those who begin as skeptics but over time experience their own journey toward faith. I discovered that the gospel of Christ would authenticate itself if given time. This made a very big difference for me when I started out as a youth pastor in Seattle. Also, I learned specific skills. Particularly useful were two speech classes I took, which I believe were so effective because my instructors chose to work with each individual student's natural speaking style, rather than try to impress a diverse group of speakers into a single mold. I was also deeply impacted by the thoughtful models of ministry and preaching that I saw in several of the great professors, particularly John A. Mackay, the president, and George Hendry, who taught theology.

All of these inputs, when added together, gave to me a beginner's confidence in the validity of the Christian message. In addition, two summer internships at First Presbyterian Church of Berkeley, where I had attended church as an undergraduate, gave me a sense of optimism about the church as an institution. I was not unaware of some of the problems of the Christian fellowship as an institution planted in a place with an address, but as I entered the profession of ministry I had not been burned by the church as institution; and for that optimism at the beginning I have always been grateful. I expected good things to happen, and they did.

Keeping the Rhythm

Of course, I had much still to learn when I left seminary and entered the parish. I remember the senior class dinner at Princeton Seminary the year I graduated. The speaker was George Buttrick, who at that time was pastor at Madison Avenue Presbyterian Church in New York City. He challenged our class, and its future pastors, in two ways. First, he urged us to be *with* our people, to be listeners in the marketplace in order to understand *where* people are and *what* they are thinking and feeling. His second word of counsel seemed to contradict the first: "When you are at Coney Island, don't tell the people of the concessions on the boardwalk, about which they know. Tell them of the mystery of the sea, about which they do not know." He went on: "Don't read only what your people are reading . . . read what your people are not reading."

Throughout my career, I have tried to follow Buttrick's advice, and three concerns have come forward as a practical result of that attempt: (1) How is it possible to find time to read about the mystery of the sea when I have so many urgent responsibilities among the concessions? (2) When I have found the time, what should I read as a pastor in today's world? (3) How do I remember what I read?

Most pastors have been given what I call the *gift of time;* that is, the privilege of organizing time with more flexibility than those in most other professions. As each of us knows, however, this gift of time has its own snares, particularly for those who are not self-starters, or who allow the hours of the week to confuse themselves into a random jumble of low-quality segments. This means that the first challenge that confronts the pastor who wants to study and read seriously is to have a clear system of weekly time management. I have found that for my own life the key to having quality time for my family, for spiritual formation, for reading, for ministry to people, for writing, and for recreation is to have a life rhythm. This means that I primarily think of time in terms of a week rather than in terms of a year, month, or day. It's no mistake, it seems to me, that the seven-day week is the biblical yardstick for measuring life in the Ten Commandments. My goal is to divide each week into a rhythm of work, rest, worship, and play. Accordingly, I work with people, but I also work alone. I worship with my faith community, but I also worship by myself. Similarly, I discuss various things with others, but I also spend time reflecting on them alone. A person is able to take in stride a high intensity of demands if there is also built into life the opportunity for an easing up of demands. I am able to enjoy rest if time allotted to rest follows real work. I am talking about a rhythm that includes fast/slow, many/few, rich/lean, exterior/interior.

I divide my own week into two major parts: I place into the first part Sunday morning through Wednesday evening, the large group meetings and worship services, also the counseling, small study group meetings and teaching sessions, and finally the church administration and staff obligations that fall to me. Thursday and Friday are days for private study, reflection, writing and reading. Friday evening through Saturday evening is family recreation time — a time for a total change of pace. My study goal each week is to have completed by Thursday at noon the sermon for the coming Sunday. When this goal is met, it means that Thursday afternoon and Friday are available for long-term study, reading, and writing objectives. I find that if the immediate teaching-preaching preparation is not completed by Thursday, then that unfinished task tends to threaten and intimidate Friday and Saturday. With this rhythm, my week is more intense at the beginning and eases up toward the end. One's time at both sides of the week is of a better quality, it seems to me, when there is such a rhythm.

The Mind Alive

Having scheduled the time, we come to Buttrick's second question: What shall I read? I believe that the rhythm principle is sound in relation to content as well as to form. I want to read intensively and also extensively, light and heavy, theologically and geologically, and so forth. As a pastor my first intensive reading-research challenge centers on the main book of my life, the Bible. For me this means first of all having effective access to the major translations of the Bible now available. It also means having access to a working library of historical background and technical books.

In order to keep myself intellectually involved in theological dialogue, I have pursued two particular reading goals. First, in regard to major theological writers, I have found that there are two ways into a heavyweight theological book: through the front door or by the window — that is, from the first page onward or through its topical or biblical reference index. Both are valid entrances into theological books. Often I find that the window route has coaxed me into reading the whole book. A second way to keep engaged with current theological discussion is through journals and magazines.

There are several authors with whom I have developed a special sort of friendship; they do not know me, but I know them. I am trying to read all that they have written. These are authors with whom I especially resonate, and it is my goal to have in my own library a complete collection of their works. These writers have become permanent friends. They are not masters of my mind, because I may not always agree with all they write; they are more like guides and companions who especially challenge me and who continue to encourage my own pilgrimage as a Christian. I feel that I understand how they think and how they approach the serious questions. I not only read these writers; I reread them.

We come now to Buttrick's final question: How am I to keep track of what I read and remember what needs to be remembered? The answer to this question begins with a way in which a pastor sees the study-reading task of ministry. Is the pastor a collector, an assembler of the conclusions of others, or is the pastor a researcher-scholar whose goal is making a creative contribution? I believe the second model is harder, but far more rewarding. All of my reading is a vital part of the total research task that goes into writing a sermon or a special teaching study. Holding on to my discoveries is vitally important.

My own method is not complicated. I have found that in order to remember what I have read, I must read carefully. Therefore, I read slowly. I take notes in my daily journal or on a separate review page, or make coded marks on the margins of the book. When I have found an unusually impressive book, I offer a small group seminar or discussion on the book. This is another way to study a significant book creatively, as well as to see it through the eyes of other people.

When it comes right down to it, a book is itself a friend, and it is best remembered when we have a sense of respect for it. When I quote from authors in a sermon, my own approach is to quote few but long — that is, to make use of only a few quotations in a given sermon, but to show respect for whatever is quoted. This means allowing the quotation to speak from its own setting; it means reading enough of the quotation that the author is really heard, and not simply used to focus upon what I am saying. This approach involves more work for the preacher homiletically in establishing the context for the quotation, but it also has the benefit of encouraging listeners to want to read that author for themselves. I have made for myself two rules for using quotations: I do not quote from a book I have not read, and I do not quote from a typed card. I either quote from memory or read from the book itself, present and visible. In this way the book is honored, and also, I believe, endorsed to the listeners. It seems to me an insult to a great book like *The Brothers Karamazov* to read selections from its great and moving chapters, now impertinently removed to utilitarian index cards. Such a great book deserves respect, not exploitation.

As pastors in the Christian church, we stand in a long and good tradition of learning and of concern for truth. Books have their unique part to play in this lifelong obedience to truth, to which every Christian is committed. I am aware that electronic media, TV, and films play an increasingly influential part in communication within the human family, but I still maintain that when it comes to the image-building of that greatest of all collectors of dreams and ideas — the human mind — there is still nothing to match a book read aloud, and especially to a child. Listen to how C. S. Lewis describes Jill's encounter with the lion Aslan: ". . . the voice was not like a man's. It was deeper, wilder, and stronger; a sort of heavy, golden voice. It did not make her any less frightened than she had been before, but it made her frightened in rather a different way."[1] No TV or film version of the Chronicles of Narnia will be able to capture or highlight the vast features of that golden lion quite so wonderfully as the human imagination itself set in motion by the words of a book. *The Book* and *books* make it possible for us to describe the mystery of the sea.

Of course, different pastors will have their own lists of favorite writers and of books that have made a difference in their intellectual and spiritual pilgrimage. My own list would look something like this, and I offer it in hopes that it may offer some of my readers some suggestions for truly enriching reading:

- Blaise Pascal, *Pensées*. This work conveys the sheer excitement of a Christian mind alive to the relevance of Jesus Christ.
- John Calvin, *Institutes*. Calvin's impressive grasp of the large outline of the gospel's meaning makes his works exciting.
- Martin Luther, *Lectures on Romans*. These are as fresh and electric today as in the sixteenth century.
- Karl Barth, *Dogmatics in Outline*. I deeply appreciate Barth's bold-

1. C. S. Lewis, *The Silver Chair* (New York: Macmillan, 1953), p. 16.

ness and his serious intention to really hear and obey the biblical text. He is the theologian's theologian.

- Dietrich Bonhoeffer, *The Cost of Discipleship.* Bonhoeffer called out to me to decide once and for all about what matters the most in my life.
- C. S. Lewis, The Chronicles of Narnia. I owe so much to C. S. Lewis, especially his wonderful mixture of surprise and the goodness of God.
- G. K. Chesterton, *Orthodoxy.* I love Chesterton's humor and ability to stir up my own imagination.
- J. R. R. Tolkien, *The Lord of the Rings.* How can anyone miss out on the journey of Frodo and Sam?
- Helmut Thielicke, *How the World Began.* I learned about preaching from Thielicke.
- Leo Tolstoy, Fyodor Dostoyevsky, Boris Pasternak, Aleksandr Solzhenitsyn, Victor Hugo. These writers have stirred me emotionally and spiritually more than all other novelists.
- T. S. Eliot, W. H. Auden, Robert Frost. These poets have given me a deep respect for words and imagery.
- Mark Twain, Pat McManus, Robert Benchley. They have given me their rich humor and insight into personality.
- Paul Tournier. He demonstrates psychological wisdom and even-handedness.
- I think the three greatest novels I have ever read would be Dostoyevsky's *Crime and Punishment,* Hugo's *Les Miserables,* and Twain's *Huckleberry Finn.*
- The most helpful book about the Christian faith for me has been Karl Barth's *Dogmatics in Outline.*
- The most persuasive case for the Christian life has been C. S. Lewis's *Screwtape Letters.*

People in Power: Making the Church Happen

"Are you a pastor?" "No, I'm just a layman."

From time to time in my ministerial career I have heard exchanges such as this, and I think it is time to think about what is going through our minds when we say, "I'm a pastor" or "I'm just a layman." The word "laity" itself comes from the ancient Greek *laos,* which simply means "people," and therefore it includes us all. All Christians are a part of the people of God, the *laos* of God. Some of us are specially ordained for teaching and pastoral tasks, but most of the *laos* will make the work of the church happen as teachers, servers, and leaders — as the volunteers who make the fellowship of Christ's people real and definite.

Lay volunteers, the ones we typically mean when we use the word "laity" or "layperson," make the church happen. They feed youth groups. They free the church financially to carry on ministry. They make up committees that hire and fire church workers and set policy goals for the congregation. They teach Sunday school classes, lead home Bible studies, and reach out to neighborhoods to share the gospel. They grow in personal faith. They love and encourage the ordained workers and pastors. And they worship Christ and give his church its concrete public expression in the world.

Of course, the *laos* of God also grow tired, sometimes slow down, occasionally panic, and even wear out. Even so, in spite of all of the challenges in ministry, the laity is just as much the church of Jesus Christ as are the pastors and paid staff. The laity is the group who volunteers their time and gifts to the ministry of Christ in the world. In fact, most of those who make up the Christian advance team throughout the world are lay volunteers, the people of God in ministry.

Tom Gillespie, former president of Princeton Theological Seminary, said at a meeting I attended recently, "Every institution has a spirit about it." The question for pastors, then, is this: Where do we find that "spirit" of a fellowship group or church? The spirit of a church, I believe, is more accurately seen among its volunteers than in the pages of its fund drive's full-color brochure. In fact, what happens in the lives of the lay Christian member of a fellowship is a more accurate measure of the character of a congregation or fellowship group than any other combination of spiritual life indicators. It is the bottom line.

Take a work crew at a Young Life camp. They work together through several weeks in the summer. The campers come and are involved in a one-week program designed for them. Nevertheless, what happens to the camp's work crew may be of more crucial, long-term significance for the total strategy of the kingdom of God than what happens with the campers. Why? The campers, like churchgoers, may experience the "spirit of the institution," but the work crew is the labor force which, by its discipleship and attitudes, shapes that spirit. If this is accurate, then we who mobilize lay volunteers need to think carefully about how to encourage these folks so that they don't burn out. In this regard, I believe that four principles apply equally to the professional Christian servant and the lay volunteer, and so I will end this essay by describing these principles, what I call "realistic expectations," "the tyranny of tiny strings," "beware of power," and "a serious and happy task."

Realistic Expectations

In the Book of Acts, the church is first described as those repentant believers who received God's forgiveness in Jesus Christ and then were united in the apostles' teaching and fellowship. Note that this definition does not exclude or excuse any members of the church from these three criteria. We are all *inadequate* individuals who repent and receive grace. We are all being *taught* so that we may grow in the content of the gospel. And we all need *fellowship* with one another.

The essential truth here is that we are either volunteers or special "apostles" (that is, "ones sent out") *not* because of our adequacy on a leadership flowchart, but because of grace. This is not to downgrade the need to develop our talents, but, talents notwithstanding, we have all become Christians by grace. Thus, the most that anyone can expect from those of us in church work is *trust* in Christ, *growth* in Christ, and *fellowship* with Christ and with other people.

Many of us, laypeople as well as pastors, suffer because we create for ourselves unhelpful expectations. We embrace an idealistic myth of what a leader is supposed to be, and then we hold ourselves up to it. And while such myths are impressive and inspiring on paper, they are usually devoid of realism and grace. For that reason, we should test every occasion in our Christian community where volunteers are involved to see if these three criteria are being met: trust in Christ, growth in faith, and fellowship with Christ's people.

I once spent a week at Laity Lodge in Texas, a Christian ministry sponsored by the H. E. Butt Foundation. On the first evening, the director, Howard Hovde, introduced each member of the lodge "family" to those of us who were guests for the week. Everyone was presented, including the maids, student summer workers, dishwashers, volunteers from town, and cooks. As he introduced each one, they told about their families, their local church involvement, and their ministries. Then they conveyed their interest in our week together, and also their hopes that we, like they, would have a growing experience at Laity Lodge. Consequently, that evening we all were bound together by a common gospel objective and a common fellowship. Burnout occurs much less frequently when those New Testament bonds are part of both paid employees' and volunteers' shared experience.

The Tyranny of Tiny Strings

A second principle holds that we each need the authority to move and flex and do what needs to be done without what I call "the tyranny of tiny strings." In 1985 my family and I took a three-week train trip across the Soviet Union. We came away from that experience with the impression that Soviet citizens didn't so much live in fear of the KGB, as many Americans imagined they did, as they lived under the tyranny of a thousand tight strings which managed even the most ordinary day-to-day movement, thereby restraining natural human flexibility, freedom, and initiative. Every decision, whether it had to do with an individual's housing, vacation, or education, had to be decided by a committee or by a workgroup leader. As a result, every move was slowed down by the bureaucratic wet cement of delayed decisions and endless procedures for approval.

Christian fellowships, too, can lose their ability to move decisively and flexibly because of the tight little strings of endless committee processes, needlessly deferred decisions, and "management-by-objective" committees which freeze action in the here and now while we wait for long-range planning surveys to come in. In every living fellowship, both large and small, there must be a creative balance which enables people to understand the larger policy goals and, at the same time, to act decisively and flexibly to meet situations without the hindrance of unnecessary institutional roadblocks.

Most of us know how refreshing it is to meet someone who is able to make a clear and definite decision without the need to check with others. Of course, every fellowship needs checks and balances in policymaking; but the "spirit of the institution" should be one of goodwill, trust, and adventure, so that the experimenters and innovators are not squeezed out but rather liberated to do concrete things under the guidance of the gospel and in the dynamic network of the fellowship. This balance happens in direct proportion to the sense of shared consensus within the fellowship about what is major and what is minor. Such a consensus comes from healthy doctrines experienced in the community of faith by people who care about each other because they have felt God's care. Christian care keeps us mellow enough to roll with the mistakes we inevitably make and yet able to act without unnecessary delay.

Beware of Power

This third principle is a necessary companion to the second. For just as we must shun the tendency to avoid making decisions, so we must, both lay volunteers and Christian professionals alike, guard against the temptation to abuse power — to be the ones who tie those strings on people and programs so that any movement requires our agreement. When we give in to that temptation, we ourselves become the oppressors of initiative and creativity, and those who work with us must either obey us, humor us, or deceive us in order to remain our coworkers. When we become preoccupied with power, our coworkers are eventually used up, one by one. Worse yet, they may resort to various games of deception in order to cope with a leader who has become intoxicated by power.

Notice the two nonproductive results. On the one hand, an abusive leadership style may reap a collection of noncreative, non-risk-taking leader-pleasers who impair a Christian fellowship's ability to meet challenges. On the other hand, overly controlling leaders may find themselves surrounded by dishonest power brokers.

How can we avoid succumbing to this temptation? We must begin with a healthy doctrine of power. In the New Testament authentic power is seen in Christ's concrete victory over sin, the devil, and death; it is the life-giving and redeeming power of Jesus. For us as Christian leaders, therefore, authentic power is not the power we are able to exercise over other people, but rather our confidence in the power of Christ. It is the authority that Christ himself has over all other powers. He is the one who by his death and resurrection has won the victory over the powers of sin and death and the evil one.

The greatest strength that we can ever know is our assurance of the permanent truth of this threefold victory and authority of Jesus Christ. We stand under his authority at all times, and therefore whatever authority is entrusted to us is itself under the constant check and balance of the law and the gospel. Such a confidence is not oppressive toward others. On the contrary, it is freeing and contagious. The great continuity of the Christian church throughout history lies not in its institutional discipline nor in its ordained pastoral authority, but rather in the gospel.

A Serious and Happy Task

The fourth and final principle applies to professionals as well as to volunteers. The key to a good ministry experience lies in recognizing that our work is both a serious task because of God's greatness and a happy task because of his companionship with us through his people. It can be enjoyment as much as a task to drive teenagers to a retreat, to wash dishes after the morning prayer breakfast, to tutor a youth who is struggling with math, or to work in a community food distribution program. The joy comes from knowing that we want to be where Christ is — serving his people, even serving strangers in his name. It is that joy of working with other Christians in service to Christ that keeps us refreshed.

Perhaps that's what the ancient psalmist meant when he said, "I would rather be a doorkeeper in the house of my God than dwell in the tents of wickedness" (Psalm 84:10).

16. Gossip: The Grace Notes
of Congregational Life

Carol L. Schnabl Schweitzer

Grace Notes: An Introduction

I have spent more than twenty years in ordained ministry. During the first fifteen I was pastor of several Lutheran congregations, even while completing graduate school, and during the last years my primary role has been that of seminary professor. With the advantages of hindsight, I am now able to reflect on my early years in the ministry with humor and a great deal more wisdom than I possessed when I began. I could have easily entitled this essay, "the things I learned *after* seminary graduation." A few introductory words about my own journey to arrive at this place are in order and will serve (I hope) to provide some helpful background information, if not encouragement, for those who find themselves in similar situations.

I *never* intended to seek ordination. I embarked on my vocational journey intending to become a full-time church musician (hence my penchant for employing musical metaphors). Four years in a conservatory didn't seem like enough preparation for a church vocation and I explored the possibility of a two-year program in a seminary. Instead, with a great deal of ambivalence, I enrolled in a four-year program which culminated in ordination. Women in ministry were still a curiosity at the time, so much so that my five-year-old goddaughter said, "but ladies can't be pastors." I struggled with this concept and wasn't at all certain that my godchild wasn't correct. I'm also a "pastoral care convert" in that I concentrated my efforts on biblical studies during my first four years in seminary — clinical pastoral education had been enough for me, or so I thought. The less-than-gentle nudge for clinical training occurred only after I found myself all too frequently in pastoral care situations that I felt ill-prepared to manage. "Why hadn't anyone ever told me it was going to be like this?" was my constant refrain. (One example of the situations that presented themselves to me: an eight year old started a fire in his bedroom that nearly destroyed the entire house; the family didn't have the resources to seek therapy, and *yes,* they were members of the congregation I served.) My formative early years in ordained ministry were in many ways a baptism by fire and the words from Isaiah 43:2 echoed in my ears, "when you walk through fire you shall not be burned, and the flame shall not consume you."

One might expect that gossip, the topic I want to address in this essay, simply served to fan the flames of the fire but it didn't. Even now, as I ponder my experiences as the *subject* of gossip, I am still moved to laughter. In many ways those first years in the ministry were and continue to be my grace notes in ministry. I use that term, "grace note," with a double meaning in mind. For those who are not musicians, *Webster's Unabridged Dictionary* describes a grace note as follows: "in music, a note added for embellishment; it is usually printed as a small note just before the note that it embellishes, from which its time value is subtracted."[1] What I wish to emphasize here is that a grace note is an embellishment with a brief time duration, but which adds something to the music in the same way that gossip adds something to church life (even if gossip is sometimes destructive). Grace notes are small but not insignificant, and if one isn't listening carefully one might miss the performance of a grace note. This is the first meaning. The designation of these embellishments implies that grace is *imparted;* thus, the second meaning.

What exactly is grace? When I taught confirmation class, my students would say things like "grace is God's love in action." I thought this was a solid beginning for thirteen-year-olds. What does *Webster's* say? I was surprised to learn that in the entry for *grace* (used as a noun), definition eleven of the sixteen listed was actually dedicated to theology: "a) the free unmerited love and favor of God; b) divine influence acting in us to restrain us from sin; c) a state of reconciliation to God; d) spiritual instruction, improvement and edification."[2] Does gossip that pertains to the minister ac-

---

1. *Webster's New Universal Unabridged Dictionary,* 2d ed. (New York: Dorset & Baber, 1983).

2. *Webster's New Universal Unabridged Dictionary,* 2d ed.

complish all these things in church life? No, of course it doesn't. I will suggest, however, that God's unmerited love and favor was often announced to me in the form of gossip. I would not want to suggest that gossip is actually God's influence restraining us from sin since most of us would, I think, be inclined to view gossip as itself somehow sinful. And it may even be the case that in some way I was reconciled, at least in my relationships with others, as a result of gossip. But it's the last part of that definition which is compelling for me. When I listened carefully to the meta-message of the gossip about me, I received spiritual instruction, was edified, and worked for improvement in the carrying out of my responsibilities. I experienced grace in these ways when I was able to *respond* to rather than *react* to what was said.[3]

The difference between responding and reacting is crucial, since it is what allows for the possibility of grace notes in the gossip. Responding (taken from Ronald Richardson's understanding of self-differentiation) is "the ability to think clearly and wisely about possible options for action and the likely consequences for each of these options; and, the ability to act flexibly within the situation on the basis of these perceptions, thoughts and principles."[4] It means I will not create a perception of threat when there really isn't any threat to my well-being in the first place. One might wonder about why there was such keen interest among church members in many of my activities. I think it centered largely on the fact that I was very young, single, female, and a *solo* pastor. All of those factors added to the interest in my private life!

Gossip: A Means of Grace

When I was a seminarian gossip was something that *happened* in the community (and it still does!) but it was not a subject given any serious academic consideration. Donald Capps,[5] Susan Hedahl,[6] and Richard

3. See a discussion of emotional reactivity in Ronald W. Richardson, *Creating a Healthier Church: Family Systems Theory, Leadership, and Congregational Life* (Minneapolis: Fortress, 1996), pp. 91-101. He states: "Reactivity is the emotional expression of people's sense of threat."

4. Richardson, *Creating a Healthier Church*, p. 86.

5. Donald Capps, *Living Stories: Pastoral Counseling in Congregational Context* (Minneapolis: Augsburg Fortress, 1998), pp. 173-201.

6. Susan Hedahl, *Listening Ministry: Rethinking Pastoral Leadership* (Minneapolis: Augsburg Fortress, 2001), pp. 88-93.

Lischer[7] are among those in different theological disciplines who recently have examined the importance of gossip as a communication form in pastoral ministry. Each has noted that the origins of the word have a spiritual or theological foundation; a "gossip" was originally a sponsor for Christian baptism and suggested a close, trusted friend relationship. Each acknowledges, too, that gossip as a form of communication is tainted because it is often used to exclude and degrade "outsiders." Contemporary uses of the word tend to center on a *person* who spreads rumors or idle talk, or on the *rumors* themselves. As Capps observes, "*idle* implies absence of announced purpose."[8] This does not prevent him, however, from arguing for gossip's positive function in ministry; he notes that social scientists do recognize that gossip "plays an important role in social exchange."[9] His own study of gossip leads him to conclude that pastoral counseling is a higher form of gossiping because the counselor attends to the "trivia" of a person's life story, which is often demeaned by others, while keeping confidences in the tradition of a godparent.

Capps is not alone in his efforts to reclaim the positive value of gossip. "Gossiping," writes Lischer, "was speech within the community of the baptized. For all its negative associations, gossip retains something of its salutary function in a small town. . . . [G]ossip is the community's way of conducting moral discourse and, in an oddly indirect way, of forgiving old offenses."[10] Here I would add that most, if not all, congregations function as small towns. Moreover, Lischer contends, "[w]hen gossip serves the gospel, it exhibits historical, moral, and pastoral dimensions."[11] He does seem here to privilege a pastoral (theological) dimension over historical or moral dimensions in arguing that gossip "no longer serves the gospel and becomes tediously destructive"[12] if the pastoral dimension is absent. If the gossip has a pastoral dimension, then the "moral discourse" of the "community seeks to integrate a person whose behavior does not enjoy historical or moral precedents. It makes allowances and adjustments."[13] In

---

7. Richard Lischer, *Open Secrets: A Spiritual Journey Through a Country Church* (New York: Doubleday, 2001), pp. 95-102.

8. Capps, *Living Stories*, p. 177, Capps's emphasis.

9. Capps, *Living Stories*, p. 180.

10. Lischer, *Open Secrets*, pp. 95-96.

11. Lischer, *Open Secrets*, p. 97.

12. Lischer, *Open Secrets*, p. 99.

13. Lischer, *Open Secrets*, p. 99.

Lischer's own situation, the community wondered aloud about how his wife's habits (e.g., she hired a babysitter in order to sit behind the garage in her bikini and read books!) might be affecting his ministry or the performance of his duties. The personal anecdote I will share momentarily demonstrates how the congregation I served sought to integrate my behavior. After all, I was the first woman to serve this congregation and to be called to a church in that town. There were *no* historical or moral precedents. I was the one making them.

Susan Hedahl elaborates even further on the positive significance of gossip in her discussion of "listening in the community." Gossip is, she says, an important form of internal communication within a congregation.[14] When listening to individuals (say therapeutically, as in pastoral care) we need to attend not only to the person but to the person in his or her context. We need to listen as if we are listening to the whole group or congregation, for the role of the gossiper may be compared to that of a public relations agent or "grapevine" manager.[15] One person (sometimes more) dares to come forward with a summary of the community's moral discourse. Like Lischer, Hedahl understands gossip to be a form of moral discourse; but she observes too that it tells us something about the construction of social relationships. How then does one "exegete" the gossip?

Hedahl summarizes the work of Jorg Bergmann[16] and offers some strategies for understanding gossip's features. We need to ask questions like: Who is the one *doing* the gossiping? Who is the one *being* gossiped about? Who is the one *receiving* the gossip? The speaker and the listener(s) are transgressors of a sort since the information they are sharing was, until this point in time, known only to the one being gossiped about. Hedahl makes the point that *"gossip occurs because people keep secrets."*[17] What is in public view of the congregation or any other social organization is generally not gossiped about. Hedahl condenses Bergmann's work, and notes that three features are constitutive for gossip to occur: *absence, acquain-*

14. Hedahl, *Listening Ministry*, p. 89.

15. Capps, *Living Stories*, pp. 189-92. Capps provides a summary of John Dominic Crossan's understanding of the positive role of gossip as a vehicle for spreading the word about Jesus.

16. Jorg R. Bergmann, *Discreet Indiscretions: The Social Organization of Gossip*, trans. John Bednarz Jr. with Eva Kafka Barron (New York: de Gruyter, 1993), as cited by Hedahl, *Listening Ministry*, pp. 89-90.

17. Hedahl, *Listening Ministry*, p. 89, my emphasis.

tanceship, and *privacy.* Gossip, she suggests in citing Bergmann's conclusions, is "a means of social control, a mechanism of preserving social groups, a technique of information management, and the social form of discreet indiscretion."[18] The following contains each of these elements. See for yourself!

The Tale of the Tropical Print Shorts

My husband, whom I had not met at the time this event took place, still remarks about the following story because he rather enjoys it. Actually, we both take pleasure in its telling and laugh about it now because it directs our attention toward the small-town nature of church life. It also underscores the public/private distinction which drives gossip as a form of information management or discreet indiscretion. I say at the outset that, fortunately, I had the good sense not to react to what was being said about me as I became the subject of gossip. How did I arrive at this wisdom? I had already begun my training as a marriage and family therapist, which included hours of personal therapy! In other words, it wasn't wisdom arrived at easily or hurriedly.

Now to my story. For the most part, when I served as the pastor of a congregation I wore suits or other appropriate attire, being sure, frankly, that not too much flesh was exposed. My skirts were all below-the-knee, and I wore loose-fitting dress slacks or dresses. Many individuals saw me primarily on Sundays, when I was attired in an alb. So there was nothing to see, so to speak. If there was a work day at church, I showed up in jeans and a t-shirt like everyone else. How I dressed on my own time, however, was a different story. This was perceived by church members as "secret information." Notice now that how I ordinarily dressed in public was not the issue (except for the time an attorney friend of mine gave me an *expensive* purple suit; but that's another story. It still hangs in the back of my closet because one day I am going to purchase a red hat to wear with it!). The issue was how I dressed at home, because that had the status of "secret information."

It was a particularly hot, humid summer afternoon in southeastern Pennsylvania. I had been washing my car in front of the parsonage on my

18. Bergmann, *Discreet Indiscretions,* p. vi, as cited by Hedahl, *Listening Ministry,* p. 90.

day off, and happened to be wearing brightly colored, tropical print *shorts* (maybe a little too short, I admit, to be worn on church property) and a tank top. It was getting late on a Friday, and as I was finishing up the florist delivered the Sunday altar flowers at his customary time. When he saw me he expressed his amazement: "Are you really allowed to dress like that?!" I no longer remember exactly how I replied, but I shrugged off his comment. This should have been my cue to use more caution. But I was only thinking about finishing my task and getting inside out of the heat and humidity. Finishing up with the car, I decided to retrieve the day's mail from the mailbox on the main road in town in my tropical print shorts. It's worth noting that the church was just across the street from the police department, senior center, and various other township buildings, in a town with a population of approximately 55,000. I served a congregation of 500 members. What were the odds that one of them would drive by while I strolled out to collect the mail? I'm sure there is someone who will read this essay that is able to do the math. At any rate, by now you may have surmised that someone *did,* in fact, drive by at that precise moment, only to see me in plain view at the mailbox in my tropical print shorts.

I am now quite certain that much of the time which elapsed from Friday afternoon until Sunday morning was spent by church members in conversation about my attire. Why? Because by 7:45 a.m. there were some members of the congregation who proceeded to inform me upon their arrival on Sunday morning, with smirks on their faces, that the word was out: *"Pastor, we heard you were in your shorts at the mailbox."* With a grin on my own face, I immediately replied, "I suppose it could have been worse. I might have been wearing a swim suit. I was washing my car." At that point, someone else entered into the conversation with, "Didn't you know she reads on the deck behind the house in her bikini?" In that moment I didn't even want to imagine how the details of the story had been embellished. I didn't wear a bikini, but if they wanted to think so . . . that was fine with me. Honestly, I was a little stunned that my shorts had created such a stir, but I worked hard not to become defensive about my choice.

One may wonder why my shorts did create such a stir. I've already shared the fact that I was the only ordained woman in town. I need to add here that the women of the church, in particular, were very protective of me and my reputation because some of the women of *other* local Protestant churches had remarked upon my arrival, "Maybe she'll build you up enough so that you can afford to hire a man next time." This comment did not sit well with the church matriarchs and they were determined to demonstrate to their friends in the community that the congregation had not made a mistake. I had momentarily forgotten an essential of church life — I represented them in the larger community.

A sense of humor and the ability to take a step off the "dance floor" of congregational life is absolutely necessary if one is going to be able to maintain a flexible and non-defensive, non-anxious perspective. In this instance I needed to be able to laugh at myself and with the members of the church, rather than to hear what was being said as criticism or as a threat to my pastoral authority. It is certainly the case that I could have gone back inside to change before I went to get the mail, but I didn't. They good-naturedly feigned shock at the scandal of the tropical print shorts, but deep down they were glad to know that I was one of them. I was beginning to relax enough so that my new location felt like a home and they like members of my family.

The Trivia Interpreted

What may at first seem like trivial details of this personal anecdote upon further examination illustrate how the various aspects of gossip come to life in a congregation having positive value. If we think about the three constitutive elements of gossip — absence, acquaintanceship, and privacy — we will begin to see how my story does conform to an academic understanding of gossip even while it illumines the vital role gossip plays in congregational life. I was not absent from the congregation in this instance; although it was my day off, I was still on church-owned property. However, my absence could be construed as time I spent apart from the membership. In general, they respected my time off as well as my privacy. This event did concern my *acquaintanceship* with them and my *privacy.* They wouldn't have talked about this incident had they not had an existing relationship with me and not been curious about how I spent my personal or private time. I was still "the new kid on the block." How, then, was "the tale of the tropical print shorts" moral discourse? Well, certainly they had seen their previous ministers wear shorts. But those pastors were men. I was a woman minister, and they needed to conduct some comparison studies concerning what was acceptable behavior for a minister who happened to be a woman in public on her day off. This was new territory to be traversed. They wondered about how my donning of tropical print shorts might affect my ministry or the performance of my ministerial obligations. And I still wonder if the florist was the first tattle tale.

Previous pastors, all of whom were male, did wear shorts in public; but denim or khaki ones with a t-shirt, not a tank top. Did the fact that I was wearing shorts, and tropical print ones, no less, influence the way members of the community at large might perceive me or the congregation? This was their concern. They were, in effect, making allowances and adjustments for my behavior, but they were also wanting, in some way, to protect me from what might otherwise be vicious tongues in the community. I never did dispose of the shorts. But never again did I retrieve the mail attired that way either. Furthermore, if I chose to wash my car, I generally did so when visiting my parents, who lived in another town. How, then, does the trivia of my experience illustrate some of the functions of gossip?

The retelling of the tale did function as a means of social control since I quit wearing *those shorts* in any location where I might be spied. I modified my behavior in response to the gossip. They were looking out for my best interest. Second, gossip as a mechanism of preserving social groups was evident in their collective fear that someone in the larger community would speak ill of me and, subsequently, of the church. My reputation needed to remain untarnished if the church was going to become more visible in the community. (Although one could argue that I had made great strides in increasing our visibility!) As an aside, despite the fact that they were located at one of the most traveled intersections in town, very few people knew the church was there because it was a tiny building situated on a large lot with a long setback from the road. Third, gossip as a technique of information management is observed by the fact that everyone now knew the pastor washed her own car and dressed for the occasion; but also, and perhaps more importantly, the pastor knew she was being observed on her day off at her own home. Finally, gossip as a social form of discreet indiscretion was at work because everyone enjoyed some levity at my expense, but they didn't wait too long before I was included. It isn't as if they had purchased an ad in the local paper announcing my indiscretion.

In addition, we ought not to forget Lischer's thesis that gossip is a way to forgive old offenses. It wasn't exactly an old offense, but I was already loved in this community and forgiven for my social indiscretion of wearing tropical print shorts at the mailbox, where anyone in this suburb could observe me. At any point in the give-and-take between me and members of the congregation, I could have opted to become angry, reactive, and defensive because the banter continued for some weeks beyond that Sunday morning; but I didn't. I listened intuitively for the historical and moral precedents embedded in the chatter. I knew that I still had much to learn from this community and they were most willing to instruct.

Gossip as Gracious Give-and-Take

Had I chosen to respond in a reactive manner, what became a grace note could have been career-ending or, at the very least, career-altering. What on the face of it may have appeared to be idle chatter and rumors was converted into grace. Like a musical grace note, this anecdote upon first reading may seem rather insignificant. However small, it was nevertheless an embellishment in my pastoral ministry. The chatter only appeared to be idle because at a deeper level it served a purpose — my edification in the responsibilities of being a pastor; and it opened up the possibility for a deeper spiritual relationship with the congregation I served. We now shared a connection we hadn't enjoyed previously. Lischer understands gossip to be a community's continuing education. The reworking of our shared stories in the form of gossip, he notes, "helps soften the edges of people who are simply too accessible to one another, who irritate one another to death, but who can't escape one another or their common history. Gossip also explains peculiarities, and tells how they came to be."[19] Lischer has it right. I was embraced as one of them, and no longer viewed as the "preppy pastor" who came from a community which was very different from the one I now lived in.

Gossip depends on oral tradition and the spoken word, which is to say that the written word is no substitute for gossip. Why? Again, I refer to Lischer's observations: "Gossip requires repetition and give-and-take. It relies on the nuanced reply, subtle changes, and intensification that occur in even the most scrupulously repeated message. These happen only in the spoken word. The printed word emanates from a central power source in

19. Lischer, *Open Secrets*, p. 96.

the town — the newspaper or the church newsletter. Gossip is decentered speech that belongs to the entire community."[20] I was the central actor in this little story but I did not own it. Needless to say, the story was repeated many times, often in a stage whisper, in the weeks immediately following my excursion to the mailbox. But I am certain that it was long ago forgotten. The details of what I was wearing were embellished and they changed over time. The changes depended on the one who was engaged in the telling and his or her relationship to me. I expect that the members of Peace Lutheran Church, which I left to attend graduate school more than a decade ago, would be surprised to learn that our shared history will now appear in print. It is their story as much as it is my story. For the many things they taught me, some of which came with my wearing those tropical print shorts, I am and will always be grateful.

Gossip Requires Triadic Relationships

Thus far, I have spoken about the subject of this gossip — me. What about the one who observed me or "stole" the information and then recounted it to a listener who also had a relationship with me? The one who witnessed my appearance in tropical print shorts eventually confessed. As a matriarch she was taking care of her "children." What is significant about that? The one who "opens the secret," as it were, or the one who does the gossiping "externalizes what is internal."[21] In my own illustration, the gossiper was someone who just happened by the church as I was headed for the mailbox. The internal or inside information was generally what I did, where I went, and, in this case, what I wore on my day off. What made this incident an externalization of what was internal is that I was oblivious to the fact that I was being watched at that moment. Now, one could argue that I should have known better, but I simply wanted to retrieve the mail before I retired inside for the rest of the day. The driveway of the parsonage was generally hidden from the view of passersby. The only reason the florist had a sighting was that he came up the very long driveway to enter the church. The matriarch had access to information that no one else had only by chance.

The gossiper does at least momentarily enjoy a raised status in the

20. Lischer, *Open Secrets*, p. 101.
21. Hedahl, *Listening Ministry*, p. 90.

community. If you want to know something, ask "so-and-so." Knowledge is power. It should come as no surprise to anyone that this particular matriarch was often the source of confidential knowledge within the community. The habitual gossiper is like the old-fashioned switchboard operator: "His or her reputation and position within the gossip triad is essentially determined by the potential and factual access he or she has to the unequally distributed information about another's private life and the extent to which the dissemination of this information is subject to socially enforced restrictions."[22] This matriarch did, in many ways, have more access to information because she was an elected member of the church governing body; but in this instance access to information was a matter of chance. If the one sharing the information does so in a destructive manner it ceases to be a ministry-enhancing grace note. But then, in all probability, the gossiper also has violated socially enforced restrictions.

Now, what of the one who engages in the listening task? It isn't gossip unless I have a relationship with the one who is the subject of the gossip. If I receive gossip then I become a "co-informer," according to Hedahl. I now share something with the gossiper that I didn't before and I'm a bit tainted, morally speaking. Hedahl reminds us of what we already know to be true: "As the pastoral leader listens to the individual and to the group, it is important to appreciate the functions gossip plays in a faith community."[23] How are those engaged in ministry to become more appreciative? We need to listen for the meanings embedded in and beneath the mere facts. We need to recognize that gossip does have a salutary function and not every story shared about the minister needs to be interpreted as a form of personal attack. We do well to reflect on such questions as these: What does it mean when these specific people of God relate this particular story or respond to a given situation at this particular point in time? Why these particular facts, these certain words, and not others? Meaning is discerned in a context.

A Few Final Grace Notes

My context, or the congregation described herein, self-identified as "blue collar." This self-identification was so intense that I nicknamed the presi-

22. Bergmann, *Discreet Indiscretions*, pp. 66-67, as cited by Hedahl, *Listening Ministry*, p. 90.

23. Hedahl, *Listening Ministry*, p. 90.

dent of the congregation "Mr. Blue Collar." Why is this important to mention here? It also became a grace note that *happened* shortly after I arrived. The congregation had my resume and had made their interpretations about it after hearing a few of my sermons. One Sunday after services, "Mr. Blue Collar" entered my office and announced, "You know, we're blue collar here." Evidently, my literary allusions were not well-received and were most definitely a source of "gossip." I could have taken offense, felt rejected, and started the search for a new call. Instead, I listened to the deeper meanings embedded in the text: they wanted a pastor who cared enough about them to take an interest in what was important in *their* lives. Message received. I had to work diligently at adopting a more narrative preaching style, but it paid enormous dividends. As Capps suggests, "[t]here is power in this freedom to enter imaginatively into the life of another."[24] As my preaching took more of an interest in their lives, our relationship deepened and so did our mutual trust. Capps concludes that without gossip there would be no gospels. The gospels are what provide us with a sense of what it means to be an "intimate of Jesus."[25]

Gossip was (and still is) the source of the grace notes in my pastoral ministry. The testimony to this truth came at my farewell banquet as I prepared to depart for graduate school. They had imparted their wisdom and were ready to let me go. I wasn't certain that I was ready to leave. After dinner was shared, the youngest child in the Sunday School came forward with a brightly wrapped package; a group gift from the Sunday School. I was asked to open it before the entire congregation with all eyes upon me. Inside, on a cushion of white tissue paper, was a hand-made stole in white with many handprints, large and small, upon it. Whenever I wear this stole I continue to be embraced. I will never forget all the lives that touched and transformed mine even as I touched theirs.[26]

24. Capps, *Living Stories*, p. 191.
25. Capps, *Living Stories*, p. 191.
26. Some of the ideas and stories contained in this essay were originally presented in a lecture during the "School for Pastors" sponsored by the Omaha Presbyterian Seminary Foundation at Hastings College in Nebraska in July 2004.

17. Three Teachers

Loren B. Mead

Miss Florence

It was a hot day. Most days were, I discovered; and no place was air-conditioned. It was over a generation ago, and it was a culture that exists today only in areas far off the beaten track. Television existed, but it didn't matter much because nobody had decent sets. Ours was a seven-inch, on which our four-year-old and two-year-old watched Davy Crockett on the wild frontier.

Her name was Florence Lucas. Everybody knew her as "Miss Florence." She buttonholed me at the post office. That was where everybody met (if you wanted to meet anybody), but many people never went there. I'd walked up the dusty main road a couple of hundred yards from my office. She was coming out; I was going in. "I need help," she said. I hadn't been in town long. It was my first pastoral appointment and about all the bishop had said about it was that it was in an area of the state with a growing industrial base. (More on that later!) I recognized Miss Florence. She lived with her bachelor brother and was a fixture of both the community and church where I'd had two or three weeks of leading the services.

My mind clicked onto its "pastoral" track. I began to think of things that "might" come up. I'd already learned that alcoholism was a kind of epidemic in the community. I thought, since I was deep in rural country, of some of Liston Pope's writing about North Carolina. I wondered about the implications of local racial issues. Nothing had been said, but I'd seen the black Baptist congregation down the road and I'd heard there was a black Reformed Episcopal congregation somewhere in town. The *Brown v. Board of Education* court decision had just been handed down, which focused on the county next to ours. I braced myself to deal with the subconscious fundamentalism I'd already discovered people lived by, regardless of what the local clergy preached. "What in the world *does* she need help with?" I thought.

Trying not to tip her off to the variety of possibilities running through my head, I said, "Well, Miss Florence, what seems to be the problem?" "I'm in charge of altar flowers for the altar guild this year," she said. "Oh, no," I thought. "What's an altar guild?" Maybe I exaggerate. I *had* heard there was such a thing. I thought I remembered that my mother had occasionally been a part of such a group in the parish in which I'd grown up. I flipped through my memory banks, but the screen came up blank. She charged ahead: "My problem is that I need to make plans for Advent and Lent, and I need to know whether we are going to have flowers on the altar then!"

I hadn't a clue. I didn't know exactly what the altar guild was and I didn't know they had anything to do with flowers. I knew there was a season called Advent and another called Lent. I knew clergy wore purple stoles around their neck at services at those times. I knew that because the clergy wives (in those days all the clergy were men and most of them had wives, even in seminary) had sewing groups at seminary to make stoles for their husbands. I racked my brain, but all the screens were still blank. Nobody had said anything in three years of seminary that gave me a clue.

So I hung there with my mouth open, not knowing what was at stake or what to say. But I knew enough to know that this was an important question, the answer to which Miss Florence was dying for me to tell her. It felt like one of those "make-or-break" moments.

What in the world was the answer? Was there some liturgical rule about this? My mind flipped to our liturgy class. Nothing. Was there some existential meaning involved? Seminarians' minds usually tried to find the existential meaning in those days. I think it was something Niebuhr was into; or was it Tillich or Bultmann? If there was any guidance there I couldn't find it. Was it from the Reformation? Maybe the Oxford movement? I had a feeling I was getting warm, but anything solid simply eluded me.

I gave up. And I saved my life and my ministry. Very humbly, I said, "Thank you for asking, Miss Florence. What did we do last year?" Pow! It worked like a charm. I didn't even know what I was doing, but I gave her something that worked.

What was really more important in the long run was that I did not really give her my answer. Actually, as I've already confessed, I didn't have an answer. It was only much later, reflecting on that experience and many others that I discovered what really happened in that short exchange, what was really important. I discovered that I didn't have to have an answer. I discovered, too, that other people *had* answers. Indeed, in many, many situations they had answers that were deeper, better, and more appropriate than anything I could think up. I didn't realize it then, but I chose a mode of ministry then that has saved me many, many times since. I discovered that ministry is less about giving out my answers and more about helping people discover their own answers. What a burden it is to have to have an answer to all the questions. How heavy it is to be the only one who *has* the answers. Or to *think* you are!

I think I came out of seminary, with its models and methods of teaching and learning, with a subconscious sense that every encounter was like a little examination. At my first vestry meeting everybody would be waiting to see if I "passed," if I got it right. That's not the fault of the seminary. It was *my* immaturity and fragile sense of identity that made me react that way. I sort of thought I was in a game with a winning side and a losing side, an adversarial game. My response to Miss Florence — which came merely out of stupidity and anxiety, not wisdom — served to turn my ministry toward being a team sport. Miss Florence wasn't my adversary, trying to catch me out. She knew stuff I needed to know. She was part of a system of ministry that I was joining. Since then, I've realized that if I *had* given her an answer, I would have been using misplaced authority to change the ministry we shared, "our ministry," into a solo project, "my ministry."

Her question was an invitation into a larger, better sense of ministry. I was ordained and installed already, but she invited me to start trying to join in *real* ministry with them. I think that's when my ordination really started to happen. Fifty years later, it's still happening! Miss Florence taught me, without knowing she was teaching me, that a minister, a pastor, a priest doesn't have to have the answers.

Fast forward fifty years. Long after it happened, I kept running into what I learned in that short exchange with Miss Florence. In the 1970s and 1980s, in research we were carrying out at the Alban Institute on what we called "Crossing the Boundary" — the boundary being the one between seminary and congregation — we kept rediscovering that theologically trained people carry all sorts of assumptions with them into their first appointment or placement. An almost universal assumption was the one witnessed to above, namely, that the minister, pastor, or priest carries with him or her the authority to *give* all the necessary answers. Somewhere along the way we are taught, or we learn, or we just observe, that the pastor is responsible for charting the course. It was only when I began to work with the idea of interim ministry — which was around 1975 — that I got hold of the basic issue. Ordained people somehow pick up a realization which gets stuck in their bones, namely, that when they go into a congregation it's their job to remake, reshape, or otherwise take control of ministry. They "own" ministry. An army chaplain articulated it most clearly when I asked him how he adapted to starting new jobs with each three-year appointment. "Well," he drawled — we were at Fort Knox in Kentucky and he sounded like a Kentuckian, or maybe an Alabamian — "I just go in assuming they never had ministry until I got there."

I began learning from Miss Florence that this was hogwash. I began learning then, and now I teach enthusiastically, that ministry is resident in the people already and that the pastor therefore has three primary tasks. The first is to enter that community of ministry sensitively, with one's eyes, ears, and self truly open to honor that ministry. The second task involves discerning how one's own special gifts for ministry might be used to strengthen weaknesses, whether in parishioners or in yourself, to adjust things that are not going well, and occasionally to encourage new things being raised up to be part of that ongoing ministry. The third task involves trying, when the appropriate time comes, to leave respectfully, without damaging either the congregation or yourself, both asking for and giving forgiveness for the life you've all shared.

Preston

His name was Preston. I remember him clear as a bell. Tall, imposing, and usually impeccably dressed, he wasn't an "every Sunday member," but more an occasional one. A few months went by without his being there even once or twice to offer his strong voice and very pleasant presence. He was a powerful man in the town. He served on the important committees. He carried himself with confidence and security. He also seemed pretty well-to-do, living in a lovely house in one of the best neighborhoods with his wife and widowed mother.

And very soon I realized that he bugged the hell out of me. This wasn't easy to face as a young pastor with his first pastoral charge — that one of my members who hadn't done *anything* to me simply bugged me. So I didn't allow myself to think about it. I "forgot" to do parish calls over there, although in those days these were an unwritten commandment for clergy. I didn't engage him in long conversations after church. At some level, I think I was ashamed of myself and really quite uncomfortable.

I got home late one night from some meeting or other. My wife Polly called to me and said, "Louise wants you to call. She called here about an hour ago." "Okay," I responded, and gave Louise a ring. Louise, incidentally, was the one who seemed to be at the center of all the networks and grapevines. She always heard things first. When I got her a few minutes later, I said, "Hi, Louise. It's Loren. What's up?" She said, "Monica just phoned to tell me that Preston's mother had a heart attack this afternoon, and that she passed away about supper time." (That reminds me. In that part of the world *nobody* ever "died," they all "passed away." Over the years there, and in other places, I discovered that every community has a language culture of its own!)

I mouthed platitudes to Louise, saying how awful that was to hear, and asking whether she had been in pain and if the family had arrived yet. It turned out that Preston was home, and that his wife, brother, and son were there, too. I mumbled something to the effect that I'd go right over.

And to my dismay, I knew I *had* to. I mean, I was the pastor. I *had* to go. When somebody's Momma dies, the pastor's *got* to go; even if it's somebody you don't feel good about, someone — it began getting clearer — who *bugs* you and, more than that, *intimidates* you, somebody who's self-confident when you're not. When somebody's Momma dies, the pastor *has* to go and *has* to give comfort and tell them about God and Jesus and heaven and angels. I mean, that's what I'm *paid* for, isn't it? Even if I'm not up to it!

Somewhere about then — as this was going through my mind — something else occurred to me. I didn't know what to say. I wasn't all that clear about how God and Jesus and death fit together. I wasn't sure what "life after death" meant. I knew my Paul and all his gobbledygook about spiritual bodies — a few things about some Greek words like *pneuma* and *sarx* — but I hadn't a clue about what I could say to this fine, imposing citizen who seemed to have it made. His *Momma* had died. What was I to tell him about that? I felt stupid. And I didn't have time to study up on it.

I recall thinking about that as I walked slowly out to my 1949 Ford.

"Maybe it won't start," I thought, "it's been hard to start all this week!" I grasped for every straw I could think of as I cranked the motor, and when it started I headed out for the mile or so trip between my house and Preston's. I went around his block twice before I stopped. Then I made myself get out of the car and start up the walkway, dragging my feet all the way. The thing that took me up that long walk was complete heresy, but it got me there. I'm embarrassed now even to tell what it was. I thought how hard it must have been for God to send Jesus into the world. Maybe I was feeling just a taste of something that connected with the Big Story. I got to the door, consciously thinking to myself "If God could do what he did, I can push this stupid doorbell." So I did. I was absolutely empty. I had no idea of what to say. I had no wisdom to impart. I was scared and not a little resentful.

Preston opened the wooden door, then pushed open the screen door. "Loren," he said, "I'm so glad you came. Come on in. I've just poured myself a drink. Can I get you one?" Then, he hugged me! Me, the stupid, inarticulate fraud on his front step. After that we went in, all of us sat down, and we talked about his mother and about him and about family and friends. We talked about hymns they'd all loved and why. He talked about his mother taking him to Sunday school when he was a boy. And somehow, in the middle of it all, ministry happened. In the talking and the telling of stories, in the laughing and, indeed, a few tears, all of us were moved. I'm not kidding that we were *all* moved. Something deep inside me, something that had sharp claws in my guts, eased off; and I became a better friend to Preston and to myself, and probably a better pastor to a lot of people from then on.

While I had been working off the assumption that I was the God specialist, and that my job was to bring God into the situation, I found out that God was already there. God didn't depend on me to fix it. Peculiarly, I also learned something almost the opposite of that. I learned that although the ministry was already in good hands and did not depend on me, when I relaxed, listened, and entered into the moment, my being there was quite important. My contributions weren't words. What helped most was something about the pastor just being there.

Manney

My strongest, early memories of being a new pastor have to do with loneliness. Some of the loneliness I experienced was circumstantial. In my day, newly ordained Episcopal clergy were assigned by their bishop to whatever job they had that commanded a salary, wherever and whatever it was. Most of us got posted to far-out, rural places with no nearby colleagues. I got sent to a small church in a place called Hell Hole Swamp. No kidding! And I found that the judicatory system and bishop, much as they tried, weren't able to help much. Let me name one thing that happened. When my bishop said I'd be posted to a place in a "growing industrial area" of the diocese, I decided to do my own data gathering. So I wrote to the state government's develop-ment office to find out what I could about the county where I'd been placed. I got hundreds of graphs and pages of data. I culled them down until I had the page that described the distribution of jobs among the population. In that county there were about 30,000 people. The data showed the following: Unemployed, 2,500; Agriculture, 11,000; Forestry, 7,000. Professionals, 500; Business and Marketing, 4,000; Education, 3,500; and so on, with several other categories listed. Finally, I got to Employment in Industry, 3. *Three!* Not three *hundred,* not *three thousand,* but *three.* Since that time I've gener-ally read information from my judicatory with a grain of salt.

The "mentor" my bishop assigned to me turned out to be both an al-coholic and a sexual predator (we called them "womanizers" in those an-cient days), and I never had a phone call or visit from him in my time there. As a result, I had two options for community with peers — ecumenical con-nections or my denominational colleagues. The ecumenical connections were very difficult to make. In very small towns the rivalry between denom-inations and congregations can be very caustic. Congregations were, *all* of them, conscious of their fragility, even those that were much larger than we were. When a new dentist and his family moved to town there was an evan-gelistic feeding frenzy among the congregations — and the pastors. One new professional who was a strong contributor could make the difference between a year in the red and a year in the black. We never talked about that, but that anxiety lay not very far below the surface. Years later, living in a university town whose professional schools spawned people moving out to be lawyers, doctors, and dentists in very small towns, I frequently urged them to prepare themselves for that difficult dimension of small-town life. To a new person in such towns, "evangelism" sometimes feels like a college fraternity's or sorority's "rush week," with more than a little psychological pressure to make the "right" choice.

Another unhelpful dimension of ecumenical collegiality was the level of prejudice we carried in us and with us. I won't tell you about the terrible things I said or thought about the extreme evangelicals among us. I am still ashamed of some of the disrespectful ideas I harbored. And I remember some of the cheap shots I took as pastor of a small Episcopal church: "Oh yes. You're the people who drink, aren't you?" And "Is it true that in your church you use *another* book?" And "You people ought to have your services at the Country Club since that's where all your members are on Sunday!" And "People say you all don't believe in the Bible, but are revisionists. Is that true?" I guess I did my best not to take offense, but it was hard to feel very trusting or collegial with people who joked about you that way. Even about the parts that were partly true!

Because it wasn't easy to find collegiality with pastors of other denominations, we organized a group of pastors and spouses from our own denomination who met monthly for covered-dish suppers and conversation. This was not something that was "laid on" for us. We had to invent it. And for some of us it meant a commute of an hour and a half each way. It wasn't long in that configuration before we discovered that meeting as couples did not give us immunity from the less pleasant parts of clergy collegiality, including our ability to be critical and unforgiving, and to become a center of gossip and backbiting ourselves. Our desire to get ahead, even of our colleagues, was sharp and often controlled us. I remember one time, after dinner, we waxed eloquent about a critical issue in denominational life, focusing on one of our colleagues who was — we were unanimous in thinking — spectacularly wrong. The conversation gradually turned nasty and personal about him. And I remember with gratitude the way one of our number, Manney, interrupted his Christian brothers and sisters. He said, "Wait a minute! What are we doing here? It sounds like we're ganging up on a guy who can't even defend himself." He went on, "We don't treat each other like this!" In saying that he called us back to ourselves. He also exercised ministry in us and to us. I learned a lot then, and I'm remembering it half a century later. A demonic spirit had taken over our fine Christian meeting. But because one in the group came to his senses and called us back, we all turned around. Isn't that what "repenting" means? We learned that we not only were in ministry, were part of God's ministry, but, more than we wished, we were deeply in need of ministry ourselves. And frequently we were resistant to it.

I've now spent more than fifty years in ordained ministry. The three lessons I've outlined here I've had to learn and relearn innumerable times.

Often the relearning has come with renewed pain and sometimes with new dimensions of awareness. I have no doubt that the learning will go on as long as I live, and that there are painful lessons yet ahead of me. But I know in my bones how true it is that I don't have, or have to have, the answers to ministry — that the people of the church have a great store of wisdom and experience to offer, to others and to me. It's a store I can learn from and contribute to.

I know also that wherever I go or wherever I'm called, the Lord precedes and follows. I do not have to carry God on my back or see myself as God's messenger. God is already there and will meet me wherever he calls me to go.

And I know this can be a lonely calling, but it is one in which we can support, strengthen, and send each other, especially if we open ourselves to our colleagues both to give and to receive.

18. Bearing a Memory, Sticking Out
Like a Sore Thumb, Expressing a Hope

Theodore J. Wardlaw

I must begin by stressing that my theological education in the late 1970s was a transformative experience — one that turned me upside down and inside out. Union Theological Seminary in Virginia received me from the ranks of the church with the admonition from a former Sunday School teacher, "Don't you let them change you!" still ringing in my ears. And then it did just that. Seminary changed me in ways that I will always appreciate. It created, almost immediately, a necessary (even if occasionally uncomfortable) distance from a lifetime of formation in a series of Presbyterian congregations in South Carolina and Georgia. It introduced me to what I then thought was a new world. I know now that in fact it was a very old world, one built upon a classical foundation of Reformed theology and ethos, biblical scholarship, church history, and the like, and infused from start to finish with an uncompromising ethic of what one professor after another called "the stewardship of the mind." Within that new-old world I was given the gift of critical distance for the first time in my life. This distance from life at the congregational level gave me room to explore, weigh, sometimes reconsider, and sometimes reinvest in a realm of theological *and* churchly values that had simply been givens prior to my time at seminary. Four years later I came out a different person.

Then, because of a graduate fellowship from Union, I spent another year at Yale Divinity School where I earned a Master of Sacred Theology degree. There, too, in a far more diverse denominational and theological polyglot in the unfamiliarity of the Northeast, I encountered yet more space for new ideas and insights to flourish. I discovered, once again, the learning environment this new space created. I felt like a kid in a candy store.

To this day, I uphold the intentional creation of such academic distance in the context of theological education as a great value. How else would seminarians come to know what they don't know? How else would they be remotely open to the idea that maybe Moses didn't write the Pentateuch, that maybe discerning the words of Jesus is more complicated than simply looking for what is printed in red? How else would they be willing to learn some new hymns, even if they aren't printed in the blue hymnal? With apologies to my earnest Sunday School teacher, seminary did indeed change me — thanks be to God — and in great measure because of the blessed space it provided between me and everything I had learned before.

All of that said, however, it was the same distance that I had to negotiate once more when moving finally from the academy back to the parish. As I look back on it now, many of us in possession of new insights from seminary-land were altogether too prematurely certain about them as we marched back across that distance as if on a grim errand. We were in possession, after all, of some bad news for the church. We had to inform the church, for starters, that preaching was probably on the way out, and that we all would have to figure out what to do in its place (show a movie? read a story?). We had much to teach the church about what it had been doing wrong, sometimes for centuries, with respect to its worship. We had to let the church know that ministry would henceforth be far more professionalized. Many of us, after all, were in possession now of Doctor of Ministry degrees earned in four years of seminary education (instead of Master of Divinity degrees earned in three). These D.Min. degrees, like M.D.'s for doctors or J.D.'s for lawyers, would place us far more solidly within the ranks of professionals possessing certain "competencies," rather than of those servant leaders from the past possessing merely "callings."

We would have to teach our parishioners to respect our newly defined boundaries regarding time. Days off would be like personal Sabbaths; and even if the clerk of session died while we were on vacation the folks back home would have to understand why we could not interrupt our seasons of renewal to return for the funeral. We would have to find ways to share with them, as they were ready to hear it, all of the many, many things that were out-of-date and would have to change. Armed with our strategies to demythologize, ecumenize, therapize, professionalize, and Schallerize, we marched back across that distance between academy and parish imagining that, at best, we would get to our destinations just in the nick of time.

Since my hope had been to go straight from Yale to an inner-city parish, my first stop was the last setting in the world that I thought I wanted — an associate pastor position in an affluent congregation in suburban Memphis. But the great and enduring value of the lessons I learned in that place revealed itself with time, and being there for three years became a deeply cherished experience. Why? *Because of what they had to teach me, once I discovered (ironically) that I, too, and not just they, needed a teachable spirit.* I learned in that wonderful church that one's theological education is never adequately imparted just in seminary, but ought to continue in every setting of ministry thereafter. This is worth remembering, by the way, in a time when seminaries are often accosted for not teaching a whole range of things, as if the church itself is not also a center for lifelong theological learning. Now I know that every congregation I served was, in very specific and important ways, a teaching congregation.

Almost immediately, that church in suburban Memphis began teaching me the first of three enduring lessons I have learned over and over again: the church is a memory-bearing institution, often more watchful than its pastors concerning what about itself dare not be forgotten.

A Memory-Bearing Community

I remember vividly the occasion when I began learning this lesson. It was a Sunday morning, shortly after my installation at Germantown Presbyterian Church in Germantown, Tennessee, and I was standing in the pulpit before the 8:30 service going over the sermon I would soon preach. A member of the chancel guild was trying to figure out where to place the flowers in the chancel. "Pastor," she finally said to me in exasperation. "Could you help me figure out where this flower arrangement will look best? Here's my problem: If I place it here in the middle of the Lord's Table, these tall stems hide the cross. But if I place it on this pedestal to the left of the table, then it throws off the symmetry of things and fights with the banner to the right and the pulpit to the left of the chancel. I could just elevate the cross a bit by putting it on top of a stack of hymnals, and then put the flowers there, but then that might block a good view of the choir. I wonder if . . ."

"Oh, it doesn't matter to me," I said brusquely, more intent on getting ready to preach than on listening to her dilemma. "Do whatever you want to do about the flowers; after all, nothing up here is that sacred."

She pulled herself up to full height and said sternly: "Young man, I was baptized at that font back there. My daughter marched down this very aisle a few years ago to get married in this very spot. Then, too soon, my husband was buried from this church. I'll thank you to remember that, as far as I'm concerned, virtually everything in this church, in this chancel, is sacred."

Her rejoinder was perhaps the first of many such encounters that startled me into examining with appropriate reverence the important role the church plays as a memory-bearing institution. There is, after all, in every church something profoundly healthy and formative embedded within the memories that it nourishes. Any minister coming in fresh from seminary and filled to overflowing with all of its "superior knowledge" would do well to check smugness at the door and to listen attentively for the evidence of what in fact is sacred, and of enduring value, in the church's memory.

In his wonderful memoir, *Open Secrets,* Richard Lischer recalls his first Sunday after being ordained and installed in his first church, a small Lutheran congregation in rural Illinois. During his preparations for worship on that Sunday morning Lischer encountered the ghastly sight of his predecessor, Erich Martin — now weakened and bald from cancer and unable to sit in a pew, and thus sprawled out in relative comfort on a chaise lounge in the sacristy. From there, he could participate in the service by watching Lischer in the chancel through a partially-opened sacristy door. There he was, dressed in his customary cassock, surplice, and stole, and lying there in the chaise lounge with a hymnal opened across his lap. Over the months to come, Lischer would become accustomed to the sight of this liturgically vested dying man worshiping in the room off to the right. "I never met anyone," he writes, "less absorbed in himself or driven by a personal agenda than Erich. Unlike the therapeutically trained cleric, Erich did not compulsively insist on being a friend or a pal to his parishioners. He was not, as one of my friends says of Protestant ministers in general, 'a quivering mass of availability.' He did not personalize his every act of ministry. Unlike ministers who make a career of getting along with people, Erich's approach was to do his duty, and to let the duties symbolize something larger and more important than his own personality."[1]

Lischer's portrait of this predecessor pastor offers a kind of paradigm

1. Richard Lischer, *Open Secrets* (New York: Random House, 2001), pp. 66-67.

of a memory-bearing church. He represents more, I suspect, than simply the anachronism that many thoroughly contemporary pastors and polemicists would paint him to be. In their arrogance and premature certainty, they might look upon him with pity. After all, he appears so clunky there in his cassock, so ignorant of Plexiglas pulpits and seeker-centered "worship centers" purposefully denuded of potentially offensive Christian symbology; so out of it as he clings hopelessly to yesterday's traditions; so unaware of how to fashion a church that simply "scratches where people itch"; so bald and cancerous and barely alive just like the twenty centuries of tradition-engorged Christianity that his dying faith represents.

But Erich Martin deserves a second, more appreciative look. Perhaps he is who, and where, we have been. Maybe he reminds us that we all drink from wells we didn't dig. Perhaps he invites us to look with reverence upon those others who have sat behind the desks we now sit behind, who have occupied the pulpits we now occupy. More than just this, perhaps he symbolizes a past which has formed us, a past which we dare not take for granted. If there are contemporary pastors who have been all too willing to forget the church's formative past (and their names are Legion), then there are also those others, too, who have been re-energized by its rediscovery, and who have found the humility not to trumpet such rediscoveries as new inventions.

As one who frequents antique stores, I have noticed across recent years an amazing market for old black-and-white snapshots from decades ago. My guess is that antique dealers scarf up these snapshots from those estate sales where the harried and maybe indifferent heirs of some departed grandmother or great-aunt gratefully unload the flotsam and jetsam that won't fit in their U-Hauls. Those snapshots bring impressive sums these days in antique stores. Sometimes I thumb through them and am moved by their sheer ordinariness. In one, several young women from the thirties pose outside a restaurant in Hahira, Georgia. In another, a hardy and grim-faced family from the early 1900s poses in front of a mud house in North Dakota. In yet another, a little girl stands to the side of a folding table bearing a birthday cake. There are ten candles on the cake, and in the background there is a camper from the forties parked amid a few scrawny trees. Maybe her family was on a cross-country trip and this picture was taken in — who knows? — Arkansas? Idaho? Wisconsin? As intriguing as these pictures are, I think there's something fundamentally sad, and instructive, about the fact that there's a market these days for the photographs of somebody else's ancestors. Does it mean that we, lost in the cosmos and disembodied from well-rehearsed stories, need to buy these snapshots, take them home, frame them and put them in our dens so as to remember that we didn't get here on our own?

Erich Martin — almost a snapshot, an antique, himself — reminds us that theologically speaking we are not orphans at all. All dressed up in his ancient vestments and parked there in that sacristy amid equally ancient accoutrements of Christian worship, he reminds us that, at our faithful best, we pastors and church people emerge from, and do our best to assist in telling, an old, old story.

And because it is not just a story about the past, but also about the present, the church's story sticks out like a sore thumb. In fact, I believe that, in these days, the essential strangeness of this story — the utter impossibility of its being easily digested by our culture — is profoundly more noticeable than it was when I was in seminary. This is the second enduring thing I have learned thus far from the church across the years of my ministry: at its best, it is fundamentally countercultural.

A Countercultural Community

If theologians like Douglas John Hall, Stanley Hauerwas, and others are right about the ongoing demise of Constantinian Christianity in North America (and I believe they are), the news of that demise came relatively late to the part of the world in which I grew up. In the years of my childhood and adolescence, the symbology of Christian faith was as much a natural part of the landscape of my social location as was being a member of Rotary. Public school was opened at the beginning of each day with a morning devotional being read over the loudspeaker, and, depending on the flavor of Protestantism subscribed to by the particular kid reading it, that devotional came straight from the quarterly booklet of one of a handful of mainline denominations. High school football games began with a prayer offered by a local clergyman, one that always ended with ". . . through Jesus Christ our Lord." The mailman invited new residents in the community to visit his church on an upcoming Sunday, and the guy selling them their home insurance was as likely as not to offer his personal testimonial. If you were the child of a local mainline pastor, as I was, you could get a "ministerial discount" at the local department store when purchasing a new pair of khaki pants or oxblood Weejuns or whatever else. The faith was as much a part of the fabric of things as Sunday lunch at the cafeteria where anyone could get ten percent off the price of the meal if they presented to the cashier the bulletin from their church. You could practically drink the water in any town in South Carolina and become a Baptist or Methodist. In my growing-up years there, I was immersed in the respectability of Culture Protestantism. The faith of the church, all mannerly and deferential, didn't stick out at all.

Seminary did not do enough to shake me of such a well-behaved faith. It was as much a stakeholder in that culture in those days, after all, as was the denomination that it endeavored to serve. We took clinical pastoral education in local hospitals and proudly donned the white coats and beepers that made us look like doctors; and some of us, I must admit, felt more culturally legitimized by those white coats and beepers than we would ever have felt by the clerical collars or pocket New Testaments of our own profession. In those settings, as in most of the internship settings we worked in, we learned the rhythms and techniques of pastoral care, careful sermon preparation, and congregational leadership. Thus armed, I entered parish ministry equipped with tools to become a useful contributor to a large, well-functioning societal machine.

But I did not learn much at all about sticking out like a sore thumb. I remember a moment in a hospital when I was serving as a pastor in a Presbyterian church on New York's Long Island. A young man in that church, a recent college graduate, had suffered a diving accident a few days earlier that had left him paralyzed from the neck down — an accident that ultimately took his life. Now he was in the intensive care unit and I was making another visit to him and to his family who had been keeping vigil there. On this particular day, his room was a flurry of activity. Several doctors and nurses were attending to him and to the various machines that were keeping him alive. As I entered the room I was sure that there was nothing I could offer that would be equal to that situation. Everyone in the room possessed an urgently-needed skill and was doing something critically necessary. The mission that had brought me there was the only thing, I was sure, that could wait until later.

His mother came over and hugged me, thanked me for coming, and, amid all of the whirring and beeping of machines and the terribly essential medical information being barked back and forth, I said to her, "Well, all I was going to do was just offer a prayer; I'll come back when things settle down a bit." She said with bold conviction, "Well, there's nothing that is needed in this room more than prayer, so at the moment you're the most important person here." Then she did something that I have never forgotten. She announced to every doctor and nurse in that room that I was her pastor, and she requested that we all pause so that I could pray with them for her son. All of the activity settled into a reverent pause, and I prayed.

This mother taught me more than she ever knew. She taught me about sticking out like a sore thumb. Certainly, in that New York congregation more than in any other church I served, I got a glimpse of what church life looks like in settings where there is virtually no cultural support for going to church. The impressive number of those who regularly gathered there for worship on Sunday mornings and who took part in the rest of that church's rich program life gained no social points or business advantages for being there. In that particularly post-Constantinian setting, where high school lacrosse teams scheduled Sunday morning games on the playing field a stone's throw away from our historic sanctuary, people like this mother who went to church or unashamedly called for prayer in a hospital intensive care unit, had a greater sense than I did of what was fundamentally countercultural about their faith. I began to see more and more clearly that so many people in our time seek from the church not so much an approach to faith that makes religious sense out of their secular life as they do access to an ancient rhythm that will be, by its very nature, jarring and peculiar; one that may even make them peculiar before it is finished with them. I began to see the contours of a faith that doesn't seek to accommodate itself to the world's rhythms and values, but seeks rather to stick out as the holy, disruptive, bizarre thing that it is. I began to see that the liturgical formula, "Remember your baptism and be glad," was one of the most dangerous and hope-filled phrases that I could ever utter to another person.

It's dangerous because a baptismal identity will make us odd, and in fundamental ways not conformed to the ideologies and lesser gods of our time. It's hope-filled — because it will give us different eyesight with which to see the world. This eyesight is rooted in the eschatological hope for a future in which the One who created the world will, in the fullness of time, complete the world — a world that we cannot complete by ourselves — and gather it all back into that One's loving arms.

We didn't dwell on such eschatological themes when I was in seminary. Mainline Protestants of that generation were a bit embarrassed by the unsophisticated ways in which certain more enthusiastic, Spirit-filled churches articulated these themes. We typecast their affirmations as too much "pie in the sky by-and-by when you die." We found them too certain about the furniture in heaven and the temperature in hell, and maybe we were right about that. But mainly, I suspect, we were leery both of the theological priorities they chose to accent and of their aesthetics. We didn't read the same scholars that they read. We didn't like the chaos of their worship services. We were put off by the gaudiness of their most celebrated television preachers. And so we recognized in them little value. Yet in so doing we maintained an approach to the faith that was finally too cerebral, too horizontal, and not rooted enough in the hope that comes from a hefty emphasis upon the sovereignty of God who is forever working God's purposes out.

So it was not in seminary, but in the last church I served before becoming a seminary president, that I learned most about a third enduring thing: the power of an eschatologically-oriented hope.

An Eschatological Community

It was near the end of the final Christmas Eve service at Central Presbyterian Church in Atlanta one particular year, a little after midnight. The darkened sanctuary was aglow with the light from a large roomful of hand-held candles lit from the Christ candle of the Advent wreath. Slowly, solemnly, the whole lot of us processed out to the courtyard to finish our last hymn.

I stood in that mass of humanity spilling out of the courtyard and onto the front sidewalk and surveyed the scene. In the foreground facing me and towering above us all was the church itself. Its windows were warm with color, its stone walls somehow secure and protective, its steeple held up to the sky the cross of Jesus Christ. Just beyond the sidewalk and across the street was the imposing front portico of the Georgia capitol building, magisterial and dramatic and topped with its gold dome. Off to my right, beyond a small park, was a view that all the worshipers facing me could see: city hall, a tall and handsome building twinkling with lights visible a block away through the bare limbs of trees.

In the gymnasium, located on the fifth floor of the church building on the other side of the sanctuary, were about seventy men. They slept, or prepared to sleep, on cots that would offer them hospitality and safety for the night and an opportunity to wake to warm breakfast in the morning. On the bottom two floors of that same building was a child development center. The next business day, some sixty or so office workers would bring their infants and toddlers there for another day of care. Beneath the court-yard upon which most of us were standing with our still-lit candles was a fully-equipped health clinic. Two days hence, it would be open again for business — its large waiting area crammed with street people, Spanish-speaking mothers with their babies, and various of the working poor in need of medical care. Behind me and rising four stories was the church's main education and office building, where children and adults gathered regularly for Christian formation, where choirs would gather the next Wednesday evening to practice, and where volunteers would gather again in two days to assist the staff of an Outreach Center located on the bottom floor. Above it all was a vast sky: clear and dark blue and illuminated with thousands of stars, some of which, upon second look, were moving gra-ciously in a large circle and waiting for the word from the control tower six miles south that it was time to land.

In that setting, on that Christmas Eve night, we lifted our candles high. In that setting, busy and prominent during an ordinary day but never more quiet and deserted than on that special night, we found our voices again. We sang together the last verse of the last hymn. "He rules the world," we sang, "with truth and grace, and makes the nations prove the glories of his righteousness and wonders of his love." Then, as the benedic-tion, we said antiphonally these words from the Gospel of John: "The light shines in the darkness." *"And the darkness did not overcome it."* Everything about that moment was shaped by God.

On many other days, though, the thought would cross my mind: How in the world can we make such a claim with a straight face? In a loca-tion like Central's, after all, at the absolute epicenter of the Atlanta metro-politan area, one needed no imagination to envision the pressing urban problems of poverty, racism, greed, inequity, neglect, and the whole long list. We were, as I liked to put it, "at the corner of Power and Powerless-ness."

Those who flocked to that church from more distant neighborhoods — for the rich worship, the compelling adult education classes, the forma-tion for children and youth, the choirs, the arts programs, the various out-reach ministries — had to learn to negotiate the urban challenges where nothing was subtle. Sometimes that meant stepping over a person sleeping in a doorway or entering a door manned by a uniformed security attendant. Sometimes it meant an uncomfortable confrontation between their own plenty and somebody else's dramatic need. Those who joined that church with a personal agenda to "fix" something quickly, like homelessness, joblessness, or some other social problem, were the ones who burned out first. Those who stayed were able to do so only because, sooner or later, even in the midst of the apparently insoluble brokenness of human beings and systems, they experienced somewhere in the life and witness of that church a foretaste of what the kingdom of God will look like someday when God is finished with it. They saw the power of eschatological hope.

I saw it too; many times, in fact, over the close to twelve years that I was there. I frequently saw it in worship, as I watched the grand procession of humanity. They were rich and poor; young and old; black and white and brown; gay and straight; conservative and moderate and liberal; high-church and low-church and almost-no-church. They came forward regularly to receive, and even become, the Body of Christ. I witnessed that hope in session meetings, as people dealt hospitably with one another, even when presented with dividing issues, because, as one person once put it to me, "If we're going to be together in Heaven, we may as well start learning to live together now." That hope also appeared in the courageous commitments the church was willing to make, collectively and individually, and without counting the costs, for the sake of things that mattered. In so many places such as these I saw a faith which is not based on evidence, but rather upon the sturdy hope for what is yet to come. It was not something I could have learned from a course called "Eschatology 101." I had to learn it from being part of the church.

Elsewhere in his memoir, Lischer paints a word-picture of his rough-hewn elders as they take their turns at distributing Holy Communion:

> Our elders had the thickest and most heavily muscled fingers I have ever seen. How they got a wedding ring over such enormous knuckles I can't imagine. Gnarled and calloused hands, textured by manure and industrial grit in equal parts, gingerly pressed the Bread of Life into the uplifted palms of their neighbors, cousins and parents. . . . I was trained to believe that Jesus was really *there* in the bread and the wine, but now I saw him with my own eyes in . . . the calluses and knuckles of the servers.

"*Body of Christ. Body of Christ,*" they said robotically. They meant the body of Jesus, to be sure, but also the body of believers. All of us. Paul warned his readers to "discern the body," which means to see Jesus' body in a new way. Not as a miracle of physics occurring in the elements, but as a miracle of community in which atoms of solitude are re-created into new families and friends. Christianity is a body religion. I had only begun to discern it.

I took such pleasure in lifting the chalice . . . when I came to the words, "Do this as often as you drink it, in remembrance of me." Because, when the light was filtering through our art-glass windows or flooding through the open doors in back, I could just see the whole congregation reflected in the silver cup. And in that congregation, the whole church.[2]

This, at its best, is the enterprise we're about, and the world is hungry for such expressions of it.

Conclusion

Such a picture of the church, as a memory-bearing, countercultural, and eschatological community, is not easily grasped in a seminary class, or three years of classes. This is not the seminary's fault. It should not be expected to prepare persons for every single nuance and eventuality which they will encounter in ministry. It should only be expected to lay a theological foundation for the practice of ministry, one that graduates leaving the seminary and entering the church will build upon for the rest of their lives.

From time to time, we apprehend the church not just as it has been but also as it will be someday. We remember, in such chastening moments, that many of the ways we would otherwise try to "manage" or "corporatize" or "reinvent" or "save" the church is only our atheistic anxiety getting the best of us. It is God's church, after all, and the truth about ministry is that we who are called to minister are finally stewards, not owners, of the whole enterprise. Through these gifts, we have the privilege of touching the future, just as surely as, from time to time, the future touches us and reminds us of the community we will be in God's good time.

2. Lischer, *Open Secrets*, pp. 70-71.

19. A Different Kind of Transition

J. Philip Wogaman

I am intrigued by the central theme of this book. I hope, and trust, that it will be helpful to the thousands who make the transition each year from seminary studies to parish ministry, seeking to make sense of the differences and similarities between the seminary world and the world outside. But I must confess at the outset that my experience of this transition may be somewhat different from that of the other writers. Many seminary professors, having completed their studies, spend years in the parish before returning to the seminary to teach. That pattern is as true today as it was in previous generations for a Karl Barth or a Reinhold Niebuhr.

But that isn't the way things worked out for me. I went through three years of seminary studies, followed immediately by three years' work on my Ph.D. While my intention through most of those years was to return to my home Methodist conference in Southern California and take a church, I was lured instead into teaching — first at the University of the Pacific (1961-66), then at Wesley Theological Seminary (1966-92), where I taught Christian ethics and served for a number of years as dean. Thus, from 1954 to 1992 my one and only pastorate was for two years in a student appointment during my last year of seminary study and first year as a doctoral student. That pastoral experience in the (then) shoe-mill town of Marlborough, Massachusetts, was formative in a number of ways, but hardly representative of what a seminary graduate would encounter in a full-time parish setting away from school.

But I finally got there! In 1992, after I had turned sixty, the bishop in Washington, D.C., asked if I would consider an appointment to Foundry United Methodist Church in downtown Washington. My wife Carolyn and

I did not linger over the decision. At our age, and with my having taught seminary for twenty-six years, we were immediately attracted to this challenge. The church, located in the heart of the nation's capital, presented unique opportunities. Having taught generations of seminary students, I figured maybe it was time for me to put up or shut up. Carolyn announced that it had just taken me longer than anybody else to get out of seminary. In any event, we said yes and plunged into the new life.

Our ten years at Foundry Church were wonderfully energizing. They also evoked new reflections on the relationship between the world of the seminary and the world of the church. Having heard seminary graduates speak for years of "the things they didn't teach us in seminary," I was tempted now to formulate my own list. But most of those things probably couldn't be taught effectively in seminary since there really are things that have to be learned through more direct experience. As I reflect now on the question whether my many seminary years really helped, I can only answer *absolutely!* Those years were immensely helpful. But to understand why, I must say a few things about different aspects of ministry as I experienced them at Foundry.[1]

The Ministry of Preaching

I begin with preaching, central in many respects to pastoral ministry. Does seminary education help with that? There are pastors who say no, but upon examination their sermons may not stand the test of time. After all, the first rule of great preaching is to have something to say. Seminary courses in Bible, theology, church history, ethics, and world religions do not concentrate on the how-to aspect of preaching. But if they are up to standard, they draw seminarians into serious thought about the content of the faith they are preparing to proclaim. If one is open to it, one can learn to think theologically, with rich background drawn from Israel and the church through the centuries. Sometimes preachers will complain that laypeople are not prepared to hear the kinds of things students pick up in seminary. I disagree. In my experience, laypeople are *hungry* for the kinds of insights seminary graduates should be prepared to offer.

---

1. Soon after retiring from Foundry I wrote a memoir of those years, published as *An Unexpected Journey: Reflections on Pastoral Ministry* (Louisville: Westminster John Knox, 2004).

But there is an important caveat: A sermon is not a lecture! One does not, in a twenty-minute sermon, attempt to use the vocabulary of Theology 101 and expect laypeople to get it. I had done a fair amount of preaching during my professorial days, usually on a one-time basis to a congregation I would not see again. I don't think I tried to lecture on those occasions, although the congregations in question might offer a second opinion. What I do know is that, upon entering into a pastoral relationship with a congregation, with responsibility to preach to the same people week after week, I found myself struggling a whole lot more with how to make the message accessible. Above all, that meant watching the vocabulary. In preparing to preach — which I attempted to do without manuscript or notes each week — I spent much time going over what I planned to say, continually refining the language to make it accessible without loss of meaning.[2] But the main point remained: try to have something to say that is worth saying. The bishop who ordained me so many years ago was a great, engaging preacher. He used to say that the worst sin for a preacher is to not be interesting. I accepted that judgment until it dawned on me that some of the worst charlatans and demagogues in history have been interesting! One wishes they had been less so! Even a dull presentation of the truth beats a compelling presentation of wickedness. Still, there's a lot to be said for presenting the gospel in an interesting, accessible way.

Most seminaries work at preparing their graduates to preach. I'm especially grateful for courses in homiletics that respect the unique gifts of different seminarians, seeking to draw the best out of each one. On those few occasions when I've taught such courses (while serving the Foundry Church), I've been impressed by the fact that all of the students do have gifts to offer through preaching. But, again, the key is to have something to say, and it is a seminary's main business to help students at exactly that point.

My own experience is a bit unique. It is one thing to go through three years or so of seminary and then begin preaching Sunday after Sunday; it is another to have spent many years as a professor, teaching, writing books, sharpening one's theological mind. There's a trade-off here. The professor may have thought many things through, but meanwhile lost the capacity to

---

2. While I sought the direct face-to-face encounter with the congregation afforded by preaching without notes, I carefully prepared a manuscript and then re-outlined the sermon numbers of times to sharpen the main points, illustrations, and transitions.

communicate effectively outside the academic world. Perhaps my experience with the transition may be relevant to students who haven't spent so many years "getting out of seminary," but it can be helpful only if students have honestly sought, in their fewer years of study, to learn to think theologically.

While at Foundry, I fell into a practice that I heartily recommend. In each of the last six summers in the church I offered the congregation an opportunity to submit written faith questions on a given Sunday to which I would respond during the following Sunday's sermon time. A small lay committee organized these anonymously submitted questions, and as they read them to me I, like the rest of the congregation, was hearing them for the first time. This invited a certain kind of spontaneity, and the exercise as a whole demonstrated (1) that it is all right to have questions, and (2) that the people were struggling with a variety of issues. Over a period of six years, I was in fact able to offer a response to all the questions that were asked, even though I could sometimes think of a better way of saying it an hour later. Still, I was quite prepared to say "I just don't know" or "I'll have to think some more about this one." Sometimes others, learning of this "faith question" exercise, would commend me on my courage, but that entirely misses the point. Any seminary graduate should be able to do this and to grow intellectually in the process.

Moreover, it is a way of showing respect for the mind of the congregation. Once, while preparing to preach a series on faith questions, I remarked to the congregation that Foundry was one of the only two churches I had ever served — the other being the small mill-town church in Marlborough. Foundry was loaded with people with advanced degrees, while the Marlborough church had only two or three college graduates. Nevertheless, I commented, I really couldn't tell all that much difference between the two churches so far as their ability to grasp theological insights is concerned! But again, that ability plays out only if the preacher employs accessible vocabulary.

Prophetic Presence

Preaching is not, however, simply imparting abstract intellectual truths. It is getting to the heart of things, seeking above all else, to have "some word from the Lord." The preacher struggles to be a prophet, one who speaks for God. Most seminaries challenge their students to cut against the grain of contemporary ways of seeing and doing things, to be, at least somewhat, countercultural. Therein may lie the most challenging aspect of the transition between seminary and the world outside. The people in the average parish are almost bound to be more captive to contemporary culture than people in the average seminary. Is it possible to bridge that gap?

My Foundry experience may not be the ideal test of that, because that church has a long tradition of grappling with issues in a progressive spirit. In that sense, it is a good deal "safer" for a prophetic ministry than many other churches. Is it really possible, in more typical settings, for a recent graduate to convey prophetic insights derived from the seminary experience? I have a mental collection of numbers of seminary graduates who have done so with a grace and effectiveness that puts me to shame.

Still, I did learn a few things about this even at Foundry. First, the cardinal rule is love of the people. I believe a congregation instinctively senses when a preacher is talking down to them or only venting his or her own hostilities. If being "prophetic" is finally about how to translate God's love into the circumstances of human life, this can hardly be done in an unloving way. From that deeper perspective, we can see that the "prophetic" word is not always even controversial. When Jesus referred to the common peasants as the "salt of the earth," that unexpected affirmation was prophetic enough, but hardly controversial. Similarly, to restore a people's sense of self-worth in our time may be a very deeply prophetic ministry, but altogether positive. That is essentially true of ministry in churches of oppressed people.

But what about the countercultural edge that really is controversial, that is, challenging the status quo comforts of privileged people? Or urging people to become more deeply involved in the social, economic, and political issues of the day? A point I came to feel instinctively is that the more controversial an issue is, the more people have a right to careful explanation of the reasons why a pastoral leader has arrived at a given conclusion. That means that one does not simply announce the conclusion; one exposes the data and the thought processes leading to the conclusion. It also means one shows respect for the thought processes of people who may disagree. In preaching on controversial issues, I tried to anticipate the disagreements. In seminary ethics classes through the years I used to urge students to try to state views opposed to their own even more convincingly than those who held them before expressing their own disagreement. I'm not sure I always followed that advice myself, upon moving into the parish setting. Nevertheless, I did mentally envisage somebody in the congregation saying "yes, but" in the midst of a sermon. Unanswered "yes, but" reactions among congregants can destroy all the rest of the sermon.

The disagreements may simply reflect a different base of experience. Any number of times, I have mentally dismissed a parishioner as hopelessly benighted, only to discover later that he or she had moved way beyond me on an issue after being exposed to the human reality. I recall one seminary student early in my teaching years who, while intellectually brilliant, seemed utterly unreachable about the problems of poverty in that era. Upon leaving seminary, this graduating student was appointed to a church in a company mill town where people were obviously suffering from blatant economic oppression. The young pastor returned to seminary to ask some of us how to organize a labor union! Sometimes the best thing is to find ways of drawing church members into actual experience through field trips, visiting speakers, or films.

Again, it can matter whether it is all done in a loving spirit. But that does not mean that prophetic ministry, even when expressed with love, is always "safe." I'm not sure that tenured seminary professors, like I was, are in a very good moral position to pressure their students to be more courageous. But it is a beautiful thing when a minister combines love with integrity and courage. Such people have sometimes suffered quite unjustly, but even so they have helped to change the world. Do they not have Jesus as the supreme example? Who of us would want to criticize Jesus for not being "effective" or a "good pastor"? Still, Jesus wept over Jerusalem and forgave those who nailed him to the cross.

Pastoral Presence

I did not have to be told, before transitioning into my Foundry ministry, that it is important to be a good pastor. Still, I learned three important things.

The first was not to be afraid. In retrospect, it's hard to see why I was at all intimidated by this aspect of ministry, but I was. In particular — I'm embarrassed even to mention this — I was anxious about making hospital calls. It wasn't that I'm afraid of the sight of blood or repulsed by images of physical distress; nor do I find hospitals in general to be alienating. My anxiety was about how I might be received by the patients themselves. Would they consider my pastoral visits to be an *intrusion,* a violation of their privacy? Looking back, now, after ten years of ministry that included countless visits to people in hospitals, I can scarcely believe that I ever thought I would not be welcomed. Indeed, in my experience a pastoral visit was *invariably* greeted with eagerness, and even sometimes with joy. I do not want to overstate this, but a pastor is often experienced as a representative of God or at least as one who can be counted upon to be a good friend. Something more: if the patient is a member of the pastor's church, the pastoral visit is seen as a representation of the community itself. I used to play on that sometimes. I would say, "The whole congregation would like to be here today, but the room is just too small. So they sent me." Of course, we both would know that most of the people in our large congregation wouldn't even have known that the patient was in the hospital, much less that they explicitly had delegated me to represent them. But in a larger sense, they really had sent me, and I had to believe that most of them were pleased to be represented in that way. In any case, we would have a good laugh over that line.

I don't know that I was particularly fearful about relating pastorally to those who have just lost a loved one, but I did come to see that there is no need to be anxious about what to say. Sometimes it's best not to say anything at all. One's presence is what counts, and if one is not anxious about saying the right thing, the needed words will come when and as they should. There are, of course, vast resources available for such occasions. Often it is the simple presence, being God's grace to people who need to be able to experience that in personal ways.

The second thing I learned is that pastoral responsibility is not just a one-on-one, individualistic form of ministry. No pastor should image this responsibility as analogous to a therapist who hangs out her or his shingle and schedules appointments in the office. Sometimes it is like that, but more often meaningful pastoral interactions happen in more ordinary settings, even such venues as a conversation in the parking lot after a meeting is over. My more important learning, though, was that pastoral responsibility is shared by a whole congregation. The individual conversations or conferences can be important. But the broader reality is of a whole congregation of mutually caring people. A pastor can do much to lead a congregation into the fulfillment of this mutual caring. That can even occur in the worship setting. Immediately upon arriving at Foundry I borrowed a practice of my longtime friend and pastor at Washington's Metropolitan Memorial United Methodist Church. During the "joys and concerns" part of the worship service, I would tell the congregation about individuals in hospital, or families that had lost loved ones, or more joyous events like weddings. Then I would ask, in each case, for a volunteer from the congregation to call or visit each of these persons or families to express the church's caring. And I would wait for somebody to raise his or her hand as a volunteer. This wasn't understood as a substitute for my own involvement, but as a way for the congregation as a whole to reach out. If a person asked not to be mentioned in this way, I would of course honor that request. But that was very rare. In most cases, people were deeply moved by this expression of the congregation's concern — ironically, that could be especially true if the caller and those being called were not previously acquainted with each other, for then it was obviously an expression of the whole congregation.

Two unexpected consequences flowed from this practice. One was that members of the congregation came to see that what was happening for others would also happen to them if their lives were impacted in special ways. The other was that visitors to the church were immediately drawn into a deeper sense that they had come into a real community. So I commend the practice. And if it would "work" in a large setting like Foundry Church, located downtown in a great city, I cannot imagine it would not prove helpful anywhere else.

The third thing I learned about being a pastor is that it is intimately related to preaching. Through the years, as I noted above, I had often preached on a one-time basis in various churches without previously knowing many, if any, members of the congregation. And then I was gone. But at Foundry, we had all been drawn together in a very special relationship. In time, as I came to know the people better, I had a much better conception of what needed to be said in order to connect with the congregation. Moreover, it became clearer to me that even when the message had to be on a controversial theme challenging the comfort zone of many in the congregation, they could at least know that the words from the pulpit were spoken by a friend and not an adversary. That fact didn't always spare me from the wrath of this or that offended parishioner, but it certainly helped.

An Invitation to Spiritual Growth

I don't know quite how to say this, but I truly found the pastoral ministry to be an invitation to grow spiritually. The reason why I'm uncomfortable in making this point is that people have preconceptions about the spiritual life that I cannot easily relate to. I am hard-pressed for an answer when somebody asks me about my spiritual life and the disciplines I use to sustain it. It isn't that I don't know the right answers; it's that they don't easily fit my experience. The expectation is that there are certain spiritual disciplines of prayer and Bible reading that are necessary. I truly believe in the importance of prayer and Bible reading, but not for show-and-tell purposes. And sometimes even prayer and Bible reading can be practiced in such a way as to lead away from, and not toward, spiritual growth. (As a humorous aside with which some of my readers will no doubt identify, my wife and I were once students at a missionary language school in Central America where the daily chapel services were dominated by pretty judgmental fundamentalists. One evening, an older missionary of my denomination commented, "We're being prayed for, viciously.")

Having said that, I want to emphasize that, on the whole, entering pastoral ministry truly is an invitation to deepen oneself spiritually. The weekly discipline of preparing a sermon, struggling with the Scripture, praying that this will truly be helpful, and above all taking the lives of the people seriously, cannot fail to affect one. I was no stranger to the theological disciplines, having taught in seminary for so many years. But I really did experience a difference in relating to a congregation on the basis of the ultimate issues of life.

An illustration. We had a weekly healing service at Foundry. We recorded no miraculous cures; indeed, numbers of the people who frequented those services early in my ministry there had died by the time of my retirement. Most of the problems addressed at the time of the laying on of hands were psychological or relational in character. Sometimes I just didn't feel spiritually ready for this kind of service at the beginning. Then somebody would come up to the kneeling rail surrounding the small chancel area and, with soft music playing in the background so our conversation couldn't be overheard by others, would pour his or her heart out and ask for my prayers. Often it was as if a whole new reality had invaded my spirit, and it could be as though the prayer, which I articulated, had come from somewhere else. Maybe that was not what we Christians describe as the Holy Spirit at work, but to me there was something very real about it. I recall one such instance, when I truly was not in the mood. There was a youngish man kneeling before me, pouring out his deep sense of personal inadequacy. I found myself taking him by the shoulders and speaking of his worth as a human being, and being confident that this was certainly a "word from the Lord."

My transition from seminary teaching to the parish setting brought to mind a classroom remark by Paul Tillich during my student days. A student ventured to ask the distinguished professor if he would comment on the prayer life of a theologian. "Vell," he said in his characteristic German accent, "ze zeologian must pray tvice as much as anybody else." At the time, I thought he was just being cute. But it came to me, as I traded the academic setting for the life of a pastor, that he had a real point. Theological thought often deals in abstractions of one kind or another. That is a necessary service by theologians to Christians and their churches. But abstract thought is also distancing, and there can be a spiritual problem for theologians when they relate to God only with distancing language. Presumably Tillich meant that prayer is needed if God is to be experienced in other than conceptual terms.

Perhaps the admonition also applies to pastors and preachers. And yet, there is something in the communication of pastor to people that leads to the deeper dimension.

I suppose I should honestly record that there are also special spiritual temptations that accompany this pastoral role. There is here the opportunity for ego-enhancement, much more I think than in the seminary setting. One can come to thrive on the praise of a congregation and to feel offended when it is not forthcoming. I am not surprised that this has led to spiritual catastrophe with some hugely popular preachers. But it does not have to be that way. The spiritual dynamics of pastoral ministry can increase one's sense of the deep reality of God and lead to the right kind of humility.

One thing that helped me at that point was to see, in a parish setting over a period of ten years, something of the flow of generations, watching children grow into youth, and older people move from vitality to weakness and then to death. Thus to realize, concretely, that we are here but for a moment in the long procession of time, and the ultimate significance of our lives rests entirely with the God of the ages, in whose presence there is no place for self-centered pretense.

The Special Expertise of Pastoral Ministry

If these points are kept in mind, there is yet another point to record about the transition from seminary to church. Often seminary students are unduly impressed, even intimidated, by the reputations and intellectual attainments of their professors. That is probably inevitable. But the danger is that freshly minted seminary students may feel that the work they are about to undertake is, somehow, inferior to that of those distinguished teachers. If one were really first-rate intellectually, one could become a professor oneself. As it is, one must settle for second-best by going into parish ministry. If I had really believed that, I certainly wouldn't have left a secure, tenured seminary post to take my place at Foundry Church!

But, having made the move, I came to a more vivid comprehension of the different form of expertise that is the hallmark of pastoral ministry. That is the capacity to draw things together, to see the interrelatedness of the academic disciplines and to connect them relevantly to practical life. That discipline of seeing the connections is, in fact, a very important form of competence — one that many specialists in the different theological disciplines do not possess at all.

The problem sometimes begins even within a seminary faculty, if the "classical" disciplines, like theology and Bible and church history, are taken to be superior to the merely "practical" disciplines, like Christian education or pastoral psychology or homiletics. I can record that this kind of faculty split has not been the case with the two seminaries I've been most associated with — Wesley and Iliff. But I have talked with people who have felt this tension in other settings. Where such a tension exists, there may be even more of a tendency for seminary graduates to feel that their work is "merely" practical and not that it represents a much-needed form of competence. Perhaps what is needed is a better sense of what St. Paul's metaphor of the "body of Christ" comes down to.

But if one is to fulfill this possibility, out there beyond the seminary walls, it seems to me that two things are needful.

The first is that one must learn to think theologically — that is, to be able to draw upon the insights and resources of the theological disciplines in addressing the problems facing individuals and their communities and the world at large. How does sin express itself in the world, and with what ultimate consequences? What is the meaning and grounding of justice? How are we to understand power, both positively and negatively? How and where can we encounter God's grace at work in human existence? Is genuine community an achievable possibility in this fallen world? How are we to understand catastrophes, both at retail and wholesale levels? Can the church and society relate positively to the findings of science? What are the possibilities and limitations of technology, seen in human terms? Such questions invite theological answers even as they force us to grapple with our ongoing experiences in the factual world.

The other point is that to become the kind of expert that pastoral ministry invites means that one must be a life-long student. I used to comment to my own seminary students that if they do not continue to study, ten years later they may as well never have gone to seminary in the first place. That may overstate the matter slightly, but the truth is that if we do not go forward we slide backward. Great pastors — and there certainly are some — continue to read, even voraciously. The reading diet is not narrowly specialized, but it does not neglect intellectually challenging books. Nor does it disdain the insights to be gained from biography, novels, and poetry. When possible, continuing study can be enriched by book study groups and by continuing education programs.

We can be deeply grateful for the seminary experience. In the lives of very many people it has proved to be the seedbed that its name implies. For many of us, it has been a time of spiritual as well as intellectual quickening. But there is no reason to fear the life that follows, nor to feel that the seminary experience was irrelevant. My own ministry of more than fifty years has involved intimate relationship with both seminary and church, and far from being in conflict, I have found them to be mutually supportive.

20. Learning to Build Christian Community: Males, Whites, Heterosexuals Wanted for Leadership

Traci C. West

For most white ministers who tell their stories about the journey from seminary to ministry, one of the privileges of being white is that a discussion of the racial/ethnic makeup of their seminaries, denominations, or first local church assignments is optional. Perhaps if someone who is not white plays a prominent role in one of their stories, his or her racial/ethnic identity is mentioned. But most often, whiteness is treated like heterosexuality and other identity labels that members of dominant groups share. It is treated as if it does not require any reflection on its meaning or the consequences it brings.

Even if whites do not discuss their racial/ethnic group identity when describing their vocational experiences of starting out in ordained ministry, issues of race definitely inform those experiences. For a white Christian minister in one of the major, predominantly white, Protestant groups in the U.S., her or his social status includes the option of being seen as an individual seminarian or pastor whose racial identity requires no particular attention. This privileged status is supported in mass media, electoral politics, public education, and elsewhere in public life where white people's whiteness is usually neither mentioned nor analyzed. The option to be seen by others in such a racially oblivious way is, in itself, an example of how powerfully white privilege shapes the vocational experiences of most white ministers. In contrast, attention to my black racial/ethnic identity, together with my gender, played a significant role in my transition from seminarian to pastor, making reflection upon it unavoidable.

But is attention to racial/ethnic identity a *good* thing? In most cases, I tend to believe that, yes, the act of calling attention to issues of race signals a morally healthy concern for historical and current political realities. In predominantly white Protestant groups, such as my own United Methodist church, it is no simple matter to discuss the racial/ethnic identity of ministers, laity, churches, or communities in a morally healthy manner. The dangers of reinforcing racial prejudice and stereotyped assumptions abound.

In this essay, I explore the moral contribution that attention to race/ethnicity and other social markers of identity can make to church culture. I concentrate on the nature and role of Christian community in the initial seminary-to-parish period of ministerial formation and appointment. How does societal concern with certain categories that label human identity help to define the nature and role of Christian community? Does this kind of concern help to define Christian community in a manner that is good for the vitality and integrity of the community? I utilize my own autobiography to explore these ecclesial and ethical questions, retracing some of the steps of my journey from seminary to parish ministry. Some of the same themes related to race and the formation of good community that are present in my seminary experiences are also found in my initiation into parish ministry. Several of those issues were already a matter of concern when my earliest teenage yearning to become a minister developed and first received its first formal confirmation from a church body.

Identity Matters

I knew that I was called to ordained ministry when I was a high school student. At the age of sixteen, I began meeting with my pastor in order to learn about the ordination process that my denomination required. I remember excitedly accompanying my pastor as he carried out his duties. I wanted to be exposed to the daily routines of a parish minister. Later, as a college student, I met with a committee in my local church to be interviewed. It was an important initial step in my ordination process. Responding to the committee's tough questions and then receiving its approval was an exhilarating experience. My mother waited for me outside the glass doors that enclosed the committee room. She told me afterwards that when she saw me slip off my shoes and tuck one foot up underneath me in the chair while talking animatedly, she knew that I was okay.

I do not remember being overly concerned about the all-white makeup of the committee. They reflected the majority of my church. I knew most of them as my former Sunday school teachers, members of the church committees I had worked with when serving as the youth representative to those committees, or as acquaintances and parents of acquaintances I had worshiped with for many years. My family had been active members of this local church for all of my life. I suppose that my confidence was also boosted by the fact that my mother hovered outside of the committee room, threatening with her very presence to make sure that these white people treated her daughter in the right way. To describe my mother as an extremely articulate, assertive, and protective parent would be a decidedly understated depiction.

At the time of the meeting, my mother and I understood that this committee was comprised of trusted members of our church family. At the same time, we also knew that it was comprised of white people whose white racial socialization could easily grant them permission to behave in a discriminatory fashion. Basic racial realities made me cognizant of perilous qualities that inhabit Christian community. Though at the time I would not have expressed my feelings with such explicit language, I was aware that my faith community was a place laden with the landmines of the white members' notions of inherent racial superiority reinforced in them by the broader society. My awareness was also accompanied by naïve optimism about how easily Christian faith could bring about social and spiritual transformation to mute such notions of superiority.

I enjoyed the opportunity to craft responses to the questions I was asked during this initial interview. For instance, the men and women on this local church committee pressed me on whether I truly believed in, and would promise diligently to teach and to uphold *all* of the Holy Scriptures, particularly in light of their injunctions about women remaining silent in the church. The committee's concern was buttressed by my candidly stated rejection of such injunctions. In addition to this topic, I remember that the committee asked me for a detailed description of my understanding of the work of the Holy Spirit.

This group was the first line of gatekeepers for the church. They were, I suppose, trying to make sure that church traditions would be preserved. But of all the traditions found in Christian Scripture, why was it that the only scriptural tradition we discussed was the one concerned with the subordination and silencing of women? I do not think that this issue would have surfaced in an interview with a male candidate, or if it had that it would have been as central a focus. This discussion about my commitment to teaching Scripture in a manner that takes into account its passages mandating women's silence also seemed to surface doubts on the part of some committee members about whether they ought to confirm a woman's call to ordained ministry. I felt that I had to assuage those doubts and prove that I had a right to be a minister, "even though" I was a woman.

My socially defined identity (as woman) seems to have been a key factor guiding the task of safeguarding the gateway to ordained ministry. If I am correct in this speculative assertion that the question about scriptural authority and the leadership rights of women does represent gendered, unfair scrutiny that would not have been applied to a male candidate, then this process was tainted with bias. Because the interview was conducted in this way, the committee and I learned that in the structuring of Christian community, unfair, discriminatory treatment based upon social definitions of human worth is acceptable for the selection of its leaders. But additionally, the committee and I learned how to do contextual, hermeneutical work as they fulfilled their gate-keeping obligation of scrutinizing my qualifications. In granting approval of my candidacy, the committee found a way to interpret Scripture such that they too rejected an explicit scriptural mandate about the subordination and silencing of women. Together we learned that the meaning of Christian Scripture and tradition is a dynamic, evolving aspect of Christian community and that we could discover new ways of understanding it.

Building Community

When I graduated from college I was thrilled to go immediately on to pursue my Master of Divinity degree. I looked forward to becoming a seminarian, to focusing entirely on preparation for ordained ministry. My seminary courses nicely built upon the work that I had begun as an undergraduate religious studies major. Whether it was in Elizabeth Bettenhausen's Christian ethics course on power, Susan Thistlethwaite's introductory theology course, or Paul Sampley's introduction to the New Testament, I was challenged to expand my understanding of Christianity in new and creative ways that would serve me well in my future ministry. Beyond the classroom, another essential element in my vocational preparation included participation in the broader seminary environment, including worship in the chapel, student activities sponsored by the women's center, and lectures by visiting scholars in nearby, related seminaries and universities.

I do not think that I had ever previously encountered as much emphasis on "building community" as I found at seminary. Whether at entering student orientation sessions, school-wide retreat planning, or various informal gatherings, administrators and student leaders repeatedly referred to "the Christian community we were building together." In these frequent references to the seminary's ethos, I received a strong message about the nature of Christian community. Christian community, the seminary taught me, is not merely a place demarcated by concrete walls, a cross, a Bible, and people who claim membership in it. "Community" must also be an identifiable lifestyle of deliberately creating shared ethical values among socially diverse people. This deliberate communal commitment involves multiple forms of ongoing, dialogical engagement reflecting upon and practicing those shared values. At this northeastern seminary in Boston, in the early 1980s, the specific ethical values that were mentioned most frequently as reflective of an authentic Christian community lifestyle were honesty, mutual respect, and social justice in church and society.

I witnessed a painful test of this understanding of moral Christian community. The seminary was embroiled in intense conflicts about its ethical commitment to an affirmative action policy that was supposed to guide the hiring of faculty and administrators. In the period just prior to my matriculation, a liberal black male and a feminist white female had been candidates for faculty positions in departments that had been the exclusive province of white males in the former case and of males in the latter. Although their hiring received the seminary faculty's approval, both candidates were treated poorly and rejected by white male university administrators.[1] In the academic year before I enrolled, the seminary had also been in turmoil over the firing of a female associate dean, who was a white feminist, by the white male dean of the seminary and his immediate hiring of a non-feminist white male associate dean to serve as her replacement.

Many of the students and faculty believed that the successful implementation of affirmative action policies represented one concrete manifestation of how the Christian community should put their shared ethical

1. The details of these conflicts are explained in Marjorie Heins, *Cutting the Mustard: Affirmative Action and the Nature of Excellence* (Boston: Faber and Faber, 1987).

values into practice. But some, primarily the seminary administrators, believed that there were insurmountable institutional impediments created by the seminary's location within a larger academic institution. The university's operating procedures, which were rigidly controlled and monitored by an idiosyncratic university president, often conflicted with the justice agenda embraced by the majority in the seminary. It seemed that for the top seminary administrators, it was simply untenable to identify a successfully implemented affirmative action policy with authentic Christian communal living. For my part, as a new student I saw the school's problem as an inability to make a choice between being a witness to its Christian commitments to social justice, or merely cloaking itself in impressive rhetoric about Christian social justice while representing longstanding and discriminatory dominant traditions of church and academy. I had an aching spiritual longing for my seminary community to make a bold witness to its Christian ideals. I had an urgent desire for my seminary genuinely to embody the legacy of its most famous social justice activist alumnus, Martin Luther King Jr. (a legacy often touted in the seminary's publicity materials).

After my first year, the conflict reached a dramatic climax. Another feminist seminary administrator, a stalwart advocate of affirmative action and racial justice, was fired and subsequently filed a lawsuit against the school. When the students and faculty found out that the dean of the seminary, Richard Nesmith, fired this member of his administrative team, Nancy Richardson, a firestorm of protest erupted on campus. Sixteen of the eighteen faculty members wrote letters to complain about the decision and ask for its reconsideration. Students wrote letters, held protests, and eventually organized an ongoing committee to support Richardson's lawsuit.

As a student, I had known Nancy Richardson as an exceedingly calm and skillful administrator who handled a myriad of student crises related to financial aid and housing. She was a petite, soft-spoken, friendly, but somewhat shy white woman, with what — to my New England-bred ears — sounded like a heavy Southern accent. She had a reputation as a person of action who knew how to bring a consistent sense of fairness and compassion to her enforcement of rules and responses to student requests. Nancy Richardson was one of the first white feminists that I had met whose anti-racist commitments were central to her self-understanding and her vocation. I was deeply impressed by the integrity of her commitment. Though I had been raised around liberal white Christians, I had previously known few white people like Richardson who did not expect my permission, congratulations, or gratitude for her expression of anti-racist commitments on a daily basis. Her expression of these values included her duties as a seminary administrator.

When he fired Richardson, the dean told her that his reasons for doing so were "pedagogical" and "ideological." To explain what he meant by "ideological," the dean referred to specific concerns related to gender and racial justice. He met with her and told her:

> You have been on the firing line, for example, say, related to the women's issue, where you quite rightly have strong objectives. . . . At the same time you are a member of an administrative team that can't always deliver and certainly haven't always delivered in the way that you, with your social ethics hat on here as a woman . . . would want. There is a kind of tension there.
>
> The second illustration — the racism issue. Again, your personal ethic and your ideological dispositions press you to want to see things move out here on the front of racism and justice. Over here, you are a member of an administration that wins and loses on that score. . . .[2]

As their meeting continued Richardson responded to these examples from the dean by defending her views.

> I think that you are absolutely right, around issues of affirmative action. I have tried to be as clear as I can be. I think that both justice and the law demand an affirmative action process, and I have tried to be as clear with you, as clear publicly in the school, as clear everywhere that I believe that is what we are about, and that's what I want to be about, and when we fail to do that, then I'm upset about that.[3]

There were differing approaches to gender and racial identity in this conflict. More precisely, there were differing understandings of how sexism and racism should be confronted — of what a just response to them requires   in a (Christian) seminary community. In the dean's view, there was a separation between an administrator's personal identity and convic-

2. Heins, *Cutting the Mustard,* pp. 71-72. This is an excerpt of a meeting that Richardson tape recorded with the permission of the dean.
3. Heins, *Cutting the Mustard,* p. 72.

tions and her public, institutional loyalties. Moreover, he believed that the latter should receive priority in all public settings. Richardson insisted on a cohesive link between personal convictions and publicly expressed institutional loyalties.

Also note that the dean offered an erroneous, but revealing, argument when attributing Richardson's support of affirmative action to her identity as a woman. He assumed that her feminist desire for the just treatment of women was automatically dictated by the fact that she is a woman. Even feminists often make a similar mistake, by assuming that based upon self-interest all women support feminist struggles for the inclusion of women in positions of power. Rather, as Richardson's insistent anti-racism demonstrated, her support for affirmative action and other socially just practices was not purely a matter of serving the self-interests of her social identity (as a white woman) and obviously not at all a matter of serving the interests of her individual, careerist ambitions (as a white woman seminary administrator). Her support of affirmative action involved a deliberate choice to pursue what she believed to be good communal interests for seminary life.

The dean's firing of Nancy Richardson exposed me to some of the peculiar traits that characterize the abuse of power by leaders in Christian communities. It illustrated how the abusive twisting of moral relations is driven by a consuming concern with appearances. I observed the ferocity of this concern in the orchestrated campaign to make sure that the appearance of Christian moral concern (in this case, the appearance of opposition to racism) was publicly presented. The dean was especially upset about the open criticism of him by students for his policies. When firing Richardson, he referred to these student concerns as "the anti-racism stuff," which he expected her either to squelch or to predict and warn him about in advance.

Another, related dimension of this kind of Christian abuse of power is the dogged insistence on the appearance of unity. Richardson had failed to ensure the public appearance of a unified school stance on anti-racism. Public expressions of dissent by the students, including a student's critical speech at commencement, made the school appear as if it was not unified in its Christian concern for social justice. In sum, I learned how the art of public presentation and a show of unity, when wrapped in uniquely Christian moral language, can take on strategic importance that trumps just practices. Through the actions of the seminary leadership that prevailed on this campus, ethical Christian practice became a matter of preserving the institution's right to maintain an exclusive ethos and excluding practices, benefiting white and male leaders.

The lessons learned from Richardson's firing were also about what Christian feminist, anti-racist courage looks like, about a willingness to stand up for inclusive practices even at the cost of losing one's job, privacy, and financial stability. As part of the student committee supporting Nancy's lawsuit, I was nurtured in the possibility of Christian community as a place where one submerges individual will and desire for individual recognition to a broader group process of justice work. Although Nancy lost the lawsuit, I found my participation in that work to be one of the most valuable aspects of my seminary education. After the lawsuit concluded, for a variety of personal reasons, I ended up transferring to another school in California to complete my seminary degree.

The Process for My First Appointment

When the day had finally come for me to have a chance to try out my leadership skills as pastor of a local church, I felt ready. It was the end of my last semester of seminary. I waited for the telephone to ring with news of my first pastoral appointment. The district superintendent finally called me to describe the church where my name was to be submitted. He was one of six official supervisors designated by the bishop and his cabinet that presided over geographic sections of the New York region where I had just been ordained. When I received the call I was both elated and very nervous. The district superintendent told me that the church was a racially integrated church in Connecticut that the cabinet believed would nicely match my own church background.

A few days later, I received another telephone call in which this same district superintendent explained to me that the church had rejected the idea of having me as their pastor and that the cabinet would try to find another assignment for me. Apparently, after hearing the district superintendent's description of me, the church committee had decided that I would *not* be a good match for them. In brief, they had rejected me for three reasons. There had been unanimous agreement among the white and black, male and female members of this committee. They did not want me because I was a black person. The church had just experienced their first black

245

pastor and it had not been a good experience for them. They did not want another one. Also, they did not want a woman pastor because they had never had one of those before and feared that it would not work out. Finally, they did not want a pastor who was as young as I was because they felt that they needed an older, more experienced minister — like the retired white male interim currently serving their congregation. I listened politely and calmly thanked this white male district superintendent for his explanation of the church's concerns about (certain aspects of) my identity. He reassured me that such things sometimes happened in this process but another appointment would likely be found for me. I am embarrassed to admit it, but when I hung up the telephone the first thing that I did was cry.

After crying and praying aloud for God's help, I started to feel angry. So far in this process of being appointed to my first full time position as a pastor, my theological, pastoral counseling, or preaching abilities that had been such a primary focus of my seminary preparation had never even been mentioned. Only my age and the social labels that marked my identity as black and as a woman were at issue. This seemed like a patently unfair and discriminatory way of operating the church. However, some aspects of my seminary education had prepared me for this experience. I had resources that ranged from insights raised in Bettenhausen's Christian ethics course on power to inspiration from Richardson's example of a Christian feminist, anti-racist challenge of unjust institutional practices.

When I listened to the district superintendent during that second telephone call I knew that I was supposed to go along with his smooth public presentation of these events as a fair and valid appointment process that the bishop and his cabinet had pursued, though regrettably it had a disappointing result. I was a twenty-four-year-old fledgling ordained deacon in the position of asking for her very first appointment to a local church. Because of the unambiguous negative response from the church in Connecticut, it was the wisdom of the bishop and the cabinet that this matter was now settled. But I could not go along with the appearance of fairness, wisdom, and closure presented to me in that telephone conversation.

I made a series of telephone calls introducing myself to individual members of the bishop's cabinet and lobbying for them to reconsider my case. Ultimately, the white male lead district superintendent, the dean of the cabinet, reversed the cabinet's acceptance of the church's decision. He consented to my view that the local church committee should have an opportunity to move beyond their previous deliberations focusing upon my race, gender, and age. They should interview me and consider what gifts and graces for ministry I might bring to pastoral leadership of their faith community. (An interview was ordinarily the follow-up step that came after the district superintendent's initial meeting describing the candidate to the church's personnel committee.)

This church appointment process, as well as my experience in seminary in Boston, illustrates a consistently interdependent relationship between the church and the broader society. Historic protests and demands by Christian leaders for civil rights helped to instigate the passage of laws in the broader society to bar racial and gender discrimination favoring whites and males, and to promote affirmative action policies to counter such discrimination. On the one hand, my experiences demonstrate how the broader society's newly legalized acceptance of these laws seems to have impacted church culture and procedures, especially when that church culture was institutionally located within the secular academy. Newly passed affirmative action laws related to hiring were instrumental in the pressure on the seminary in Boston to move beyond Christian lip-service in its response to racism and sexism. On the other hand, the church's exemption from the state's laws, including those that bar racial and gender discrimination, seems to have allowed the church freely to embrace unjust discrimination in its process for hiring a local church pastor. In Christian church culture there is frequently a commitment to longstanding social norms of inequality and prejudice that elevates the worth of some while diminishing the worth of others. This commitment was embraced with religious tenacity in both the aggressive anti-affirmative action policies of my seminary in Boston and in the passive acceptance of a local church's racial and gender parochialism by the New York area United Methodist Church superintendents. Yet Christian resistance to these supremacist values is also a part of this story about ministerial formation.

It was because I wanted to try actively to fight church discrimination that I found myself sitting in the room with members of the local church committee who had rejected me. After insisting on having this interview, I remember sitting there wondering: "What was I thinking?" The white male dean of the cabinet had become a genuine advocate for me and personally presented me to this group. The committee was eager to begin questioning me. As for me, I was very sleepy. I had traveled on the cheapest "red-eye" flight from California to New York and had not had a chance to take a nap before the interview. After two and a half hours of a very amicable meeting, I recall the district superintendent saying, "Shall we conclude now or take a break and continue?" To my chagrin the committee members agreed that we should take a break and continue. At the district superintendent's suggestion, I offered a prayer to conclude the first part of the meeting and begin the break. In the end they voted to hire me.

One of the questions that the chairperson of the committee asked me that night was about whether or not I would charge members of the church for counseling them. This question seemed rather odd to me at the time but I did not hesitate to respond that I could not imagine any circumstances under which I would do so. I later learned that this concern related to a complaint against a previous pastor. This question, however, like many of the others that the church members asked that night, was concerned with how I would use my power. They wanted to know if I knew how to support and build Christian community with honesty and respectful treatment of them. While a commitment to social justice was not part of their criteria for a pastor, it was clearly an intense part of our interactions. Forcing my presence on them that night represented a negotiation over socially just communal practices. The issues of honesty, mutual respect, and socially just practices in Christian community (and in the broader society) had been the focal point of much of my seminary work.

I believe that a continual, communal process of honing these core values sustains the hope and faith church leaders need. Church culture can seem hopelessly mired in the hypocrisy of rhetoric about building just and loving communities that witness to God's grace, but with accompanying practices that belie this rhetoric. This is especially true of Protestant denominations like my own United Methodist Church. It continues to expand an institutional commitment to teaching the superiority of its heterosexual clergy and laity over its gay and lesbian church members who are called to ordained ministry and laity who seek to have their marriages and families receive equal pastoral care to what heterosexual members sitting alongside of them in the pew receive. As a candidate for ordained ministry or as a new pastor there is a temptation to assume that in light of such fractious realities the wise and prudent strategy is one that maintains the appearance of unity in the church. However, in my experience, trust — a basic ingredient needed for sustaining the integrity of relationships — is eroded by such dishonesty and by abuse of power that follows from the efforts by leaders to pretend that nothing is wrong.

Whether it is one's maleness, whiteness, heterosexuality or another label that society creates to differentiate certain human traits and the social status they deserve, these identity labels play varying but significant roles in the moral ethos of church cultures. Even when it seems like local or denominational church culture expects the usual unjust, prejudiced-based relations to be reinforced by its leaders under the guise of maintaining the appearance of Christian unity, another kind of leadership is possible. Admittedly, the necessary confrontations that such an alternative kind of leadership would involve may prove personally costly. These confrontations may be painful for all those who choose to pursue and advocate for what is too often relegated to devalued categories of human worth, including those who enjoy forms of privileged status and still choose to do so. There is, nevertheless, a deep spiritual hunger for new models of ordained leadership that engender honest, fair, and respectful treatment of people in the church and broader society. This kind of leadership should not be attempted without a support network of family and friends as well as a lot of prayer.

21. What a Minister Is to Do

Wallace M. Alston Jr.

The memory of my first day on the job as the sole pastor of a small Southern church in the early 1960s remained with me until the day I retired and kept me ever searching for an answer to the question: What is a minister to do?

I had received a call from a church of some three hundred members and no other paid staff, located in a small, conservative town in North Carolina, where racial segregation was being challenged and integration resisted by educated people as well as the uneducated, by the rich as well as the poor, sometimes by means of a demeaning epithet, sometimes by means of violence to life and property. I was the beneficiary of a fine theological education from outstanding institutions in Richmond, Cambridge, and Zurich. I had been taught to use the Greek and Hebrew languages to exegete a text and to craft a sermon. I had read and studied under some of the finest theologians and biblical scholars in the world. But when I entered the minister's office on my first day as pastor of that church, shut the door behind me, and took my seat behind the desk, I was struck by the fact that I did not know what to do.

The transition from academic life, where institutions provide hospitable contexts for nurturing ideas and communities, to the isolating and often lonely life of a minister can be daunting indeed. In the past, there had been parents, teachers, senior officers, and mentors of one sort or another to provide guidance and direction. I had not realized to what degree I had taken for granted a structured context of expectation. Now there was no requirement, no standardized guideline, and no one to tell me what I was to do. I was, humanly speaking, my own boss, as long as it was perceived that I was doing an adequate job. But what was the job? How were the job and the successful doing of it understood by the members of the church? What did they think they were paying me to do? Was their perception of the matter the same as mine, and if not, how was I to survive? More importantly, were the biblical and theological assumptions that informed the members of the church, however vague and unformed, compatible with my own; and if not, what was I to do?

These questions and others like them, which were the daily companions of many pastors in the racially segregated South in the 1960s and 1970s, raised the deeper issue of human transformation. Can racism be supplanted by love? Can people be changed? Is radical change in assumption, perspective, and way of life possible? Wherein lies the power to change? The testimony of the Bible seems to be that human transformation, though never inevitable, is always possible. But it became abundantly clear early on in my ministry that human transformation could not be coerced. Defenders of the segregated social order often argued that you could not legislate morality, and they were not entirely wrong. You could legislate public morality by changing the law and criminalizing brutal social behavior, but you could not force a change of heart. That would happen only by suasion. Pastors of churches in these turbulent times soon came to realize that the only power they possessed to effect change in their churches and in the society at large was the power of suasion. This realization alone motivated many ministers to rediscover two different but closely related aspects of pastoral identity: the pastor as politician and the pastor as theologian. These two aspects of pastoral practice, informing my own sense of what the minister is to do over the next three decades, continue to be essential parts of effective ministry today.

The Pastor as Politician

Seminaries and divinity schools rarely do what it takes to prepare their students to meet what they are likely to find when they become the pastor of a church. It is not that these institutions are opposed to the inclusion of such preparation in their three-year M.Div. curricula. It is that they are crippled by the absence of people on their faculties who have firsthand knowledge of pastoral ministry. The porous boundary that once existed between the pastoral ministry and the teaching ministry, which meant that a pastor would often be called to teach on a seminary faculty and that a seminary teacher could be expected to have experience as pastor of a church, disappeared with the emergence of the professional guilds. As a result, even the pastoral or practical disciplines in the theological curriculum are now taught by people who may hold doctorates in the discipline, but who have never actually done it in any sustained and disciplined fashion. Preaching is regularly taught by people with doctorates in homiletics, for example, but who have never preached Sunday after Sunday, year in and year out, to a particular congregation. The same might be said of Christian education, pastoral care and counseling, to say nothing of Bible and theology. Seminary and divinity school faculties which lack the experience, insight, and theological acumen of men and women with sustained pastoral experience can hardly be expected adequately to equip the student headed for the pastorate to foresee and to pre-think what lies ahead.

What lies ahead must be analyzed from below as well as from above. From above it may be true that the church is the people of God, chosen before the foundation of the world, the body of Christ, "the fullness of him who fills all in all" (Eph. 1:23). Yet viewed from below it also must be acknowledged that the church is a voluntary association. This means that, however you choose to interpret it theologically, individuals choose to participate in the life of a church of their own volition, not because of some compelling external force. A critical development in religious institutions during the last four or five centuries has been the gradual shift from forms of necessity and coercion toward voluntarism. Today, church membership, attendance at worship and religious education, adherence to church doctrines, and the amount of financial support given in support of the institution, to a great extent, are matters of voluntary and private decision. If an individual fails to derive benefit from a particular church, or if a person disagrees with its theological orientation or ethical position on a controversial issue, he or she is free to leave that church and join another, or to withdraw from church altogether.[1]

These observations, while they may appear to some to be flogging the

1. I first became aware of the importance for ministerial practice of these two ideas, the church as voluntary association and the minister as politician, in 1970 by reading *The Church, the University, and Social Policy,* The Danforth Study of Campus Ministries, vol. II (Middletown, Ct.: Wesleyan University Press, 1969), particularly the papers by Jeffrey K. Haddon ("The House Divided") and by James Gustafson ("Political Images of the Ministry"). The discussion which follows depends heavily on and is indebted to these papers.

obvious, lead to an inevitable conclusion that begins to shed light on the question of what a minister is to do. That is to say, it follows from an understanding of how voluntary associations work that the effective functioning of such institutions depends on the formation of a basic consensus among the membership as to the meaning, purpose, and direction of the organization. A person who is either ignorant of or out of accord with that for which the organization stands, and who derives from participation in it little or nothing that gives meaning or purpose to life, is unlikely to continue to participate. Similarly, if the negative factors involved in participation are perceived to outweigh the positive, membership is likely to be curtailed.

Pastors, especially young pastors who enter upon their first call with idealistic expectations, must come to terms with the absence of unanimity in Protestant opinion and with the conflict which afflicts the church as a consequence. To be a pastor is to live within an environment of confrontation, disagreement, argumentation, and dispute. The very nature of the church as a voluntary association; a commitment to the liberty of the individual conscience and to the freedom of speech; the lack of theological unanimity in the church; the absence of a central authority whose task it is to regularize doctrine; the diversity of opinion, background, and needs of the laity; the difficulties of communication; and the sheer stubbornness of people all militate against the formation of that basic consensus that is so crucial for the proper functioning of a voluntary association. The task of leadership is to evoke that measure of unanimity that does exist into a somewhat unifying force and to move the community toward a consensus around normative assumptions and goals.

We have all been tempted at times to compare the ministry with other learned professions, particularly with medicine and law, when in fact the social situation of the minister is quite different from that of the physician or the lawyer. This case of mistaken identity sometimes leads ministers to assume a measure of entitlement and importance which is not warranted. Medical care and legal expertise are things people in our society cannot do without. The doctor gets his patients when they cope with a physical malady that drives them to seek medical care. Likewise, the lawyer gets her clients when they must come to terms with some facet of the law. The physician does not have to make a case for the importance of medical care. The attorney does not have to make a case for the importance of legal advice or advocacy. Both are provided a place and a constituency by virtue of personal or social need.

The same cannot be said of the Christian ministry. Ministry has no inevitable place in the order of things. A constituency is not provided the minister by virtue of social necessity. The minister must build and maintain a constituency if a ministry is to be pursued. The minister must have access to people who are willing to give him a hearing in order to have an effective ministry in any given place. The pattern of ministerial leadership, therefore, is more like that of a politician interested in pursuing progressive reforms in a conservative district than it is to that of a doctor or lawyer.

To remain in office without being the mirror image of the electorate, to be the pastor of a church without simply reflecting the mentality of the congregation, is the essence of the political process. While doing what it takes to maintain sufficient support within the constituency to remain in office, the effective political leader also seeks to shape and reshape the consensus of the constituency in the light of the normative convictions held. The conscientious politician is always accountable, not only to an immediate constituency but also to certain normative convictions about the nature and meaning of things that drive the policies espoused. The effectiveness of political leadership is judged by the leader's ability to direct the consensus of those to whom she is immediately accountable in the light of these normative convictions.

Similarly, the task of the minister is to shape the consensus of a church in the light of the convictions the minister holds and on the basis of which the minister was ordained and called to serve. If this is to happen, the minister must be able to articulate these convictions in private as well as in public, with the necessary prerequisite of knowing what they are. A lack of clarity about the sources, convictions, and contemporary relevance of the faith which the church represents leads not only to the minister's inner chaos but also to confusion on the part of the church. Just as the politician does not need to be a legal philosopher in order to govern well, so the pastor does not need to be a scholar in order to have an effective ministry. But just as the politician needs a set of convictions which inform the policies put forward, so the pastor needs to be clear about the theological presuppositions and assumptions that lie behind the pastor's preaching, teaching, pastoral care, and church administration. Being clear about theological presuppositions and assumptions is what theology is all about. The political task of the ministry is done with integrity when the pastor finds his primary identity as a theologian.

The Pastor as Theologian

The crisis of the contemporary church, at least in part, is occasioned by the hiatus between academic theology and church theology, between the theology of the classroom and that of the congregation. Academic theology is an indispensable and highly valued servant of the church. The achievement of a high degree of competence in such things as the Bible and the history of Christian thought, and the capacity to make use of these sources for the purpose of contemporary reflection, requires rational analysis as well as a mastery of languages, texts, ideas, cultures, and intellectual biographies. It also requires the maintenance of a certain critical distance if one is to discern the true from the less true and both from the utterly false. Bridging the gap between the academic study of theology and the confessional interpretation of theology, between the critical distance that rational analysis requires and the personal devotion that Christian witness calls for, is not easy. It is accomplished only with great skill.

To make matters even more complex, there is a tendency on the part of denominational seminaries, especially those that exist in the shadow of secular universities, to compete or at least to prove themselves intellectually worthy by exchanging confessional teaching for programs resembling general religious studies. Seminary faculties are increasingly educated in university graduate programs, where detachment, disinterested analysis, and dispassionate judgment are the legitimate tools of academic research. They are often called to faculty positions in denominational institutions without possessing either the basic M.Div. degree or a thorough knowledge of the tradition within which they are called to teach, and without ever having served as pastor of a church. It is not surprising, therefore, that whereas seminary teachers once taught and wrote as "doctors of the church," for the most part they now write for their peers within the guild as their primary constituency. It is also not surprising that there has been a sharp decline in recent years of the pastor-theologian.

The word "minister," when used by the church, means *"minister verbi divini,"* servant of the Word of God, and makes absolutely no sense whatsoever apart from the assumption that the pastor as well as the teacher is called to be a theologian. I regret that the terms "pastor" and "preacher," to say nothing of the mildly degrading "reverend" and the bloated "doctor," seem to have overtaken the term "minister" in popular parlance. The minister is pastor and preacher, but also teacher, a function of ministry that is often downplayed. "Instead of catering so exclusively to what are usually described as 'pastoral needs' (though the term often cloaks institutional busywork)," writes Douglas John Hall, "ministers today are recalled to the teaching office. If the minister of the congregation is not herself or himself in some sense a theologian, we cannot expect lay persons to reflect some measure of the sort of informed thoughtfulness that is needed if we, as church, are to find a way into the future."[2]

We have two or three generations of church members today, many of whom were influenced by parents and teachers of the 1960s, who rejected the ways and wisdom of the past and are thus relative strangers to the Christian tradition and ignorant of the content of the Bible. Some communions have been more diligent than others in the task of traditioning, but chances are that none of them measure up to even the minimal standards of catechesis that were once taken for granted in these denominations. Having no Curia and no universally accepted criteria for the standardization of doctrine, one wonders how the church is to build a theological consensus capable of undergirding its mission in and to the world. I seriously doubt that it is possible to do so apart from the recovery of a learned ministry that approaches preaching, teaching, pastoral care, and church administration as theological occasions. If that is so, then what does that mean for what a minister is to do?

The first thing a minister is to do if she intends to be a pastor-theologian is to find ways in congregational life, both formal and informal, to give the Bible to people, enabling them personally to identify with the language, stories, and convictions of the church. The Protestant Reformers insisted on translating the Bible into the language of the people. They were convinced that ordinary people could read, understand, and apply the Bible to their daily lives. They also contended that theology should be in the language of the people. Hence they rejected the specialized language of the academy in favor of the language of the church.

To say that what the minister is to do is to teach the Bible may seem obvious, but the fact remains that it is not happening in many churches. One reason for this may be that seminary graduates themselves cannot always be counted on to know the Bible. It was a sad day for the church when many theological seminaries decided to eliminate or to subordinate the

---

2. *The End of Christendom and the Future of Christianity* (Valley Forge, Pa.: Trinity Press International, 1997), pp. 48-49.

study of Greek and Hebrew from their requirements for graduation. There is a depth of biblical knowledge and insight that is only gained by the study of the Bible in the original languages. One of the things the pastor-theologian is to do is to study the Bible diligently and daily, and to do so for its relevance to his own life as well as in preparation for preaching and teaching it to others. The other thing the pastor-theologian is to do in this regard is to devise ways of engaging members of the church in reading, studying, praying, singing, and confessing the Bible, until it becomes as intimate to them as the air they breathe, even to the point of being the story of their lives.

The second part of the task of the pastor-theologian is to familiarize the congregation with the important theological moments, insights, and personalities in the history of the church. Whether or not a particular church embraces or uses the creeds of the church, members of the church should know what they are, where they came from, and why they confess what they confess. If a minister of whatever tradition does not have a life-long love affair with the creeds of Christendom, she is missing something rich and rewarding. If members of the church do not know the creeds as liberating documents that stand over against the desacralizing and dehumanizing forces of the prevailing culture, thrusting life out onto new boundaries of expectation and hope, they too have missed something profoundly important and exciting. Likewise, there is no reason that church members should be unfamiliar with the likes of Justin Martyr, Origen, and Augustine; Catherine of Siena, Thomas Aquinas, and Julian of Norwich; Martin Luther and John Calvin; Paul Tillich, Karl Barth, and Dietrich Bonhoeffer. Each Christian should know that he does not begin *de novo* with the Christian faith, that men and women of great heart and mind have held and kept the faith with integrity and courage long before they were born, and that they can draw strength from the great examples of the past.

A former teacher of mine, with whom I often disagreed but to whom I will be forever grateful for his compelling advocacy of the vocation of the pastor-theologian, would frequently say, "Any minister who does not have at least some of the members of the congregation reading serious theology is simply not doing the job." I think there was never a time in my thirty-five years of ministry in congregations that I did not have one theological study group or other in process, often meeting in my home on weekday evenings. It is part of what a minister is to do if a general theological con sensus is to be built and nurtured that, while never approaching unanimity, will nevertheless grant to the pastor sufficient understanding and support for an effective ministry.

Third, the task of the pastor-theologian is to equip people to think theologically. In its broadest sense, theology is critical refection on the meaning of human existence and the nature of the universe. Christian theology is critical reflection about the meaning of human existence and the nature of the universe in the light of the revelation of God in Jesus Christ as attested in Scripture, in dialogue with how Christians have thought about these things in the past, and in conversation with contemporary experience.

All people live by faith. Augustine, claiming that "to believe is to think with assent," noted more than once that there is a faith commitment in all understanding.[3] To be human is to live by faith. There is no other option. The events of life compel us to act on the basis of faith commitments, be they explicit or implicit, conscious or unconscious. Each day we make decisions based on some sort of faith assumption concerning such things as the meaning of life, the worth of a person, and the distinction between right and wrong, good and evil. If to be human is to have some kind of theology, then it follows that everyone in some sense is a theologian.

Theology as the vocation of each and every human being is based on a threefold foundation. First is the testimony of the Bible. It is implicit in Jesus' admonition to consider the lilies, how they grow (Matt. 6:28). It is explicit in the great commandment to "love the Lord your God . . . with all your mind" (Matt. 22:37). The Apostle Paul insisted that the believer should take "every thought captive to obey Christ" (2 Cor. 10:5) and the author of 1 Peter declared, "Always be ready to make your defense to anyone who demands from you an accounting for the hope that is in you" (3:15). What this amounts to is the calling of the Christian to love God with the mind. Not doing so is irresponsible and can be dangerous.

Second, theology is grounded in the nature of faith itself. Faith seeks understanding or intelligibility, as Anselm of Canterbury said in the eleventh century. This is so in part because of the nature of a human being as

---

3. "On the Predestination of the Saints," *A Select Library of the Nicene and Post-Nicene Fathers of the Christian Church,* vol. V (New York: The Christian Literature Company, 1887), p. 499. See also "On the Profit of Believing," *A Select Library of the Nicene and Post-Nicene Fathers of the Christian Church,* vol. III, pp. 359-60.

an intelligent being, and in part because it is the nature of faith to bring all things into an intelligible, coherent whole.

Third, theology is required by the mystery that encompasses all created things. Human life is lived within certain boundaries or brackets, the most obvious of which are birth and death. Within these boundaries much can be known and done, many problems can be solved, and many new discoveries made, but the meaning of the boundaries themselves and what, if anything, lies behind or beyond them remains unknown. Many people, when confronting a boundary situation, be it the birth of a child or the approach of one's own death, the experience of some great joy or incomparable beauty or intolerable pain, sense a Presence that can only be addressed as "Thou," in whose presence they experience incomparable awe and reverence. Theology is reflection on these varied experiences on the boundaries of life in the light of faith in God.

The task of the pastor-theologian is to help people do this. More specifically, it is to give people the resources, the conceptualities, and the language that might enable them to understand their own lives as well as all of life in the light of the revelation of God in Jesus Christ. This will be possible only if a minister understands her own life and vocation in this way. A congregation will quickly spot a fake. It will be obvious if the minister is pursuing a career rather than a calling. When pastoral occasions are understood as theological opportunities, when even the most mundane and routine work of a church is undertaken with expectation and receptiveness, not only does the church grow in faith and understanding, but its members begin to see what a theological interpretation of life looks like and are more likely to claim that perspective for themselves.

Nathan Pusey, a past president of Harvard University, once referred to the minister as "the professional of whom all other professions stand most in need." One might quibble with the identification of the minister as a professional, and surely non-professionals need what the ministry has to offer as well, but the conviction behind Pusey's comment is one that ministers need to hear. In his speech at the dedication of the Speer Library of Princeton Theological Seminary, Dr. Pusey noted that

> the enduring first need of the church is for a learned ministry, for a continuing succession of those scholar-teachers who shall not need to be ashamed and shall not fail to help the churches to do their work in the world because they will have been qualified rightly to divide the

word of truth. . . . Many circumstances of our lives suggest that today the informed, compassionate, understanding scholar-minister is the professional of whom all other professionals stand most in need, whether they know it yet or not, for it is [the minister's] function to speak to them of that kind of redemption or redirection which alone can give acceptable meaning to their efforts and which it is in the gospel's power, helped by a truly learned ministry, widely to mediate.[4]

Concluding Thoughts

Before concluding, two things, often neglected by seminaries and divinity schools, deserve brief mention. The first is criticism and critique. Few ministers are prepared in advance for the amount of "flack" they routinely receive as the pastor of a church. Ministers are generally sensitive souls who enter the ministry for love's sake. They do not become pastors of churches because they like to argue or enjoy a fight. Most enter the ministry intent on binding up wounds, not inflicting them. What they often find when they begin their ministry is that they have entered a hornets' nest in which they are under constant scrutiny and subject to judgment regardless of what they do or do not do. Ministers are highly vulnerable to criticism and critique. I have never known a minister who did not inwardly hemorrhage at times when subjected to sharp and pointed expressions of dissatisfaction in the congregation in the form of personal criticism.

The church is a grand and glorious institution in many ways. I have given my life to it and would do so again. But the church can be and often is very petty. Its membership includes many fine, intelligent, highly motivated, well-balanced people, who will forever be among the minister's best friends and from whom he or she will draw incredible strength and encouragement. But also included in its membership are all sorts and conditions of people with various needs, motives, weaknesses, problems, and degrees of suffering, who often try to use the church to compensate for some unresolved issue or other. These are the people for whom the minister can do no right, who target the minister for unkind criticism, and who can be a thorn in the minister's flesh. For one, it will be her preaching that

4. Reprint of "The Dedication of the Robert E. Speer Library," October 8, 1977, Princeton Theological Seminary, Princeton, New Jersey.

is the problem; for another, it will be his failure to visit or otherwise to exercise proper pastoral care; for yet another, it will be some administrative inadequacy.

If to be forewarned is to be forearmed, my warning is that criticism and critique go with the pastoral territory, not only because of the diverse makeup of the church's membership, but because such things as the sanctity of the individual, particularly of "the least of these," freedom of speech, and the duty of the disturbed conscience to say "no" when it is deemed that "no" needs to be said, is rooted in the Christian faith itself. Criticism and critique of the minister are to be expected in every church, be it large or small, urban or suburban, sophisticated or unsophisticated. Part of the task, a piece of what the minister is to do, is to develop strategies for coping with criticism, for it will surely come, finding ways of drawing it into the whole process of human interrelatedness and dialogue that has always been a part of the movement of the church into the future.

Sometimes the criticism invites equally determined response, which, if done in a way that does not close the door on possibilities of reconciliation, may begin a conversation in which both parties consider an alternative point of view or even a change of mind. At other times it must be admitted that the criticism is just and right and must be taken to heart. Once after I had expressed my anger at having been criticized for a particular course of action, a friend and member of my church asked me how I thought God speaks to a minister. "God speaks to us through you," she said. "Have you ever considered the possibility that God may speak to you through the criticism you receive from members of your congregation?" Sometimes that may be so and the minister must remain open to that possibility. At other times it may not be so. It is then that the minister must previously have developed strategies for survival that will enable him to proceed without bitterness with the task at hand.

The final thing that might be said before concluding is something about one of these strategies. It is one that I have found to be important, especially in those times when all is not well and one is in some measure under fire. This strategy concerns the continuing nurture of the minister's own mind and heart, doing whatever it takes and taking whatever time it takes to nurture that lively sense of the presence of God on the basis of which he or she first discerned a call to ministry and responded. Ministry is a depleting vocation. This depletion can leave a person vulnerable to burnout and open to the attractiveness of the various "tricks of the trade" if she does not acknowledge that staying close to the sources and convictions of the faith in ways that enable the living God to replenish the spirit and renew the soul is part of the ministerial task. Feelings of guilt for reserving time for this in the minister's daily routine are inappropriate. It is what a minister is to do.

When I accepted the call of a Presbyterian church in Princeton, New Jersey, I received a note from Dr. George A. Buttrick, a venerable minister who had for years been a mentor and personal friend. He concluded the note with a benediction of sorts, which read, "Joy and Peace and Power to you . . . but not too much peace." He had no need to worry. The pastorate does not allow a minister too much peace. What it does allow is a lifetime of opportunities to explore the riches of the peace that the world cannot give, but that comes to people as a gift in extraordinarily interesting, moving, and encouraging ways. The challenge and joy of the Christian ministry, and particularly of the pastorate, is incomparable. The privilege of being a part of the giving and receiving of the peace of Christ in the context of a Christian church, however ambiguous and complex it may be, is rewarding beyond measure and never ceases to provide fresh and intriguing insights into what the minister is to do.

22. Blooming Where We Are Planted

Kathy Dawson

Theological and Practical Education

Many people over the years have asked to hear my call story or to know why on earth I would choose to go to seminary, but until I was approached about writing a chapter in this book, I had never been asked for my graduation story or how I ended up in a particular church and what that was like. When I think back to my transition from seminary to ministry there are two recurring themes that both aided and hindered my work in the church: experience and support. In this chapter I will highlight the influence of these two factors on my calling while I tell my story.

Both experience and support can be seen as I left my home in California to pursue my first theological degree at the Presbyterian School of Christian Education in Richmond, Virginia. Coming as a second-career student, I brought with me nine years of experience teaching in the public schools. I also brought a variety of volunteer work in the church as an elder, teacher, children's choir director, and young adults' event planner. My faith had been nurtured through worship, Christian education, and adult Bible study. Having been a member of several churches in southern California, I had a set notion of what church looked like and didn't look like in medium to large, white, mainline congregations. Of course I would not have put all those descriptors on my experience at that time, because I naïvely thought that the church(es) I had grown up in were the way everyone who was Christian worshiped. I made my experience the norm and judged all future encounters with difference against my early Christian experience.

I knew that the transition from teaching school to preparing for ordained ministry would mean a physical move as well as a spiritual one — from California to Richmond, Virginia, where I knew no one.

I did not go alone, however. Three close family friends decided to make the long drive with me. We loaded two cars and car top carriers with everything that could fit in a small dorm room, and the rest of my belongings went into storage. We spent a week driving across the United States and having all sorts of adventures. Despite the fun and excitement of that trip, though, what I remember most about this transition was crying the last evening in the last hotel room before having to say good-bye to my friends. These were friends who had nurtured my faith in evening Bible studies and lifted me up when my mother had died suddenly. They would continue to play a long-distance part of an emerging support network for ministry that was only just beginning.

The degree I earned at the Presbyterian School of Christian Education led to a second degree at Columbia Theological Seminary in Decatur, Georgia, where my experience in education and the support of friends would continue to play a part in my growing sense of becoming a pastor. This time I would not have to say good-bye to all of my new friends, as several made the transition with me from one school to the other. We had all been a part of the same prayer group in Richmond and started a similar weekly gathering in Decatur.

The experience in education and Christian education that I had brought from California and Virginia was also valued in Georgia. I soon began working part-time as the interim director of Christian education for a large, white, affluent Presbyterian congregation to the north of Atlanta. I enjoyed being able to put into practice what I was learning in the classroom. The children, youth, and adults with whom I ministered were a good grounding for the heady world of theological study. Yet this was a church in transition. They had recently lost their long-time senior pastor, and so I had the growing experience of working under three successive interim pastors. This meant that I was doing many things out of the norm for a part-time interim D.C.E.

My most enduring memory from this period was the Ash Wednesday service I planned from the then-new *Book of Common Worship,* complete with ashes. My experience told me that anything that involves a new learning requires a lot of preparatory education. So I scheduled a Wednesday night supper about the service, in which we burned pieces of paper on which we had written the things that separate us from God. These would then become the ashes used in the service the following week. I instructed the choir. I talked about it on several Sundays prior to that Wednesday. I even instructed the congregation before the worship began on that evening. It was a beautiful service. I was deeply touched when a young woman brought one of the elderly members of the congregation to the front and helped him place ashes on his forehead. As the parishioners left silently out the back doors and the choir descended to the choir room, I took a deep breath and felt wonderful about God's presence in this new thing.

Then a woman met me as I was cleaning up the chancel area, her voice becoming louder and louder as she told me first that I had no business becoming a minister because I was catholicizing the Presbyterian Church and second that she would no longer attend this congregation. She indicated that if her husband chose to continue to come to the church in her absence I would have caused a divorce in their family. Quite a lot to swallow for a soon-to-be seminary graduate! I was devastated and wondered if this was what ministry was all about. So I called on my support, both my long-distance friends as well as the weekly prayer group on campus.

I tell this story not to scare the reader away from ministry or to caution theological seminary students or graduates never to try anything novel. I tell it by way of illustrating one of the blind spots caused by my teaching experience. I expected instruction to convert people to embrace a new ritual, much as I had taught young children new mathematical concepts or vocabulary words. The embodiment of faith, however, is not something that can be taught until one is ready to receive it. Some found the symbol of ashes transforming in their relationship to God. At least one did not. I'll never know what prompted that woman to have such a strong negative reaction to this particular service, but I don't think I would change my choice if I had it to do over again. I can now look back and remember others' faces, all the people coming forward joined by beautiful music and the sense of communal confession.

Time has made the imposition of ashes less strange to those unaccustomed to them in Protestant worship. Time also showed that the woman who found it so offensive that evening did not leave the church permanently and was also willing to call on the pastoral staff for hospital visitation several months after the service. Being able to pray with trusted others during this time brought God into the conversation, taught me that I was entering a different world, and gave hope through perseverance. I have not given up on rich and different liturgy, continuing to seek new ways to acknowledge God's presence in worship and seeking to be faithful. Yet I also acknowledge that there are those who find great spiritual nourishment in the familiar and traditional forms of worship.

The Interview Process

As I prepared to complete my seminary education, I found myself grateful for the opportunity and experience I had received by working and attending classes at the same time. Surely I now knew what was expected of me in ministry and had no illusions that this was to be an easy calling. What I had not anticipated, again, was how my experience and the support of friends and colleagues would influence this next step.

There is nervous energy, bordering on the frantic, around graduating seniors in seminary as they seek their first call. I was no exception. Having a degree in Christian education and about to receive another in divinity, I was a popular candidate among churches searching for associate pastors of Christian education. I kept a file box of church information forms by the phone, so that when a pastoral nominating committee would call unexpectedly, I would be able to choose the appropriate folder and know to whom I was speaking and be able to recall their church's story.

I still saw myself as emphasizing educational ministry, so even though I was a woman, many larger churches were happy to talk with me because the job descriptions for their open positions were very similar to those I had seen as a director of Christian education. So how to choose? Through prayers of discernment, I determined that my gifts in teaching and pastoral care were where God was most strongly leading me. In reading church information forms, I looked at things like the congregations' church school attendance statistics, curriculum choices, and the balance between administrative responsibilities and time for teaching and pastoral visitation. I also looked at opportunities for preaching. How many times a year did the position call for me to be in the pulpit? Did expectations mesh with the amount of preparation time allotted for preparing a meaningful and faithful sermon? I wanted to preach, but not every week nor even every month. I knew that the teaching moment, the give and take between learner and leader, was where I most nearly felt the Holy Spirit working for growth and transformation. This will not be the same for every person or call, but part of the work of seminary or divinity school is internal discernment, listening for the unique place to which God is calling you.

After all this internal work, I was thoroughly convinced that God was calling me to a particular new church development in Tennessee. The position sounded ideal. I could birth a Christian education program with no voices saying, "This is the way we've always done things." The phone interviews we had were very promising. I liked these people. They liked me. I was sure that once we met face-to-face our mutual searching would be over and I would be able to claim this wonderful challenge as my own. Members of the pastoral nominating committee were coming to campus to interview several of us when a freak ice storm hit, postponing their arrival.

In the meantime, another church called and was very persistent. This church was an established church in Mobile, Alabama. I had never been to the state of Alabama. When they called, not only did I have to pull out their folder from the box, but also a map to see where Mobile was. Their senior pastor was also a board member and wanted to meet me while he was on campus. Our meeting happened during that ice storm. It was a brief conversation, simply exchanging information forms, but I agreed to travel to Mobile for an interview should the occasion present itself.

As you might anticipate, the trip to Mobile and the rescheduled interview for the church in Tennessee occurred at the same time. I had a ticket to Mobile in hand, but was devastated that I would miss the interview with the other church. However, when I arrived in Mobile, I felt almost immediately that I had been mistaken — that it wasn't Tennessee where I was supposed to be, but rather Mobile, Alabama. I could say it was the wonderful seafood, the warm congregation members, the beautiful facility, or the collegial sense of a team ministry approach that changed my mind. But really it was a deep-down, gut-level sense that this was the place that God wanted me to be. I basically agreed to the position, pending the committee's interview with one last candidate, before I even left Mobile. It was only when I got home and listened to fellow students in their protracted negotiations with their calling churches that I realized I hadn't even asked about salary or benefits. I guess I simply trusted that God would provide what was needed and that certainly turned out to be the case.

Kathy Dawson

Transition to Mobile

Being Presbyterian, I couldn't just simply pack my bags at graduation and head to Mobile. There were ordination exams to pass; a final exit interview to schedule with my presbytery in Riverside, California; and an oral examination to undergo in my calling presbytery of South Alabama. There was also the awkwardness on campus. How could I rejoice in my call to ministry when so many of my brothers and sisters were still interviewing? It would be nice if God would speak to everyone on the same day and all the potential ministerial candidates were automatically matched with their ideal congregations, but God doesn't work in a computerized fashion. The call process is often messy and seemingly unfair. No one likes to receive (or to write, for that matter) letters of rejection, but it's even stranger to receive letters of rejection from churches to which you didn't apply! Sometimes churches receive recommendations from a variety of sources both on and off campus. These unsolicited letters of rejection continue to come even when you've accepted a call, and always are disconcerting. Having a supportive prayer group to listen, laugh, and cry through the call process was an important part of my experience.

There were also decisions to make about where the ordination service itself would take place. The year was 1994, and this latter decision was difficult to negotiate because at that time in the Presbyterian Church (U.S.A.), it was normally the calling church and presbytery that handled ordination services for Ministers of Word and Sacrament. However, my long-distance support network had sustained me through two degree programs on the East Coast, but they were in southern California and were unlikely to be able to make the trip to Mobile. Therefore I decided that I wanted to be ordained in California and installed in Alabama. After working out the details of polity, etiquette, and timing, the plan was approved by both churches and presbyteries. I was delighted to be able to celebrate with my family, friends, and former colleagues in California from different parts of my life. It was truly a wonderful commissioning and anointing that blessed the experiences that had prepared me for this ministry in this new place. The installation service was equally memorable, as it introduced me to people who became important in forming the pastor that I was to be.

Ministry in Mobile

There were two of us that came from seminary to the staff that same summer. My fellow associate pastor, his wife, and their growing family would all become very influential partners in making the transition between seminary and this first ordained call. It was beneficial in these early days of ministry to have another newly called pastor with whom to share impressions and confusion. Although our job descriptions were distinct, we found areas of common interest and divided our labor accordingly.

Here is an example of how we worked. "Youth ministry coordination" was on my job description, but the middle school and high school youth met simultaneously. Either I would need to change the meeting night for one of the groups, a problematic prospect given that siblings often came together and were in separate groups, or bounce back and forth between the two groups, never really being a part of either. This latter option was alien to what I thought was most transforming in youth ministry — relationships. At the same time, my colleague was wrestling with the fact that involvement with youth was not part of his job description, when he had enjoyed working with youth in the past and had real strengths in this area. So we talked and presented a new alternative to our senior pastor and governing body. We would share responsibility for the youth groups. I would meet consistently with the middle school youth and my colleague with the high school youth. I would be responsible for coordinating the calendars, sending out joint publicity, and planning shared events. This redefining of responsibilities meant a more faithful experience for all, especially the youth.

This worked so well that we collaborated on other programs as well, like confirmation. I would teach the confirmands; my colleague would train their mentors. We would jointly plan events that involved both groups. I discovered through these cooperative ventures that written job descriptions are the best guesses of pastoral nominating committees about how ministry can best be done in churches, but that it takes the God-given gifts of the actual person to see how these will be lived out. In my case, this reshaping of expected ministries was made much easier by the fact that my colleague and I were arriving at the same time. Neither of us was already set within particular responsibilities or boundaries, so we could both draw on our personal experiences and gifts to determine the configuration of responsibilities that would most benefit the church. This would have been much more difficult to achieve as the only newly ordained pastor coming into an established staff.

Sometimes, too, there were things not on the job description that the church needed and which matched my passions and gifts. For instance, the church's nursery had not previously been considered part of the Christian education program and thus was not mentioned in the call form I received. Nevertheless, the nursery was in need of extra staff attention. As in many churches, it was staffed mainly by parent volunteers and by youth who wanted to avoid worship. There were always announcements being made begging for people to sign up for a turn in the nursery. I knew from the training in human development I had received during my theological education that a consistent caregiver is important to a child's growth and development, including his or her spiritual development. I suggested that we have at least one paid professional nursery worker, along with volunteers, so that parents could feel confident in leaving their young children in the church nursery and so that the children would have a loving familiar face to see each Sunday. At first we contracted with an agency, but they were unable to consistently send the same individual every week. After much searching, we found the right person. At the same time, we beautified the nursery and brought it under the umbrella of the congregation's Christian education program. Volunteers were now Christian educators, having an infant/toddler curriculum that could be used with the children in the nursery during the worship service their parents attended. This was one of many times that I would bring my experience in theological education into the daily work of the church. The practice of doing so was formed back in the Atlanta church when I was both attending classes and doing ministry.

Embracing such a method of reflective practice is an important part of the transition between classroom experience and ministry in the church. We constantly bring our previous experiences into our present practices, so learning to reflect consciously on both is helpful and necessary. Indeed, not reflecting on our experience can lead to unconscious assumptions that cause us and others pain.

Let me illustrate this last statement by broadening the context of my first call into the community. Mobile is a Gulf Coast city with a rich history. Like other Gulf Coast cities, it has waved many national flags, including French, Spanish, and American. The region's religious history is consistent with its national heritage, with its two dominant strands of

Christianity being Roman Catholic and Southern Baptist. What this meant for a woman pastor coming into the region was that I had very few clergy colleagues of my gender. I didn't perceive this to be a problem when I left seminary, even though I knew that I would be the only ordained woman in the presbytery and the first one for this particular congregation, though they had other female staff members. After all, I had both male and female friends in seminary. And there I had been graded on the content of my work, not my gender. At the time, I couldn't understand female students who seemed to need exclusively female support from fellow students and female professors.

If I had reflected on my own experience background, I may have listened to these women's stories and been better prepared for the gender issues that arose in my first call. I realized in retrospect, having come from positions wide open for women, like elementary school teaching and directing Christian education programs, that I was ill-equipped to deal with gender discrimination and exclusion in my new calling. These instances were, for the most part, not overt or mean-spirited, but simply showed the church trying to deal with a new paradigm at the same time that I was learning this new role of pastor.

The church was very welcoming of my presence, not only in Christian education but particularly in pastoral care, a responsibility that all three clergy on staff shared. Women especially seemed to enjoy the time I made for lengthy hospital visits and for listening to their stories. The problem within the church mainly manifested itself during the six times a year that I would step into the pulpit. At the end of the service, I began to notice a consistent pattern in the way that people would respond to me as they left the sanctuary. They almost always would mention something about my appearance — my stole, my hair, my shoes, even my posture. It wasn't until my third year of ministry that we began having conversations about the actual content of the sermons.

As a teacher I could rely on the constant feedback and reading of non-verbal cues from my students. But as a preacher, I hadn't a clue whether any of my sermons were touching the lives of parishioners. Finally, I had to give up the wondering and simply try to present the gospel faithfully, hoping that despite my disconcerting appearance the Word of God would have its way.

It surprised me that older women had the most difficulties with my pastoral identity. Now, in listening to the voices of my women colleagues and women students, I am hearing that perhaps these women's own thwarted dreams of becoming a pastor may have been responsible for some of their discontent. I heard through others in the church that a group of women had given me a nickname, "Little Girl Preacher." At least I felt good about the last part of this nickname. If they could call me a preacher, their notions of what was encompassed by this title were beginning to change.

Let me share one final story that encapsulates this change. The church I served was part of an ecumenical consortium of five churches in Mobile that shared a Meals-on-Wheels program and a yearly Thanksgiving service. Traditionally, the Thanksgiving service was held at one of the five churches and another of the five senior pastors was invited to deliver the sermon. One particular year the hosting congregation's pastor decided that he would expand the list of participants to include the choirs and associate pastors of each of the churches as well. All were issued invitations, except for me. I had to make the decision of whether to attend the service as a worshiper or simply stay home. As painful as it was I decided to attend the service. The combined choirs sang beautifully. The liturgy was rich, with ten male pastors reading Scripture and leading liturgy. After the service I saw a number of choir members. One of them was a woman who had openly told me some time ago that while she valued my ministry, as a former Southern Baptist she had some real problems with seeing me in the pulpit. At this event, however, she came up to me and said, "You know it just didn't look right to not see a woman in the chancel area." Change comes slowly, but often at powerful moments.

Throughout these early years of ministry, it was crucial for me to find new support and to maintain old connections. This church was a great crucible of learning, from the teamwork amongst the clergy staff to the wonderful lay personnel and volunteers. Outside the church there was not an organized network amongst other clergy and Christian educators, so I drew on the experience of monthly educator luncheons in Atlanta to begin a similar venture in South Alabama. Unlike the Atlanta lunches, which were more programmatic, with speakers and discussion, our monthly gatherings were simply a way to connect and not feel so isolated in ministry.

Having attended a traditional residential seminary, I had become accustomed to living in community with a group of people similarly positioned in life. One of the most difficult transitions was leaving that community to live on my own. There wasn't anyone's door on which I could knock at the end of the day and simply debrief a difficult situation. As a pastor, I was often involved in emotionally wrenching situations that called on me to develop new spiritual disciplines and practices in order to stay connected to God and emotionally healthy in the midst of ministry's challenges. Again my long-distance network of family, old and new friends, and former mentors would be drawn on in times of particular challenge, but it was difficult to create those same kinds of relationships close at hand without violating confidences or putting my call at risk.

Despite the difficulties inherent in ministry, I have found it to be a deeply nourishing calling. When it came time to pursue my next call to ministry in an academic setting, I left this church with mixed emotions. I was excited to pursue the dream of a teaching ministry, planted in my heart when I made that first journey from California to Virginia. Yet I had grown into the role of pastor of a local congregation and loved the consistency of standing alongside a faithful people as God worked in their lives from birth through death and beyond. The transition from local church pastorate back into the academic world had as many regrets and joys as the transition between seminary and the church.

I still keep my hand in the local church, coming full circle as a volunteer once more and as a faculty member in the theological institution where I received my Master of Divinity degree. The church where I currently worship is different from those in which I ministered. Over the years, I have grown to appreciate the unique mission of smaller congregations that are not so program-driven. Diversity of culture, age, and socioeconomic status has also become more important to me in seeking a worshiping faith community than they were when I left California.

There are seasons of the church year when I long for the worship and educational world of the local pastor and seasons of the seminary year when I can't imagine my present calling more suited to God's purposes for my ministry. We bloom where God has planted us, sometimes drawing on previous harvests of experiences, and always needing the care and feeding of others, especially the One who has called us.

23. Between Two Worlds

William H. Willimon

In retrospect, my first year as a pastor was perhaps the most painful, frightening year of my entire ministry. Part of the terror that I experienced was my fear of failure, not simply to fail at being an effective pastor (I had little means of knowing what being "effective" would look like), but rather my fear that I had failed to discern God's will for my life. What I had thought was that my tortured, gradually dawning, wrestled-with "call to the ministry" might be revealed as something other than God's idea. Looking back, I realize now that the early bumps and potholes that I experienced during the course of that first year were so disconcerting because each one of them made me wonder, *Maybe my friends are right. Maybe I don't have what it takes to be a pastor. Perhaps the church really is a waste of my life.*

As it turned out, I received more confirmation of my vocation in that first year than invalidation. Wonder of wonders, God really did occasionally speak through me to God's people, God really did sometimes use me to work a wonder, and God's people — some of them — really did respond to my ministry. I came to realize that much of my consternation was due not to my own lack of preparation, or to inadequacies in me or in the church, but rather to a move I was making from one world to another.

I recently heard Marcus Borg of the errant Jesus Seminar chide us pastors for protecting our congregations from the glorious fruits of "contemporary biblical scholarship." There's a brave new world of insight through the historical-critical study of Scripture! Don't hold back from giving the people in the pew the real truth about Jesus as it has been uncovered by contemporary biblical scholarship and faithfully delivered to you in seminary biblical courses! He implied that even the laity, in their intellectual limitations, can take the truth about Jesus as revealed by Professor Borg and his academic friends.

Yet it seemed not to occur to Professor Borg that contemporary biblical scholarship, because it is asking the wrong questions of the biblical texts, and even more because it is subservient to a community that is at odds with communities of faith, may simply be irrelevant both to the church and to the intent of the church's Scripture. Sometimes the dissonance between the church and the academy is due not to the benighted nature of the church, but rather to the limited thought that reigns in the academy.

It took me a long time to learn this. As I said, I remember experiencing that dissonance in my first days in my first church in rural Georgia. I was the freshly minted product of Yale Divinity School, now forlorn and forsaken in a poor little parish in rural Georgia. My first surprise was how difficult it was to communicate. It was as if I were speaking a different language. As I preached, my congregation impassively looked at me across a seemingly unbridgeable gulf.

At first I figured that the problem was a gap in education. (Educated people are conditioned to think this way when dealing with the uneducated.) I had nineteen years of formal education behind me; many of them had fewer than twelve. Most of my education involved lots of writing and talking, whereas they seemed taciturn and reserved.

I was impressed that they knew more about some things than I. Mostly, they talked and thought with the Bible. They easily, quite naturally referred to Scripture in their conversation, freely using biblical metaphors, sometimes referring to obscure biblical texts that I had never read. If they had not read the masters of my thought — Bultmann, Tillich, and Barth — then I had no way to speak to them. I had been in a world that based communicating upon conversations about the thought of others, rather than worrying overmuch about my own thoughts. I realized that my divinity school had made me adept in construing the world psychologically and sociologically (that is, anthropologically) rather than theologically. The only conceptual equipment my people had was that provided by the church, whereas most of my means of making sense were given to me by the academy. Their interpretation of the world was not simply primitive, or simple, or naïve, as I first thought. Rather, they were thinking in ways that were different from my ways of thinking. I came to realize that we were not simply speaking from different perspectives and experiences; it was as if we were speaking across the boundaries of two different worlds.

When a theologically trained seminary graduate like me confronts the sociological reality of the church, when a new pastor, schooled in a vision of the church as it ought to be, has his or her nose rubbed in the church as it is — that's the kind of collision that is the concern of this book. The leap between academia and ecclesia can be a challenge.

I want to avoid a characterization of the challenge as a leap between the goofy ideal (ecclesia as portrayed in the thoughtful academy) and the gritty real (ecclesia as it is in all its grubby mediocrity). Sometimes new pastors say, "Seminary did not prepare me for the true work of ministry," or "There is too great a gap between what I was told in seminary and what the church really is."

Nor do I want to put the matter in a way that privileges academia over ecclesia, as if to imply that to theological schools and seminaries has been given the noble vision of the real, true, faithful church whereas it has been given to the church the grubby, impossible task of actually being the church, putting all that highfalutin theological theory into institutional praxis.

The challenge is not to stretch oneself between the ideal and the real, or between the theoretical and the practical; the challenge is in finding oneself in the middle of an intersection where two intellectual worlds collide. True, there is often a disconcerting disconnect between the questions being raised in the seminary and the answers that constitute the church. Yet there may also be the problem that the seminary is preoccupied with the wrong questions, or at least questions that arise from intentions other than the Kingdom of God and its fullness.

The Seminary's World

To be sure, it's risky to attempt to characterize so complex and diverse a phenomenon as "the seminary." My characterization arises out of nearly thirty years on a mainline Protestant seminary faculty and visits, in the course of time, to over forty different theological schools. Some of my books have become standard texts in the curriculum of a few dozen seminaries, so I know at least a large part of the world of the seminary.

I am helped, in attempting to generalize about theological education, because the world of the seminary is more uniform and standardized than the world of the church. Seminaries, be they large or small, conservative or liberal, have more in common with one another than they do with the churches they serve. They have patterned their internal lives, constructed their curricula, selected their faculties, and have expectations of their students that are based more on the models of other seminaries than on the mission of the church. That's only one of the problems of theological schools.

Seminaries, at least those in our church, labor under a growing disconnect between the graduates they are producing and the leadership needs of the churches these graduates are serving. This disjunction causes friction in and sometimes defeat of the transition between seminary and church for new pastors. For example, most Protestant seminaries have organized themselves on the basis of modern, Western ways of knowing. The epistemology that still holds theological education captive is that which was borrowed from the modern university — detached objectivity; the fact/value dichotomy; the separation of emotion and reason with the exaltation of the latter as the superior means of knowing; the sovereignty of subjectivity; the loss of any authority other than the isolated, sovereign self paired with subservience to the social, cultural, and political needs of the modern nation-state.[1]

That's saying a mouthful, but it is an attempt to depict the intellectual "world" of the theological school, a world that has a tough time honoring both the intellectual restrictions of academia and the peculiarly sweeping mandate of the church of Jesus Christ.

The word "seminary" means literally "seed bed." Seminary was meant to be the nursery where budding theologians are cultivated and seeds are planted that will bear good fruit, God willing, in the future. Trouble is, seminaries thought they could simply overlay those governmentally patronized, culturally confirmed ways of academic thinking over the church's ways of thought, and proceed right along as if nothing had happened between the seminary as the church created it to be (a place to equip and form new pastoral leaders for the church) and the seminary as it became (another graduate/professional school).

In the world of the contemporary theological school, faculty talk mostly to one another (as Nietzsche noted long ago, no one reads theolo-

---

1. The best history of what happened in our seminaries in the twentieth century is Conrad Cherry, *Hurrying Toward Zion: Universities, Divinity Schools, and American Protestantism* (Bloomington, Ind.: Indiana University Press, 1995).

gians except for other theologians), and faculty accredit and tenure other faculty using criteria derived mainly from the modern, secular research university. While the seminary desperately needs faculty who are adept at negotiating the tension between ecclesia and academia, faculty tend to be best at bedding down in academia. The AAR (American Academy of Religion) owns theological education.

One last disconnect I'll mention: The seminary, by its nature, is a selective, elitist institution, selecting and evaluating its students with criteria that are derived from educational institutions rather than the ecclesia. In one sense, a theological school should be selective, astutely selecting those students who can most benefit Christ's future work with the church. Trouble is, when criteria are applied that arise from sources other than the Body of Christ, we have the phenomenon of the church's leadership schools cranking out people who have little interest in or equipment for service to the church as it is called to be. If college departments of religious studies were not in decline, there would be something to do with the best of these seminary graduates. If the U.S. Post Office were not holding its employees more accountable for their performance, the rest of them would have promising careers.

For instance, when my district superintendents and I interviewed a group of soon-to-be graduates in one of our seminaries, we were distinctly unimpressed with their responses. Here we were before them saying, in effect, "We are a declining organization. We are looking for people who will come into the United Methodist ministry, take some risks, attempt to grow some new churches and new ministries, and help lead us out of our current malaise." Yet the seminarians we were conversing with struck us as mostly interested in being caregivers to established congregations, caretakers of ministries that someone else long before them had initiated, and in general, to be people who were attracted to our church's ministry precisely because they would never, ever have to take a risk with Jesus.

When I was critical of the students we were meeting, one of the pastors with me said, "Look, you have people who have spent a lifetime in school learning nothing more than how to be in school. They have been taught by tenured faculty who have given their lives to doing well in academia and thereby getting tenure and never having again to take a risk in their lives. Faculty who are not held accountable for their performance or results are not likely to educate clergy who are focused on accountability or results."

When seminaries appoint faculty who have little skill or inclination to traffic between academia and church, is there any wonder why the products of their teaching find that transition to be so difficult? Alas, what many graduates do is quickly jettison "all that theology stuff" that seminary attempted to teach and relent to the "real world" of the congregation, the rest of their ministry simply flying by the seat of their pants. The seminary may self-flatteringly think of itself as the vanguard of the thought of the church when in reality it is an agent for the preservation of the church's boring status quo.

The Church's World

Seminarians who have been schooled in modern, Western notions that they are primarily individuals, detached persons whose main source of authority is their own subjectivity, have thereby been inculcated into the unchristian notion that they should think for themselves. What a shock to enter their first parish and find that church is essentially a group phenomenon, an inherently traditioned enterprise. Our most original thinking occurs when we think not by ourselves, but with the saints. The best thing that seminary has done for its graduates, if it has done its work, is to introduce them to the burden and the blessing of the church's tradition, to form them into advocates for the collective witness of the church, and to make believe that the church is God's answer to what's wrong with the world. Yet the way that the seminary engages the witness of the saints makes it difficult for new pastors to think with the saints.

For example, Scripture, the tradition of the church, has a privileged place in the communication of the church. Pastors are ordained, ordered to bear that tradition compellingly, faithfully, quite unoriginally before their congregations, not primarily so that their congregations can think through the tradition, but rather so that they can in their discipleship incarnate Christian truth. We pastors are not free to rummage about in the recesses of our own egos, not free to consult other extra-ecclesial texts, until we have first done business with Scripture and the great tradition. Alas, too much of today's theological training (arising out of the German university of the nineteenth century) places the modern reader above the texts of the church, assuming a privileged, detached, and superior position to the church's historic faith. The academic guild stands in judgment upon the texts, raising questions about the texts. Thus it comes as a jolt for the seminarian to graduate and to find him or herself cast in the role of the ordained, the official who leads the church not in detached criticism of these texts but rather in faithful embodiment of the sacred texts.

In my book *Pastor*[2] I observed that many seminarians tend to be introverted, reflective, personal seekers after God whereas the church is heavily politicized and communal. Pastors are supremely "community persons," officials of an institution, leaders whom the church expects to worry about community and group cohesion with a Savior whose salvation is always a group phenomenon. The seminarian who is trained occasionally to write a speech for a group of individuals, sometimes to do one-on-one counseling, to form intense personal relationships within a conglomerate of individuals, finds herself flung into a politically charged, complex organization, a family system that requires astute knowledge of group dynamics and wise leadership of a divisive group of people who have been caught in the dragnet of God's expansive grace in Christ. When Chrysostom argued his own inadequacy to be a pastor or bishop, it was precisely this public quality of Christian leadership that he cited as the reason why he did not have what it takes to be a pastor.

Sadly, too often the seminary has taught its students to step back from the Christian tradition and its Scriptures, to reflect, to learn to critique, and actively to question. True, such stepping back and critique are developmentally appropriate for the formation of the church's leaders. Yet when the seminarian becomes a pastor, she takes her place as leader of an organization that has goals like embodiment, engagement, involvement, participation, and full-hearted commitment, embrace of the enemy, hospitality to the stranger, group cohesion, *koinonia*. The whole point of discipleship is not cool consideration of Jesus, but rather following Jesus. The person who fails to make the move from being the lone individual confronting the faith and tending his or her own spiritual garden, to the role of a public leader of a group, is the person who will have a tough time in the first parish.

Today many describe the ordained ministry as "servant leadership." The peculiar service that the church needs from those ordained is that they step up, lay aside their own spiritual quandaries, and speak for the church to the church. They must, as the bishop tells them in the ordinal, "take au-

---

2. *Pastor: The Theology and Practice of Ordained Ministry* (Nashville: Abingdon, 2002).

thority," cultivating in themselves the habit of thinking more about the community and its needs than their own. Students who have been enculturated into the world of the academy — in which students must defer and submit to the authority of the professor, who has submitted to the authority of the academic guild — sometimes have difficulty standing up in a congregation and, in service to the community, taking charge, casting a vision, and taking the time and doing the work to build a group of allies who will join the pastor in moving toward responsibility for Christ's mission into the world.

I therefore tell seminarians upon their graduation that they are not just taking on a new job, they are moving to a new world. One of the most important shifts in theological education in the last few decades has been the shift away from students who, having been nurtured by the church — through years of Sunday school, church camp, church youth group — are then handed over to the seminary for preparation for being pastors. An increasing number of seminary students arrive at seminary having had minimal exposure (if any) to the church and its ministrations. This shift has necessitated seminaries developing courses that not only introduce seminarians to the pastoral ministry but also to the church itself. (In the middle of my third class session on baptism, after a question by a student, I asked the class, "How many of you have actually seen a baptism performed?" Just over half the class said yes.)

I expect this book on transitions from seminary to the parish is needed more than ever because the challenges in that transition may be greater than ever. Recently, when I asked a group of our best and brightest new pastors what they would like most from the church and from me as their bishop, I was surprised to hear them all respond, "Supervision!" They yearn for help with the move between these two worlds because they realize the inadequacy of their preparation. Churches and judicatories must take this move more seriously and must develop better means of mentoring and supervising new pastors through this process.

Some Specific Suggestions

As someone who now works with new pastors on that move from the world of the theological school to the world of the parish, I have some specific suggestions:

1. Devise ways to learn to speak their language. Laity sometimes complain that the young pastor, in sermons, uses "religious" words like "spiritual practice," "liberation," "empowerment," "intentional community" (this is an actual list a layperson collected and sent to me) that no one understands and no one recalls having heard in Scripture. Such "preacher talk" makes the pastor seem detached, alien, and aloof from the people and hinders leadership.

2. At the same time, prepare yourself to become a teacher of the church's peculiar speech to a people who may have forgotten how to use it. This may seem contrary to my first suggestion. My friend Stanley Hauerwas says that the best preparation for being a pastor today is previously to have taught high school French. The skills required to drill French verbs into the heads of adolescents are the skills that pastors need to teach our people how to speak the gospel. Trouble is, most seminarians are more skilled, upon graduation from school, to be able to describe the world anthropologically than theologically. They have learned to use the language of Marxist analysis or feminist criticism better than the language of Zion. We must be persons who lovingly cultivate and actively use the church's peculiar speech.

3. Keep telling yourself that the difference in thought between the laity in your first parish and that of your friends back in seminary is not so much the difference between ignorance and intelligence; it's just different ways of thinking that arise out of life in different worlds. I recommend reading novels (Flannery O'Connor saved me in my first parish by writing stories that sounded like they could have been written by one of my parishioners) in order to appreciate the thought and the speech of people who, while having never been initiated into the narrow confines of the world of theological education, are thinking deeply.

4. Remind yourself that while the seminary has an important role to play in the life of the church, it is the seminary that must be accountable to the church, not vice versa. It is my prejudice that, if you have difficulty making the transition from seminary to parish it is probably a criticism of the seminary. The Christian faith is to be studied and critically examined only for the purpose of its embodiment. Christians are those who are to become that which we profess. The purpose of theological discernment is not to devise something that is interesting to say to the modern world but rather to rock the modern world with the church's demonstration that Jesus Christ is Lord and all other little lordlets are not.

5. Be open to the possibility that the matters that were focused upon in the course of the seminary curriculum, the questions raised and the arguments engaged, might be a distraction from the true, historic mission and purpose of the church and its ministry.

6. On the other hand, be open to the possibility that the church has a tendency to bed down with mediocrity, to accept the mere status quo as the norm, and to let itself off the theological hook too easily. One reason why the church needs theology explored and taught in its seminaries is that theology (at its best) keeps making Christian discipleship as hard as it ought to be. Theology keeps guard over the church's peculiar speech and the church's distinctive mission. There is something within any accommodated, compromised church (and aren't they all, in one way or another?) that needs to reassure itself: "All that academic, intellectual, theological stuff is bunk and is irrelevant to the way the church really is." The way the church "really is" is faithless, mistaken, cowardly, and compromised. It's sad that it is up to seminaries to offer some of the most trenchant and interesting critiques of the church. Criticism of the church ought to be part of the ongoing mission of a faithful church that takes Jesus more seriously and itself a little less so. I pray that your theological education rendered you permanently uneasy with the church. Promise me that you will, throughout your ministry, never be happy with the church.

7. I pray that you studied hard in seminary, read widely, thought deeply because you are going to need all of that if you are going to stay long as a leader of the church. Your life would be infinitely easier and less complicated if God had called you to be an accountant or a seminary professor. Most of the stuff that you read in seminary will only prepare you really to grow and to develop after you leave seminary. Think of your tough transition into the parish as the beginning, not the end, of your adventure into real growth as a minister. Theology tends to be wasted on the young. It's only when you run into a complete dead end in the parish, when you are aging and tired and fed up with the people of God (and maybe even God, too) that you need to know where to go to have a good conversation with some saint in order to make it through the night. Believe it or not, it's much easier to begin in the ministry, even considering the tough transition between seminary and the parish, than it is to continue in ministry. A winning smile, a pleasing personality, a winsome way with people, none of these are enough to keep you working with Jesus, preaching the Word, nurturing the flock, looking for the lost. Only God can do

that and a major way God does that is through the prayerful, intense reading, study and reflection that you can only begin in three or four years of seminary.

8. Try not to listen to your parishioners when they attempt to use you to weasel out of the claims of Christ. Much of the criticism that you will receive, many of their negative comments about your work, are just their attempt to excuse themselves from discipleship. "When you are older, you will understand," they told me as a young pastor. "You have still got all that theological stuff in you from seminary. Eventually, you'll learn," said older, cynical pastors. Now it's, "Because you are a bishop, you don't really understand that I can't. . . ." God has called you to preach and to live the gospel before them and they will use any means to avoid it. Be suspicious when people encourage you to see the transition from seminary to the parish as mainly a time finally to settle in and make peace with the "real world." Jesus Christ is our definition of what's real and there is much that passes for "the way things are" in the average church that makes Jesus want to grab a whip in hand and clean house.

9. The next few years could be among the most important in your ministry, including the years that you spent in seminary, because they are the years in which you will form the habits that will make your ministry. That's one reason why I think the Lutherans are wise to require an internship year in a parish, before seminary graduation, for their pastors and why I think that a great way to begin your ministry is as someone's associate on a team ministry in a larger church. In a small, rural church, alone, with total responsibility on your shoulders, in the weekly treadmill of sermons and pastoral care, if you are not careful there is too little time to read and reflect, too little time to prepare your first sermons, so you develop bad habits of flying by the seat of your pants, taking short cuts, and borrowing from others what ought to be developed in the workshop of your own soul. Ministry has a way of coming at you, of jerking you around from here to there, so you need to take charge of your time, prioritize your work, and be sure that you don't neglect the absolute essentials while you are doing the merely important. If you don't define your ministry on the basis of your theological commitments, the parish has a way of defining your ministry on the basis of their selfish preoccupations and that is why so many clergy are so harried and tired today. Mind your habits.

10. Get some good mentors. I believe that ministry is a craft. I am unperturbed when new pastors sometimes say, "Seminary never really taught

me actually how to do ministry." I think seminary is best when it instills the classical theological disciplines and exposes to the classical theological resources of the church, not so good at teaching the everyday, practical, administrative and mundane tasks of the parish ministry. One learns a craft, not by reading books, but by looking over the shoulder of a master, watching the moves, learning by example, developing a critical approach that constantly evaluates and gains new skills.

Selecting a mentor can be your greatest challenge as a new pastor. Few experienced pastors have the training or the gifts for mentoring a new colleague. The "Lone Ranger" mentality afflicts many lonely pastors and their work shows the results of their failure to obey Jesus' sending of the Seventy "two by two" (Luke 10:1). Some senior colleagues are often threatened by your youth, or your idealism, or your talent, seeing their own failures and disappointments in the light of your future promise. You will encounter those experienced pastors whose main experience has been that of accommodation, appeasement, and disillusionment with the meager impact of their ministry. They have a personal stake in robbing you of your youthful energy and expectation for ministry. Their goal is to get you to say, "Well, I thought that ministry in the name of Jesus would be a great adventure but now I've settled in and turned it into a modestly well paying job."

Yet asking someone to be your mentor, to look into your life, to show you how to do ministry as they have done it, is one of the most flattering and affirming things you can do for a senior colleague. The Christian ministry is too tough to be done alone. There is something built into the practice of Christian ministry that requires apprenticeship from Paul mentoring young Timothy to Ambrose guiding the willful Augustine, to Carlyle Marney putting his arm around me and saying, "Here's what a kid like you has got to watch out for." In my experience, one of the most revealing questions that I can ask a new pastor is, "Who are your models for ministry? Whose example are you following?"

One of the most decisive examples given to me, in my first months of ministry, was a negative one. I was attending my first Annual Conference. Between one of the sessions, an older, self-presumed wiser pastor took me aside and said, "Son, you seem ambitious and talented. Let me give you some advice that I wish someone had given me when I was at your age. Buy property at Junaluska." (Lake Junaluska was a retreat center, now Methodist resort, near our Conference.)

"Property at Junaluska?" I asked in wide-eyed stupidity.

"Right. Doesn't have to be a house. Perhaps start with an undeveloped lot. Eventually move up to a home at Junaluska," he continued.

"I went skinny dipping in the lake at Junaluska when I was on a youth retreat, but I never really liked the place," I said.

"Name me one man on the bishop's cabinet who doesn't have a house at Junaluska," he responded before moving on to offer advice to some other promising young pastor.

I thought to myself, "Four years of college. Three years of seminary. Three years of graduate school for the purpose of a lousy mortgage at Lake Junaluska. This is what it's all about?"

That interchange was one of the most significant in my first days as a United Methodist minister. It was encouragement for me to lay hold of the vocation that had taken hold of me. Standing there in the lobby of the auditorium, I prayed, "Lord, you have my permission to strike me dead if I ever degrade my vocation as that guy has degraded his."

That I am here today, over thirty years after my transition from seminary to the pastoral ministry, writing this essay, suggests to me that I kept the solemn vow I made that day. More likely is that the Lord is infinite in mercy, full of forgiveness, and patient with those whom the Lord calls to ministry.

24. Lessons Learned

Allan Hugh Cole Jr.

Introduction

A person who edits and writes a final chapter in a multi-authored book enjoys at least a couple of advantages that the book's other authors do not. One advantage has to do with the wisdom garnered from reading what those other authors have written. Considering what others have put forth may, indeed should, lead us to think in broader, richer, deeper, and perhaps altogether new ways about all kinds of matters having to do with the subject at hand — which is to suggest that what others have said should shape what we ourselves might have to say. That has certainly been the case for me here. Reading what each of these gifted and thoughtful contributors has offered in the essays preceding this one has taught me much. Consequently I am indebted to them for the insights I might offer.

Another advantage to editing and writing a final chapter to a book like this one springs from the ability to see the whole project and in turn to offer up what has not yet been identified, discussed, or debated that may very well have a place in a collaborative conversation that the book seeks to promote. In other words, I have the benefit in this concluding chapter of simply trying to put before readers a few additional items that they may chew on after having enjoyed an already satisfying smorgasbord of tasty, nourishing, and sustaining food. Like the other authors herein, my reflections grow out of my own experience in ministry and I hope they will benefit those moving in their own vocational journey from mid-terms to ministry.

Allan Hugh Cole Jr.

Beginnings — Endings — Beginnings

My life in pastoral ministry officially began on October 9, 1994, when I was ordained by the Presbytery of Long Island to serve as pastor of the Presbyterian United Church in Schaghticoke, New York, a largely rural community tied historically to dairy farming in northern Rensselaer county, about twenty miles from the city of Albany. It was said of this lovely community, in a joking way that turned out to be no joke, that if you'd lived there forty years you were still a newcomer — which is to say that its shared history, customs, and expectations ran deep, in and out of church life.

As I recall, I had already been serving as pastor in Schaghticoke for about six weeks, but the ordination service, conducted by members of the judicatory that had nurtured me as an "inquirer" and "candidate" for the office of Minister of Word and Sacrament, made my position official; so much so that I would not have to invite a nearby retired pastor to celebrate the Lord's Supper the first Sunday in November, which I did have to do in October, and I could also baptize a couple of children whose families were eager to have that done and had been patiently awaiting the new pastor's arrival.

As a twenty-six year-old nascent minister, with degree in hand from Princeton Seminary and undoubtedly more passion than wisdom to draw on, my entry into ministry was joined with lots of ideas, too many romantic visions to recall, and also some measure of courage that I trusted would serve me and those I was called to serve well, as together we walked down our vocational paths for the benefit of God and the world. To put it bluntly, I had big plans for this ministry.

As it turned out, my stay in this congregation and community was quite brief — much more so than I would ever have envisioned. The strong tug of additional study, bolstered by deepening feelings of loneliness, isolation, and a corresponding vocational confusion, prompted a return to school after a little over one year, first at the Columbia University School of Social Work for another master's degree and then at Princeton Theological Seminary for doctoral work in pastoral theology. I relished much about ministry and the pastoral life in that first year, including the relationships I formed with church members and people in the broader community, the discipline (tough though it was) of preaching each and every week after having only written a handful of sermons while in seminary,

288

and also simply learning more and more about how to lead in the church, with all its challenges and rewards.

Yet I also struggled profoundly with leaving the world of the seminary and entering the world of the small, rural, and seemingly dying church, one that had placed high hopes for the future on my youthful vigor, fresh ideas, and expressed desire to stay for a while. Upon arriving I shared those same sentiments. Yet as my romantic visions of serving as a small-town pastor, residing in a pre-1900 colonial home, and living in a region whose beauty was simply breathtaking began to ebb, giving way first to strong feelings of isolation, then to boredom, and thereafter to a kind of vocational disorientation, I became restless in my calling, disillusioned with the pastoral life, and probably a bit depressed as well. Writing my resignation letter and meeting with the session one evening in late spring remains one of the more difficult and painful experiences I have had, in ministry or otherwise. Collective high hopes turned to communal disappointment over dreams unrealized and potential unfulfilled.

I know now that my experience is not all that unusual. Many new pastors struggle with all kinds of challenges that come with *leaving* the familiar and, at times, "cocoon-like" comfort of a seminary community — which in the course of three or more years' time tends to provide a significant measure of social, intellectual, and vocational support — and *entering* into a new community that operates with a different history, alternative norms and values, and cultural and place-specific expectations that may not have been thoroughly considered even if they were not altogether unforeseen. In too many cases, my own included, those challenges eventuate in feelings of isolation, loneliness, and uncertainty over whether one has misunderstood one's calling.

While my experience may not have been uncommon, then or now, I had not previously considered any of the challenges I faced in the pastorate, either while I was in seminary or while moving into my first pastoral position. Moreover, I cannot recall these matters ever being broached in seminary courses or internships, or as I progressed through the ordination process in the Long Island Presbytery. In fairness to those preparing me for ministry, I think the cultural shift involved in moving from the greater New York City area — in my case that included Long Island and Princeton — to a rural community of approximately 800 people was much more extreme than what may be typical in the way of requisite cultural shifts. Even so, the point I wish to stress is that this shift and its challenges took me largely by surprise. Moreover, I have spoken with enough new ministers over more than a decade since holding my own first ministry position to believe firmly that a number of them have had a similar experience and that still other new ministers will.

Interestingly, some twelve years later I think I could be happy in a community like Schaghticoke. I am simply in a different place and have different likes and needs than I did at age twenty-six. But at that time I felt in my first ministry call like a fish out of water; and that certainly compromised both my happiness and, I am sure, my effectiveness in ministry. I remember Ted Wardlaw, president of Austin Seminary, once remarking that many ministers have at least one pastorate that lasted too brief a time. That was surely true for me in Schaghticoke, and for many years I felt guilty for leaving a congregation after too brief a time when they had put great hope, trust, and confidence in my leadership and our partnership. Leave I did, though, after about fifteen months of service. I left to go back to school and to re-evaluate my vocational path.

I returned to pastoral ministry about one year later and remained there for the better part of the next seven years. While completing my social work studies I served as interim pastor of the Glenwood Presbyterian Church in Glenwood Landing, New York, a beautiful little town on the north shore of Long Island. Then, after moving back to New Jersey and completing residency requirements for my doctoral degree at Princeton Seminary, my wife, Tracey, and I moved to Long Island once again, to the south shore town of Massapequa as I accepted a call to serve as senior pastor of the Massapequa Reformed Church. I remained there for four years, leaving only after feeling a strong sense of call to full-time teaching at Austin Seminary.

In a sense, then, I have actually made at least two, and perhaps even three, transitions between the academic world and the world of the church. With each one I have learned much about God, the church, the ministerial life, and surely myself, which I believe has served to make me a more competent and faithful minister today. The reflections that follow arise from experiences tied to each of those transitions and to what I have learned along the way.

Lessons Learned

Maintaining Sensitivity to Feelings

I learned very early in ministry the necessity not merely for maintaining theological acuity, clarity, and commitment in one's pastoral work — important though all of that is — but for remaining at least equally sensitive and wise with respect to personal feelings, others' and one's own. My lesson came a few weeks following ordination, after I was called upon to officiate at a funeral for the first time. The deceased was not a member of the congregation I served. In fact, he did not belong to any congregation and had not for most of his life. Nor had he lived in the vicinity for quite some time. For several decades he had lived on the West Coast. Nevertheless, he had both roots and surviving family members in the Schaghticoke area who expressed a desire for him to be buried nearby. That desire prompted a funeral director in the city of Troy, located about twelve miles away, to phone me and ask about my availability and willingness to "do the service." As we spoke, he explained that since neither this man nor his family belonged to a church, the plans were for the service to take place in the funeral home's chapel with a "brief" graveside service to follow. As I discovered, this was not at all unusual practice in that region, even among those who did belong to congregations. In both Upstate New York and on Long Island, funerals frequently took place in funeral homes as opposed to the church.

I recall feeling quite nervous when speaking with the funeral director. Though excited to have the opportunity, even privilege, to engage in this sacred aspect of pastoral ministry — one I had thought a good deal about even though I had not yet done it — I also dreaded it. That dread centered largely on the fact that I did not really know what to do. I had never taken a seminary course on how to lead a funeral service (or any service for that matter) and I felt quite unprepared.

I should note that several such courses were offered by my seminary and that many students wiser than I took them. However, I did not take those courses because, as I recall, I wanted to take advantage of enrolling in more pastoral care and counseling courses. Consequently, when it came to leading various kinds of services, funerals included, I had to learn what to do and how to do it by reading on my own and employing a trial-and-error approach. While that approach may have some benefit, it also can lead to making unnecessary mistakes and, in my case, increased anxiety that previous coursework and practice likely would have toned down. Hence, let me say here that I would advise those reading this book *before* graduating from seminary to think very seriously about taking at least a basic worship course before their entry into ministry, one that affords the opportunity to learn not only "what to do" but as importantly "why to do it" with respect to all sorts of worship-related occasions, including funerals, baptisms, celebrations of the Lord's Supper, weddings, ordinations and installations of church officers, and others. It may very well make your pastoral life, and the lives of those you presume to engage in ministry, less laden with mistakes and more rewarding.

Of course, on this occasion (and most others I can think of) more immediate than the concern for focusing on "what to do" in the funeral service itself should have been the concern for "what to do" — or perhaps better stated "how to be" — *before* the service, especially as I prepared to meet a grieving family for the first time. I had learned from my pastoral care courses the importance of forming some beginning pastoral relationship with a family I'd never met. Though embryonic and presumably short-lived, that relationship would serve as a basis for offering a warm and supportive presence during the family's time of loss and need. That, I knew, remains a worthy objective for pastors to strive to meet; and that was my goal in this case. In light of that goal, I wish I could say that I made use of what was taught to me in those extra pastoral care courses — that I had acted on "what to do" and "how to be" in ways more conducive to competent and faithful pastoral work. After all, the members of this family had no congregation or pastor of their own. Their history with the church may very well have been ambivalent if not painful. And they had requested, for whatever reason, that their family member have a funeral led by the local Presbyterian minister. So the table was set for me to offer several significant things on my very first occasion to journey pastorally with a family who had loved and lost, including a ministry of presence, an open and supportive ear, and just as importantly, a hospitable witness on behalf of the church of Jesus Christ.

I never got to offer any of that, however, for the following reason. After hanging up the phone I immediately went to the Presbyterian Church's *Directory for Worship* seeking guidance on how to begin thinking about the funeral service, my anxiety rapidly climbing. I fairly quickly stumbled upon the following: "In order that attention in the service be directed to

God, when a casket is present it ordinarily is closed."[1] I decided then and there that I needed to speak again with the funeral director, in order to make sure that this "ordinary" practice would be maintained in the funeral home's chapel setting. The last thing I wanted was to commit a theological false start as I left the pastoral starting blocks. After patiently listening to my rationale, which included language about "the Reformed tradition," "keeping the primary focus on God," and "my denomination's constitutional requirements," he said, "I'll share what you've communicated here with the family." We hung up. A few minutes later I received a call from that funeral director's assistant, whereby she thanked me for my willingness to provide the funeral service, "especially on such short notice," and informed me that the family had decided to make other arrangements.

It did not take long for me to realize what had happened. As a conscientious new pastor, my desire to be "theologically correct" according to my tradition's norms — a desire which, incidentally, probably grew as much out of my anxiety as my more noble motivations for upholding theological "purity" — had trumped my pastoral sensitivities, practicalities, and wisdom. I wish so much that I had opted to focus more on what I actually had learned in my pastoral care courses about "what to do" and "how to be" while forming relationships and building rapport with persons in their time of need; and I wish I had opted to focus less, or at least to move that focus farther down the road, on the issue of the closed casket. I remain convinced to this day that I was theologically astute on that occasion. I had it more or less right with respect to my tradition and stood on good theological and ecclesiastical ground when making my wishes known to the funeral director and the family. But I was equally insensitive with respect to what the grieving family members' wishes may have been, and that led to a lost opportunity for ministry. On this, my first occasion to be pastoral at the time of a death, I needed a reminder that ministry, at least on occasions like this, tends to require as much in the way of personal connection and warmth as it does in the way of theological precision and exactitude, and maybe even more. If I had gone ahead with the funeral with the casket remaining open, I may very well have had subsequent opportunities to talk with the family about the Reformed tradition, a God-centered way of life, and even our beloved constitution in the Presbyterian Church (U.S.A.). As

---

1. "Directory for Worship" (W-4.10005), *Book of Order: The Constitution of the Presbyterian Church (U.S.A.) Part II* (Louisville: Office of the General Assembly, 2006).

it turned out, I waited several more months for another funeral and the opportunity to do it better. And by the way, no one from that funeral home requested my services again.

Adopting a Theology of Suffering and Death

A second lesson I learned also relates to occasions of death, especially when joined by great suffering, and common ensuing questions about God's presence, concern, power, and availability in its wake. While the lesson presented itself during my first two pastorates in Schaghticoke and Glenwood Landing, I learned it most profoundly in what I would call my third transition from midterms to ministry, when I returned to Long Island from my second stay in Princeton to serve as senior pastor of the Massapequa Reformed Church. The lesson: ministers must adopt for their ministry a clear and working *theology of suffering and death.*

It typically takes very little time for new ministers to come face to face with human anguish and with death. That may involve a very old person who dies peacefully in her sleep after living a full and largely pleasant life without illness or personal pain. It could be connected to a middle-aged man ill with his third bout of cancer in five years whose body hangs on to life by a thread amid death's tightening grip. It may very well have to do with a horrific auto accident that tragically ends the lives of several high school boys one cold Saturday night. In any of those situations, or others like them, a pastor learns quickly the necessity for having thought about suffering and death, for having clarity about that thinking, and for communicating something about God to those who need pastoral care — whether individual persons, families, or larger communities.

I first became aware of this matter's importance when, about six months or so after the incident with the funeral director, a pillar of the church died at a ripe old age after a brief illness. I became most acutely aware of its essential place in the minister's personal faith and pastoral practice when, feeling simultaneously stunned and inept, I looked out upon a congregation of bewildered and hurting souls on the evening of September 11, 2001, many of whom had not yet heard from spouses, parents, children, and other loved ones who worked in lower Manhattan either in or around the World Trade Center. I never needed to have some sense of where God is in suffering and death — incomplete and inadequate though it was — more than I did on that dreadful day in the life of my ministry, when too many persons from my town, neighborhood, and church community came face to face with a kind of human suffering and sorrow that they might have imagined but certainly never experienced in such a personal way, and when scores of those same persons, their families, and others looked to the church and its leadership for some measure of calm and light in the midst of a dark storm.

While it is never easy to watch those we love suffer or die, most of us seem to accept death more readily, with fewer questions and protests, when old people who live full lives are "called home" by "natural causes" to be with God, and less readily when untimely or comparatively violent illnesses and deaths come about, especially among younger persons. In a sense, the former are the easier kinds of deaths that ministers encounter in ministry; the latter, the more difficult. And while most ministers, pray God, will not be called upon to offer perspective, counsel, and companionship through death and suffering on days like 9/11 and its aftermath, ministers frequently extend care to persons who suffer and die as well as to those who grieve and mourn. Consequently, in preparation for ministry, new ministers would do well to think about these matters intentionally, deeply, faithfully, and courageously.

Years before September 11, 2001, as I journeyed for the first time with a family whose loved one had died, and then for a second, and then for a third, it occurred to me that I had never really considered — much less settled on — my thoughts relating to what actually happens to us when we die. More specifically, I had never given much attention to what theologian Jürgen Moltmann calls "personal eschatology," including where the dead are and if and why it makes a difference whether one embraces belief in the resurrection of the body as opposed to the immortality of the soul.

My need for more clarity on these matters grew out of parishioners and family members raising questions and making statements amid the suffering or death of a loved one for which I had little to offer in the way of perspective, much less provisional answers. Included in those questions and statements were the following: "Is he okay?" "How do I know that she's with God, and what exactly does that mean?" "Will I see my brother again in heaven?" "I know Grandma is looking out for all of us now, an angel watching over us." "His soul is with God, right, even though his body lies in the ground?" I learned fairly quickly that simply listening to the questions and daring to live into them with those asking them is as important as attempting to offer definitive answers to what may in the end be unanswerable. Indeed, pastoral care seems to me to involve companioning others into the deepest mysteries of God, life, and living, more than nailing down explanations of or solutions to those mysteries. Yet I also learned in my ministry that becoming familiar enough with what various thinkers in the Christian tradition (one's own and others) have had to say about these things, so that we may offer up at least a qualified response for questioners to consider, goes a long way toward providing the presence, comfort, and assurance that people tend to want, need, and expect in ministers. While it would be beyond the scope of this essay and book to delve in depth here into my own working theology of suffering and "personal eschatology," let me suggest a few resources that I think offer sound guidance as one investigates and eventually settles into one's own thinking about these things.

With respect to questions about human suffering, particularly those related to God's presence, concern, power, and availability in its wake, I have been helped most by reading and pondering Dietrich Bonhoeffer's *Letters and Papers from Prison;* Jürgen Moltmann's *The Crucified God;* Gerhard O. Forde's *On Being a Theologian of the Cross;* and Stanley Hauerwas's *God, Medicine, and Suffering.*[2] Though differing in significant ways, each of these thinkers writes thoughtfully and powerfully about the inescapable mystery of human suffering and God's role in it, and also the futility in attempting either to explain suffering or to justify it with an appeal to what has classically been termed arguments from the problem of "theodicy." Moreover, each advocates in varying ways the better alternative of clinging to trust in the God who in raising Jesus from the grave has promised ultimately to overcome death and suffering. Each contends that neither death nor suffering has the final say because the cross of Christ has said otherwise. Bonhoeffer put it this way when considering human suffering and where God is in it:

> God let himself be pushed out of the world on to the cross. He is weak and powerless in the world, and that is precisely the way, the only way,

2. Publication information for these books is as follows: Dietrich Bonhoeffer, *Letters and Papers from Prison,* enlarged edition (New York: Touchstone, 1997); Jürgen Moltmann, *The Crucified God: The Cross of Christ as the Foundation and Criticism of Christian Theology,* trans. R. A. Wilson and John Bowden (Minneapolis: Fortress, 1993); Gerhard O. Forde, *On Becoming a Theologian of the Cross: Reflections on Luther's Heidelberg Disputation, 1518* (Grand Rapids: Eerdmans, 1997); Stanley Hauerwas, *God, Medicine, and Suffering* (Grand Rapids: Eerdmans, 1994).

in which he is with us and helps us. Matt. 8:17 makes it quite clear that Christ helps us, not by virtue of his omnipotence, but by virtue of his weakness and suffering.[3]

Concerning "personal eschatology," I would suggest Jürgen Moltmann's *The Coming of God: Christian Eschatology* (especially Part II), and also his more current and briefer treatment of the subject, *In the End, the Beginning: The Life of Hope*.[4] The former provides an in-depth look at how various theologians, philosophers, psychologists, and poets have thought about the kinds of questions mentioned previously that pertain to eternal life, heaven, and body and soul after death. While Moltmann includes his own constructive take on these matters, one need not adopt his views to appreciate his treatment of the subject and his discussion of various thinkers and positions. Moltmann will provide readers with a good sense of the lay of the land as they map out where they themselves will travel en route to constructing their own working theology of life, death, and life after death. I strongly urge new ministers to read each of the books I have cited as they reflect on, and are called upon to help others think through, similar questions and concerns. Doing so, I believe, will help new ministers gain more confidence, speak with greater candor, and relate with deeper compassion.

Developing a Sense of Humor

A third lesson I learned had nothing to do with death, suffering, or adjoining sadness but just the opposite, namely, humor. I came to realize the indispensable value of taking what I do in ministry with utmost seriousness while not taking myself all that seriously! To say it another way, I have learned the importance of developing a sense of humor — including about ministry, about those with whom one serves in ministry, and also about oneself as minister — as a "divine" remedy for the pain, misery, and injustice that life too often includes.

In a wonderful book, *A Time to Laugh: The Religion of Humor*, Don-

---

3. Bonhoeffer, *Letters and Papers from Prison*, p. 360. Note that Moltmann cites this same passage in *Crucified God*.

4. Jürgen Moltmann, *The Coming of God: Christian Eschatology*, trans. Margaret Kohl (Minneapolis: Fortress, 1996); and *In the End, the Beginning: The Life of Hope*, trans. Margaret Kohl (Minneapolis: Fortress, 2004).

ald Capps makes a compelling case for why we need humor in religious life. He claims that humor bears many gifts, serving among other things as a "saving psychic resource" that informs "soul maintenance." This suggests that a need to find humor in life, indeed to be humorous, lies at the very core of what it means to be and to live as a person. If so, then humor would seem to lie too at the heart of what it means to be and to live as a minister serving persons. Other particular qualities (or gifts) of humor that Capps gives attention to include its capacity for informing, or helping to create, both personal and group identity; its manner of serving as a means for expressing intimacy between persons; and also its power to help re-frame a given situation or perspective so that a new situation or perspective, presumably a more pleasant or helpful one, might be adopted. As Capps wisely notes, "humor itself is soulful."[5] If so, we would do well to pay close attention to its presence and potential in our ministry lives.

Will Willimon has recognized the inseparable relationship between humor and the religious life too, evidenced by an amusing little compilation of religious humor he published some years ago titled *The Laugh Shall Be First.* I have observed on more occasions than I can recall the accuracy of Capps's and Willimon's claims, by which I mean that humor has provided bonding, healing, and a way for "seeing" life and its events differently and better. I have seen how a quick-witted comment at a committee meeting helped move a group forward just as members were growing tense because of an impasse, resulting in a renewed appreciation for one another. I have witnessed laughter's curative balm at funerals, when loved ones simultaneously wiped tears of sadness and joy as they recalled this or that funny or odd thing about the one who had died. As men have gathered for a communion breakfast, workday, or some other church event, chiding one another or, as they say in New York, engaging in "breaking one another's chops," I have recognized how much affection can come with that and how it forms and sustains deep friendships over a lifetime. Moreover, I have grown both personally and vocationally from learning how to find humor in my own missteps, and, in finding that humor, daring to share it with others.

I do not mean to suggest that ministers should strive to become stand-up comedians, taking any opportunity they have to develop their

---

5. Donald Capps, *A Time to Laugh: The Religion of Humor* (New York: Continuum, 2005), p. 103.

material. That gets tiresome quickly for those in their "audience." Similarly, I am not at all a fan of ministers who tease people insensitively. I have seen that happen on too many occasions and few things are more off-putting. What I am advocating is that ministers simply learn how to become comfortable in their own skin. That seems to me to involve recognizing, accepting, and daring to laugh about never getting it right, saying it well, or thinking it through with anything close to perfection, just as we renew our passion for and commitment to becoming the minister and person God has called us to be.

I say this for two main reasons. First, my experience has been that ministers frequently believe, or may be led to believe, that they must not show much, if any, vulnerability. In other words, ministers must have it together and keep it together at all times, which is to say that ministers cannot be human. Such tendencies likely have something to do with idealizing church life and setting extremely high standards for church leaders. Second, though I am all for high standards, for all persons in the church, I am convinced that human beings, including those gathered together as congregations, really do not want perfect ministers. By that I mean those who always get it right, constantly have it together, never fumble a word or phrase, never overlook a hymn or prayer, and certainly those who fail to preach a god awful sermon on occasion. Congregations do not really want any of that. What congregations want, which is what we all finally want, are at least two things: connections with God and other human beings, including the minister; and to be accepted as we are, warts and all, by ministers, by fellow spiritual travelers, and surely by God.

Though at times we will look upon others and see them as different from us in particular ways, at our better moments those others and their differences — especially their growing edges or shortcomings — help us to see ourselves as we really are, namely, as "people on the way" or, if you like, works in progress. As each of the Synoptic Gospels remembers Jesus saying, "Those who are well have no need for a physician, but those who are sick." If so, then it is finally those who *do not* have it all together, who are infirm in some form or fashion, whom God in Jesus Christ seeks. Those same persons must, in turn, live accepting their need to be sought. While the nature and degree of imperfection may vary from person to person and also within the same person, learning to become more comfortable with those imperfections in a humorous way reminds us that we are all in the same boat. We learn to accept others' shortcomings as we learn to accept our own. In accepting them, we may even come to find them funny in their own way — and not merely funny but distinctively our own. For, as Capps reminds us, the author of Proverbs declares that "a cheerful heart is good medicine, but a downcast spirit dries up the bones."

One of the more thoughtful things anyone has ever said to me in ministry is, "Allan, you don't really act like a minister." I understood her to mean then and now that I could live as one who takes my vocation with the utmost seriousness that it deserves, while at the same time living as one who takes myself with the utmost humor it warrants. I hope that I am right about that. If not, the laugh is on me.

Contributors

Wallace M. Alston Jr. served as director of the Center of Theological Inquiry, Princeton, New Jersey, for nine years prior to his retirement. He has also served as pastor of several congregations, including Nassau Presbyterian Church, Princeton, New Jersey; First Presbyterian Church, Durham, North Carolina; and First Presbyterian Church, Auburn, Alabama. He holds honorary degrees from Centre College, Danville, Kentucky, and Moravian College, Bethlehem, Pennsylvania, and is the author of many articles and several books, including *Reformed Theology: Identity and Ecumenicity* (with Michael Welker; Eerdmans, 2003); *The Church of the Living God: A Reformed Perspective*, rev. ed. (Westminster John Knox, 2002); and *The Church* (Westminster John Knox, 1984), part of the Guides to the Reformed Tradition series.

Ray S. Anderson is senior professor of theology and ministry at Fuller Theological Seminary, Pasadena, California, and teaching pastor at Grace Lutheran Church in Huntington Beach, California. He has published over twenty-five books, including *The Seasons of Hope* (Wipf & Stock, 2008); *Marriage and Family Ministry in a Postmodern Context* (Wipf & Stock, 2007); *An Emergent Theology for Emerging Churches* (InterVarsity, 2006); *The Soul of God: A Theological Memoir* (Wipf & Stock, 2004); *The Shape of Practical Theology: Empowering Ministry with Theological Praxis* (InterVarsity, 2001); and *The Soul of Ministry: Forming Leaders for God's People* (Westminster John Knox Press, 1997). He also serves as a contributing editor for the *Journal of Psychology and Theology*. He is ordained in the Evangelical Free Church of America and has over 45 years of pastoral and teaching experience.

M. Craig Barnes serves as senior pastor at the Shadyside Presbyterian Church in Pittsburgh, Pennsylvania, and also as Robert Meneilly Professor of Pastoral Ministry at Pittsburgh Theological Seminary. Previously he served as senior pastor at the National Presbyterian Church in Washington, D.C. He also serves on the Board of Trustees at Princeton Theological Seminary, Princeton, New Jersey. His books include *Extravagant Mercy: Reflections on Ordinary Things* (Vine Books, 2003); *Searching for Home: Spirituality for Restless Souls* (Brazos Press, 2003); *Sacred Thirst* (Zondervan, 2001); and *Hustling God: Why We Work So Hard for What God Wants to Give* (Zondervan, 2001).

Elizabeth F. Caldwell is the Harold Blake Walker Professor of Pastoral Theology at McCormick Theological Seminary, Chicago, Illinois, where she teaches in the field of religious education. She is an ordained minister in the Presbyterian Church (U.S.A.) and the author of several books, including *Shelter, Nurture, and Spiritual Fellowship of the Children of God* (Witherspoon Press, 2006); *Leaving Home with Faith: Nurturing the Spiritual Life of Our Youth* (Pilgrim Press, 2003); *Making a Home for Faith: Nurturing the Spiritual Life of Your Children* (Pilgrim Press, 2000); and *Come Unto Me: Rethinking the Sacraments for Children* (Pilgrim Press, 1996).

Allan Hugh Cole Jr. is Nancy Taylor Williamson Associate Professor of Pastoral Care at Austin Presbyterian Theological Seminary, Austin, Texas. Previously he served pastorates on Long Island and in Upstate New York. Author of numerous articles on topics related to pastoral care, pastoral counseling, and pastoral theology, he is also author of *The Spirituality of Boys: Losers, Loners, Rebels* (with Donald Capps and Robert C. Dykstra; Westminster John Knox Press, 2007); *Good Mourning: Getting Through Your Grief;* and *Be Not Anxious: Pastoral Care of Unquiet Souls* (Eerdmans, forthcoming). He is an ordained minister in the Presbyterian Church (U.S.A.) and a licensed social worker.

Pamela D. Couture is vice-president for academic affairs and dean at Saint Paul School of Theology, Kansas City, Missouri. She has written and edited several books, including *Child Poverty: Love, Justice, and Responsibility* (Chalice, 2007); *Blessed Are the Poor? Women's Poverty, Family Policy, and Practical Theology* (Abingdon, 1991); *Seeing Children, Seeing God: A Practical Theology of Children and Poverty* (Abingdon, 2000); and *Pastoral Care and Social Conflict* (with Rodney J. Hunter; Abingdon, 1995). She is an elder in the Northern Illinois Conference of the United Methodist Church.

Kathy Dawson is assistant professor of Christian education at Columbia Theological Seminary in Decatur, Georgia. She is an ordained minister and certified Christian educator in the Presbyterian Church (U.S.A.). Her most recent publication is *Confessing Faith: A Guide to Confirmation for Presbyterians* (Geneva, 2006). She is also co-editor of Columbia Seminary's online journal, *@ this point: theological investigations in church and culture*, which may be found at: www.atthispoint.net.

Carrie Doehring is associate professor of pastoral care and counseling at the Iliff School of Theology, Denver, Colorado. Her books include *The Practice of Pastoral Care: A Postmodern Approach* (Westminster John Knox, 2006); and *Taking Care: Monitoring Power Dynamics and Relational Boundaries in Pastoral Care and Counseling* (Abingdon, 1995). She is ordained in the Presbyterian Church (U.S.A.), a diplomat in the American Association of Pastoral Counselors, and a licensed psychologist in Massachusetts and Colorado.

Michael Jinkins is academic dean and professor of pastoral theology at Austin Presbyterian Theological Seminary. A minister in the Presbyterian Church (U.S.A.), he has served as pastor in several congregations in Texas and Scotland. He is the author of many articles and books, including *Letters to New Pastors* (Eerdmans, 2006), *Christianity, Tolerance, and Pluralism* (Routledge, 2004), *Transformational Ministry: Church Leadership in the Way of the Cross* (St. Andrew Press, 2003), *Invitation to Theology* (InterVarsity, 2001); and *The Church Faces Death: Ecclesiology in a Post-Modern Context* (Oxford, 1999).

L. Gregory Jones is dean and professor of theology at Duke University Divinity School, Durham, North Carolina. A noted scholar, teacher, and church leader, he is the author or editor of thirteen books, including *Resurrecting Excellence: Shaping Faithful Christian Ministry* (with Kevin Armstrong; Eerdmans, 2006); *Everyday Matters: Intersections of Life and Faith* (Abingdon, 2003); and *Embodying Forgiveness: A Theological Analysis* (Eerdmans, 1995). He writes a regular column, "Faith Matters," for *Christian Century* magazine, for which he is also an editor-at-large. He is an ordained minister in the Western North Carolina Conference of the United Methodist Church.

Susan Pendleton Jones is director of field education at Duke Divinity School in Durham, North Carolina. She is an ordained minister in the Western North Carolina Conference of the United Methodist Church, serves on its Board of

Ordained Ministry, and chairs the Order of Elders. During her twenty years of ordained ministry she has mentored more than twenty candidates for ordained ministry. She has also served several local church appointments, including as senior pastor of a 1000-member church in Baltimore, Maryland. Recently she has co-written (with her husband Greg) two books and developed accompanying videos for the United Methodist Publishing House's new "Living the Good Life Together" series.

James F. Kay, a minister in the Presbyterian Church (U.S.A.), is the Joe R. Engle Professor of Homiletics and Liturgics and director of the Joe R. Engle Institute of Preaching at Princeton Theological Seminary in Princeton, New Jersey. Among his books are *Christus Praesens: A Reconsideration of Rudolf Bultmann's Christology* (Eerdmans, 1994), a sermon collection, *Seasons of Grace: Reflections from the Christian Year* (Eerdmans, 1994), and an edited volume, *Women, Gender, and Christian Community* (with Jane Dempsey Douglass; Westminster John Knox Press, 1997); *Preaching and Theology* (Chalice Press, 2008). He currently serves as editor of the journal *Theology Today*.

Cleophus J. LaRue is the Francis Landey Patton Associate Professor of Homiletics at Princeton Theological Seminary, Princeton, New Jersey. An ordained minister in the National Baptist Convention of America, he has served congregations in Texas and New York. He is author of *This Is My Story: Testimonies and Sermons of Black Women in Ministry* (Westminster John Knox, 2005), *The Heart of Black Preaching* (Westminster John Knox, 1999), and editor of *Power in the Pulpit: How America's Most Effective Black Preachers Prepare Their Sermons* (Westminster John Knox, 2002).

Thomas G. Long, the Bandy Professor of Preaching at Candler School of Theology at Emory University, has taught preaching for over twenty-five years. A minister in the Presbyterian Church (U.S.A.), he has served congregations in Georgia and New Jersey. He is the author of textbooks on preaching and worship, collections of sermons, and biblical commentaries on Matthew and Hebrews. His other books include *The Witness of Preaching*, 2d ed. (Westminster John Knox Press, 2005); *Testimony: Talking Ourselves into Being Christian* (Jossey-Bass, 2004); *Beyond the Worship Wars: Building Vital and Faithful Worship* (Alban Institute, 2001); and *Something Is about to Happen: Sermons for Advent and Christmas* (CSS, 1996).

Loren B. Mead is a consultant, writer, teacher, and founding president of the Alban Institute in Washington, D.C., and an ordained priest in the Episcopal Church (U.S.A.). He holds honorary degrees from the University of the South, Sewanee, Tennessee; Virginia Theological Seminary, Alexandria, Virginia; and Berkley Divinity School, Yale University, New Haven, Connecticut. His ministry experience spans over fifty years, in the United States and abroad. His numerous publications include *A Change of Pastors* (Alban Institute, 2005), *Financial Meltdown in the Mainline?* (Alban Institute, 1998), *Five Challenges for the Once and Future Church* (Alban Institute, 1996), *Transforming Congregations for the Future* (Alban Institute, 1994), and *The Once and Future Church* (Alban Institute, 1991).

Bonnie J. Miller-McLemore is E. Rhodes and Leona B. Carpenter Professor of Pastoral Theology at Vanderbilt University Divinity School, Nashville, Tennessee. She is an ordained minister in the Christian Church (Disciples of Christ) and author of several publications, including *Faith's Wisdom for Daily Living* (with Herbert Anderson; Fortress, 2008); *In the Midst of Chaos: Care of Children as Spiritual Practice* (Jossey-Bass, 2006); *Let the Children Come: Reimagining Childhood from a Christian Perspective* (Jossey-Bass, 2003); *Feminist and Womanist Pastoral Theology* (with Brita Gill-Austern; Abingdon, 1999); and *Also a Mother: Work and Family as Theological Dilemma* (Abingdon, 1994).

Earl F. Palmer is senior pastor of University Presbyterian Church in Seattle, Washington, and also serves on the board of trustees at Princeton Theological Seminary and New College Berkeley, Berkeley, California. He has authored numerous books, including *Trusting God: Christian Faith in a World of Uncertainty* (Regent College, 2006); *Family-Based Youth Ministry* (with Mark Devries; InterVarsity 2004); *Laughter in Heaven: Understanding the Parables of Jesus* (Regent College, 2004); *The Humor of Jesus: Sources of Laughter in the Bible* (Regent College, 2001); and several commentaries on various books of the Bible. He has over fifty years' experience in pastoral ministry.

Stephanie Paulsell is the Houghton Professor of the Practice of Ministry Studies at Harvard Divinity School, Cambridge, Massachusetts. An ordained minister in the Christian Church (Disciples of Christ), she is the author of *Honoring the Body: Meditations on a Christian Practice* (Jossey-Bass, 2002) and editor of *The Scope of Our Art: The Vocation of the Theological Teacher* (with

305

L. Gregory Jones; Eerdmans, 2002). She teaches in the areas of religion and literature, ministry studies, and Christian spirituality.

Anthony B. Robinson is a pastor and teacher in the United Church of Christ. He is the author of a number of books and articles on ministry, the church, and leadership, including *Called to Be Church: The Book of Acts for a New Day* (Eerdmans, 2006); *What's Theology Got to Do With It? Convictions, Vitality, and the Church* (Alban, 2006); *Transforming Congregational Culture* (Eerdmans, 2003). He lives in Seattle, Washington, where he is president of the northwest regional leadership formation and education program of the Columbia Leadership Network. He has taught at Seattle Pacific University and Seattle University.

Carol L. Schnabl Schweitzer is assistant professor of pastoral care at Union Theological Seminary and Presbyterian School of Christian Education, Richmond, Virginia. She has particular interest in the care of ministers and is currently writing a book about unresolved grief in ministers' lives and how it shapes their responses to conflict. She is an ordained minister in the Evangelical Lutheran Church in America and a trained marriage and family therapist. She has served congregations in southeastern Pennsylvania.

Theodore J. Wardlaw is president and professor of homiletics at Austin Presbyterian Theological Seminary in Austin, Texas. He has served on the board of trustees at Union Theological Seminary and Presbyterian School of Christian Education, and on the board of visitors at Johnson C. Smith Theological Seminary in Charlotte, North Carolina, and Presbyterian College in Clinton, South Carolina. He has served congregations in Tennessee, Texas, and Long Island, New York. Most recently, he served for almost twelve years as senior pastor at Central Presbyterian Church in Atlanta, Georgia. He has been active for many years in the Presbyterian Church (U.S.A.), at local, regional, national, and international levels.

Traci C. West is associate professor of ethics and African American studies at Drew University Theological School, Madison, New Jersey. She is the author of *Disruptive Christian Ethics: When Racism and Women's Lives Matter* (Westminster John Knox, 2006) and *Wounds of the Spirit: Black Women, Violence, and Resistance Ethics* (New York University Press, 1999), and editor of *Our Family Values: Religion and Same-Sex Marriage* (Praeger/Greenwood, 2006).

She is an ordained elder in the United Methodist Church and previously served in campus and parish ministry in Connecticut.

William H. Willimon is bishop of the North Alabama Conference of the United Methodist Church, Birmingham, Alabama. Formerly he served as professor of Christian ministry and dean of the chapel at Duke University, Durham, North Carolina, where he remains a visiting faculty member at the Divinity School. He has authored nearly sixty books, including *Conversations with Barth on Preaching* (Abingdon, 2006); *Thank God It's Friday: Encountering the Seven Last Words from the Cross* (Abingdon, 2006); *Sinning Like a Christian: A New Look at the Seven Deadly Sins* (Abingdon, 2005); *Pastor: The Theology and Practice of Ordained Ministry* (Abingdon, 2002); and *Resident Aliens* (with Stanley Hauerwas; Abingdon, 1989).

J. Philip Wogaman is former pastor of Foundry United Methodist Church in Washington, D.C. He is also professor emeritus of Christian ethics at Wesley Theological Seminary, Washington, D.C. Most recently, he served as interim president at the Iliff School of Theology in Denver, Colorado. A past president of the American Theological Society, he is author or editor of seventeen volumes, including *Faith and Fragmentation: Reflections on the Future of Christianity* (Westminster John Knox, 2004); *An Unexpected Journey: Reflections on Pastoral Ministry* (with Kenneth Carder; Westminster John Knox, 2004); *Christian Perspectives on Politics* (Westminster John Knox, 2000); and *From the Eye of the Storm: A Pastor to the President Speaks Out* (Westminster John Knox Press, 1998).

Karen Marie Yust is associate professor of Christian education at Union Theological Seminary and Presbyterian School of Christian Education in Richmond, Virginia. Her publications include *Taught by God: Teaching and Spiritual Formation* (with E. Byron Anderson; Chalice, 2006); *Nurturing Child and Adolescent Spirituality: Perspectives from the World's Religions* (Rowman & Littlefield, 2006); *Real Kids, Real Faith: Practices for Nurturing Children's Spiritual Lives* (Jossey-Bass, 2004); and *Attentive to God: Spirituality in the Church Committee* (Chalice, 2001). She is ordained with ministerial standing in the Christian Church (Disciples of Christ) and the United Church of Christ.

Index of Names

Agee, James, 32
Aisenberg, Nadya, 167, 167nn., 168, 168n.
Aleshire, Daniel, 67, 67n., 72
Alston, Wallace M., ix, 250, 301
Ambrose, 285
Anderson, E. Byron, 307
Anderson, Leon, 175n.
Anderson, Ray S., vii, 27, 37n., 301
Anselm of Canterbury, 258
Anthony, Susan B., 124
Aquinas, Thomas, 257
Armstrong, Kevin R., xxi, 24n.
Auden, W. H., 185
Augustine, 5, 134, 170, 257, 258, 285
    Augustinian, 53

Barnes, M. Craig, viii, 104, 106, 301
Barth, Karl, 3, 23, 33, 82, 83, 136, 180, 184, 185, 225, 257, 275
Benchley, Robert, 185
Bergmann, Jorg R., 195, 195n., 196, 196n., 202n.
Bernard of Clairvaux/Bernard, 40, 47
Berton, Pierre, 2
Boff, Leonardo, 5
Bonhoeffer, Dietrich, 28, 29n., 32, 32n., 83, 180, 185, 257, 296, 296n., 297n.
Borg, Marcus, 274, 275

Bourg, Florence Caffrey, 166n., 168, 168n.
Brown, Robert E. C., 12
Buechner, Frederick, 83
Bultmann, Rudolf, 205
Burrows, William R., 174n.
Busch, Eberhard, 33n.
Buttrick, George, 181, 182, 183, 262

Caldwell, Elizabeth F., viii, 65, 302
Calvin, John, 6, 82, 82n., 83, 86, 86n., 88, 113, 184, 257
    Calvin's commentary, 82
Campbell, Will, 83
Capon, Robert Farrar, 83
Capps, Donald, 193, 193n., 194, 194nn., 195n., 203, 203nn., 298, 298n., 300, 302
Carder, Kenneth, 307
Carroll, Jackson W., xxi
Catherine of Siena, 134, 138, 257
Cherry, Conrad, 277n.
Chesterton, G. K., 81, 81n., 185
Chrysostom, St. John, 82, 82n., 83, 85, 85n., 280
    Sermons, 82
Coalter, Milton J., 68n.
Cole, Allan Hugh Jr., ix, xvi, 287, 302
Copeland, M. Shawn, 177, 177n.

Index of Names

Index of Subjects

Abuse of power, 244
Age, 73, 76, 96, 98, 130, 247
AIDS, 45
African Methodist Episcopal (AME), 75
Alban Institute, 304
America/American(s), 3, 23, 24, 51, 55,
  56, 63, 122, 125, 160, 163, 188
  African American(s), 117, 122, 123, 124,
    127, 306
  American Council on Education, 168
  Euro-Americans, 55
  Central America, 233
  Native American, 62
  North America(n), 2, 3, 58, 93, 94, 218
Anabaptism, 58
Annunciation, 132
Apprentice(s)/ship, 25, 133, 285
Austin Presbyterian Theological Semi-
  nary, xvi, 290, 302, 303, 306
Authority, 1, 37, 38, 85, 90, 125, 253, 277,
  280-81
  Authority of the church, 34
  Pastoral authority, 125
  Scriptural authority, 240

Balance, 135
Baptism(s)/Christian baptism/Baptize,
  6, 33, 36, 57, 63, 109, 192, 194, 220, 281,
  288, 292

Baptist(s)/Baptist Church(es), 29, 75, 79,
  141, 142, 146, 147, 148, 150, 219
  American Baptist, 76n.
  Baptist Church of Christ, 152
  Black Baptist/Black Baptist Church,
    141, 150, 204
  National Baptist Convention (of
    America), 144, 304
  Southern Baptist(s), 57, 148, 271, 272
Baylor University/Baylor, 147, 148
Berkeley Divinity School, 305
Bible, x, xviii, 1, 6, 7, 11, 33, 35, 39, 42, 63,
  66, 82, 90, 115, 134, 142, 182, 211, 226,
  235, 251, 252, 255, 256, 257, 258, 275,
  305
  Bible commentary/ies, 131, 137
  Bible reading, 233
  Bible stories, 54
  Bible study/ies, 14, 131, 132, 133, 134,
    180, 186, 263, 264
  Bible's teaching, 34
  Biblical faith, 180
  Biblical healing stories, 136
  Biblical languages, 149
  Biblical Studies, 150, 152
  Hebrew Bible, 49
Black, 245
  Church, 142, 145, 148
  Male, 241

312

230, 258, 259, 274, 275, 277, 278, 280, 282, 283, 284, 285, 296, 297, 299
Authority of Jesus Christ, 189
Brothers and sisters in Christ, 89
Christ's mission, 281
Christ's people, 186, 187
Christ's (concrete) victory, 189
Christ's (future) work, 278
Church of Jesus Christ, 52, 292
Cross of (Jesus) Christ, 221, 296
Disciples of Jesus Christ, 161
Fire of Christ, 140
Gospel of Jesus Christ, 52, 60
Humanity of Jesus, 34
Intimate of Jesus, 203
Jesus' admonition, 258
Jesus' body/body of Jesus, 224
Jesus' Greatest Commandment, 117
Jesus' ministry, 30, 131
Jesus Seminar, 274
Life in Christ, 110
Minister of Christ, 38
Name of Jesus, 285
Peace of Christ, 262
Power of Christ, 189
Revelation of Jesus Christ, 62
Stories of Jesus, 73
Teachings of Jesus/Jesus' teachings, 117, 138
Words of Jesus, 214
Jewish synagogue/synagogue, 117, 118
John, Apostle/Book of John/Gospel According to John/Gospel of John, 31, 33, 34, 71, 90, 98, 107, 222
Johannine, 80
Johnson C. Smith Theological Seminary, 306
Jonah/Book of Jonah, 11
Jordan (River), 106, 108, 109
Journey(s), x, xv, 74, 107, 108, 109, 110, 111, 125, 135, 137, 148, 163, 180, 185, 191, 237, 238, 287, 292
Judicatory/ies, xviii, xx, xxii, xix, 16, 18, 22, 26, 92, 210, 281, 288

Kingdom, 84

Lay:
Lay leaders, 21, 36
Layperson(s)/Laypeople/Laity/Lay personnel/Layman, xviii, xix, 63, 185, 186, 187, 226, 238, 248, 272, 274, 282
Lay volunteers, 186, 187, 272
Leadership/Leader(s)/Leading, vii, xi, xvi, xviii, xx, xxi, xxii, 9, 13, 14, 18, 19, 20, 21, 22, 35, 36, 37, 38, 63, 66, 68, 76, 84, 92, 102, 115, 120, 127, 128, 129, 135, 139, 140, 142, 145, 151, 156, 158, 159, 160, 162, 165, 168, 172, 176, 186, 187, 189, 219, 240, 241, 244, 245, 249, 254, 277, 278, 280, 283, 290, 295, 299, 306
Leaving the familiar, entering the new, 289
Liberation theologians, 154
Life, 7, 33, 68, 69, 76, 77, 80, 90, 108, 109, 142, 143, 144, 154, 169, 182, 229, 251, 259, 290, 296, 297, 298
Church life, 98
Family life, 123
Life cycle, 94, 95
Life experience, 93, 95
Parish life, 112
"Lone ranger" pastor/mentality, 23, 285
Loneliness, 15, 19, 24, 25, 288, 289
Lord, 49, 72, 75, 116, 154, 180, 212, 218, 258, 282, 286
Lord's Font, 62
Lord's Prayer, 136
Lord's Table, 52, 62, 215
Vessels of the Lord, 21
Word from the Lord, 228, 234
Love, 29, 31, 63, 82, 98, 108, 117, 118, 137, 138, 156, 169, 186, 230, 251, 258
Luke, 132
Lutheran(s)/Lutheran Church, 55, 56, 169, 191, 201, 216, 284
Lutheran Seminary, 93

Mark, 34, 35

Marriage/married, 13, 20, 34, 53, 92, 96, 118, 126, 196, 216, 306

Marriage movement, 126

Mary/Virgin Mary/Blessed Virgin, 1, 40, 132

Mary's call, 132

Mary's decision, 132

Mary Magdalene, 139

Master of Arts in religion, 147

Master of Divinity/M.Div., xvi, 5, 45, 95, 141, 214, 240, 251, 255, 273

Master of Divinity students/M.Div. student, 69n., 90, 127

Master's degree/Master's degree program, 105, 114, 133

Master of Theology/Master of Sacred Theology, 6, 213

Master's in Pastoral Theology, 93

Matthew, 258, 297, 304

McCormick Theological Seminary, 65, 69n., 76, 302

McGill University (Montreal, Canada), 90, 93

Mennonite, 75

Mentor(s)/ed/Mentoring/Mentoring group, xv, xx, xxii, 17, 19, 21, 24, 25, 29, 32, 38, 92, 97, 100, 101, 102, 103, 120, 154, 158, 159, 162, 163, 180, 210, 269, 284, 285, 303

Mercy, 30, 31, 32, 38, 87, 286

Methodist(s)/Methodist Church/United Methodist Church, 119, 120, 121, 122, 124, 126, 150, 219, 225, 231, 238, 247, 248, 278, 285, 286, 302, 303, 304, 306, 307

Micah/Book of Micah, 72

Minister(s) of Word and Sacrament, 112, 268, 288

Moses, 2, 36, 108, 110, 214

Law of Moses, 35

Moses' job, 109

Muslims, 53

Mystery, 151

NAACP (National Association for the Advancement of Colored People), 142

Narcotics Anonymous, 131

Narnia/*Chronicles of Narnia*, 41, 120, 184, 185

Nationality, 76

New College Berkeley, 305

New Testament(s), 49, 55, 188, 189, 219, 240

Greek New Testament, 132

Old Testament (professor), 149

Omaha Presbyterian Seminary Foundation, 203n.

Ordained/Ordination(s), xii, xvi, 32, 45, 48, 53, 63, 84, 86, 92, 93, 94, 96, 97, 98, 100, 104, 105, 106, 119, 120, 121, 125, 138, 141, 160, 186, 190, 191, 192, 206, 207, 210, 211, 216, 237, 238, 240, 246, 248, 254, 268, 269, 270, 271, 279, 280, 291, 292, 301, 302, 303, 304, 305, 306, 307

Ordination process, 91, 100, 104, 113, 238, 289

Orthodox Judaism, 117

Pacific School of Religion (Berkeley, CA), 53

Pastoral:

Appointment, 204, 245

Authority, 198

Care, xx, xxi, 21, 36, 45, 66, 91, 93, 99, 131, 143, 145, 160, 169, 191, 248, 252, 256, 261, 271, 284, 291, 293, 302, 303, 306

Caregiver, 92

Charge, 152, 208

Consciousness, 121

Counseling/Pastoral counseling, xx, 45, 47, 108, 120, 182, 194, 246, 248, 252, 291, 302, 303

Dimension(s), 194

Disciplines, 252

Index of Subjects

Experience, 15, 29, 143, 144, 146, 148, 225, 252
Focus, 84
Formation, 113, 114
Gentleness, 87
Imagination, 18, 86, 95, 96
Insights, 49
Instincts, 125
Interactions, 231
Leader(s), 128, 159, 160, 161, 162, 163, 229, 277
Leadership, 128, 156, 158, 247
Life, viii, xx, 25, 172, 179, 288, 289
Ministry, 13, 16, 17, 20, 25, 33, 36, 38, 60, 65, 88, 110, 141, 144, 148, 158, 160, 163, 175, 194, 200, 226, 232, 233, 234, 235, 236, 251, 281, 286, 288, 290, 291, 301, 305
Nominating committees, 106
Practicalities, 293
Practice/Practice of Pastoral Ministry, 5, 17, 251, 294
Presence, 14, 230
Psychology, 235
Relationship, 227, 292
Responsibility/ies, 147, 231
Search committee, 161
Sensitivities, 293
Theology, 29, 121, 288, 302, 303, 305
Toolbox, 157
Transition, 13
Tyranny, 63
Visit(s), 231
Vocation, 80, 84
Wisdom, 293
Work, 104, 291, 292
Paul, Apostle/St. Paul, 5, 28, 29, 35, 68, 87, 109, 208, 224, 235, 258, 285
Pedagogy/ies, 101, 102, 128
Participatory pedagogy, 101
Pedagogies of contextualization/Contextual pedagogy, 100, 101, 102
Of formation, 100, 101, 102
Transformative pedagogy/ies, 102

Pentecostal(s), 75, 150
"Personal eschatology," 295, 296, 297
Peter, 107
1 Peter, 258
Ph.D./Doctor of Philosophy, 53, 122, 147, 225
Pittsburgh Theological Seminary, 301
Practical theology/theologians, xx, xxi, 28, 33, 35, 59, 66, 112, 127, 149, 165
Practical disciplines, 252
Practical education, 263
Practical experiences, 180
Practical ministry, 3
Practical theological foundations, 132
Practical training, 93
Practice(s) of ministry/Ministry practices, xi, 4, 22, 23, 45, 56, 67, 101, 102, 132, 133, 134, 135, 149, 152, 224, 305
Preparation for (pastoral) ministry/Ministry preparation/Ministerial preparation, 100, 133, 141, 152, 154, 295
Presbyterian(s)/Presbyterian Church, xv, 9, 51, 56, 57, 58, 75, 79, 86, 89, 90, 91, 97, 99, 100, 104, 105, 150, 154, 155, 179, 180, 181, 213, 215, 219, 221, 262, 263, 264, 265, 268, 288, 290, 292, 301, 302, 305, 306
Presbyterian Church (USA), 65, 92, 268, 293, 302, 303, 304, 306
Presbytery, 57, 97, 100, 103, 105, 105n., 106, 154, 268, 271, 288, 289
Princeton Theological Seminary/Princeton/Princeton Seminary, viii, 53, 59, 141, 147, 148, 151, 152, 179, 180, 181, 186, 259, 260n., 288, 289, 290, 294, 302, 304, 305
Princeton University, 106, 180
Promised Land, 36, 107, 108, 109
Holy Land, 63
Protestant(s), 57, 73, 93, 116, 160, 197, 216, 220, 237, 238, 248, 253, 265, 276, 277
Protestant Reformers, 256
Protestantism, 218

320

Index of Subjects

Travelers, 299
Virtues, 178
Spirituality, 66, 103, 157, 162, 165, 169, 171
St. Jude, 1
  St. Jude's Roman Catholic High
    School, 116
Sunday(s), xix, 8, 10, 20, 30, 37, 39, 42,
  50, 52, 54, 60, 63, 68, 71, 72, 83, 88,
  108, 110, 111, 119, 130, 142, 143, 150, 151,
  153, 182, 186, 195, 196, 197, 200, 203,
  209, 211, 214, 215, 216, 218, 219, 220,
  227, 228, 239, 252, 265, 270, 281, 288

Ten Commandments, 61, 181
Theodicy, 296
Theological:
  Analyses, 102
  Answers, 236
  Arena, 106
  Arguments, 145
  Assumptions, 251, 254
  Book(s), 182
  Camps, 106
  Commitments, 284
  Content, 114
  Course of study, 6
  Curriculum, 7, 252
  Degree, 263
  Dialogue(s), 138, 182
  Discernment, 144, 282
  Disciplines, 194, 233, 235, 285
  Education/Religious education, x, xi,
    xviii, xx, xxi, 2, 4, 5, 17, 52, 53, 54,
    66, 67, 70, 74, 75, 76, 91, 96, 101,
    102, 112, 113, 135, 141, 149, 152, 169,
    175, 214, 215, 263, 270, 276, 277, 278,
    281, 282
  Educator(s), xix, 165
  Exactitude, 293
  Fire, 118
  Foundation, 141, 194
  Framework, 180
  Hook, 283
  Ideas, 6

Ideology, 73
Implications, 89
Insight(s), 53-54, 145, 257
Interpretation, 259
Knowledge, 2, 5
Learning, 215
Lesson, 89
Library, 51
Mind, 227
Moments, 257
Novice, 28
Occasions, 256
Opportunities, 259
Orientation, 252
Personalities, 257
Perspective, 73, 143
Precision, 293
Presuppositions, 254
Priorities, 221
Professorate, 53
Question, 165, 169
Reflection, 113, 144
Resources, 285
School(s)/Divinity school/Seminary/
  Institution(s), xvii, xviii, xix, xxi,
  xxii, 2, 4, 5, 7, 9, 28, 76, 104, 113,
  170, 256, 260, 267, 273, 276, 277, 278,
  281
Simplicities, xi
Skills, 144
Students, xxiii, 56, 67, 105, 265
Study/ies, 69, 70, 90, 91, 93, 94, 98,
  101, 102, 105, 134, 180, 264
System, 6
Teacher(s)/Teaching, 169, 170, 175
Textbook, 6
Theory/ies, 173, 276
Thought, 146, 234
Training, 279
Unanimity, 253
Understanding, 136
Vision, 144
Worldview, 3
Writers, 182